great pets!

great pets!

An Extraordinary Guide to More Than 60 Usual and Unusual Family Pets

by Sara Stein
Photographs by Edward Judice

The mission of Storey Publishing is to serve our customers by publishing practical information that encourages personal independence in harmony with the environment.

Edited by
Deborah Burns, Lisa Hiley, and **Nancy Ringer**

Cover and book design by
John Bidwell, Bidwell Design

Art direction by **Meredith Maker**

Book production by **Karin Stack**

Illustrations by **Sara Stein**,
except for **Alison Kolesar**: 28, 31, 50 left; top
and bottom, 154

Cover photographs by **Edward Judice**,
except for macaw, ferret, and dogs on back
cover and spine by ©Photodisc/Getty Images.

Interior photographs by **Edward Judice**:
ii, 20, 22-23, 29, 43, 48, 51, 53, 55, 60-62, 64,
66, 74, 75, 77, 81, 84, 100, 102, 106, 108, 111-
115, 118, 122, 124, 130, 134-136, 148, 151, 156,
164, 166, 168-175, 178, 180, 182, 184, 188-196,
202, 206, 213, 214, 230, 235, 240, 245, 253,
256, 259-261, 266, 275, 285, 286, 291, 292,
296, 345, 346

Additional photographs by:
© Artville/Getty Images: 69, 70; © David
Aubrey/ CORBIS: 308; © Annie Griffiths
Belt/CORBIS: 278, 281; Ric Butterfield/
www.mynahbirds.com: 144; © Hugh Clark;
Frank Lane Picture Agency/CORBIS: x; © W.
Perry Conway/CORBIS: 140, 199; © Pablo
Corral V/CORBIS: 90; © Philip James Corwin/
CORBIS: 177; © Tim Davis/CORBIS: 109;
© Spencer Grant/Painet: 121; © Eric and David
Hosking/ CORBIS: 160; © George McCarthy/
CORBIS: 16; © David A. Northcott/CORBIS: 46;
©Photodisc/Getty Images: i, iii, vi-ix, 3, 5, 21,
44, 49, 52, 56, 58, 65, 79, 83, 97, 107, 125, 165,
185-187, 205, 207, 212, 216, 227, 233, 237,
242, 250, 254-255, 262-263, 265, 267-268,
270, 272, 277, 289, 293, 348, 358; © Robert
Pickett/CORBIS: 95; Giles Prett: 1, 15, 26, 30,
32, 36 ; © John M. Roberts/CORBIS: 82;
© Royalty-free/CORBIS: 4, 10-12, 41, 220, 276;
© Rob and Ann Simpson/Painet: 17; © Dale G.
Spartas/CORBIS: 248; Karin Stack: 264;
© David Toase/Photodisc/Getty Images: 92;
© Sabine Vollmer von Falken: 25; © Stuart
Westmoreland/ CORBIS: 155; Hugh Wiberg: 6;
© Staffan Wistrand/CORBIS: 163.

Printed in the United States by
Von Hoffmann
10 9 8 7 6 5 4 3 2 1

Special thanks to:
Thom Smith, Scott Jervas, and Lisa
Lewis at the Berkshire Museum,
Pittsfield, MA; Green River Farm,
Williamstown, MA.

**And thank you to the following
models:**
Mollie Berman with Tzippy, Spike,
and Tookie-Tookie (birds); Sofie
Brooks with Clara (dog) and goats;
Sara Campainha with gerbils; Ariel
and Seth Carthou with snakes;
Caleb Des Cognets with Stella (dog);
Eliza Dewey with baby bearded
dragon; Anya Eckhardt with kittens;
Melody Edwards with Gerome
(snake); Taylor French with Tailspin
(Russian tortoise); Billy George and
Emma Kane with chickens; Sara
Harris and Phoebe Long with Lila
(dog); Alexa Hiley with Maizie (dog)
and Oreo (bunny); Megan Hiley with
William (cat) and snakes; Ben and
Nick Krant with Chumly (dog); Kara
and Kasey Leslie with toad, fish,
frog; Cleo Levin with Olivia (guinea
pig); Zach Long with Annie (hamster); Tess McHugh with Daisy
(dog); Dillon Payne with S'mores
(bunny); Jessie Payton with Kimmie
(cat); Simone Rodriguez with Izzy
and Peaches (baby rats);
Christopher Rougeau with ferrets,
lizard, hamster; Ruth Thier with
Brownie (dog); Sarah Wong with
Russian tortoise.

Library of Congress Cataloging-in-Publication Data

Stein, Sara Bonnett.
Great pets! : an extraordinary guide to usual and unusual family pets /
Sara Stein.
p. cm.
Originally published : New York : Workman Pub. Co., 1976.
Summary : Discusses the characteristics of various types of animals that
may be kept as pets and gives instructions for their care.
   Includes bibliographical references (p.   ).
   ISBN 1-58017-489-2 (alk. paper)
   1. Pets—Juvenile literature.   [1. Pets.]   I. Title.
SF416.2.S7 2003
636.0887—dc21

2002013689

to Igor and Ralf

Who hated to have me leave out the vampire bat and wanted you to know the following: Vampire bats bite toes and noses painlessly, have an anticoagulant saliva, and can lap up their own weight in blood.

many thanks

To my children, for taking after me.

To guests and relatives who may have suffered from my love of animals, specifically: for Ringo, who sat on the chandelier and dropped his droppings on the Thanksgiving dinner, I apologize. For Pest, who chewed through the freezer cord and cost us a side of beef, I apologize. For escaped crickets who chirped in the night, for snakes who fell from rafters, for geese who hissed at relatives, for tortoises who got stuck behind the washing machine, for goats who ate cigars and cats who ate hamsters, and for all the animals who make the weekly grocery list read "mealworms, overripe banana, crickets, chow, hamburger, seed, spinach, mice, bonemeal, kidney, hay . . . ," I apologize. But I'm not really sorry. And after reading through this book, I think you will understand why.

contents

first words

From time to time in my life, I have wanted to make a pet of nearly every animal imaginable. At 10, I saved up my allowance for a horned toad. At 25, I had a monkey. At 30, I raised a coyote. At 35, my husband prevented me from buying a wallaby. And right now I am resisting everything from a kinkajou to a burro.

Why aren't these animals in this book? Because they are too difficult or not worth the trouble. The horned toad died for lack of ants, and the monkey died of dysentery. The coyote grew up wild. Wallabies are nervous, kinkajous sleep all the time, and burros are unresponsive. For these animals and hundreds more, the work is too great, the reward too little, and the guilt at failure too high a price to pay. The realistically chosen pets in this book should be enough to satisfy the whims and talents of any animal lover.

Everyone's idea of a pet is somewhat different. Whether your idea is a wild chipmunk who comes each afternoon for food, or a caterpillar kept overnight, or a lizard who lives in a homemade desert, or a mouse who rides in a pocket, or a parrot who falls in love with you, or a dog who does what you tell it, or just a gaggle of geese in the yard, you'll find it here.

But before you rush out to get a pet, use common sense. There is a summary included for each of the permanent pets in this book, telling you at a glance the diet, housing, care, special problems, and life span of each animal, and how tame you can expect it to become.

Use the summaries to help you compare one animal with another. Use it to check your expectations: Don't get an animal that requires more care than you want to give, don't get one that will love you less than you wish, and don't get one that will bore you within a month. Be honest with yourself; we have been honest with you.

Sooner or later, with any pet you choose, you'll run into a problem for which we have no sure answer. When a pet gets sick or behaves strangely, who can help? Zoos and nature centers are often both informed and reliable. Like you, they are faced with the difficulties of maintaining animals under artificial conditions of captivity. They too have sick snakes, lethargic lizards, and nervous birds. Don't be afraid to call and ask for advice.

Surprisingly, the best resource of all might be your own neighbors. In our small community, we have a naturalist who is an expert on snakes and amphibians; tropical fish collectors who know about aquarium problems and fish diseases; an advertising executive who breeds exotic birds; a teenager who keeps dozens of different lizards; plus pigeon racers, rabbit breeders, goat milkers, chicken farmers, dog trainers, and raccoon, skunk, and flying-squirrel owners. The combined knowledge of all that experience is there for the asking in our neighborhood, and maybe in yours, too.

Veterinarians are trained to care for cats and dogs. They are not trained to care for boas or gerbils, and except in rural areas, they can't help you with a goose or a goat, either.

For the most part, pet stores can't help you. A pet store is a business, not a service. Pet store dealers are not experts in nutrition, environment, disease, animal behavior, natural history, or even the scientific names of the pets they sell.

Pet books are not, on the whole, reliable. I have read books that tell me snakes split their skin along the belly before they shed, that rats turn cannibal if they are fed meat, and that a dog will stop chasing cars if water is thrown on him. I haven't observed any of these statements to be true.

Yet no matter what resources are at hand, when you have a question, you may find, as I have, that you never get the same answer twice. Much of the time, answers contradict my own experience. The best advice may be that you should experiment. Listen, read, try this, try that, and wait and see. For instance, we often offer a delicatessen of foods to new pets. Individuals differ enormously: We have several parrots who stick with spinach, apples, and a variety of seeds, but we have another who eats meat, eggs, cheese, and pizza.

We have raised the heat in a terrarium to see whether it would increase a lizard's appetite. We have stopped a puppy's training for a while to see if a rest would increase his enthusiasm for learning commands. We have tried providing a new toy for a screaming parrot, a cave for a nerv-ous spider, a sleeping shelf for a restless snake, and more exercise and a swim in the bathtub for an irritable iguana.

Occasionally, the results are dramatic and immediate. The parrot quit screaming when he received a new toy, and the iguana stopped snapping at us. Other times we weren't sure what effect our experiments had on the health, disposition, or ultimate fate of a pet. So, like veterinarians, pet store dealers, zookeepers, and other pet book authors, I can't tell you everything either.

You may also run into problems with equipment, food, and housing. Commercial cages may not be designed well for cleaning or for removing and replacing your pet. Many are badly made, too. We've tried to give you practical homemade alternatives.

Other commercial products may not be much better. Manufacturers make siphons that barely bend, water bottles that leak, exercise wheels that jam, and thermostats that kick off when an airplane flies overhead. They also manufacture many things you definitely don't need: dog rainboots, hamster treats, parakeet mirrors, and snake-carrying bags.

On the other hand, there are things you do need that are hard to find: a good soaking dish for a snake, lab chow for rodents, cork rafts and smooth stones for turtles, large perches for parrots, and tiny harnesses for ferrets. We've tried to give you either clues on where to look or directions for how to improvise.

Pets in the Wild

It's not hard to imagine that long before the first animal became a pet, some prehistoric child used to throw his bone to the edge of the forest and stay to watch some prehistoric wolf, ears pricked, toes set to run, snatch it for a snack. That cave child was already treading along the path of pet owner. That wolf was already nosing itself into a collar.

Soon the same wolf (or the same squirrel, or the same crow) came to the edge of the woods every day. And soon the child became fond of the animal and came to think the animal was fond of him. And eventually, his great-granddaughter fashioned the first collar, and her great-great-grandson built the first fence, and his great-great-great-grandnephew wove the first cage. Finally, about 12,000 years ago, tamed wolves became known as dogs, and many other once-wild animals — cows and horses, sheep and goats, pigeons and chickens, cats and mice — gradually moved from the wilderness to human habitations.

Just because the fruit of our ancestors' affection and ingenuity is now available from farms and pet stores, there is no reason for you not to start again at the beginning. You can make friends with certain animals in the wild, as long as you are careful.

A wild animal is considered to be any animal that lives in nature by its own resources. If its resources include an ability to locate people scattering bread crumbs in the park, or garbage cans with ill-fitting lids, that does not change the fact that it is a wild animal. Pigeons, mice, and ants, all of whom have found living quarters as close to city dwellers as window ledges, baseboards, and sidewalk cracks, are wild creatures. Squirrels and ducks and many other birds live happily in city parks. Beyond the city in even the closest suburbs, rabbits, chipmunks, skunks, raccoons, and opossums are common. Coyotes, foxes, and black bears also have found ways to live quite close to humans, though we may not see them very often.

Favorite Foods at a glance

The foods suggested here are not recommended as a steady diet for wild animals. The animals mentioned in this chapter are well equipped to feed themselves, and their diets include many things that we can't or shouldn't provide, like live prey, rotting meat, insects, pond weeds, and wild grass seeds. These suggestions include foods that are convenient for us to supply and that won't be harmful if fed in small quantities. Cookies, candy, and other sweets should never be fed to wild mammals.

PIGEONS: Broken-up stale bread or crumbs.

DUCKS: Broken-up stale bread, cracked corn.

SONGBIRDS AND WOODPECKERS: Commercial birdseed, sunflower seeds, suet (raw beef fat), peanut butter.

HUMMINGBIRDS: Sugar-water (1 part plain white table sugar to 4 parts water).

SQUIRRELS: Peanuts in the shell, other nuts, dried corn on the cob, raw or popped popcorn.

CHIPMUNKS: Sunflower seeds, peanut butter, acorns, hickory nuts.

RABBITS: Raw greens and vegetables.

EARTHWORMS: Organic fertilizer.

ANTS: Crumbs of cakes and cookies, sugar, bits of raw fruit.

This chapter tells you how to make friends with certain animals by feeding them. But a caution: Wild animals bite if you try to pet them or hold them, and many wild animals carry diseases you can catch. Feed certain animals, and watch them, but don't try to touch them. Also, many states have laws against capturing and feeding wildlife, so check with your county extension service or a nature center near you before you start your career as a junior naturalist. In fact, nature centers are an excellent place to learn about wild animals in your area. Many of them have collections of wild creatures that have been injured and can't live without human help.

Pigeons in the Park

Every city has its pigeons, and these rather silly, strutting show-offs are creatures of habit. Go to the park or square where you see pigeons. Watch until you find out what time of day a flock of them arrives. This is likely to be morning, not late in the afternoon. Pigeons take off from work early, retiring to their home roosts long before sunset. Bring a bag of old bread or birdseed with you and feed the birds.

Go to the same place at the same time every day, and the flock will soon learn to expect you and your food. After a while they will not be afraid of you. The boldest of them (when you have found it, why not give it a name?) may come to perch on your shoulder or arm to peck at the crusts and crumbs you offer. Little by little, other individuals will follow suit, and you will soon recognize quite a few pigeons by their colors and by their personalities.

Pigeons recognize one another, too. Although the flock might seem to you a disorganized bunch of birds, it is actually a structured society. Most adult males are mated for life to a hen. The most aggressive cock has fought for and won the most favorable roosting spot in the flock's sleeping area, and the best nesting spot, too. He shares both with his hen. You might be able to recognize this bird as the one who flies down to feed first, the one who pecks at his food most vigorously.

In the wild flocks of the city park, some pigeons will have iridescent neck plumage, while others will be quite plain. Many people think the more colorful pigeons are the males, but in fact you can't tell a pigeon by its feathers. If you like knowing which are males and which are females, watch your flock during the months of February through July, when courtship is in progress. The males are the ones who strut, puff, bow, fan, gurgle, coo, and chase. The females are the ones who get chased. If you can identify the boldest cock, you can recognize his wife as well. She is the more modest bird he is showing off to.

If after all your observing pigeons still seem like silly birds to you, feel justified. They are living relatives of the dodo. The dodo, a flightless giant extinct now for 300 years, looked like a huge squab (baby pigeon), with pathetic little wings and an oversized horny beak. Since dodos had no natural predators on the island of Mauritius, where they lived, they never learned to

flee from danger, and they would stand around and allow themselves to be clubbed to death by humans for food. Several other members of the family — the extinct passenger pigeon and the nearly extinct crested pigeon — were wiped out by the same trusting behavior on their part and the same merciless behavior on the part of humans. Most other animals have wisely learned to distrust us.

I know of a pigeon named Charlie who was rescued as a nearly naked squab from a railroad trestle in New York. She was raised by hand and for 18 years has been an affectionate and charming house pet who lives loose in a room of her own and travels happily in a small carrier when necessary. She gets along fine with the dog (though the cats are kept away!) and interacts with her owner by making a variety of coos, chortles, and even a barking sound. In addition to taking a daily bath, Charlie loves music and responds to singing.

Homing pigeons can fly 2,600 miles to return to their homes.

Parent ducks that are used to accepting food from humans will teach their young ducklings to do the same.

Ducks on the Pond

Some wild ducks — mallards in particular — can be approached the same way that pigeons can. Do it while they are nesting in late spring and early summer, because they are bound to stay in a relatively confined area during nesting time. Ducks will eat bread, but the proper food if you want to give them a good diet is cracked corn (available in feed stores and in some pet stores).

Watch first to see where ducks come up to shore. Leave some corn there and go away (wild ducks are afraid of strangers). Keep leaving food in the same place. After a few days, watch the ducks from a distance.

Gradually, as the days pass, move closer and closer. You should finally be able to watch the ducks from only a few feet away if you sit still so they are not alarmed.

In many towns and cities, wild ducks live year-round in ponds at parks or other public places and become nearly tame from being fed by humans. While it is fun to see them waddle ashore for food, remember that even though these "tame" ducks seem like pets, they are still wild animals that must survive on their own. A friend feeds a flock of mallards over the winter in a small pond beside his driveway. These ducks have become so eager for his daily corn delivery that they now approach any passing car. This is amusing to watch, but the fact is that they have become so dependent on being fed that they no longer know how to feed themselves over the winter. He must now feed "his" flock (which numbers over 30) every morning regardless of the weather, and his cost in corn has become considerable.

Some places discourage you from feeding wild ducks and geese because they can become nuisances if there are too many of them. As you know if you've ever walked near a pond where gaggles of geese are gathered — they leave a lot of goose poop behind them.

THE EXTINCT DODO
The dodo was a large, flightless bird that lived on Mauritius, an island in the Indian Ocean. European settlers hunted it for food, and it became extinct by 1681.

A Kindly Stepmother

Many years ago, a naturalist named Konrad Lorenz went the limit — he became a mother duck. This is easier than it sounds. Ducks and many other animals have critical periods early in their lives during which a particular event triggers a lifelong habit. This is called imprinting. In ducks, the first sight and sound of the mother trigger in the hatchlings an instinct to follow her. Once the image of the mother duck is imprinted in their minds, the babies will unerringly waddle or swim after her wherever she goes.

Lorenz discovered that if the first quacking, waddling creature the hatchlings see is an elderly plump man with a beard — in this case, like Lorenz — the ducklings will forever after waddle or swim after that elderly plump man with a beard.

And that's not all. Lorenz could also convince unhatched ducklings that it was time to break their shells. Unknown to man, ducklings have been speaking to their mothers from inside their shells for thousands of years. And for thousands of years, each baby has awaited its mother's answering quacks before venturing into the world. Lorenz learned not only to mother his flock of ducklings across meadows and down village streets, but also to talk (or quack) his babies into hatching in the first place.

Birds at the Birdfeeder

You can attract birds to eat at your birdfeeder whether you live in the city or in the country. But there will be differences in which birds you can attract. To find out what each bird looks like and where it is heading, find a good field guide, one published for your part of the country. During spring and fall migration, birds may fly in flocks of thousands, over obstacles as tall as Mount Everest and as far as from the northern tip of North America to the southern tip of South America. Birds may reach speeds of up to 60 miles an hour and cover as much as 400 miles a day. The largest migrating flocks ever seen by humans were those of the passenger pigeon, now extinct. The birds blackened the sky in flocks stretching in a swath a quarter-mile wide for a distance of two miles.

Most wild birds won't tolerate interference with their nests — and it is against federal law!

Feeding Birds by Hand

If you live where winters are cold, and if you are patient and persistent, you can persuade winter birds, especially chickadees, to eat from your hand. Begin on a cold, sunny, still morning, ideally in February. Do not put birdseed in the feeder that day. Place a large mitten on a chair near the feeder and fill its palm with sunflower seeds (hulled are the best) or broken-up nuts such as cashews, pecans, or walnuts. Birds will soon discover and devour the food. The next day, put the mitten on your hand, sit in the chair, and fill your hand with food. Be very still as birds swoop toward you. They may not eat from your hand the first day, but they will soon grow used to you.

House sparrow

Downy woodpecker

Tufted titmouse

Chickadee

Slate-colored junco

Blue jay

Cardinal

SOME POSSIBLE VISITORS
Feeding stations with seed attract many kinds of birds. These birds are some of the most common visitors you'll see.

The Lovely Hummingbird

If you live in the suburbs or in the country, even that fairylike jewel of birds, the hummingbird, can be encouraged to come to your home for dinner during the spring and summer months. Though hummingbirds eat primarily insects during the breeding season, many flowering plants — bee balm, cardinal flower, columbine, foxglove, hosta, and lupine among them — attract them throughout the warm months.

Hummingbirds will accept substitutes for nectar. You can buy a commercial hummingbird feeder or make your own. Find a small, empty, well-rinsed bottle. Wrap a wire around its neck and hang it from a nearby bush or in a potted plant. Tie a bright red ribbon around it because that will make it look like a flower to hummingbirds. Red is supposed to be their favorite color. Make a mixture of 4 parts boiling water to 1 part plain white sugar (never use honey or brown sugar). Keep the bottle filled with the sweetened water (the liquid itself does not need to be colored). This mixture will spoil, so clean out the bottle every few days and replace the sugar-water.

If there are hummingbirds around you, especially if they have already noticed pots of bright

Hummingbirds are attracted to trumpetvine flowers and their honeysuckle relatives.

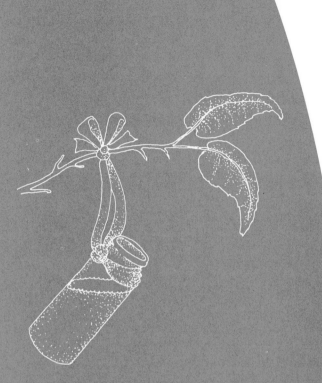

Tie a bright red ribbon around the feeder to help attract hummingbirds to it.

flowers on your patio or a flower bed in your yard, they will come to hover over the bottle and sip the sugar-water. They seem to come mostly late in the afternoon, just before dusk.

An interesting way to provide another food source for them is to leave a very ripe banana or other piece of fruit near the feeder. This will attract fruit flies and other small insects for the birds to enjoy.

If you watch carefully, you'll notice that not only do hummingbirds fly forward and hover motionless in the air, but they also are the only bird in the world that can fly backward. You won't see more than the blur of the wings' movement, as they flap at the rate of 50 times per second!

But many birds can be attracted to the backyard with food. In recent years some naturalists have complained that feeding birds during the winter satisfies their appetites so well that the birds don't bother eating harder-to-find insect eggs and larvae. They think that this might contribute to plagues of leaf-eating caterpillars the following spring. Woodpeckers, for instance, eat such foods as beetle grubs during the winter if they are not gorged on suet. Other naturalists, though, claim that birds continue to seek their natural diet even if fed by humans. You might check with the Audubon Society for their opinion. My compromise is to begin feeding around Thanksgiving and to put away the feeders when the first insects emerge in spring.

In the winter birds need high-energy fatty foods to help them produce enough body heat to keep warm in the cold. Peanut butter and raw suet (the crackly dry fat from beef) substitute for fat grubs and larvae; sunflower seed, thistle seed, and corn substitute for oily wild seeds. The easiest feeder of all is a nylon mesh bag filled with lumps of suet. You may be able to get it free if you know a butcher, but if not, it is inexpensive even at a supermarket.

The fattiest — but the most expensive — seeds are those of oil sunflower. Goldfinches and purple finches prefer tiny thistle seeds. Sprinkle cracked corn on the ground for ground-feeding birds like mourning doves, pheasants, juncos, various sparrows, and wild turkeys. Crows are usually too cautious to feed while you are watching them, but every winter at my house, one clever crow figures out how to unhook my wire suet basket from the tree and flies off with it. See page 300 for instructions on making bird feeders.

Animals in the Yard

Other wild creatures that tend to live around the haunts of people may eventually wander into your life and will return to your yard if you feed them. Don't put food on the doorstep, patio, or porch. Watch them out the window, enjoy them at a distance, but remember: No matter how unafraid they may become, these are not potential house pets. Here are a few you may meet in your backyard.

Baby raccoons are adorable, but like most wild animals, they don't make good pets.

Rabbits

Alas, the best way to invite rabbits is to plant vegetables that you absolutely don't want them to eat. Vegetable gardens almost always have to be fenced against rabbits and that other greedy vegetarian, the woodchuck (or groundhog). If you see rabbits in your yard — and would like to see more of them — offer them what might otherwise be compost: the outer leaves of salad greens, cabbage cores, and carrot greens. Put these raw vegetables out while they are still fresh, in a spot where you have seen rabbits nibbling.

Rabbits do, in fact, breed like rabbits: Each female may have several litters from spring through summer. You'll notice, though, that you may have abundant rabbits one year and almost none the next. That's because they are a favorite meat of predators like hawks, foxes, and coyotes — and also pet cats. The predator, having located a rich population of rabbits, may feed on them for weeks until there are too few left to bother with. Those "too few," however, promptly multiply, and the cycle begins again.

Raccoons

You might look out the window one night and see a raccoon finishing the sandwich you dropped by mistake that afternoon. Since the bold raccoon is not one to turn down a reliable meal, you can get it to come and eat in your yard every evening simply by leaving out food. Raccoons prefer meat to vegetables, but I don't recommend leaving smelly chicken scraps out where rats and carrion flies — not to mention your neighbor's dog or cat — can also find them. Try fruits and berries and the occasional treat of a raw egg still in the shell.

Be aware, however, that raccoons can carry rabies, which is a very dangerous disease. Dogs and cats can be vaccinated against it, but if bitten by a wild animal, humans must undergo a very unpleasant series of shots to prevent it. If your unvaccinated cat or dog is bitten by a raccoon, it will certainly have to be quarantined to make sure it doesn't develop rabies, and it may even have to be put to sleep, since there is no cure. Given their curious nature, raccoons can get so used to people that they become persistent and even aggressive in their search for handouts. As adults, they are not friendly. So make sure that your raccoons have to go out and make an honest living, finding the grubs, crayfish, bird eggs, and other things that are their natural diet, so they won't become pests.

If you have a dog, keep it in after dark, because it may attack the raccoon and vice versa. If you leave out any fruit for the raccoon, set out a pan of water, too. Raccoons love to wash their food before they eat it, and their hands afterward.

A friend who serves raccoons the day's table scraps on her patio found uninvited skunks sharing the handout. One evening she saw a red fox eating right alongside a family of raccoons. Just remember that animals don't know for whom the meal was intended, and you may receive visitors

> **Some years, oak trees produce a bumper crop of nuts, a valuable winter food for raccoons, deer, turkeys, and squirrels. When that happens, you can easily gather a huge batch from the woods to serve out during the winter.**

you wish would stay in the woods. Since raccoons climb but skunks and foxes cannot, you might make a feeding platform that nestles in a tree crotch.

Squirrels

The designs of many birdfeeders are squirrel-proof (although most squirrels can figure out a way to get into most birdfeeders). But this seems unfair, because squirrels need to eat too. And squirrels are in some ways more fun than birds. If you make a move near the window while birds are feeding, they fly away. If you open the window while a squirrel is feeding, it may walk in to see if you have even better food in the cupboard.

That's not something you want to encourage. I tried it once with a squirrel that climbed the fire escape to get snacks I left for it on the windowsill of a city apartment, and I soon found it no cuter than a rat invading the pantry. Outdoors, it is possible to get squirrels to come quite close to you for a treat of peanuts, sunflower seeds, or crackers. Just be patient and sit very still while the squirrel decides whether or not it can trust you. Don't make any quick movements. Whatever you do, don't try to pet squirrels that come near. They have very sharp teeth and they bite hard!

The opossum has a *prehensile* tail. In other words, its tail is adapted to grasping, like a hand, so that it can hang from tree branches upside down.

Chipmunk

Chipmunks

Chipmunks are usually far too nervous to come close to you the way squirrels and raccoons will. However, since they always use the same paths, once you have spotted a chipmunk's run, you can leave food on it and have a pretty good chance of watching it eat dinner. We had one trained to look on a certain rock on summer afternoons for its daily treat of sunflower seeds. The chipmunk must have been watching for us, as it never failed to hop onto its rock when we came outside.

Opossums

I'm convinced, admittedly with little supporting evidence, that opossums get up later than raccoons, and long after my bedtime. I've seen plenty of possums (short for opossums) ambling across the road late at night, but only once saw one at twilight without benefit of headlights. That one lived in the city of Elizabeth, New Jersey, half a block away from an apartment building, and it was intent on opening my aunt's garbage can. Possums and raccoons love to open garbage cans and both make an awful mess to be cleaned up the next morning. Sometimes the only way to keep out both of these creatures is to place the cans inside a wooden bin with a heavy lid.

Opossums

Opossums, or possums, as they're usually referred to, are among the most primitive of mammals. In fact, the first mammals that evolved from warm-blooded and probably fur-covered reptiles 180 million years ago may have looked and behaved much like today's possums.

Like possums, these first mammals would have been nocturnal — a good way to avoid day-hunting, flesh-eating predators. Like possums, they would have relished eggs — an easy food to come by in a world populated with multitudes of egg-laying reptiles. And like possums, the first mammals would have been small — small enough to be inconspicuous, to find a variety of homes, and to hide out from reptilian predators.

The success of the possum is due to the fact that it never bothered specializing. It's not a fussy eater. The possum still eats eggs and whatever dead animal meat or live insect food is available. It's still small enough to live inconspicuously out in the forest or as close to humans as 100 feet from the henhouse. But possums do have a serious problem caused by their low metabolism rate: They move slowly. They have a hard time making it across busy streets in time to avoid any oncoming cars. They also sleep deeply and "play possum," a comatose state produced by fear that makes them look dead so that predators ignore them.

An opossum

Keep your distance from possums. Like raccoons, they can carry rabies, and the adults are not friendly.

Unlike raccoons, which prefer fresh meat, possums enjoy even rotting meat that has become mighty disgusting to us. They also go for soft fruits like melon, grapes, and strawberries. Leaving out fruit is certainly worth a try if you want to catch a glimpse of a mother with her babies. She has as many as 12 or 13, and they each cling to a teat while finishing their embryonic development inside her marsupial pouch. When the babies are old enough, they ride on their mother's back. The mother curls her tail down toward her head, and the babies curl their tails around her tail to hold on.

A Plague of Whitetail Deer

A friend of mine used to feed the deer. She figured that if she fed them during the winter, they would not need to chew the buds off her rhododendrons or browse the wildflowers in her woods.

She was wrong. All she achieved was an increase in the local deer herd and a decrease in those wildflowers that they ate — in fact, the deer exterminated nearly half the wildflower species. Her cultivated ornamentals also suffered badly. (Because we feed our plants fertilizers, they offer better nutrition to deer than does their usual diet of forest twigs and saplings.) As a result of dwindling habitat and a lack of natural predators, the deer herds in our area are now 10 times larger than could be supported on wild land, and the woods are now so overbrowsed that no seedling trees are left to replace their elders.

The same emotions that drive us to feed chickadees urge us to feed Bambi, but feeling sorry for hungry animals is not always sufficient guidance for their care.

Don't feed the deer!

Earthworms by the Dozens

We discovered a wonderful way to make an earthworm farm that you might like to copy. We bought a bag of organic fertilizer to fertilize the lawn and garden and forgot to put away the bag where it belonged. We left it out on the lawn so long that eventually it sat through a big rainstorm. Then when we tried to pick up the bag, it was in such bad shape that it disintegrated.

It became too much trouble to scoop up the fertilizer, so we left the heap there for a year. When we finally dug down with a shovel under the fertilizer, there were dozens of earthworms, all grateful that we had fed them so well.

Earthworms can be used for fishing or redistributed into the garden, where they will aerate the soil and do the flowers or vegetables a lot of good. If you have ever wondered why earthworms come up out of the ground after a rainstorm, the answer is so simple it escapes most people — it's so they won't drown!

Each of these earthworms is fertilizing the other.

Ants Everywhere

On a summer afternoon, when it's too hot to be running around, find an anthill and do some ant watching. Drop a bit of food — some grains of sugar or cookie crumbs — close to the nest. Wait.

Worker ants have found the entrance hole to their partly destroyed nest and struggle to carry back their pupae.

Sooner or later some ant will stop acting like it's in a terrible rush to get nowhere and will start to pull the food toward its nest.

Now try moving some of the food to about three feet away from the nest. Wait. Sooner or later the ants will stop looking like they don't know which end is up and will start to move in a double line to and from the source of food, each carrying the largest piece possible back to the hill.

Now try another experiment. Put a big piece of a leaf right on top of the entrance into the anthill and wait. Sooner or later the ants will stop acting like they are working against one another and remove the leaf. With a small stick, gently knock a little sand from the top of the anthill down into the hole. Wait. Sooner or later the ants will start to emerge, each with a tiny grain of sand in its mandibles, and rebuild until the hill looks as undisturbed as when you first came upon it.

If by mistake you step on an anthill or knock over the mound, the results are instantaneous. The ants will scurry like crazy all over the place, each carrying in its mandibles an oval white pupa (the cocoon stage of ant young). Because the ants are upset, they will bite, so it is best to stay back and out of their way. Sooner or later the ants will stop running around like crazy and start moving in the same direction. If you watch long enough, you will see them excavate down to their entrance hole, carry their pupae back under the earth, and reconstruct the hill all over again.

The next morning, when all the ants have settled into their new home, feed them some more (but try not to knock down their home again!).

Going Buggy

There are lots of other bugs that are interesting to watch on a hot summer afternoon. See if you can find a ladybug munching on aphids in a rosebush, or try to follow a bumblebee as it wanders from flower to flower. If you can get close enough to a busy bee, you might be able to see it packing bright yellow pollen onto its legs for the flight back to the hive.

If you have the chance to rescue a drowning moth, bee, or fly from a pool or pond, put it where you can watch how it carefully cleans itself up and dries off before it flies away.

If you want to study insects, all you have to do is head outdoors and keep your eyes open.

The Elusive Flicker

Downy and hairy woodpeckers, and even the stunning red-bellied woodpecker, all come to my winter feeder, but flickers don't. However, these dramatic woodpeckers do come to my terrace right outside the kitchen door. The terrace is made of flat stones set in sand where many ants have built their nests. Flickers come to gobble up ants as they rush up to rebuild their eroded nest after summer rainstorms.

Watching the flicker hunt ants, seeing the red-tailed hawk zoom in on a meadow vole, or observing the great blue heron as it stalks the pond shore for frogs is a lot more satisfying than listening to the tame chickadees scolding me when I've failed to replenish their sunflower seeds.

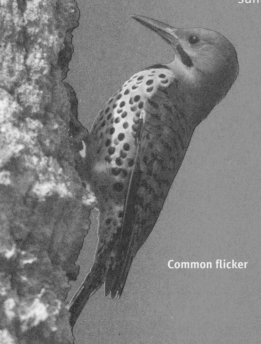

Common flicker

Providing Habitat

Delightful as it may be to feed a peanut to a squirrel or an egg to a raccoon — and even though the dream of taming wild animals is very appealing — there is another way to appreciate wildlife without interfering with its wildness. That way is to provide natural habitat.

Animals need more than the snacks you can offer them. Like us humans, they need shelter from the weather, safety from predators, and nearby water as well as a greater variety of food than we can possibly offer. Lawns do not supply these needs. You'll see hardly any butterflies in suburbs where the landscape is mostly lawn; they need nectar flowers to drink from and many other kinds of plants for their caterpillars to munch on. You won't see toads, either, unless there are spring pools where they can lay their eggs and loose stones or leaf litter where they can burrow in to hide. Mice have a hard time hiding where grass is mowed short, and mowing prevents grass from forming the seeds that they and other creatures prefer to eat. Even common birds that come to feeders may leave in spring to raise their families where there is more brushy protection, enough bugs to feed their young, and a choice of fruits through the summer.

Four Ways to Provide Habitat

If your family is considering installing new plantings around the yard, here are some that will make your property more attractive real estate for wildlife.

Instead of a hedge that has to be clipped, plant a **hedgerow** of native fruiting species such as dogwoods, virburnums, junipers, blueberries, and wild roses (but not invasive multiflora roses). Hedgerows provide not only fruit, but also insects — ladybugs and fireflies, for instance — as well as nesting sites, protection from predators, and shelter from the winter wind.

A hedgerow is even more productive if it is fronted by a **meadow garden.** Meadow gardens are made up of native grasses and flowers that are adapted to your local region. They do not need to be watered or sprayed against insects, and unlike garden plants imported from other countries, they bloom and ripen seed at just the times that animals most need them.

A milkweed plant is a veritable palace for a variety of insects. Monarch butterflies lay their eggs on the underside of the plant's leaves, and these eggs hatch into caterpillars that eat only milkweed. Spiders spin delicate webs between the leaves, aphids and ants climb the plant's stems, and bees and butterflies visit the milkweed flowers.

Another vital source of food and shelter is **leaf litter.** Instead of raking up fall leaves under shade trees, let them accumulate. Many moths and butterflies, and some amphibians too, overwinter in leaf litter. Myriad tiny insects live under the leaves, and these are the mainstay of salamanders' diet.

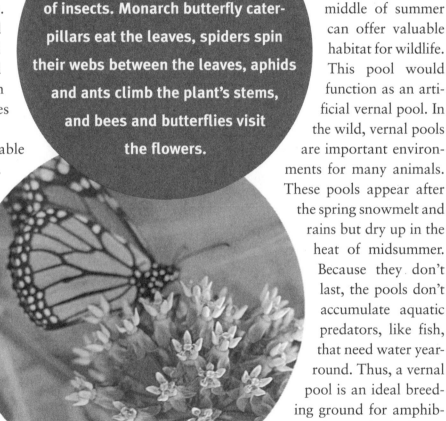

fact

A milkweed plant is a veritable palace for a variety of insects. Monarch butterfly caterpillars eat the leaves, spiders spin their webs between the leaves, aphids and ants climb the plant's stems, and bees and butterflies visit the flowers.

Unless you have wetlands nearby, you might consider adding an **artificial pond** to your yard. It doesn't have to be fancy, and it can be small enough to keep filled by hose. Even a puddle-size pond is big enough to house tadpoles, hatch dragonflies, provide drinking water, and give birds a bath. (See also bird boxes, page 142.)

Even a small pool that dries up by the middle of summer can offer valuable habitat for wildlife. This pool would function as an artificial vernal pool. In the wild, vernal pools are important environments for many animals. These pools appear after the spring snowmelt and rains but dry up in the heat of midsummer. Because they don't last, the pools don't accumulate aquatic predators, like fish, that need water year-round. Thus, a vernal pool is an ideal breeding ground for amphibians, whose tadpoles have a better chance of surviving with fewer predators (provided they mature before the summer dry-up!).

You'll be surprised how making these changes increases the number and variety of creatures that can live wildly in a cultivated yard.

Animal Tracks

Look for animal tracks in fresh snow, sand, or mud. When you find a track, see if you can read the story in the snow. Where was the animal going? Was it alone? Expert trackers can tell whether the animal is male or female, how recently it ate, how long ago it left the track, and exactly what it was doing.

If there's more than one track, measure how far apart they are. You may be able to follow the tracks for some distance.

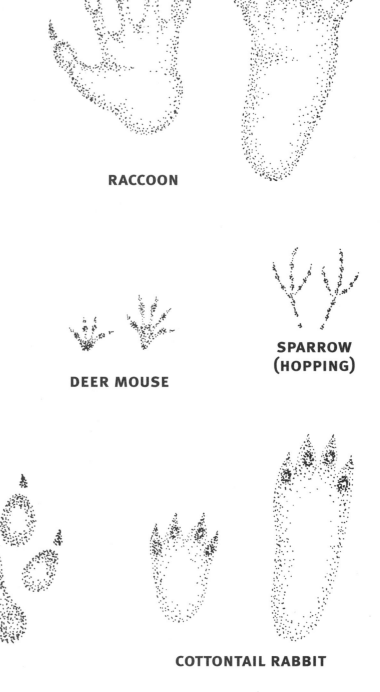

RACCOON

SKUNK

DEER MOUSE

SPARROW (HOPPING)

DOG

COTTONTAIL RABBIT

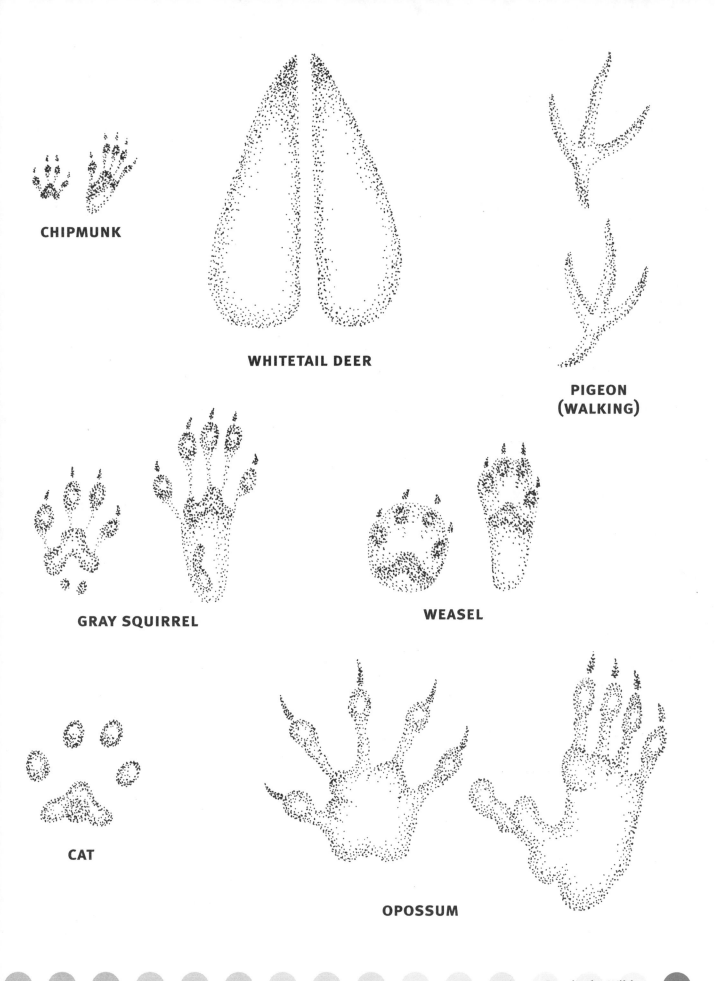

CHIPMUNK

WHITETAIL DEER

PIGEON
(WALKING)

GRAY SQUIRREL

WEASEL

CAT

OPOSSUM

Overnight Pets

Many pets you happen upon can't live with you for long. You can't give them the kinds of food they must have or the special environment they must live in. Or your parents may not want permanent pets. If you start a kind of hotel for animals, however

— a stopping place for overnight pets — you can watch them for a while and then let them go. You won't feel too sad letting them go because you know you'll be able to find other pets another day.

The different sorts of homes in the chapter "Ready Homes Construction" (page 293) can be the rooms in your hotel. The most useful are the vivariums. Other useful temporary cages are a cake-pan cage, a bug house, and a cheesecloth-covered jar. You will not have to worry about meals because your guests will not be staying long.

There are a few animals in this chapter that could live with you longer than a night. In those cases, we'll tell you where in this book to find information on housing and feeding them.

It's very, very important to return overnight pets to the exact location you found them. It's not enough to return a salamander to "the woods" or a mouse to just any rock wall. Many of these creatures inhabit very small territories that are the only home they know, and to return them to strange land in someone else's territory is to leave them as lost and vulnerable as you would be if someone collected you from your Brooklyn home and returned you to San Francisco.

It's fun to have animals in our homes, but it's also fun to visit them in their homes. Before you capture any animal for an overnight visit, spend some time observing it in its natural habitat. Look for a variety of creatures in tidal pools, at the edge of a pond or swamp, in a meadow, or by a big tree in the woods. If you settle down quietly for a while, you might see some interesting feeding or courting behavior. Make a habit of going back to the same place every few days and noting the different things you see as the seasons change.

Overnight Guests
at a glance

SEA URCHINS, STARFISH: Ocean, underwater in rocky areas at lowest tide.

JELLYFISH: Ocean, floating near or on surface.

BABY FISH, SNAILS, CRABS, BARNACLES: Ocean, tidal pools during low tide.

FROG EGGS: Pond, floating close to shore in shallow areas.

SPIDER EGGS: In or near spider webs, or close to ground along foundation walls or bottom edge of clapboards and shingles.

SALAMANDER EGGS: Pond, attached to sticks or other debris lying underwater close to shore.

TADPOLES: Pond, along bottom in shallow areas.

CRAYFISH: Pond or shallow stream, hiding under submerged rocks or logs, buried under mud.

FRESH-WATER SNAILS: Pond or stream, clinging to rocks or logs below water surface.

MINNOWS: Pond, in schools in protected shallow areas close to shore.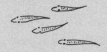

WATER TURTLES: Near or in fresh water. Sunning on rocks or logs. Turtles crossing the road in spring are almost always females heading for a nesting site, so this is not the best time to collect them.

NEWTS (SALAMANDERS): Pond, in deep or shallow water.

BEETLES: Under rocks and logs, in burrows under soft earth.

FIREFLIES: Open areas near shrubbery or woodland.

GLOWWORMS: On the ground under shrubbery.

MOTHS: On window screens outside lighted rooms, around outdoor lights.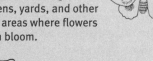

BUTTERFLIES: In meadows, woodland clearings, gardens, yards, and other open areas where flowers are in bloom.

CHRYSALISES: Hanging from twigs in leafy growth.

CATERPILLARS: On trees and shrubs, toward branch tips, often under leaves. Hanging by threads from tree branches. On tree trunks.

COCOONS: Inside curled or bent leaves. Under dead bark. Along twigs. On undersides of rocks and fallen logs.

SPIDERS: In or near webs around outdoor lights, hose outlets, house corners, window frames.

WALKING STICKS: "Imitating" twigs along smaller branches of trees and shrubs.

PRAYING MANTISES: In meadows and hedgerows. In flower gardens where plants are infested with aphids.

GRASSHOPPERS: On ground in open rocky or dirt areas, on grass stalks in meadows.

KATYDIDS: On grass stalks in meadows.

TREE FROGS: Clinging to roots, trunks, or branches of trees and shrubs near water in spring. During summer months, often heard if not seen in woods far from water, sometimes high up in trees.

SALAMANDERS: In moist woodland, under stones, rotting logs, exposed tree roots. After rain, red efts walk in the open. The adult form of the red eft is the spotted newt, which inhabits ponds and shallow water.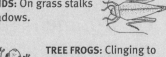

TOADS: Often hide near rock steps, walls, house foundations. Same areas at night (but more active).

LAND SNAILS: Damp grassy areas along foundation walls. Under exposed tree roots, logs, stones. In places where common, often seen on stone and wooden walls following rain or heavy dew.

SNAKES: In sunny areas atop rocks, on low leafy branches, along roadways.

LAND TURTLES: Walking in woodland, crossing roads; sometimes appear in gardens and damp meadows.

DEER MICE: Trapped in drawers, kitchen pails, dog-food and birdseed bags. Running along the base of rock walls or other protected paths. More active at night.

CHIPMUNKS: Eating on or running along rock walls, exposed tree roots, or rock formations at the edge of woodland.

Sea stars, or starfish, can live only a day in an aquarium.

Beachcombing

A saltwater aquarium is a complicated thing. The water needs to be kept at the same temperature as that of the ocean water the creatures are accustomed to, and it must be filled with much more oxygen than freshwater ponds — or freshwater aquariums — have. Splashing waves and pounding surf add a great deal of air to ocean water, and ocean creatures depend on high levels of oxygen dissolved in their water.

There are really only a few saltwater animals you can keep as permanent pets without a lot of experience and expertise. But luckily, anything you find in a saltwater tidal pool is accustomed to sun-warmed and stagnant water during the period between high tides. Tidal pools form when high tides fill crevices and depressions in rocks with seawater. As the tide recedes, the water is left behind, to be renewed only as the tide comes in again. Tidal-pool creatures will live for a night in ocean water, either in a bucket or in a tank. But you must return the animals to their natural homes the next morning.

Go to a rocky area of the shore at low tide. Wear sneakers and long pants to protect your feet and legs from sharp barnacles and watch out for slippery moist rocks (especially when they are covered with seaweed). Bring two buckets with you: one to collect overnight pets in and the other for extra ocean water. You will need a net to catch the animals (except for snails and sea stars, which you can pluck easily from the sea). You can use the kind of net that pet stores sell for moving fish from tank to tank (see page 89) or you can make your own out of any netlike cloth (cheesecloth, gauze, tulle) and a bent wire coat hanger.

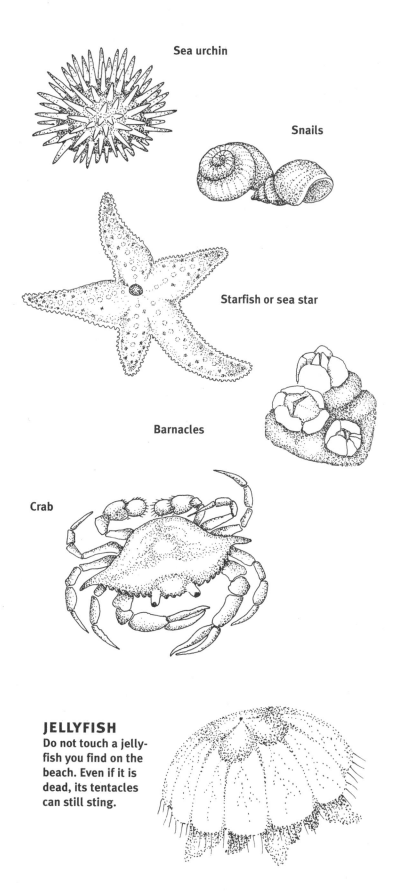

Sea urchin

Snails

Starfish or sea star

Barnacles

Crab

JELLYFISH
Do not touch a jelly-fish you find on the beach. Even if it is dead, its tentacles can still sting.

At low tides in rocky areas you may find sea urchins and sea stars, both of which will live for a while (a very short while for northern species!) in stagnant ocean water. Jellyfish can be found almost anywhere, but many have poisonous tentacles that sting like nettles or leave an itchy rash. You may find small fish, a variety of snails, and baby crabs. There will almost undoubtedly be barnacles, but it is impossible to pry them off rocks without crushing the animal inside. Instead, look for a small portable stone with barnacles on it. The barnacles may look dead to you, but if you wait patiently, they will open and you will see their tiny tentacle-like cilia (actually modified feet) waving about in the water, pulling particles of food into their mouths. Barnacles' shells led naturalists to believe these creatures were mollusks, relatives of clams and snails. But the barnacle is actually a relative of crabs and lobsters.

Collect the animals you want in one of the buckets. Add some of the plants that grow in the tidal pool, especially ones that are attached to small stones. For even greater success, transport cold-water animals in a Styrofoam container (picnic cooler) and add ice (in a separate bag) The animals will appreciate the additional oxygen available to them at cooler temperatures. Fill the other bucket with fresh ocean water.

Bring the creatures and the bucket of ocean water home. Pour fresh ocean water into a jar or small tank until it is about half full. Pick the stones and plants out of the other bucket and put them in the tank too. Now you should be able to recapture your pets with the net and add them to the tank. At first nothing much will happen, but after a while the barnacles will open and the snails will move. If you have found a small crab, try feeding it a tiny bit of raw hamburger or fish, but only to observe its eating habits. Overfeeding overnight guests will pollute their water.

The best time to look for interesting animals at the seashore is when the ocean is at low tide.

Pond Hunting

Freshwater pond and stream creatures can stay with you longer than saltwater animals can. But the more stagnant the water you look in, the better, because the animals that live there will already be adjusted to a small amount of oxygen in their water. Stagnant ponds, for example, are low in oxygen; rushing streams are high in oxygen.

To go pond (or stream) hunting you will need two buckets, a couple of plastic gallon milk jugs, and a sturdy plastic container with a lid. You'll also need a net. If you can't find a proper water collecting net, use a modified butterfly net, a homemade coat-hanger net, or a window-screen sieve. The illustrations on page 27 will show you how to make these.

Fill both your buckets and the plastic milk jugs with pond water before you begin hunting. Put the pets you find in one bucket. Since this bucket will also get full of weeds and mud, use the second bucket and the jugs of clear water to fill the aquarium or jar you set up at home.

At the Pond

Ponds and stream pools are more difficult to see into than tidal pools, especially after you have tried to catch something and muddied the water. A good way to look into muddy ponds and streams is to make a simple "viewbox." Cut off both ends of a coffee can and stretch a piece of plastic wrap over one end, securing it in place with a rubber band. You can make a more durable version by attaching a sheet of clear plastic to a plastic tube with epoxy. When you place the "window" end of your viewbox below the surface of the water and look through the can or tube, your vision will be greatly improved.

If it is early spring, take a good look for frogs' or salamanders' eggs before you do anything else. They are masses of jelly with dark spots in them — round spots if the eggs are young and more and more tadpole-shaped as the eggs mature. The egg masses float and tend to be within arm's length of the shore. Check along the length of old branches and twigs sticking up from the water, too. Salamanders attach jellylike egg masses to sticks under the water.

Look along the edges of the pond for freshwater crayfish. They are pond-bottom animals, and since they are more or less mud-colored, they are rather hard to see unless they move. They also tend to hide under stones, often in rocky brooks, where nearly every other rock conceals a small

When hunting in streams, look for small pools of water trapped behind rocks or logs. Crayfish and other stream creatures are most likely to live in these quiet places.

crayfish. With a long stick, lift a stone or prod the mud here and there. If you see a crayfish, try to catch it in the net. Place the net behind it and then frighten it into it with a stick or another net. Notice how it reacts to being caught. Another technique is simply to drag your net across the bottom, swishing it through the water as you bring it up to clear some mud out of it, and see what you catch. You may bring up water snails this way, too.

By now you have probably heard the *plops* of several frogs getting back into the water fast. You could have caught them with your hands while they were still on shore, but you can catch them with the net just as easily. Look for their noses sticking up from the water and swoosh the net in front of them. Frogs are becoming less common in many places, so be frugal! Collect only one or two, and be sure to bring them back the next day.

A variety of creatures can be tempted to the surface of the water with bread crumbs. If you can swim well enough to make this a safe adventure, find a rock that sticks out into deeper water or lie on the end of a dock, if you're lucky enough

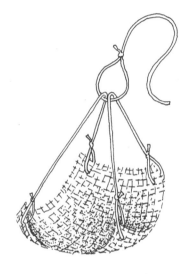

SCREEN SIEVE
Attach strings to the corners of a piece of window screen to make a handy sieve.

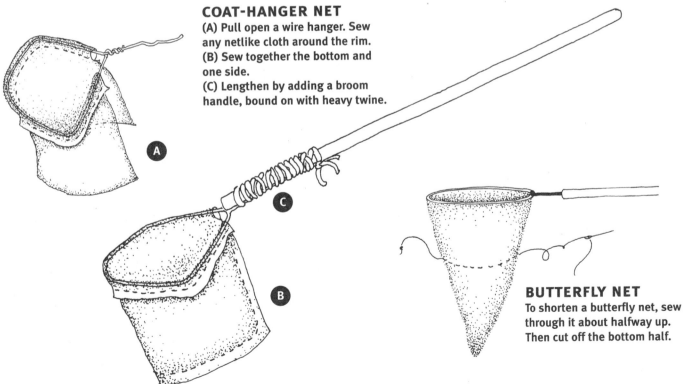

COAT-HANGER NET
(A) Pull open a wire hanger. Sew any netlike cloth around the rim.
(B) Sew together the bottom and one side.
(C) Lengthen by adding a broom handle, bound on with heavy twine.

BUTTERFLY NET
To shorten a butterfly net, sew through it about halfway up. Then cut off the bottom half.

to have one. Then sprinkle bread crumbs on the water and watch carefully to see what comes to eat. Small fish will almost certainly nibble. You may also get newts, small brown salamanders that hatch in the water, emerge to live on land for a while (as red efts), and go back to the water again to breed as adults. If you are very lucky, baby turtles will come to eat too. (It's best not to remove them from the pond.)

Keep feeding until you feel there is a good chance that a swoop of the net will get you something, and then give it a try. The creatures are very fast. It may take you awhile to catch one.

Sometimes you can fish for newts, crayfish, and even baby turtles by attaching meat to a thread. The animals are caught simply because they hold fast to the meat long enough for you to pull them toward the surface. Net them while they are still under the water. Meat for these creatures includes earthworms, slugs, and insects, but bits of raw beef or chicken taste good to them too.

As you catch the animals, put them immediately in the bucket you have reserved for collecting. Remember to keep one of the buckets aside with only clean pond water in it. You will have to keep any frogs you find in the plastic freezer container with the lid on for now. They will jump out of the bucket if you put them there.

A NOTE OF CAUTION: When handling thin-skinned animals like salamanders and frogs, use the net as much as possible and make sure your hands are very clean. Dip your hands in pond water before handling them, since wet hands are safer for the animals. The salt and oil from our skin is harmful to these sensitive creatures, and too much handling by human hands can injure or even kill them. In addition, toads and red-bellied newts can secrete chemicals that are irritating.

At Home

Here's a quick tip. Go to the pond, fill your jugs with water, and bring them directly home. Pour the water into the tank and get the tank all set up. Then go back to the pond to collect your animals. That's the way aquarium keepers do it.

If you already have an aquarium prepared at home (see page 317), you're all set. If you don't, pour the clean pond water into your tank once you get home. Now, with a ladle or cup, little by little start to empty out the bucket that has your pets in it. Remove any weeds you can by hand. As you approach the bottom, you will be able to see better what pets are in there and scoop them out one by one with a small net.

You can move your frogs into the aquarium too, but you will have to cover it or they will jump out. Let adult frogs go after a day. If you have found frog eggs in the course of your pond hunt, you can keep them until the eggs have become tadpoles and have squiggled out of their jelly. Keep them in water from their home pond so they recognize it when you release them. They need to learn the "home smell" of their local

habitat and the "family smell" of their siblings in order to continue their normal lives. Some species of tadpole can be kept until they are frogs (page 105). A good and inexpensive way to feed tadpoles is to buy canned spinach. Open the can, feed a little to the tadpoles, cover the can with plastic wrap, and store in the refrigerator.

Keep the water in your container fresh by removing some every day and replacing it with extra water brought home from the collecting spot. Gallon-sized plastic milk jugs — thoroughly rinsed (no soap!) — are ideal.

When the tadpoles have become frogs, you'll have to let them go too, because from then on

NEWTS

Newts have a fascinating life cycle. The female lays eggs in a pond, and these hatch into underwater larvae with gills. After a few months they crawl onto land, where they live as bright red efts for up to three years. They return to the water to breed, living there for up to four more years.

they need to catch and eat more insects than you can provide. Your other overnight guests should stay only for a couple of days before being released right where you found them.

BULLFROG
Some people think the male bullfrog says *rivet;* others think it says *jug-o-rum.* Either way, it calls only during its spring and early-summer breeding season.

Bug Collecting

Various sorts of insects can stay in your hotel for a few days. To collect them, you will need a jar with a lid and a piece of cardboard big enough to cover the jar's top. You might also want a butterfly net; you can hunt with just your hands and the jar, but it's more difficult. Any of the insects described in this chapter except butterflies can stay in a bug cage (page 302) or in a jar covered with cheesecloth (page 303). Butterflies injure their wings by trying to escape confinement. Keep them in a net or jar only long enough to identify them, then give them back their freedom.

Most bugs don't bite and can be held in your hand for observation.

You can also hunt butterflies and dragonflies and identify them without capturing them at all. The technique is like birdwatching: You "hunt" with binoculars. Unlike binoculars used by birders, the kind you want for butterfly watching will focus on nearby objects. They should clearly magnify your quarry at distances of just a few feet.

Getting to Know You

Part of the fun of collecting overnight guests is to find out their names. Buy or borrow from the library field guides to help you identify them. There are many field guides — general ones for insects, spiders, or amphibians, as well as specialized ones just for butterflies or caterpillars. The two most popular series are the Peterson and the Audubon Society field guides. The Peterson guides have illustrations; the Audubon guides use photographs. I find illustrations more helpful than photos, but the Audubon guides often give more — and more interesting — information.

An often forgotten but still wonderful series is the old Golden Nature Guides. Naturalists recommend them for both children and adults.

Beetles

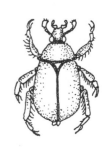

Many kinds of beetles live on or under the ground. You can often find them by lifting rocks or rotting logs. When you find a beetle, put a jar upside down over it and slip the cardboard under the jar's opening, trapping the beetle inside. Turn the jar upright so that the beetle falls to the bottom, and put on the lid.

You can try feeding the beetle raw hamburger meat. If you observe it eating (most likely at night), you could keep it several days. If it is not eating, let the beetle go after a day, in the same place that you found it.

Fireflies

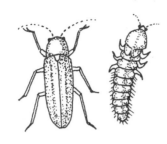

June and July are the months for collecting fireflies and glowworms, both of which are actually beetles. Like all beetles, fireflies spend "childhood" as grublike larvae, then rest for a while as hard-shelled pupae and usually emerge as winged adults. Glowworms are an exception; they are the wingless adult females of certain sorts of fireflies. Glowworm males are ordinary flying fireflies. For other kinds of fireflies, both the males and the females fly.

Firefly and glowworm flashes are signals, lighting the way from male to female in mating season. Both males and females light up by a reaction between two chemicals called luciferin and luciferase. You will not be able to notice it, but male and female signals are different, allowing the two sexes to recognize one another. Each species uses a pattern of flashes unique to its kind. An expert once told me that he'd identified over 40 species of fireflies in my vicinity. Just time their flashes with a stopwatch, he suggested to me. I couldn't see how I could keep my eye on a firefly and a stopwatch at the same time (nor is there a field guide to flash patterns), but you might want to try.

To catch fireflies and glowworms you need only your own hands, because fireflies fly slowly and predictably and glowworms can only crawl. Of course, you will need a jar to put them in, too. You can't miss seeing fireflies, but if you wait until it is really dark, you will have trouble grasping them because they light up only briefly and are invisible in between their bursts of light. Luckily, they begin to fly about at dusk; if you go out then, you can spot a firefly when it lights up and still be able to track it with your eyes when it

turns off. Look for them in grassy areas and in fields at the edge of woods. Keep your eye on one firefly at a time. Catch it carefully in midair with your hands and put it in your collecting bottle.

Look for glowworms down on the ground under shrubbery. They stay lit for longer than the winged fireflies do, and they also tend to light up when you disturb them. So if you see a glow and then it disappears, run your hand lightly along the ground where you think you saw the worm. She may light up again so you can catch her.

When you have caught as many of these insects as you want, replace the top of the collecting bottle with a piece of cheesecloth held on with a rubber band; the cheesecloth allows fresh air into the jar. You can enjoy watching your insects that night, but let them go the next day. Most will live for only a few days longer, and females must hurry and lay their eggs to produce more fireflies for you to enjoy next year.

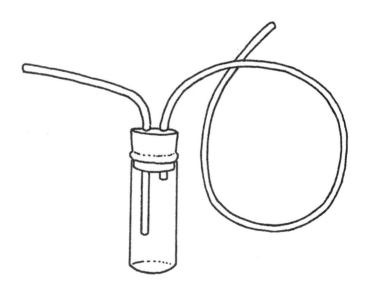

A clever tool for collecting insects is an "aspirator." The tube on the left is moved close to the insect. The collector sucks on the tube on the right and a vacuum is created, drawing the insect into the collection jar. A screen or cloth over the end of the right-hand tube prevents the insect from being drawn into the collector's mouth.

Guidebooks can help you identify what type of butterfly or moth a caterpillar will become. This one is a painted lady.

Butterfly Versus Moth

The popular names *butterfly* and *moth* have no particular scientific basis. However, in popular terms, butterflies fly in the daytime, have a curled-up tubular proboscis for sipping nectar, and have slim, knobbed antennas. Their caterpillars (larvae or larvas) don't spin cocoons but form hard shells (called chrysalises) in the pupal stage. Moths (except for sphinxes and their relatives) are mainly nocturnal, don't have obvious mouth parts (though some eat pollen), and have feathery, fringed antennas. Their caterpillars (larvas or larvae) spin cocoons in the pupal stage.

Caterpillars

Before a moth is a moth (or a butterfly a butterfly), it is a caterpillar. *Caterpillar* is the popular name for a moth or butterfly larva. Being a larva is the first stage in these insects' lives; it is the form in which they hatch from their eggs.

The caterpillar hatches from its egg looking much like an adult caterpillar, only smaller. As it eats and grows it may shed its skin several times, but it still looks like a caterpillar. To turn itself into a lovely flying creature, every cell in its body will move to another location within its body or else disintegrate completely, only to be rebuilt into totally new cells and structures. The change is so drastic that the caterpillar must go into an outwardly lifeless-looking state — called the pupal stage — while its body self-destructs and reconstructs.

While in the pupal stage, the insect is called a pupa. But because its shape, its organs, its chemistry, and its very cells are all becoming something else, it is hard to say what a pupa is. It is not a

IDENTIFYING CATERPILLARS
A caterpillar sheds its skin four times before it enters the pupal stage, and each time its color pattern may change. These changes can make caterpillars hard to identify.

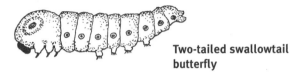
Two-tailed swallowtail butterfly

Isabella moth

Carpet moth

Black swallowtail butterfly

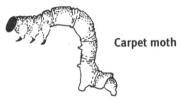

Sphinx moth

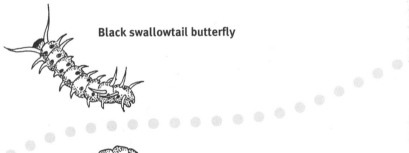
Monarch butterfly

Tussock moth

caterpillar and it is not a moth or butterfly; instead, it is a mass becoming a body.

Most caterpillars that will become moths spin a silken cocoon around their bodies to protect themselves while they are pupae. The larva of the silk moth spins a continuous silk thread 1,000 feet long. It takes 25,000 cocoons to make one pound of silk cloth — and a ton of leaves to feed the caterpillars!

Caterpillars that will become butterflies develop a shell-like skin beneath their caterpillar skin; the caterpillar skin is then shed. The pupa is called a chrysalis. The hard skin protects the developing pupa and is broken only when the butterfly splits it and climbs out. At first the butterfly's wings are folded and limp, but the butterfly unfolds them and they gradually harden in the air. Don't touch a butterfly right after it emerges — you could damage its wings permanently, making it unable to fly.

Caterpillars, unlike moths, eat a lot. If you collect a caterpillar from a leaf that it is eating, you may be able to feed it fresh leaves from the same plant or tree. (Many if not most caterpillars are specialized feeders, meaning that they'll eat only certain plants.) You can even get a small bottle of water, put a branch with leaves from the tree or plant into it, and put the whole thing in your bug

house (page 303) for the caterpillar to eat. Get a new twig from the same kind of tree when it has eaten those leaves. If your caterpillar doesn't eat, let it go within a few days.

It is hard to feed a caterpillar enough of its preferred food that you can keep it, but the common woolly bear, which will grow up to be a yellowish brown Isabella moth, eats so many sorts of vegetation that it is a good candidate for a longer-staying guest. If you are lucky enough to have found a caterpillar that has finished most of its eating, or if it will eat what you offer, you may see it prepare for the drastic changes that will turn it into a moth or butterfly.

Butterflies

Throughout history, people have loved and admired butterflies. The Aztecs, for instance, believed that dead people came back to visit as butterflies. Their god Quetzalcoatl, they believed, was first a chrysalis and then a butterfly. Some Native American tribes call butterflies "flying flowers" because of their marvelous colors.

It is not true that if you touch a butterfly its powdery scales will come off and it will no longer be able to fly. The fact that the scales come off easily may help butterflies escape from sticky situations like spider webs. The scales do form the color patterns on the wings. The butterfly can still fly without them, but the lack of color may make it harder for it to find a mate.

You can make your garden a paradise for butterflies by planting the right nectar flowers. Try

fact

Many caterpillars are specialized feeders, meaning that they'll eat only certain kinds of plants. You can help butterflies survive in the wild by planting in your yard the certain plants that caterpillars in your region of the country like to eat.

Metamorphosis of a Moth

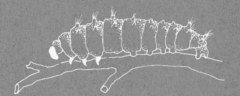

1 **EGG**
A caterpillar hatches from its egg.

2 **LARVA**
It eats and grows, shedding its skin four times.

3
The caterpillar begins to spin its cocoon. The silk comes from its mouth.

5
Inside the cocoon, the caterpillar skin is shed, revealing a new pupal skin.

4 **COCOON**
A finished cocoon is secured to a twig.

6 **PUPA**
Under the two flap-like folds, wings are developing.

7
The pupal skin splits and the moth climbs out. Its wings look small and shriveled.

8 **ADULT**
The moth pumps fluid from its body into its wings to expand them. Metamorphosis is finished.

aster, bee balm, butterfly bush, cosmos, lavender, marigold, parsley, phlox, purple coneflower, sage, and zinnia. Let wild plants like milkweed, Queen Anne's lace, thistle, violet, and yarrow grow in your yard.

Along with nectar, butterflies need water and shelter. If you have a birdbath, set a couple of stones in the water to create a resting place for butterflies. A woodpile is a perfect natural "apartment building" for overwintering butterflies and chrysalises.

Bringing Up Butterflies

In the wild, only one out of ten monarch butterflies survives to become an adult. Fortunately, it's not difficult to raise your own, and you may have a much better success rate.

The best way to start is by collecting monarch eggs, and the second best way is by collecting caterpillars. Look for both on the undersides of milkweed leaves in gardens or fields. The eggs will be tiny, milky white, and firmly attached to the leaf. Cut the leaf with the egg on it and place it in a screw-top jar or other lidded container. Keep the jar out of sunlight. Every day, add another leaf from the same plant, so the hatching caterpillar will have fresh food to eat. If you see a black dot at one end of the egg, that might be a clue it's about to hatch. The newly hatched caterpillar will be so tiny you may not even see it at first, but it will grow amazingly quickly.

The caterpillar has bold yellow and black stripes. Once you have one, either one that has hatched from an egg or one you found, it's time to give it lots of its favorite food — fresh milkweed leaves. You can move the caterpillar into a plastic bottle with a piece of netting secured to its top with a rubber band. Continue to provide it with fresh leaves every day as it grows. Remember to keep the container out of the sunlight.

The Netting Technique

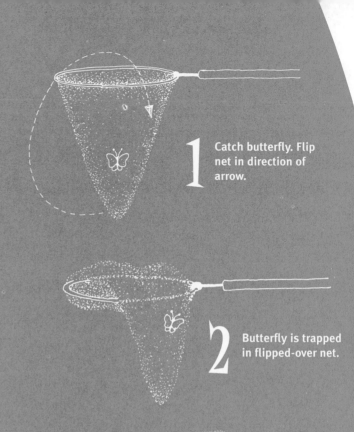

1 Catch butterfly. Flip net in direction of arrow.

2 Butterfly is trapped in flipped-over net.

To use a net, sweep it in an arc around you over the top of the grass. End the sweep with a twist of your wrist to flip the net over the side of the net's metal rim, forming a pouch of netting. The creatures you have swept up will be caught in the pouch. Look at what's in the pouch before you try to get anything out. If there's a bee in there, flip the net open and let everything out.

Try again. If you catch only one or two insects you want to keep, you can carefully slip your hand into the pocket of the net and gently pick out the creatures. If you have caught many insects, or very small ones like leafhoppers and ladybugs, don't try to pick them out one by one. Instead, follow the directions in the illustration and then quickly get the jar lid on.

Grasshoppers, katydids, praying mantises, walking sticks, ladybugs, and leafhoppers can all live in a bug house for a few days.

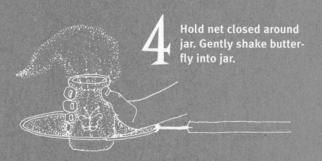

3 Hold net closed. Bring jar up underneath.

4 Hold net closed around jar. Gently shake butterfly into jar.

Ladybug

Leafhopper

5 Cover jar with cloth and rubber band.

When the caterpillar is ready to metamorphose into a butterfly, it will fasten itself to the top of the container. Soon it will form a green chrysalis with gold sparkles on it. It will take up to two weeks for the pupa to transform. During this time, you can remove all the milkweed leaves and add a twig for the butterfly to perch on.

Finally the big moment comes. You'll know metamorphosis is almost complete when the chrysalis turns dark (look closely and you'll see the monarch's wings). Soon the butterfly will be perched on the twig, unfolding its damp wings and filling them with fluid for its first flight. Keep the butterfly until it has flown inside the jar, so you know its wings are ready. Then, as soon as it's warm outside, take the jar outdoors and release your butterfly. Congratulations!

Moths

You will find a variety of moths, different ones at different times during the spring and summer, on the window outside a lighted room at night. The light — electric, oil lamp, candle, or, way back in history, the caveman's fire — attracts moths, ensuring that male and female get together. In some species of moths, the female emits an odor to attract males, too. A male hawk moth can smell a mate from as far away as six miles.

If moths come to your window, try to catch one by using a jar as a net. If you can scoop one up, cover the top quickly with a piece of cardboard. Although moths are easy to catch in your hands, by doing so you will rub the tiny colored or iridescent scales from their wings and bodies and they will not be pretty anymore.

Moths may have a very short life — sometimes only a day or two — so it's best to let your moth go before the following morning so it gets a chance to live in freedom, to mate, and, if it is female, to lay eggs. Don't even bother trying to feed it. Butterflies sip nectar from flowers, but most moths don't eat at all. You may have heard of moths eating wool clothing; the damage is actually done by larvae when they hatch from eggs the female moth lays in woolen fabrics.

Making Your Own Insect Cocoon

Cocoons themselves aren't exactly pets because there is no creature to be seen until it emerges from its cocoon. But you can, if you are careful, remove a pupa from a cocoon and watch it slowly develop into its adult form. (On the other hand, you can't remove a chrysalis's skin without injuring the butterfly pupa.)

First make an artificial cocoon by putting a layer of cotton in a small box and keeping a second layer of cotton to put over it. Then carefully remove the thin cocoon with your fingers and, if necessary, small scissors and tweezers, revealing the pupa underneath. The pupa is still very soft, so be careful when you pick it up. Place it on the bottom layer of cotton, cover it with the second layer, and close the box.

Every few days, check the pupa. You will see that little by little the shapeless body is developing into an adult insect — either male or female. Its legs, the wings on its back, its eyes, and its antennas all begin to form. Generally it will also change from white or pale tan to the color of the adult it is growing to be. As it changes, you may be able to guess what sort of insect it is becoming.

Watch out — moths are not the only insects that make cocoons. If you can see that a pupa resembles a wasp or hornet, take the cover off its box before it is quite finished and put the box under a rock outdoors. That way it will be able to get out of its artificial cocoon, and you won't get stung by the baby you raised. Let any insects go when they have grown up, so they can lead their normal lives.

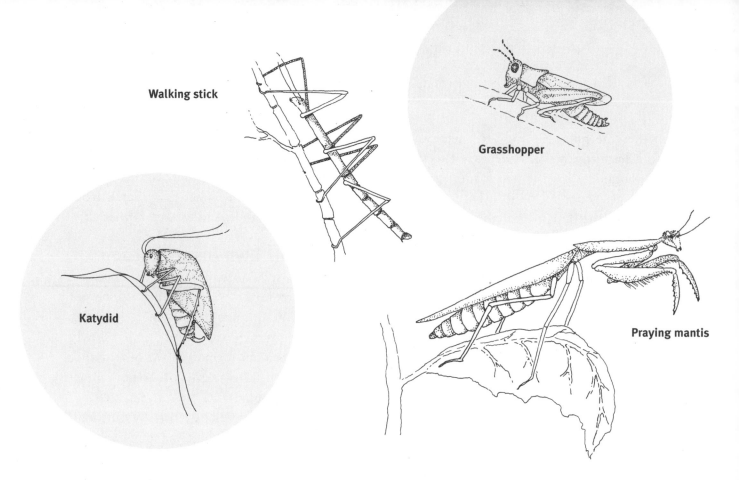

Walking stick

Grasshopper

Katydid

Praying mantis

Spiders and Sticks

Many spiders and "sticklike" insects make interesting guests. Observe them for only a day or two, and then return them to where you found them.

Spiders

Spider eggs are easy to find and fun to raise. Most egg cases are round. You will find them in spider webs in the grass, in windows, in corners of your basement or garage, or near the foundation of your home.

Gently pluck the egg case from the web and put it in a small box. Place a lid on the box, and check it every day. When the babies hatch, take the box outdoors, remove the lid, and let them climb out. You will be able to watch the hundreds of tiny spiderlings emerge to spin their first webs and start their new lives.

Walking Sticks, Praying Mantises, Katydids, and Grasshoppers

August is the best time of the year to look for walking sticks on tree branches and praying mantises and katydids in shrubbery or in meadows, where grasshoppers also live. Take a jar or a sturdy plastic container (and its lid) with you.

Praying mantises are easiest to find in the late summer or fall because that is when they are large enough that you can spot them. The adults die in the winter, leaving behind only their egg cases. The baby mantises hatch in spring, but they are so small that you won't usually see them.

Each of these creatures is camouflaged in a different way. Walking sticks look like a twig. They almost never move. Praying mantises and katydids are green to match leaves and grass. Some grasshoppers are mottled tan or gray to be invisible against rocks or bare dirt.

If you can't spot any of these insects, try making a wholesale sweep through meadow grass with a butterfly net.

Grow Your Own Praying Mantis

Praying mantis egg cases, hard to find in nature, can be bought by mail. They are sold because the adult insect is valuable as a predator of aphids and other garden pests. In fact, mantises are so valuable that in many states there is a fine for killing one. Check out gardening and lawn supply catalogs or look for ads in the gardening section of newspapers or in gardening magazines.

During the winter the egg cases must be kept either outdoors or in the refrigerator to provide the dormant period they require before hatching. When spring comes, put them in a bug jar (page 303), where a hundred or more babies will hatch within a few weeks.

Unlike moths and hornets, praying mantises and all their grasshopper relatives do not go through larval or pupal stages. The babies are called nymphs and are tiny replicas of the adult insect, except that their wings are barely formed and they can't yet fly. The nymphs will shed their hard skins many times in order to grow to adult size.

You may keep the nymphs in your bug jar for a day or two to watch them, but then let them go outdoors so they can feed on the live insects they need. If you don't release them, they'll begin to eat each other. You will be rewarded by seeing your praying mantises from time to time outdoors, where they will grow to a hefty four inches while voraciously ridding your garden of small nuisances.

Amphibians

Spring Peepers and Other Tree Frogs

These thumbnail-sized acrobats, found east of the Mississippi, are a lot of fun to watch. Spring peepers are among the smallest of frogs and have adapted to living in trees by clinging with suction-cup pads on the ends of their toes. For advice on catching peepers in the spring, when you can hear them calling, see the instructions on page 79. If a peeper is going to stay with you for a night or two, it needs only a large jar with a cheese-cloth top held on with a rubber band. Place a thick layer of damp moss at the bottom of the jar first so that your guest's skin will not dry out. Stick some small branches into the moss for the frog to climb on.

Salamanders

If you want to find a salamander, look under rocks, rotting logs, and decaying leaves in woodlands. You may have to turn over a lot of logs and stones before you find one. Raking up old leaves often turns up salamanders, especially the large spotted salamander. And sometimes salamanders emerge from hiding just after a rain, when they are able to keep themselves moist. Then your hunting may be less work.

Like tree frogs, salamanders can live for a while in your woodland vivarium, where their skins can stay moist. (If their skin dries out, they will suffocate and die.) But they will tend to stay hidden most of the time, so you might want to just watch them in the wild for a few minutes instead of bringing them home.

If you do keep a salamander for a few days, place a layer of damp moss in the bottom of the jar. Most of the insects and other small prey that salamanders eat live in woodland soil and leaf litter. Soil and leaf litter you collect from the woods may contain enough prey to feed a salamander for a night or two, but no longer. If you want to keep your salamander for a more extended stay, see the information on pages 75–76.

Toads

Toads are common amphibians in some areas and are very easy to catch. They need water, which you can pour into a jar top sunk into the sand or soil of your vivarium. Some people have succeeded in feeding a toad by jiggling a bit of hamburger meat on the end of a broom straw to make dinner look alive. It could be fun to see if this works. You can also try feeding it live crickets (sold at pet stores) or earthworms (sold at fish bait shops). But you will still not be able to keep the toad for long simply because you will not have the patience to feed it the dozens of insects it may eat in a single day.

When you release your toad, be sure to put it back exactly where you caught it. Toads are territorial, and your temporary pet probably had an

TIP

Salamanders, usually hidden in or against the cool earth in shadows, are adapted to cooler temperatures than most frogs are. A frog might do very well in your room, but a salamander could find it much too hot.

The idea that handling toads can give you warts is only a myth. Be sure to wash your hands afterward, however, because if the slimy fluid on the toad's skin gets in your eyes, it will hurt.

Ezra and the Slugs

In Maine, my young grandson Ezra once found a banana slug. Slugs are shell-less relatives of snails, and banana slugs are a polka-dotted species that grows to six or seven inches long. Of course Ezra wanted to keep "his" slug, especially when he noticed that it was chewing on some dried rice that clung to the freezer container he was using for collecting. (Slugs chew with a circular set of teeth called a radula.)

Ezra took the slug home, and his father made a mossy terrarium to house it. In a few days, they noticed he/she was protecting a big batch of jelly eggs. Then the eggs hatched into three dozen baby slugs. Then the mother/father laid another batch of eggs — and then another.

By the time the family had grown to nearly a hundred, winter had set in and there was no way to release them. The slugs had to be fed on cornmeal, rice, and lettuce leaves all winter before they could be released to their natural environment. Meanwhile, the terrarium had to be cleaned often of the slimy trails these creatures leave wherever they go (picture removing the huge family every week or so in order to wash their home!). Let this be a lesson that "overnight" guests can easily overstay their welcome.

But why did we not assume the egg-layer was a female? That's because slugs can produce either eggs or sperm, or they can produce both and fertilize themselves.

established place to live. In fact, you can encourage a toad to claim territory in your garden by building a toad home; simply half-bury a clay flowerpot on its side in a sheltered spot and wait to see if a toad moves in.

By the way, don't worry about getting warts from toads, though again, for their own good, you shouldn't handle them excessively. They may urinate in your hands when upset, but neither their urine nor their bumpy skin causes warts. The toad's bumps are skin glands that keep its breathing pores moist and secrete an irritating substance. The poison can make a dog's mouth foam for hours, but it doesn't hurt human skin. It can be harmful, though, if it gets in your eyes or mouth!

Mollusks

Snails

As you look for salamanders, frogs, and toads, you're likely to find land snails, especially after it rains. They are mollusks, not amphibians, but they share similar environments. Land snails can stay in a jar covered with cheesecloth and will eat lettuce. If you want to keep a land snail longer than a few days, page 69 tells you how. Freshwater snails, by the way, can live permanently in an aquarium, and they're more entertaining to watch than you might think.

Reptiles

Snakes

Among the common and harmless snakes you may happen upon are the garter snake and the ring-neck snake. Also harmless but less common (and protected in some states) are the hog-nosed snake and the green snake. The rat snake, black snake, and king snake are biters. If you're not familiar with local snakes, study a field guide before you go snake hunting. Pay more attention to memorizing the poisonous than the harmless varieties, and don't hunt before you're sure you can identify all the poisonous ones. A visit to a local nature center or natural history museum could be helpful.

Once you have studied up on these reptiles, wait for a nice hot sunny day for your hunt. Snakes like to sun themselves in the open. Bring an old pillowcase or sock and a rubber band with you — it's the best way to carry around a snake.

Catch a snake by grasping it firmly just behind the head. Otherwise, it may twist around to bite you. Don't catch a snake by stepping on it, because your foot could easily tear its skin or break a bone. Garter snakes, when annoyed, emit

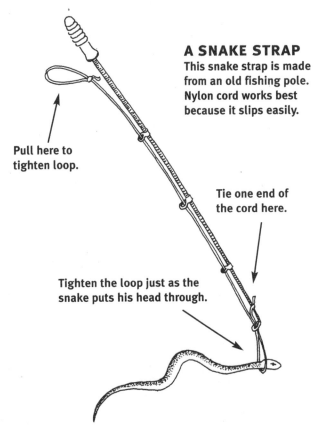

A SNAKE STRAP
This snake strap is made from an old fishing pole. Nylon cord works best because it slips easily.

Pull here to tighten loop.

Tie one end of the cord here.

Tighten the loop just as the snake puts his head through.

To use a snake strap, lay the noose on the ground in front of the snake's head. Pull on the cord to tighten it as the head comes through and the noose is just behind the head. The advantage to a snake strap is that it is longer than your arms so you don't have to be as close to the snake to capture it. The less close you are, the less chance there is that you will frighten it.

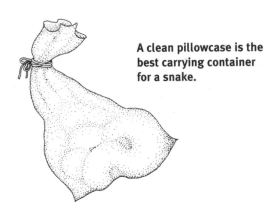

A clean pillowcase is the best carrying container for a snake.

really stinky stuff from glands at the base of their tail. The smell is so repulsive that it will make you gag — which, of course, is the point of this defense against predators. This has happened to me only once, though. I was showing off to guests by handling the snake too much.

You have to be quick to catch snakes because they will slither back into their hiding places under rocks and tree roots quickly if they sense you coming. Move slowly and very softly; snakes can "hear" the vibration of your footsteps. Any of the snakes I've mentioned would be safe for a week in your vivarium (page 304).

Snakes can do without food, but don't forget to provide your guest with a crockery dish of drinking water. It will begin to suffer from hunger in about a week, and that is the time to let it go. Release it in the same spot where you found it.

Box Turtles

Box turtles are woodland creatures. (They're not water turtles, though they do sometimes go into shallow brooks and ponds.) They could make wonderful pets if there didn't happen to be a law against keeping them. There aren't enough box turtles left for you to keep one in captivity.

You can recognize a box turtle by its hinged shell, which can close its front right up from the belly. Instead of taking the turtle home with you, be very patient and quiet, and you'll be able to observe the turtle going about its business. If you startle it, it will disappear into its shell, but you can be pretty sure it won't run away. Box turtles remain in their own home territory all their lives, so you'll have a good chance of seeing it again.

Birds

The most tempting, and often most disastrous, overnight guest is the adorable fledgling (young bird) that has fallen from its nest. Our maternal and paternal instinct to feed that gaping mouth is nearly as strong as the parent birds'. But the bird has a better chance of survival without human help. Even if you are successful in keeping a baby bird alive, it will most likely die when released because it has become human-dependent — or just too friendly!

If you find a fledgling that has tumbled from its nest and can't fly, the kindest thing to do is return it to its nest if you can, or leave it where you found it if you can't. It's not true that the parent birds will abandon a fledgling if it smells of humans; in fact, most birds have a very underdeveloped sense of smell. But they may abandon it if there are too many people around.

Some birds recognize their baby only if it is in the nest. But many mother birds know perfectly well where a fallen fledgling is, and they will help it find a hiding place on the ground and continue to feed it until it can safely fly. In fact, for many birds, leaving the nest before actually being able to fly is a natural part of growing up. The biggest enemies to fledglings, besides people who try to rescue them by bringing them home as pets, are cats. If you do leave a fledgling on the ground, try to convince nearby cat owners to keep their pet indoors for a few days so the bird will be safe.

Of course, if someone brings you a fledgling and can't remember exactly where he or she found it, you will have to try to feed it. Try mushed ripe banana or other soft fruits, raw hamburger, bits of earthworm, softened dog food, or bread soaked in egg yolk, offered at the end of a toothpick. But be prepared for failure.

Baby birds don't usually survive when cared for by humans. So don't "rescue" a baby bird unless you have no other choice.

Small Mammals

Deer Mice (White-Footed Mice) and Chipmunks

Deer mouse

These small mammals don't take to captivity, but you can catch them and watch them for a few hours. Be aware that they might carry deer ticks. The only way to catch them is to trap them. Look for a Havahart trap, available at hardware stores, which doesn't harm animals. It is a wire-mesh box with a bait platform in the middle and a trapdoor at each end. The bait platform releases the trapdoors when the animal steps on it. These traps come in various sizes — the smallest one is the right size for chipmunks and mice.

Chipmunks are active during the day, and deer mice mostly at night. They will both come to traps baited with peanut butter. If you have caught a mouse or a chipmunk and want to do more than just observe it inside the trap, have a wire cage (page 330) ready. Put the trap into the cage. Put in something else that will serve the animal as a good hiding place — a box with a small hole in it, a sock, or a toilet-paper tube. Open the trap and get the top back on the cage quickly. When the animal comes out, it will very likely go into the hiding place you have provided. It should be safe then to reach in and remove the trap.

Sometimes mice and chipmunks are too nervous to eat, but you could try a few sunflower seeds or some peanut butter and see what happens. A young animal might be calm enough to eat and stay with you for a few hours, but neither mice nor chipmunks make happy or trustworthy pets.

Always release the animal in the same place where you caught it.

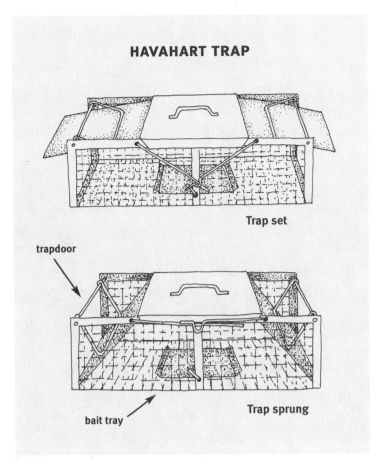

HAVAHART TRAP

Trap set

trapdoor

bait tray

Trap sprung

Shrews

Short-tailed shrew

By accident you may catch a shrew in your trap. A shrew looks like a longish mouse with a shortish tail. They are among the tiniest mammals in the world, the smallest weighing only ¼ of an ounce. To make up for its size, however, the shrew is extremely fierce. Some have poisoned saliva with which to kill their prey.

There is no hope at all of keeping a shrew for even a few hours. The shrew needs to eat nearly three fourths of its body weight in insects and other live prey each day. It can starve to death within hours. When frightened, a shrew may collapse and die of shock within minutes. If you find a shrew in your trap one morning, open the trap instantly and cover it with leaves or a rag so the animal doesn't die of fright before it can figure out how to escape.

Vivarium Pets

This chapter is devoted to small (and some not so small) but otherwise miscellaneous creatures that need special environments to live in. Their world is a vivarium. A vivarium is any container, such as a tank, a jar, or a glass bowl, that re-creates a suitable land or semiaquatic environment for a particular creature.

Tanks, jars, and glass bowls, because they are enclosed by glass walls, can be made into miniature environments quite different from the inside of your home. Birds and mice, although they live in cages, must still get along with your household thermostat, your dry winters, and your humid summers. But a desert iguana won't eat unless the temperature in its world is 90 degrees, a tree frog can't breathe if its skin gets dry, and an anole drinks only dewdrops. Because each of these animals needs such a special environment, we don't recommend trying to keep any but salamanders and tree frogs together in the same vivarium.

Vivariums make it possible to keep representatives of much of the animal kingdom as pets. Frogs and salamanders, for instance, are amphibians, descended from the first fish that learned to walk on land. Their early life is most often spent living like fish in the water, sometimes breathing through gills. Although they develop lungs as adults, most of their breathing is done through their moist skin. A dry frog or salamander quickly suffocates.

The lizards in this chapter look similar to salamanders, but they are reptiles, a completely different branch of the animal kingdom. Tortoises are reptiles too, and extraordinary ones. Their shells are actually bone covered, with a thin horny layer similar to the stuff fingernails are made of. At some time in ancient history, more than 200 million years ago, the backbone of the tortoise's ancestor began to grow outside its skin to form a covering over its back. Most members of the tortoise family can pull themselves into their shells

Vivarium Pets
at a glance

Bearded Dragons *PAGE 53*

ADULT SIZE: Up to 24 inches.

HOUSING: 60-gallon tank for adult, screen top, incandescent and fluorescent light fixtures. Gravel, sand, or newspaper for flooring.

SPECIAL REQUIREMENTS: Basking area with temperature from 90 to 105 degrees F as well as cooler area of tank. Branch or rock to climb on.

DIET: Insects, baby mice, dark leafy greens. Supplement with other vegetables and vitamin/mineral powder.

CARE: Mist with water once or twice daily. Clean old food and droppings out of cage regularly. Change all substrate every two or three months.

TAMABILITY: Docile and friendly if handled properly, easy to care for.

LIFE SPAN: Five to ten years, depending on care.

Skinks (Blue-tongued) *PAGE 54*

ADULT SIZE: Up to 20 inches long.

HOUSING: Optional incandescent light. Indoor/outdoor carpet, newspaper, bark mulch (make sure it's not getting eaten) for flooring.

SPECIAL REQUIREMENTS: The blue-tongued skink is relatively easy to keep. Other varieties of skink may have different requirements — do your research on the kind of skink you decide to buy.

DIET: Omnivorous, so feed a variety of vegetables and fruits, with low-fat canned dog food, slugs, mealworms, earthworms. An occasional pinkie mouse will be appreciated.

CARE: Feed every two or three days, pick up droppings and leftover food. Clean and refill water dish daily.

TAMABILITY: Become very accustomed to humans, and are easy to handle. May learn to come to front of cage when they see you.

LIFE SPAN: Can live as long as 20 years.

Desert Iguanas *PAGE 56*

ADULT SIZE: 12 to 16 inches.

HOUSING: Minimum 30-gallon tank, screen top, incandescent and fluorescent light fixtures. Calcium carbonate for flooring.

SPECIAL REQUIREMENTS: Desert environment, high temperature, ultraviolet light.

DIET: Raw spinach and other dark leafy greens, small amounts of fruit, mealworms.

CARE: Feed and pick up droppings and leftover food daily. Mist with plant mister twice a week.

TAMABILITY: Become calm with handling, eat readily from fingers. Not affectionate; older males can be aggressive. Not as easy to keep as other lizards, and hard to find.

LIFE SPAN: Three to four years, but could be longer with excellent care.

Carolina Anoles *PAGE 59*

ADULT SIZE: Six to eight inches, including tail.

HOUSING: 10-gallon tank (larger for more than one anole), screen top, fluorescent light fixture, potted plant. Orchid bark or commercial tropical soil mixture for flooring.

SPECIAL REQUIREMENTS: Ultraviolet light. Drink from water droplets only. Love to climb, so provide branches, etc., in cage.

DIET: Mealworms and other insects. The insects must themselves have had a proper diet before being fed to your lizards.

CARE: Feed, sprinkle water for drinking on plant daily. Rake up droppings and water plant weekly.

TAMABILITY: Stressed by handling. Some may become calm with handling and accept food from fingers. Not affectionate. Move rather quickly.

LIFE SPAN: Two to three years.

Land Tortoises
PAGE 61

ADULT SIZE: Can get as big as a dinner plate, depending on species.

HOUSING: 20-gallon tank for a baby, but will need increasingly larger quarters with room to move around (some may need an actual room or large outdoor pen), full-spectrum fluorescent light fixture, crockery water dish. Optional incandescent light. Mixture of loam (topsoil) and soft sand (play quality) for flooring.

SPECIAL REQUIREMENTS: Depends on species; some need more dryness, others more humidity. Many need access to water for soaking. Most are sensitive to incorrect conditions. They have very specific lighting and dietary needs. Many experts consider tortoises among the most difficult of reptiles to keep in captivity.

DIET: Dark green leafy vegetables, ripe fruits, some insects, prepared pellet diet, calcium supplements.

CARE: Feed, pick up droppings and leftover food, clean and refill water dish daily. Take out of cage for exercise at least once a week; more often is better. Take outdoors for exposure to some sunshine as often as possible.

TAMABILITY: Become very accustomed to humans, but don't like being handled. May recognize owner and beg for food.

LIFE SPAN: With good care, can live 10 to 25 years or longer. However, many tortoises die in captivity within months from improper care.

Tarantulas *PAGE 65*

HOUSING: 5½-gallon tank, screen top, incandescent light fixture. Optional gravel for flooring.

SPECIAL REQUIREMENTS: Desert environment, high temperature.

DIET: Live crickets or other large insects.

CARE: Check water daily and replenish if necessary. Feed two or three times a week. Remove insect carcasses and droppings as necessary. Clean up webbing weekly.

TAMABILITY: Become calm with handling. Will not bite unless startled, teased, or cornered.

LIFE SPAN: Females will live up to 25 years. Males tend to be shorter-lived (six to eight years).

Land Snails PAGE 69

HOUSING: Cheesecloth-covered jar.

SPECIAL REQUIREMENTS: High humidity.

DIET: Discarded outside leaves of salad greens.

CARE: Wash out jar and replenish leaves daily.

TAMABILITY: Not tamable.

LIFE SPAN: Three to five years.

Ants PAGE 70

HOUSING: Homemade glass-and-wood ant vivarium or commercial ant farm.

SPECIAL REQUIREMENTS: Soil from home nest area or commercial substitute to build nest in (included in price of commercial ant farm).

DIET: Dead insects, cake crumbs, fruit, nuts, honey.

CARE: Feed and remove leftover food daily.

TAMABILITY: Not tamable.

LIFE SPAN: Workers die within a few months. Queens live several years and continue to produce new workers during their lifetime.

Field Crickets PAGE 73

HOUSING: Cheesecloth-covered jar or screen-and-can cage.

SPECIAL REQUIREMENTS: None.

DIET: Moist bread and cereals, soft fruits, soft sweet vegetables.

CARE: Feed and clean cage daily.

TAMABILITY: Not tamable, but chirp at night.

LIFE SPAN: A year or less.

Salamanders PAGE 75

HOUSING: 5½-gallon tank, glass cover. Optional filter system for large species.

SPECIAL REQUIREMENTS: Moist woodland or semiaquatic environment, high humidity.

DIET: For small species, home-raised fruit flies. For large species, commercial shrimp pellets.

CARE: Ventilate tank daily. Feed large species daily, replenish fruit fly colony for small species weekly. Mist plants, clean filter, or wash soaking dish weekly, depending on type of woodland or semi-aquatic setup you use.

TAMABILITY: Not tamable.

LIFE SPAN: Three to four years.

Tree Frogs PAGE 76

HOUSING: 5½-gallon tank, glass cover, crockery soaking dish.

SPECIAL REQUIREMENTS: Moist woodland environment, high humidity.

DIET: Home-raised fruit flies; larger ones can eat crickets.

CARE: Ventilate tank daily. Replenish fruit fly colony weekly. Mist plants and wash soaking dish weekly.

TAMABILITY: Not tamable.

LIFE SPAN: Three to four years.

Hermit Crabs PAGE 80

HOUSING: Medium-sized homemade cake-pan cage, crockery water dish or 5½-gallon tank, screen top, crockery water dish.

SPECIAL REQUIREMENTS: Bark or substitute for climbing, assortment of shells for crab to choose from as it grows.

DIET: Raw leafy vegetables and greens, prepared pellets, bits of lunch meat (nothing raw, and remove promptly if not eaten).

CARE: Feed, replenish water, and clean up leftover foods daily. Wash cage once a month.

TAMABILITY: Not tamable.

LIFE SPAN: Two years or more.

Fiddler Crabs PAGE 80

HOUSING: 5½-gallon tank, screen top, crockery water dish. Gravel for flooring.

SPECIAL REQUIREMENTS: Deep, damp sand to burrow in.

DIET: Raw leafy vegetables and greens, prepared pellets, bits of luncheon meat (nothing raw, and remove promptly if not eaten).

CARE: Feed, replenish water, clean up leftover foods daily. Either wash and sterilize or replace sand monthly.

TAMABILITY: Not tamable.

LIFE SPAN: Two years.

Bearded dragon

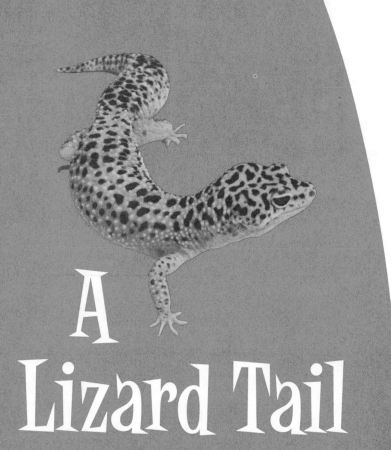

A Lizard Tail

Geckos and anoles have one thing in common: If you catch them by the tail, or sometimes even if you just press on the tail, the tail comes off. It isn't your muscles that have pinched off the tail but the lizard's own muscles. Pressure stimulates muscles between each vertebra to contract suddenly, parting the skin and bone at the same time that other muscles close off the artery to prevent bleeding.

Losing its tail is a clever form of self-defense. The tail keeps wiggling for a few minutes, fooling a predator into thinking it has caught something interesting. The lizard, meanwhile, is long gone and will soon have grown a new tail, although it won't be as pretty as the original.

Lizards shed their skin at intervals, but not in one piece like snakes do. The skin peels off in ribbons that run down the length of the lizard's body. Lizards may shed only once or twice a year or as often as every month. When and how they shed is controlled by chemicals in their body, called hormones, and not by how fast they're growing. No one knows exactly what triggers the hormones that cause lizards to shed.

for protection, and one, the box turtle, can shut the door behind as well. The door is a hinged section that closes up neatly against the top shell.

At about the same time that the tortoise was creating its shell, the world's most numerous, and some say most successful, animal group was evolving: the arthropods. Families in the arthropod group include crustaceans like the hermit crab, arachnids like the spiders, and insects like ants and crickets.

The habits of arthopods can barely be believed. The common hermit crab not only finds a mollusk shell to shelter its unclothed tummy, but also attaches to it a bit of live sponge. The sponge grows to cover the shell, effectively disguising the crab from enemies. Spiders spin webs, build trapdoors, twirl lassos at their prey, construct underwater homes, and manufacture parachutes on which they float for miles. Ants build cities, farm crops, and raise livestock.

Even the common land snail, an unassuming mollusk, can perform extraordinary feats. In 1846 an Egyptian land snail was glued to a piece of cardboard and sent to the British Museum as a natural history specimen. In 1850 staff at the museum soaked the cardboard in water to melt the glue so they could remount the specimen. The snail crawled away, after four years without food, water, or exercise. It had sealed in moisture with a hardened mucous plug at the shell entrance, as snails do in a dry season, and lowered its food and air needs, as other animals do when they hibernate.

None of these pets is the sort that follows you about the house or nudges you for affection. The reward is in being able to share a little in the life of a strange creature enabled to live in your world by the special environment of a vivarium.

Bearded Dragons

I've never owned one of these charming lizards, but I'm told they make wonderful pets for the first-time reptile owner, something that cannot be said of all the species discussed here. Bearded dragons become calm and even friendly with handling. They got their name from the skin under their chins, which is slightly spiky. When aroused or annoyed, both sexes will puff up their throats, making the spikes stand out. Males tend to have much darker beards than females do.

Housing

Because they grow to be about two feet long, bearded dragons need a lot of room. A 60-gallon tank is big enough for one adult. So the lizard can bask, include a rocky area where the temperature falls between 90 and 105 degrees Fahrenheit. The dragon must be able to escape the heat as it regulates its body temperature, so also create a cooler spot with perhaps some rocks or crevices for the lizard to hide in. A tree branch or log makes a good climbing area.

Cover the floor of the tank with newspaper (which needs to be changed frequently), sand, pea rock, or aquarium gravel. Mulch, bark, and corncob litter are not recommended because they might promote bacterial growth. You'll need to pick out droppings and uneaten food several times a week and replace the entire layer of flooring as needed.

Like all reptiles, bearded dragons need full-spectrum lighting so they can synthesize vitamin D_3 and properly absorb calcium. Alternatively, you can expose your pet to sunlight for at least 30 minutes every other day.

Food

Bearded dragons are omnivorous and should be offered a variety of foods, including crickets, mealworms, and pink or fuzzy baby mice. They also need plenty of greens and other vegetables, chopped fine and offered every other day. Crickets should be dusted with a vitamin/mineral supplement — more frequently for younger animals. Don't offer too much food at once to juvenile dragons. Several small meals are preferable, and make sure not to feed a young animal crickets or mealworms that are too large for it to digest easily.

Bearded dragons don't drink from bowls very readily, so you should mist your pet once or twice a day to ensure that it is properly hydrated. Provide water in a shallow dish (a jar lid works well) in case your dragon learns to lower its head to get a drink. Change the water daily.

One reason bearded dragons make such great pets is that they seem to enjoy being gently patted.

Skinks

The information we include here pertains to the blue-tongued skink. There are several other varieties, so do your research before you purchase a particular species. Different kinds of skinks have different housing needs and diets, depending on their native land. While we never kept skinks ourselves, I understand that they make docile and friendly pets, unlike some other kinds of lizards. If handled gently from a young age, they will learn to sit happily on your shoulder or lie cradled in your arms. They are fairly intelligent and curious creatures, and they will enjoy exploring safe areas of your home and yard (always under the strictest observation, of course).

Blue-tongued skinks are solitary and should not be housed in pairs. Other types of skinks may be happy living together, though usually two males will fight over their territory. Skinks are not arboreal (tree dwellers), so they need more horizontal space than vertical room for climbing. They like to burrow into the substrate (flooring) of the cage, so make sure it is deep enough for them to hide in. Don't use sand for flooring, because the skinks might eat it; mulch or torn newspaper is safer. Your pet will also appreciate a box of some sort to retreat to. As with all reptile homes, a skink cage should never be left in direct sunlight.

Skinks are native to Australia, New Guinea, and Tasmania. They don't need a great deal of humidity in their environment, but they should always have clean water available to them. Feed your skink every two or three days, making sure to dust one meal a week with extra calcium. If you're feeding your skink dog or cat food, stick with a high-quality brand made of beef or chicken. Pinkies (baby mice), slugs, earthworms, and mealworms also make up part of a healthy varied diet. To encourage your skink to eat its veggies, try chopping up greens such as spinach and romaine lettuce and mixing them with the dog or cat food. Your lizard will also relish treats such as kiwi, berries, and cantaloupe.

Because skinks are still imported into this country, before bringing a particular skink home, find out where it came from and what its medical background is. Skinks can carry worms and other parasites, so have your new pet checked out by a vet who is familiar with reptiles.

To prevent disease, keep your skink's cage clean. Wash the cage, as well as the skink's dishes and other equipment, regularly with a diluted disinfectant. One part bleach to 10 parts water is a cheap and effective disinfectant solution. Do not use oil-based cleaners such as Lysol and Lestoil; they're not good for reptiles. Dry the cage and all the equipment well before replacing the skink in its home.

fact

Blue-tongued skinks are among the friendliest of lizard pets. If handled gently from a young age, they will learn to lie cradled in your arms or sit happily on your shoulder. They are tame, intelligent, adventurous, and curious creatures.

Desert Iguanas

Desert iguanas are handsome lizards. Though they are able to move fast, they don't scurry and only occasionally leap. Their bodies grow to about 5 inches in length, but the tail can be twice that long, making the adult a full 15 inches long. Desert iguanas are colored a brownish gray, with mottled markings and stripes that resemble the background of their native American Southwest desert environment.

In nature, the desert iguana's life is ruled by extremes of temperature only a handful of animals have managed to cope with. They live in burrows from which they don't emerge until late in the morning, when the desert has heated up. As the temperature rises to heights that would kill other reptiles, iguanas may seek shade, but they return to their burrows only as the heat approaches 115 degrees Fahrenheit. By late afternoon they are out foraging for food again. They are probably most active, and most comfortable, between 90 and 100 degrees.

Our own desert iguana is named Agatha. We don't really know her sex and haven't found a way to tell. She just looks female to us, and so that is how we refer to her. Outside her vivarium Agatha enjoys walking about, climbing up arms, and nestling under hair. If she is warmed up enough to be hungry, she eats mealworms right from our fingers, chewing on them at length before she swallows. The chewing seems not in order to break up the worms at all, but only to get them headed in the right direction. She attacks spinach like a small dinosaur, enthusiastically ripping off great mouthfuls of vegetation and chomping realistically. I say "realistically" here because at other times she may stand so still for so long that one isn't sure she is real. This "freezing" behavior is probably a protection against predators. Were she that still against a brownish gray background, Agatha would be invisible.

In the vivarium, Agatha has a daily routine that reproduces to some extent a natural life. At night she sleeps in the shade and coolness of a slanted rock cave. She climbs her branch during the day to bask in the heat and light above. When she is hungry, she actually takes a stroll to her food dish to see what's there.

Housing

To prepare a home for a desert iguana, set up the desert vivarium shown on page 304, including the screen top. Because these lizards regulate their body temperature by moving around, a fairly large enclosure is needed — a 30-gallon tank is the minimum, and a 40- to 60-gallon tank is recommended. Arrange rocks to form a shaded hiding place. Provide a leaning branch so the lizard can get close to the heat and light when it needs to bask. You will need a jar top to serve dinner in, and recently we have discovered that our lizard likes to soak in a crockery dish of water sunk into the gravel. We don't know that this is necessary, just that she likes it.

Equip the vivarium with a thermometer, as suggested on page 307. Use the ultraviolet light setup described on page 306 and the incandescent fixture described on page 306 for heat. Raise the temperature to at least 90 degrees, and preferably as high as 100 degrees, by using the incandescent fixture during the several hours of the day that include your iguana's feeding time. The heat raises the lizard's activity level enough to make it an eager eater. Use a full-spectrum light such as a Vita-Lite (see page 306) the rest of the day; it will keep the temperature of the tank near 80 degrees. At night, heat the tank only if the room temperature drops below 65 degrees.

Clean the iguana's vivarium of leftover food after every feeding. Pick up dry droppings from the surface of the gravel as you notice them. There won't be many, and they don't smell.

Food and Water

The rule with any relatively unusual pet like a desert iguana is this: Offer a delicatessen. Several books describe the desert iguana as exclusively vegetarian. One prescribes a diet of dandelion leaves and blossoms. Agatha eats spinach and mealworms — seven at a meal. She loves ants. There are reports of these iguanas eating desert cactus blossoms, various insects, the meat from dead animals, and even mouse droppings. Our best advice is to try several kinds of leafy vegetables and fresh herbs, soft

Our Agatha

No doubt the healthiest desert iguanas would be ones you caught wild in America's southwestern deserts. But when we first got Agatha from a local pet store, she was almost as immobile as a statue. If she raised a foot, it might stay raised for 10 minutes. We soon began to think she was the only creature in existence who could double as a robot.

We wondered how such an animal could survive in nature, unless her immobility was a ruse to convince a predator she was already dead. In fact, Agatha looked dead every morning. She fell asleep in assorted postures that suggested a crushed rib cage and broken limbs. Sometimes all four legs were stretched straight behind her flattened body, as if she had just emerged from under a truck tire. We would turn on her incandescent sun. Five minutes passed. An eye opened. A head lifted. A paw assumed a normal position. Her chest rose from the ground. She was alive. Sooner or later the heat would fill her body with enough life that she would nibble half-heartedly on a spinach leaf.

Luckily for Agatha, we didn't think any lizard should act this way. If we had thought this was normal desert iguana behavior, Agatha would eventually have died from vitamin deficiency and dehydration. The pet store had advised room temperature, no water, vegetarian diet. So you can see you'd better do your own research. In this case, several different books on reptiles and desert animals gave us clues about providing sunlight, water, and a delicatessen approach to diet. Now Agatha doesn't at all resemble the dried-up, lethargic lizard we brought home. She has turned into a perky plump worm-gobbler.

fruits, and both mealworms and crickets (available at pet stores). When your lizard has shown its preference, you can reduce its diet to the two or three things it likes, offering other choices every once in a while just in case it changes its mind. If your lizard refuses to eat anything at first, raise the heat in the vivarium to 110 degrees, then try again.

Agatha eats best when we offer her food every other day. The amount she eats seems to have more to do with the temperature in her vivarium and how frequently we let her out for exercise than with any routine daily need. If she is kept warm and allowed to exercise, she eats a small leaf of spinach or about seven worms per meal. If the mealworms are offered with spinach, she eats only the worms. So we offer spinach for one meal, worms for the next. Since mealworms dig into the sand, die, and begin to smell, we put them in a jar top to prevent escape.

Mealworms are the larvae (or grubs) of a small beetle. They will live for weeks — without changing into fat-shaped pupae and then into adult beetles — if they are kept in the refrigerator.

No one, not even a professional naturalist, has ever observed a desert iguana drinking water. This does not mean that iguanas don't need water; it only means that we don't know how they obtain it. Agatha was definitely dehydrated when we got her — her skin was loose and dry. Once we figured out what she liked to eat, she began to regain "normal" skin tone (normal for a lizard, that is).

Although vegetation in the diet provides some water, some lizards are also able to absorb water through their skin. With that in mind, we spray Agatha with a plant mister several times a week. I don't know if it helps, but she seems to like it. And recently, as I mentioned earlier, she has taken to soaking herself in a crockery dish of water.

Lean a branch against one wall of your iguana's vivarium at an angle low enough that your pet can climb it. When the iguana wants to bask in the heat of the light fixture, it will climb up the branch and settle in for a nap.

Carolina Anoles

The Carolina anole, native to our southern states, is another lizard that can live in a dry vivarium. These attractive little lizards are popular pets and relatively easy to keep, though they become stressed if handled too much. Although it is not a true chameleon, the anole shares one characteristic: It can change its color. The anole's range of color is not nearly as dramatic as that of a chameleon, and no patterns are possible, but an anole can change within three minutes from brown to a bright grass green. The off-white belly stays off-white.

A color change may camouflage the lizard, but only if it happens to be in the right place when the change happens. Color change is triggered not by the surrounding scenery but by temperature. At 50 degrees an anole is always brown. As the temperature rises to 70 degrees and beyond, it turns bright green if it is in the shade or in the dark. In bright light it will stay brown. Above 86 degrees it turns pale green and stays that way regardless of light. The color changes help regulate the lizard's body temperature. Dark colors like brown absorb heat. Light colors like green reflect heat. In addition to heat and light, emotions can also make an anole change color. In a fight, the winning anole turns green and the loser fades to brown. We had a Cuban anole, a large relative of the Carolina, that turned brown when you bothered him and green when you gave him a grape.

Anoles are much faster in their movements than desert iguanas, and more sudden in their decisions. We've lost a few anoles by carrying them around on our head or shoulders outdoors. While we thought they were happily resting, they actually had their eye on a leafy branch above. The leap to freedom is so quick and light that you can't feel it happen. There was a transient fashion in the last century for wearing an anole on a woman's lapel. The anole was attached by a little chain collar to a pin in the lady's dress. This seems like a cute idea, but no one sells lizard leashes these days.

The male anole can fan out the skin at his throat, a feat he employs both to attract a female and to warn off a rival male. When light shines through the fan of skin, it appears bright red. No smarter than other lizards, a male anole will make great displays of head nodding and throat fanning at his own reflection in a mirror.

Perhaps because of its ability to change color, anoles are often called chameleons by circuses and pet stores, but they aren't. Anoles are not even near relatives to that curious, curly-tailed African lizard. True chameleons come complete with dragon horns and pop eyes that move separately from each other. Their tails curl like a spiral and can hold on to branches like monkeys' tails. Their tongues are sticky and longer than their bodies. A chameleon can catch a fly by

fact

When an anole is preparing to do something active like eat or fight, it basks in a warm spot to raise its temperature. It may change from green to brown in order to warm up; the darker color absorbs more heat.

extending its elastic tongue and then retracting it complete with stuck-on fly into its mouth.

In case this description makes you want to by-pass the common anole and get to the wonderful chameleon, you will find them for sale. But they are very difficult to keep alive in captivity and they do not make good pets for most people. Because of this, it seems a shame to encourage pet stores to sell these animals; resist buying one, so you won't have to watch it die before its time.

Housing

The vivarium for an anole can be the same as for a desert iguana, but at least one plant should be added. Choose a low, leafy variety, and one that will do well with water sprayed on its leaves. An African violet is a good choice. Sink the pot into the gravel so the plant looks like it's growing there. The plant will be used as a watering station, since anoles drink from droplets only.

Anoles are arboreal, so provide your pet some branches for climbing and plenty of places to hide. Your anole will need to be able to move from the warmer to the cooler parts of the tank.

Incandescent light won't be necessary. Use only full-spectrum light, which will keep the heat high enough and also provide the equivalent of natural sunlight.

Anole droppings are rather small. Use a fork to rake the sand clean once a week.

Anoles are excellent climbers. In their native habitat in the South, you might spot them on tree branches, fences, or walls. To give your anole somewhere to climb, place at least one small branch in its tank.

Food and Water

Carolina anoles eat many kinds of insects. They are so agile and quick that in the summer you can put them on the window screen and watch them leap on flies and moths that have accumulated there. You can catch spiders or unwelcome insects like cockroaches for them. During the winter, rely on store-bought mealworms, served up in a jar-lid platter. The largest male anoles might tackle a store-bought cricket too, and spiders that live in the house all winter are welcome dinners. Anoles eat only live meat, so raw hamburger, while just as healthy as insects, will not do. Anoles don't eat vegetables.

Giving a Carolina anole water is a slight problem. In nature, anoles drink dewdrops or raindrops from the leaves of plants. A pet anole cannot learn to drink from a water dish. Water has to be sprinkled into the vivarium each day, but since water droplets sink quickly into the gravel or drip off the rock, your anole may not have time to drink before the drops disappear. That's the reason for the small leafy plant suggested for this vivarium. Spray the plant daily with a mister or sprinkle water onto it with your fingers, making sure that water isn't building up on the floor of the cage. The natural wax on the leaves will keep the water in droplets for the lizard to lap from.

Land Tortoises

All tortoises are turtles. Turtles that live on land are usually called tortoises, but otherwise they are hardly different from water turtles. Tortoises, like all the turtle clan, have become a big "no" in the pet market since it was discovered that this family of reptiles can carry a bacterium called salmonella. Salmonella causes diarrhea in humans. It is

only unpleasant in adults but is often very serious in young children and infants. However, both land tortoises and water turtles checked for salmonella by the Department of Health are now available.

Land tortoises make particularly good vivarium pets if care is taken about their environment. The elongated, the red-footed, and the Greek tortoises are good choices. Pet stores may sell young ones that are only three to four inches long or adults that may be five to six inches long.

Tortoises are among the most ancient of reptiles, and how they evolved is still a mystery. The earliest fossil tortoise, a full 200 million years old, is virtually identical to the Galápagos Islands tortoise of today except it weighed close to one ton. In other words, no one has dug up a fossil that shows a pre-tortoise reptile just beginning to develop a bony shell; researchers have found only perfectly finished tortoises that, except for their gigantic size, would look normal today. As an aside, this is also true of another reptile, the snake. No one has yet found a fossil snake with little tiny legs — a missing link connecting a lizard to a serpent.

Good nutrition is very important for turtles. If they don't have the right kind of food, their shells will not grow properly. A deformed shell can never be repaired.

Claims about tortoise age records are extraordinary. They've been said to live more than one hundred and fifty years. Allowing for exaggeration and the fact that such claims have not been proved, scientists still think the tortoise is the longest lived of all animals. So if you bring one home, you're making a big commitment.

Tortoises can make wonderful pets, but they are not easy to keep healthy. As you must with all reptiles, do your homework carefully before purchasing a tortoise. Make sure you know what type of turtle you want (some species get quite large and do better if housed outdoors, which is a problem in many climates). It is far preferable to buy a captive-born tortoise than one that was caught in the wild. Wild-caught reptiles tend to be stressed, prone to internal parasites and other ailments, dehydrated, and underfed. You will avoid many problems by starting out with a healthy animal.

Housing

Dryness is normal for land tortoises, all of which come from very dry climates. The desert vivarium (page 304) is a proper home; the 10-gallon size is better than the 5½-gallon, and larger tortoises will need even more room. Tortoises don't climb, so you won't need a branch. The screen top is not necessary either. The leaning rock is a good idea because it provides a shaded corner, but be sure there's enough room for the tortoise to walk behind it and get out again. To prevent a leaning

> In the wild, most land tortoises get most of their water from the plants they eat. In captivity, it's necessary to provide water in a dish set into the sand or gravel of the tank.

rock from falling on a clumsy tortoise, glue a small wood block to the tank floor with epoxy glue. Position it out from the wall as a wedge for the rock to rest against. Push sand over it so it's not visible. Sink a water dish into the sand with the rim barely above the surface. Tortoises lean down to drink.

Because tortoises look so indestructible, people often fail to keep them warm enough. The tortoises in pet stores are young and delicate and usually succumb to respiratory disease if kept in an unheated vivarium. Daytime temperature should be 80 degrees, with normal room temperature (65 to 70 degrees) at night. An 80-degree temperature can usually be obtained with just full-spectrum light (page 306). Tortoises must have this ultraviolet light unless you are supplementing their diet with ready-made vitamin D foods like cod-liver oil. If the ultraviolet light doesn't keep the vivarium warm enough, add incandescent light as needed (page 306).

Pick up droppings as they occur, and remove leftovers after each meal. Change the water and wash the water dish daily.

Once a tortoise has survived infancy, its health is less of a worry. Adult tortoises over five years old can live free in a home or apartment as long as they have access to a warm spot, like a sunny corner or a radiator. Keep a low pan of drinking water available all the time. In really warm areas like Florida and southern California, people keep adult pet tortoises all year long in a fenced yard. They have been known to learn to nudge their owner's feet when they get hungry.

Food and Water

Tortoises are about as omnivorous as we are — they eat fruits, vegetables, meat, and even eggs. However, some species are more vegetarian than others, so research the individual needs of your pet. Offer a selection of dark leafy vegetables like spinach and romaine lettuce and ripe fruits like tomato, pear, banana, and chopped apple. Corn on the cob is a favorite. Include raw hamburger in the diet and try occasional snacks of raw fish or raw chicken. Although a tortoise can go for weeks without food, that does not mean it should. Feed your tortoise once every day. A reluctant eater can sometimes be encouraged to eat by dyeing a light-colored food like banana with red or yellow vegetable dye.

Pet tortoises will become accustomed to humans, and some even learn to recognize their owner, but most don't like to be handled overly much.

Tortoises need extra calcium if they are to grow well in captivity. There are several ways to provide it. Bonemeal (sold at plant stores as a fertilizer) and pulverized eggshells are good sources of calcium; try sprinkling them over the hamburger meat. You can even pound up the cuttlebone sold for birds in pet stores. Two times a week is often enough for the calcium additive.

If you don't use the full-spectrum light so that your tortoise can manufacture its own vitamin D, you'll have to mess with cod-liver oil, which contains vitamin D. Occasionally a tortoise will open its mouth and let you put a delicious drop right in. More often, it will merely consent to eat its hamburger with a drop of cod-liver oil on it. A drop a day is recommended.

A tortoise will drink from a dish sunk into the gravel so that its rim is almost level with the surrounding surface. It doesn't lap the water but drinks with a sucking and swallowing movement. Be sure the water is deep enough for the tortoise to put its snout in.

Incidentally, if your tortoise makes a clicking noise, it is probably grinding its teeth.

Illnesses

If your tortoise gets a respiratory disease, the symptoms are inactivity, a runny or bubbling nose, and noisy breathing, which you can hear if you lean your head close.

Keep the temperature at 80 or even 85 degrees. Use a powdered form of Terramycin (available from a veterinarian) or a bird antibiotic (available from pet stores). Following the recommended dosage for birds, dissolve the medicine daily in the tortoise's drinking water. To be sure it gets enough, sprinkle about half the same quantity on its food. If the antibiotic is in tablet form, you will have to crush it with a spoon first. Check with your vet before giving medicine.

Tarantulas

Another of the larger vivarium pets is both interesting and useful. It is interesting in that it is a large spider called a tarantula. It is useful in that it keeps away unwanted guests. In fact, we recently read of a jewelry store owner who keeps a tarantula in his window display at night. He used to be robbed frequently; he's never robbed anymore.

People's fear of the tarantula is due not only to some deep-seated and ancient horror of the beast but also to a totally unfounded belief that tarantulas are deadly poisonous. This is not so. Tarantulas, like most other spiders, secrete a salivary fluid that is injected through their fangs into their victim. The saliva contains digestive enzymes. The enzymes digest the prey from the inside out, reducing the tissues to liquid. The spider then sips its dinner neatly from the undigested shell. Its secretions definitely kill insects and even young birds and mice, but its bite causes only local pain and swelling in humans. The malicious rumor that tarantulas are deadly to all probably came from a mix-up between the American tarantulas and some European spiders that are the real bad guys.

There are around 800 varieties of tarantulas, and they don't all have the same basic needs. Some are arboreal and need branches to climb on, while others prefer to burrow into the earth. Some species need much higher humidity than others do. You can buy tarantulas at pet stores and from suppliers on the Internet, but you should do your homework first to figure out what kind you want and what you will need to provide to keep it healthy.

Our tarantula measures five inches from toe to toe. She is a painted tarantula, native to the deserts of our Southwest, and though she's not as large as some of the South American varieties, her bright orange stripes make her the most colorful member of the family.

We've named our tarantula Mary. How do we know she is a girl? We don't — it's a guess. Male tarantulas have special complicated mouth parts that are simpler in females, and in many species, males have small hooks on their front set of legs. Both sexes have a hole (or vent) behind where their eight legs emerge. The female lays her eggs through the vent. The male picks up a package of sperm from his vent with his special mouth parts and inserts the package into the female's vent to fertilize her eggs before they are laid.

Mary, like all American tarantulas, has eight eyes, eight legs, a little pair of mouth parts called pedipalps on either side of her mouth, and fangs. She allows us to pick her up and walks freely on us. She has never bitten, reserving her bites for potential dinners only. We use caution basic to animal handling, however. When we pick up Mary, we do so from behind using two hands as scoops. No animal likes being cornered.

We don't bother her when she is hungry or when she is molting. Hunger makes anybody grouchy. Molting's worse. In a spider, molting is much more complicated than simply climbing out of a tight skin. Each molt is accompanied by radical cell destruction, construction, and rearrangement inside the spider's body. After a molt, and

there may be as many as nine in some species, a spider is a different creature inside as well as outside. During the final molt in a male or female spider's life, its internal reproductive organs are manufactured. It's enough to make anyone want to bite.

For some spiders, growing up to sexual maturity means the approach of death. Females may die after their eggs are laid, and in a few kinds of spiders the female kills and eats the male after mating. Most male tarantulas live only between a few months and a couple of years. But female tarantulas continue with their adult lives for a long time, living frequently to the ripe old age of 25.

Housing

Our tarantula vivarium is about the same as the desert iguana's. Mary has a rock to hide under, gravel under her feet, and an incandescent sun in her sky. The full-spectrum light isn't necessary. The incandescent light is used to heat her environment when the house is cold. A good average daytime temperature is 70 to 75 degrees. At night you can let the temperature drop to the 60s. Don't be fooled by the apparent immobility of a resting tarantula — a screen top is necessary. Tarantulas can jump out of a tank in a flash.

Some tarantulas have needs different from Mary's, so make sure you know what your particular spider should have. For some species, for example, this environment would be much too dry.

We keep water in a small dish sunk to its rim in the gravel. We were told to keep a bit of sponge in the water dish. Our tarantula strokes it with her

fact

Like tarantulas, wolf spiders have excellent senses of vision and touch. To catch prey, they don't spin webs but, rather, hunt. A large wolf spider will eat crickets. If you can't afford a tarantula, you can catch and keep a wolf spider instead.

pedipalps but we don't know whether she's drinking or washing her face. But in case that's how she drinks, we don't dare remove it. Several times a week we change the water to keep it clean.

Though tarantulas do spin webs, they don't inhabit them the way other spiders do. When she's done eating, Mary spins a neat case around the shell of her finished dinner and pushes it to a corner of her cage, away from the entrance to her rock burrow. She similarly encases her own weekly bowel movement. Both prey and bowel movement can be picked out by hand whenever you notice them. Stray webbing gets left about on the surface of the gravel; we remove it with a fork when we see it.

We thought plants would look nice in Mary's home and at first placed an array of cacti and succulents in small sunken pots in the gravel. The job of keeping them free of webbing was too annoying, however, so we removed some and made her home simpler. The cage should be thoroughly cleaned out two or three times a year, or anytime you notice a buildup of excess moisture, mites, or other problems.

Food and Water

Tarantulas hunt insects and small animals such as baby birds and mice. They can leap as far as three feet when attacking prey. Mary does well on

Molting Mary

At the beginning of one summer, Mary suddenly refused to eat. Three weeks went by without a cricket. She acted sluggish but was jumpy when touched. My son swears she kicked him. Then she began to turn blue. Her normally pinky beige glow faded to a leaden hue, and her hair dropped out. We called several vets, one of whom had once examined a tarantula with a sore toe, but none of them had advice to offer. It was time for summer vacation, so we left Mary to board at our friendly neighborhood pet shop with our commiserations. "Don't feel bad if she dies," we said. "We know she is very sick."

All summer no one had the nerve to call and find out Mary's fate. When we got back, we went gloomily to the pet store to hear the bad news. Just as we thought, our friend held out to us a plastic bag with Mary's remains. We caught a glimpse of dried legs, an abdomen, fangs. Then he pointed to the shelf. There was Mary, bigger, brighter, hairier than ever. She had molted. We don't know yet if that was Mary's final, grown-up molt, but if she ever stops eating and turns blue again, we'll at least know what to expect. The plastic bag of spider exoskeleton worked well as a show-and-tell item in school.

You should be extra careful around your tarantula during and right after a molt. Avoid handling her during this time and don't give her food for a few days after she sheds, because she needs time for her new skin to dry and toughen up. She could actually be harmed, even by a cricket, because she is so vulnerable right after molting.

store-bought crickets, usually three or four a week. She either drinks or bathes or both at her water sponge. We've had her for over a year now, and she appears to be in excellent health.

A greater problem than keeping Mary in good health is keeping the crickets alive. She won't eat them if they're dead. Crickets sold for food must have food of their own to survive. Keep them in a coffee can, with holes punched through the plastic lid for ventilation. Sprinkle cornmeal in the bottom for them to eat, and add a slice of apple or potato for both food and moisture. Keep the can in a warm place — near a radiator in winter. With this method, we just barely manage to keep the crickets alive for one week's food supply.

Plumb out of crickets one day and suspecting Mary was hungry, we caught two wolf spiders for her dinner, a large one and a small one. They're similar to tarantulas in that they hunt and leap on their prey. We put both wolf spiders in Mary's cage. In a twinkling, the large wolf spider leaped upon the small one. In another twinkling, Mary leaped upon the large wolf spider. It was nature in the raw.

But the event gave us the idea that if you can't afford a tarantula, you can catch a large wolf spider instead. They hang about under baseboards in the house, in basements, and outside near foundations, coming out mainly in the evening to hunt. It is not hard to catch one in a jar and then slip the lid under the opening. A large wolf spider will eat crickets. A friend of ours found a wolf spider living behind a piece of scrap lumber in his basement. Instead of capturing it, he taught the spider to come out for dinner. He feeds it mealworms from his fingers.

Land Snails

Even a mollusk can be a pet. The ordinary garden snail, a relative of all the seashell creatures and of clams and mussels, eats well and stays healthy in captivity. Look for snails in the grass along a damp wall or foundation, and in the woods under rocks and rotting logs or at the base of trees.

A snail is such a common, taken-for-granted, everyday critter, few people ever wonder how it gets its shell. The snail makes it — rapidly when it is young and growing fast, slowly as it approaches its natural size limit. Take a magnifying glass and look carefully at your snail's shell. Between the spiral grooves, you'll see the shell is a series of tiny bands. Each band represents a thin layer of a special fluid secreted by the snail. The fluid hardens upon exposure to air, forming a new band at the shell opening. The shell begins at the center of the clockwise spiral pattern. As the snail grows, it adds new layers at its shell opening to accommodate its size.

In hot dry weather a snail may shut itself up completely. It seals its shell entrance with an air-hardened substance. Thus protected from loss of moisture, it can estivate (be inactive during dry, hot weather) for several months.

The part of a snail's body that makes contact with the ground is called a foot. Its mucus-smoothed, wavelike motion isn't very efficient, but its slime protects it from rough ground. Snails really are the slowest animals; the slowest move at about 23 inches an hour.

The long stalks on top of the snail's head are tipped with light-sensitive pigment and serve as eyes. The shorter stalks more toward the front of its head are touch-sensitive feelers. Both move in every direction and can be retracted into the head.

Housing

A snail prefers a climate more moist than your home. A jar-sized vivarium (page 303), naturally humidified by the moisture in a lettuce leaf, takes care of that. Ventilation is essential; don't substitute a pierced jar lid for the cheesecloth top suggested on page 303. Never leave a jar vivarium in sunlight. Even one hour of sun can heat up the inside like a greenhouse and kill your pet in short order. Snails prefer damp shade, anyway.

Every day, remove the snail and its food from the jar and rinse out the jar well with fresh tap water. You may have to use a sponge too, since the mucous trails left by the snail are quite gooey and hard to clean. The black spots are droppings. Dry the jar so there is no extra moisture to invite decay. Put in a fresh lettuce leaf for humidity, plus whatever other snack is on the day's menu.

Food and Water

Small as it is, a snail has a mouth, called a radula, equipped with powerful teeth that can chomp through even tough vegetation. The easiest diet to feed a snail in captivity is leafy lettuce (but not iceberg). It wouldn't hurt to also offer other leafy vegetables, such as spinach and watercress. If you have the patience, you'll be able to watch your snail eat its way along the edge of a leaf or chomp holes in its middle. If you remove the lettuce and look at the chomp marks carefully, you can actually see the pattern of tiny teeth.

Snails don't drink. They get their water from the leaves they eat. Be sure to replace these leaves before they dry out.

Ants

Ants are among the few insects that are truly social. Each colony is composed of three kinds of ants: a queen, winged males, and wingless sterile female workers. Most colonies keep only one queen. As winged males and new winged queens come to maturity, they fly from the nest to mate. Sometimes these flights happen all at once over a wide area and the sky is filled with "flying ants," coupling in the air and then falling to the ground still attached to one another.

The males have a short life. They fly, mate, and die. Mated queens, however, immediately dig small nests of their own. They bite off their wings if they have not already fallen off, lay their first eggs, and raise them to adult workers. Then the workers take over the running of the new colony.

Workers, all the crawling ants you are likely to see, extend the nest, keep it clean, protect it from enemies, forage for food and water, and bring back the liquefied meal in their crops (stomachs) to feed to the larvae in the nest. Ants that have been out foraging also share their regurgitated food with ants that have been too busy in the nest to go out, as well as with the queen, who for the remainder of her long life — as much as 15 years — will be too busy laying eggs to take care of herself or her offspring in any way.

Getting the Ants

You can buy ants from a variety of places, including through the mail (check the Internet for sources), but the colony you get probably won't contain a queen. If you'd rather try for a long-lived colony plus the chance to see eggs develop through larval and pupal stages into full-grown ants, you will have to hunt your own. You will need a white cloth about the size of a pillowcase, two jars with lids, a pair of tweezers, a pointed hand trowel, and a friend.

Ants are amazing! Different types keep slaves, harvest crops, raise aphids, and have armies.

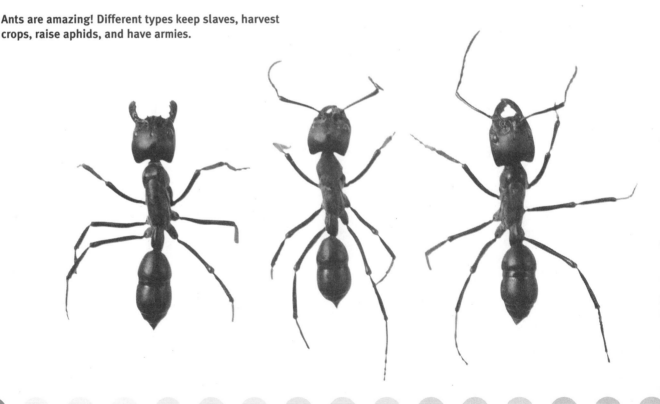

ANT DEVELOPMENT

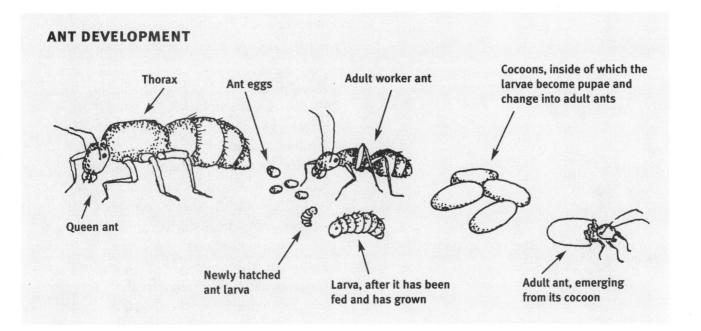

Thorax

Ant eggs

Adult worker ant

Cocoons, inside of which the larvae become pupae and change into adult ants

Queen ant

Newly hatched ant larva

Larva, after it has been fed and has grown

Adult ant, emerging from its cocoon

Many common species of ant make good pet colonies. The smallest red ants may be too little to see well, but the larger rust or black dirt-dwelling species are fine. Look for a small anthill that is built in soft dirt or sand and will be easy to dig up. The structure of the nest can go quite deep into the soil, and the queen either is already in or soon will depart to the deepest recesses. She's the one you're after.

Lay the white cloth next to the anthill. Bravely take your spade and in one deep scoop lift the anthill and the soil beneath it onto the cloth. Ants will be all over the place in a second, some dragging oval white pupae with them. Now look for the queen. She may be larger than the other ants, but not necessarily. Another clue is the size of her thorax (the portion of the body between the head and the abdomen, or what we would think of as the chest). The queen's thorax is larger than the other ants'. If you see a group of ants dragging around another ant, that may well be the queen. The ants are attempting to get her back into the deep part of their nest. If you don't see the queen,

take your time about picking up other ants before you start to search the nest.

Use the tweezers to pick up a few dozen ants and put them in one of the jars. Do this carefully so you don't crush them. If you can, identify by body type the important different kinds of ants that make up a colony. A colony is most effective when it is fully equipped with workers as well as with eggs, pupae, and larvae. Eggs, pupae, and larvae exude chemical substances that mature ants appreciate and that are important to the organization and daily work of a colony. Put each of the pupae the ants are carrying in the other jar to protect them from the overexcited ants. Later, you can add to the pupa jar any eggs and larvae you find as you excavate the nest. Your friend should be helping you with all this.

When you have the ordinary ants you want safely in one jar and some pupae in another, start to excavate the nest for the queen, some eggs, and some larvae. By this time the queen will be at the very bottom of the nest. Dig carefully, following along tunnels with the point of the trowel. If you

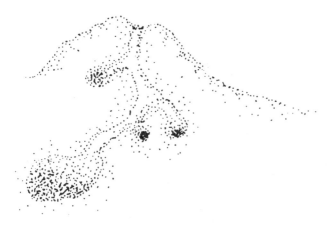

As ants start their tunnel, they carry up grains of dirt to form the hill.

find the queen, put her in the same jar with the eggs, the larvae, and the developing pupae.

If you don't find the queen in this nest, you have a choice: Either settle for this generation of ants and the next that will develop from the eggs or throw out your catch and start again on another nest. You can't use a queen from another nest, as she will be murdered by the colony.

If you have not yet added soil to your ant vivarium, you have time to do so now. The ants will appreciate having soil taken from near their nest. Add some soil from the nest itself if you can. It will smell like home to the ants.

There are two ways to transfer your ants into the vivarium without getting ants all over the house. The first is to refrigerate them in the jars for a few hours until they move sluggishly and are easy to handle. The second way is to dump them from the jar into a sinkful of water. They won't drown, but they'll be easy to pick up from the surface of the water — gently — with tweezers. Once in the vivarium, the ants will usually set right to work building a new home.

Watching the industry of ants is exhausting. Some ants excavate whole cities hundreds of feet in extent and housing half a million individuals.

Your labors in catching the ants can't begin to match the industry you're about to witness.

Housing

An ant colony can be kept in a tall narrow glass vivarium filled with soil taken from the vicinity of the ants' nest or with an artificial substitute. Since the ants have only a narrow space in which to work, many segments of their tunnels and rooms will run along the glass. You can see the construction and the builders themselves as they work. Instructions for making an ant vivarium are on page 315, or you can buy one in a pet department or order one by mail.

The homemade ant house has cardboard sides to keep light from the ants' tunnels when you aren't watching them. The commercial ant houses don't come with cardboard sides. Add your own by cutting cardboard to fit. Attach the cardboard to the top of each side with masking tape.

Food and Water

Since captive ants can't forage for food, you have to feed them. Ants eat a balanced diet of dead insects and sweet food. Dead mealworms or flies will do for the insect food. Tiny bits of nuts, cake crumbs, sweet breakfast cereals, honey, and fruits will do for sweets. Water is also necessary to an ant environment. A good way to provide both water and honey is to keep a small square of sponge moistened with honey-water in the feeding area. Replenish the sponge with a few drops of water and a drop of honey each day.

Remember, ants have tiny stomachs. Try not to overfeed them. Ants will store their food if there is too much for them to eat. Don't give them a surplus for storage, since it can decay, grow moldy, and ruin the colony. Clean up leftovers and add new food by reaching in through the hole at the top of the vivarium with tweezers.

Field Crickets

Crickets, another type of insect, have been kept as pets for centuries in China. The traditional Chinese cricket home is a tiny bamboo cage, complete with sliding door. A cricket in a cage, like a cricket on the hearth, was considered good luck in China, as it was in Europe and in America. For people who didn't want the live pet, cricket doorstops and cricket doorknockers provided a substitute. The real thing is easy to keep.

Only the male cricket sings. The sound is made by a process called stridulation, in which one surface is rubbed against the other. The male grasshopper "fiddles" by rubbing his wing against a leg. The male cricket, on the other hand, uses only his wings. He leans forward, lifting his wings above his back, and rubs a scraper under the upper wing against a file on the lower wing. You can produce a similar sound by rubbing the back of a knife against a regular metal file. It won't sound as pretty as the cricket's chirp, but it's the same idea.

Crickets sing, like birds sing, to announce their whereabouts to female crickets and to warn other males away from their small territories. You can recognize the male cricket because he has no ovipositor, the long tube used for egg laying that sticks out the rear end of females. Young male crickets can't sing until their wings are big enough to cover their back. Most field crickets are mature with full wings by late July or August.

A cricket in captivity can live through the winter and occasionally into spring and summer. His chirping is pleasant but persistent during the night. If it drives you crazy, you may have to lock him out of your bedroom.

fact

You can tell what the temperature is by counting the number of times your cricket chirps in one minute. Divide by 4 and add 40 — the answer should be quite close to the current temperature in degrees Fahrenheit.

Catching a Cricket

Pet stores sell a tan-colored cricket as live food, but this species is difficult to keep alive more than a week or so. If you have no other choice, you can give it a try, following the suggestions given for keeping a tarantula's dinner alive on page 68. The dark brown or black field cricket is a much better pet, and sings more enthusiastically.

Wait until August, when crickets are full grown and chirping, to collect your new pet. At nightfall arm yourself with a flashlight and a jar. Listen for the *crick-crick* sound of a cricket. Favorite haunts of crickets are typically dark and damp, often close to a source of food. Look for them on the damp earth at the base of a foundation, especially where garbage pails are kept, or in other dampish spots in long grass, at the base of rocks or the trunks of trees. We've had our best success at the base of a well near a compost heap where rotting vegetation, dripping water, protective grass, and a masonry wall make a fine world for crickets.

When you locate the sound, walk slowly toward it. When the sound stops, stop walking;

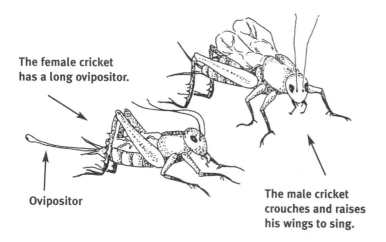

The female cricket has a long ovipositor.

Ovipositor

The male cricket crouches and raises his wings to sing.

wait until you hear the chirp resume and then proceed again. The sound of your footsteps will make the cricket stop singing over and over again. But sooner or later he will chirp again, even when you are only inches away. When you're quite sure you're almost stepping on him, turn on your light and start searching, pulling grass or leaves apart with your hands until you find him. Place your hand over him loosely. Then gently close your whole hand around him. Don't ever pick up cricket by a leg — their legs come off easily. Let the cricket drop from your hand into the jar. Then turn the light on him and make sure you have found a male. Remember that he's been singing in order to get a lady friend to join him, and if she's arrived, you may have caught her instead of the male.

Housing

The screened cage and the bug jar, on pages 302–303, are excellent homes for a cricket. You must keep the humidity high by placing a small square of moist sponge at the bottom of the vivarium. The vivarium should be rinsed out every day to get rid of leftover food and droppings. Dry it so there aren't puddles, but don't forget to rinse out and replenish the moistened sponge. While you're cleaning the vivarium, you can keep the cricket in an empty jar or can.

You can keep crickets as pets or as food for bigger pets.

Food and Water

Once safely home and settled into a cage, your cricket might be hungry. Crickets eat a large variety of foods, including other insects. They'll enjoy bread moistened with milk, as well as soft foods like banana, cooked sweet potato, tomato, and moistened cereals. Drinking water isn't necessary.

Salamanders

Because salamanders have the same general body shape as lizards, people often think they are reptiles. But salamanders are amphibians, hatched in the water as tadpoles, living only part of their lives in moist land areas, and going back to the water to mate and lay their eggs. Salamanders don't have scales as reptiles do; their skin is smooth and always damp.

There are several common salamanders you might easily find in the woods in the eastern half of this country. Elsewhere they are more rare. Many pet stores sell nonnative types of salamanders. Before you buy one, do a lot of research to make sure you know exactly how to take care of it. Some species can live for decades, so you are making a big commitment! If you plan to catch a salamander yourself, first check with your local wildlife service to make sure you're allowed to keep it. Some native salamander species have become rare or even endangered, and it is against the law to capture them.

The morning after a rain you may find salamanders walking about, but ordinarily they shy away from the dry outdoors and stick to their damper hideouts. Their native haunts are in woodlands, under rocks and rotting logs. Turning over rocks and logs will eventually uncover one if you are persistent.

Be careful not to handle your pet too much. Salamanders breathe through their delicate skin and will suffocate if they get too dry. The oils and dirt on your hands may be harmful to them, and some species exude toxins that can be irritating to humans.

Catching a Salamander

Salamander species are often very local and you will have to look at a field guide to amphibians for your area of the country to see which kinds live near you. The most dramatic are the larger species like the black and yellow polka-dotted salamander, which can grow to six or seven inches in length. If you catch a young one, you could have it as a pet for 25 years — its normal life span.

Another larger salamander is the yellow- or light olive-blotched tiger salamander, which at 13 inches is the largest salamander you will find on land in the world. It would still look meager compared to the largest water-dweller — the giant salamander of Japan measures five feet, weighs over 20 pounds, and may live for 50 years.

Salamanders live under rocks and rotting logs. After a rain, they may come out to enjoy the damp woodland floor.

Smaller species include the marbled salamander and the striped two-lined salamander. Both can be found on land. The common newt, another small species, is a brown water creature in its adult stage but a bright red spotted beast when in its juvenile land-dwelling stage. These youngsters are called red efts.

Housing

The moist woodland vivarium described on page 309 is a suitable home for salamanders. If you find one of the large species like the yellow polka-dotted salamander, you'll have to add a sunken crockery dish for it to soak in, or instead make one of the other semiaquatic environments suggested on page 312.

Salamanders are most unlikely to climb out of their home unless there is an obvious route, like a leaning branch. They can't climb glass walls. When weather is humid, you can remove the glass top to give ventilation. When the weather is dry,

remove the top once a day and wave fresh air into the vivarium before replacing it.

The semiaquatic vivarium needs no top. No misting is necessary in a semiaquatic tank, but mist once a week if you are using a sunken water dish in a woodland vivarium. Clean the bathing dish, if you have one, at least once a week, and refill it with fresh water.

Any of the salamanders can share their home with other salamander species or with tree frogs.

Food and Water

The smaller salamanders can eat only small insects. These are very hard to collect. The easiest substitute for wild bugs is a fruit fly colony, in which adult flies continue to lay eggs, the eggs become larvae, the larvae hatch into adult flies, and the whole process starts all over again. This whole life cycle takes only 10 days. See the box on page 78 for instructions on how to start a fruit fly colony.

Larger salamanders will eat shrimp pellets, a fish food available in pet stores. Drop food daily on the surface of their bathing pond.

Tree Frogs

The spring peepers of the East and the Pacific tree frogs of the West are both tiny arboreal (tree-dwelling) frogs whose long toes are equipped with sucking disks that allow them to cling to trunks and branches. No bigger than a thumbnail, these amphibians are noisemakers all out of proportion to their size. The male's mating call is enormously amplified by an inflated throat sac, which looks very much like a bubble-gum bubble. It's only by following the sound that you have a chance of finding these tiny, shy creatures.

Start Your Own Fruit Fly Colony

Start a fruit fly colony in warm weather when the flies are abundant. Use a baby-food jar as the container. Moisten the bottom. Crush a little overripe banana into the bottom of the jar. Wait until it begins to attract fruit flies — the tiny, slow-flying critters that hover over decaying fruit. Don't let either the fruit or the bottom of the jar dry out. When fruit flies have been swarming over the jar for several days, you can put the jar in the vivarium. Eggs will be laid in the fruit, and more flies will be available soon. Each adult female lays 3,000 eggs!

A fruit fly colony in a baby-food jar.

To keep a fruit fly colony going outside the vivarium, use a larger jar, like a mayonnaise jar. Instead of putting the fruit directly in the jar, put it in two small containers such as bottle caps. Put the filled bottle caps in the bottom of the jar.

Once some adult flies are inside, cover the jar with a thin cloth held in place with a rubber band. Each week you can remove one of the bottle caps to the vivarium, where a new crew of flies will hatch. Replenish the jar with another fruity bottle cap.

A few flies might escape when the top is open, but on the whole they prefer to stay where their dinner is. They aren't aware that they are about to become dinner themselves.

A fruit fly colony in a cloth-covered jar. Each bottle cap will contain eggs that hatch and grow into flies in the vivarium.

Green tree frogs from the Florida area are commonly found in pet shops, as are gray tree frogs, which appear to be a southern subspecies. Tropical species of tree frogs are also very popular.

Catching a Tree Frog

As evening falls in mating season, most likely April, you will hear a chorus of peeping from every damp spot around. The sound is a high-pitched *peep-peep-peep,* and it comes from the throats of the male tree frogs. Take a flashlight and a jar with a lid and follow the sound. As with cricket hunting, your footsteps will temporarily make the tree frogs stop their peeping. They will start again if you stop walking.

When you're close to a particular *peep-peep-peep,* turn on your flashlight and examine the tree trunks near you. Once you see a tree frog, it is not hard to catch it in your hands. Transfer it to the jar and close the lid. Try to get your peeper into his vivarium soon so his breathing pores don't dry out.

Housing

Tree frogs would probably do best in one of the semiaquatic vivariums suggested on page 312, but they may also be kept in a moist woodland vivarium. They can live with any of the salamanders. Add branches for the frogs to cling to.

A glass cover is absolutely necessary. Tree frogs are acrobatic jumpers and climbers; their suction pads allow them to climb glass walls. If a tree frog escapes from its moist vivarium into the dry house air, it will surely die. Amphibians do much of their breathing through their moist skin.

A dry frog suffocates. Toads are one of the few amphibians that can live in dry areas; they moisten their own breathing pores with mucus produced in the bumps or "warts" on their skin.

Other than water changes or filter cleaning in your semiaquatic vivarium, the only maintenance task is to ventilate the vivarium every day by carefully removing the glass top and waving fresh air inside. If you are using a woodland vivarium, mist it with water once a week.

Food and Water

Feed tree frogs fruit flies, exactly as for small salamanders. If you can get a look at the frogs feeding, you'll notice that they catch insects on the wing with their long, sticky tongues. Misting will take care of the frogs' water requirements.

fact

Most tree frogs have wide disks on the ends of their toes that help them cling tightly to branches, tree trunks, and the walls of a vivarium. If you don't keep a lid on your pet's home, you'll soon find it climbing the walls of *your* home.

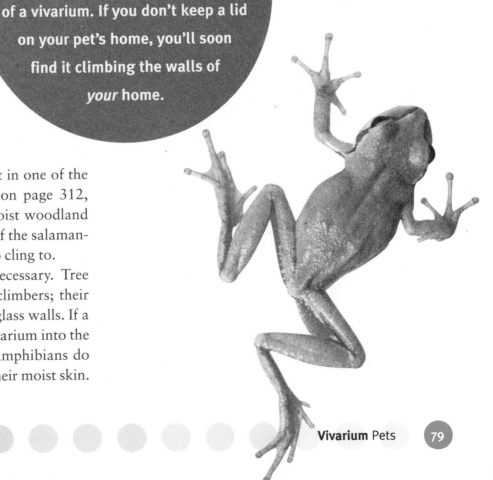

Hermit and Fiddler Crabs

Few crustaceans (such as lobsters, crabs, shrimp) are popular as pets, but the hermit crab (or tree crab) has many admirers. Although the creature itself is nothing much to look at, it clothes itself in a mollusk shell and becomes as lovely as the shell it chooses. One crab I know of lives in a Venetian pearl shell.

Behind the hermit crab's hard-shelled head and claws, its body is completely soft. It is shaped in a spiral, twisted to fit snugly in a discarded mollusk shell. It can pull its body almost completely into this borrowed house, and it is probably the excellent protection the shell provides that has allowed several species of hermit crabs to leave the water and live on land. Some even climb trees, and are popularly known as tree crabs.

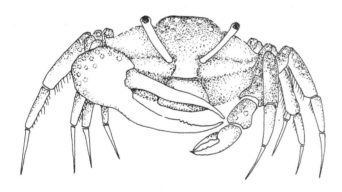

In actual size a fiddler crab is only about as big as a 50-cent piece.

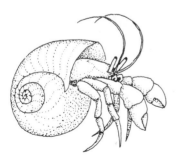

Hermit crabs that live in water attach a bit of live sponge to their shell. The sponge grows to cover the shell, becoming an effective camouflage.

Fiddler crabs are less dramatic but still satisfyingly peculiar. The males of this species have developed a super-big claw — usually the right one — that they wave about comically both to entice females and to threaten other males. They scuttle on the beaches at low tide, picking up anything that might be edible and waving frantically at real or imagined dangers. The sight of a tiny fiddler crab holding a cigarette butt aloft on a North Carolina beach is among my favorite memories.

Fiddler crabs are among those animals that have an incredible internal clock. For instance, they change colors — dark in the daytime and light at night — but they do it by the clock, regardless of how light or dark you make their quarters. In nature, they burrow into their holes during high tides and scramble out to look for food during low tides. Even when kept as pets thousands of miles from their native seashore, they still emerge from their burrows at low-tide time. Since low tides come at somewhat different times each day, this is a remarkable feat. Even more remarkable, you could live in Ohio and still know, by your fiddler-crab-clock, precisely when low tide is in the area where your pet was originally caught.

Choosing a Crab

Both crabs are quite common — hermit crabs along almost any shore and fiddler crabs from temperate to tropical beaches. Both are also available in pet stores from time to time.

Housing

Hermit crabs must have an assortment of new shells to choose from as their bodies grow. Depending on which species of hermit you have, the shells might be as small as little snail shells or as large as an orange. It is best to provide a whole

Hermit crabs need a variety of shells, in different sizes, to choose from while they grow.

pile of snail-shaped or pointy-shaped shells. Pet hermit crabs will fuss with this pile, pushing the shells here and there, trying on this one and that one for size.

Hermit crabs enjoy climbing and would be happier with a wire-mesh cage, like the cake-pan cage on page 330, than with a glass tank. If you'd rather use a tank, provide large pieces of bark or a slanted surface of wire-mesh hardware cloth for the crab to climb around on.

Fiddler crabs need moist sand in which to live and dig their burrows. Use a 5½-gallon tank, filled with at least six inches of sand to provide enough digging space. In nature, burrows may be as much as a foot deep. Keep the sand moist — about the consistency of the seashore after the tide has gone out. Don't flood the sand, since fiddler crabs are air-breathing and can drown.

For either pet, be sure to use a cover — the cake pan, or a screen top to fit the tank. Sink a small water dish into the sand for drinking water. The top of a glass jar would be about the right size.

Clean the cage of leftover foods every day, and refresh the water dish. Moisten the fiddler crab's sand as necessary.

The moist sand that the fiddler crab requires is somewhat difficult to keep clean. A safe routine is to remove all the sand every month, rinse it well, and bake it in the oven at 300 degrees for at least an hour. The heat will kill bacteria and help prevent decay in the damp sand. Then put the sand back in the crab's tank.

Food and Water

Like most crabs, both hermits and fiddlers are scavengers, which means they eat almost anything. Lettuce, spinach, seaweed, or water plants provide their vegetable needs, but it is best to offer small bits of raw hamburger or raw fish — even dog or cat food — also. Cleanup is more of a problem with meat than with vegetables.

Both crabs need fresh water to drink, although the fiddler crab may satisfy at least part of its thirst by filtering water from the moist sand.

Aquarium Pets

Water pets live in aquatic vivariums called aquariums. A few water pets are in-between pets. A turtle, for example, can live in a semiaquatic vivarium as happily as it would in an aquarium. A red eft will eventually leave the land and take to the water, just as a tadpole will eventually leave the water and take to the land.

Almost all the characters you'll read about in this chapter can live together in a single tank. Take, for example, a large goldfish, a small turtle, a couple of bullfrog tadpoles, a garbage-collecting crayfish, and an algae-eating snail. All these creatures should be able to find neighborly harmony together in an aquarium just as they might in a small pond in nature. You might add to this aquatic crew a whirligig beetle or a water strider, letting it skim across the surface of the water. These insects aren't exactly pets; you can't feed them their natural food and they may eventually get eaten by an enterprising goldfish. But here we have a fish (the goldfish), a reptile (the turtle), amphibians (the bullfrog tadpoles), a crustacean (the crayfish), and a mollusk (the snail). Might as well add an insect, too.

Since you can't climb into an aquarium to make friends with a fish, you have to be content with what contact can exist between you from either side of a glass wall or a watery surface. Most of the time that means just watching. Some of the things a fish does — those constant gulping motions, for instance — may look silly to us, but they have a purpose. Other things a fish does are remarkable but unnoticed — not slamming into rocks in the dark, for instance. Watching is more fun when you know a little more about fish.

Fish gulp all the time because that's how they breathe. The gulped water is pushed from their mouths out through their gills (the flapped slits just behind the fish's head), where tiny blood vessels absorb dissolved oxygen from the water. The water is then sent back out to the tank by the gill

Aquarium Pets
at a glance

Goldfish

PAGE 87

COMET GOLDFISH

FANTAIL GOLDFISH

BLACK MOON GOLDFISH

HOUSING: 10-gallon tank, filter system. Optional gravel, plants.

SPECIAL REQUIREMENTS: None.

DIET: Commercial granular or flake goldfish food. Optional supplement, lettuce, water plants, brine shrimp, tubifex worms.

CARE: Feed once or twice a day. Clean filter box once a week. Refresh water by siphoning four times a year.

TAMABILITY: Come for food at signal; may eat from fingers.

LIFE SPAN: Three to four years average, but can be as long as 10 years.

Guppies

PAGE 93

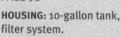

HOUSING: 10-gallon tank, filter system.

SPECIAL REQUIREMENTS: None.

DIET: Commercial granular or flake guppy food. Optional supplement, brine shrimp and tubifex worms. Gravel, plants.

CARE: Feed once or twice a day. Clean filter box once a week. Refresh water by siphoning four times a year.

TAMABILITY: Come for food at signal.

LIFE SPAN: Two to three years.

Water Turtles

PAGE 96

HOUSING: 10-gallon tank to start with, fluorescent light fixture. Optional filter system.

SPECIAL REQUIREMENTS: Dry land area as well as deep water area, ultraviolet light.

DIET: Commercial shrimp pellets or canned cat food. Supplement with calcium, raw fruits and vegetables, raw meat, or earthworms.

CARE: Feed, clean up leftover foods daily. Clean optional filter box weekly or clean tank weekly. Refresh water in filtered tank by siphoning four times a year.

TAMABILITY: Become calm, but don't enjoy handling. May come for food at signal.

LIFE SPAN: Most baby turtles die within months from improper care. With good care, they can live for decades.

Crayfish *PAGE 102*

HOUSING: 10-gallon tank, filter system. Optional gravel, plants.

SPECIAL REQUIREMENTS: Rock to hide behind.

DIET: Leftover vegetable and meat scraps.

CARE: Feed daily. Clean filter box once a week. Refresh water by siphoning four times a year.

TAMABILITY: Not tamable.

LIFE SPAN: Five years.

Water Snails

PAGE 103

HOUSING: 10-gallon tank. Optional gravel. Water plants.

SPECIAL REQUIREMENTS: None.

DIET: Algae that form on tank walls, or water plants.

CARE: Supply fresh-water plants several times a year if no algae in tank. Refresh water by siphoning four times a year.

TAMABILITY: Not tamable.

LIFE SPAN: Three to four years.

Tadpoles

PAGE 103

HOUSING: 10-gallon tank, filter system. Optional gravel, plants.

SPECIAL REQUIREMENTS: None.

DIET: Leftover salad greens, raw meat scraps.

CARE: Feed daily. Clean filter once a week. Refresh water by siphoning four times a year.

TAMABILITY: Not tamable.

LIFE SPAN: Become frogs within weeks or, in the case of bullfrogs, in one to two years.

Crayfish

flap, and the next gulp of fresh water pushed in. Goldfish are among the fish that can survive in stagnant water low in oxygen. They can gulp air directly. When you see your goldfish coming to gulp at the top of the tank other than at feeding time, it is gulping air to push through its gills. Goldfish normally breathe this way some of the time, but if they start to do it often, your water may be too low in oxygen. Check your filter to be sure bubbles are coming from it, or get a stronger pump. If the filter seems to be working fine, it may be time to replenish the water (page 322).

Goldfish are quite nearsighted, but they can see colors. Fish as a whole don't hear sound waves very well, but they can feel vibrations keenly. When you tap on a tank, the vibrations hit the fish like shock waves. The shock makes them acutely nervous and uncomfortable. Don't tap fish tanks! A fish can smell with pits that look like nostrils on its snout. More marvelous is the fish's sense of taste; it is located in taste buds similar to those on your tongue, but these may be scattered all over the fish's body. In other words, a fish can taste its dinner long before it gets into its mouth.

Beyond sight, hearing, touch, taste, and smell, fish have a sixth sense that is almost beyond our ability to imagine. Look at the side of your goldfish. A thin line, called the lateral line, runs the length of its body. Inside the line is a canal filled with fluid, connected by many other smaller canals to the fish's entire body surface. These canals sense the movement of the water. If water flow is interrupted by an obstacle — another fish, a rock, a bump in the mud — it bounces back, causing ripples. You can see similar bounce-back ripples in a pond where water touches a rock or when you toss a pebble into the water. The same movements exist underwater. Fish can read the complicated patterns set up by both bottom contours and the movements of other creatures. They

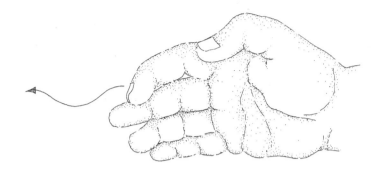

This is how to swim your hand like a fish.

can feel the shape of the water around them. Even in pitch black darkness or in muddy waters, fish don't bump into one another or into rocks or plants or sandbars.

Breeders have changed the normal streamlined shape of goldfish; the fantails and Moors are not good examples of fish built to swim fast. But looking at the comet goldfish as an example, you can see that its narrow body, pointed toward the nose, is made to cut through water. Mucous glands under its scales coat its body with a slippery substance that cuts down on friction.

A fish moves through water in the same way a snake moves along the ground. Its body and tail curve to form a loop. The rear edge of the loop pushes against the water. The fish is pushed forward. You can see the way the movement works more easily in a snake, and even feel that backward push by putting your hand against the rear edge of a snake's loop. Most fish move so fast that this movement is hard to see.

A goldfish's top (dorsal) fin helps hold it upright. You can see how this works by holding your hand flat and perpendicular to the floor, as if it were a fish in water. You'll find that it's easy to wiggle your hand forward but hard to tip your hand sideways. When a goldfish is swimming slowly, it raises its top fin to keep from tipping. Its side fins move about to stabilize the fish, too.

Swim Bladder

You don't see fish having trouble staying near the bottom or top of the tank. They don't fall to the bottom as you do after a jump or float to the top as you do after a dive. Fish have a swim bladder inside their bodies that constantly adjusts their buoyancy. You can fool around with a plastic bottle in a bathtub to see the way the air-filled swim bladder works.

Fill the bottle two-thirds full of water and screw on the top. The bottle is the fish, the air the swim bladder. If the bottle floats to the top, add some water. If it sinks to the bottom, pour out a little water. Keep adjusting the air until the bottle floats submerged. That's the condition of a fish. If it needs to float higher, it will take more air into its swim bladder to decrease its density. If it wants to float lower, it will let air out to increase its density. Balloonists and submariners maneuver up and down in the same way.

It was the swim bladder, by the way, that ultimately allowed the first fish to leave the water. The air-containing bladder evolved over millions of years into lungs. The lungfish that still exist today use lungs instead of gills, coming up to the top of the water to breathe.

Some species are born with gills but lose them entirely, just as many salamanders do. The mudskipper is a fish that not only breathes through lungs but also climbs mangrove trees along the shore to hunt for insects. It lives in mangrove swamps in the Pacific, and in Asia in the Indian Ocean, leaving the water for hours at a time to climb trees with its limblike front fins. A naturalist once told me that he never got used to coming to a swampy shore and startling dozens of fish that dropped from the trees with a splash back into the water's safety.

A bottle will float under the water like a fish if you carefully adjust its weight by adding water. This glass bottle needed only a little water. Plastic bottles require more.

Fish that can walk on land like the mudskipper and its relative the mudhopper look like a cross between a fish and a salamander.

But when it swims fast, the fish folds down its top fin to streamline itself. It keeps its side fins tucked flat too, except to help it when it needs to change direction or put on the brakes.

Goldfish

The goldfish was bred from the common carp of Asia long ago. The whole carp family is hardy and adaptable, and the goldfish can live a long life — up to 50 years — in captivity. Although most goldfish no longer resemble the bulky, brown, bewhiskered carp, one large Japanese breed, the koi, has kept the typical carp whiskers and can live year-round in outdoor pools. Koi and other goldfish are safer in an indoor tank, though. A friend keeps goldfish in a tiny cement-lined pool in her garden. One day, four fish were missing; the next day, only a few were left. On the third day, early in the morning, she spotted a great blue heron finishing off the rest. Another summer, a raccoon fishing at the pool ate all her goldfish in a single night (he left behind wet footprints).

Choosing a Goldfish

There are several types of goldfish to choose from. The common goldfish is the comet. It is pleasingly plain: fish-mouthed, fish-shaped, and fish-tailed. The next fancier model is the fantail, which is sometimes called a veiltail. This fish has two tails, the result of a mutation. In the best specimens, the two tails grow to be four to five inches long. Fantails have a shorter, plumper body than that of comets. Between their fat bellies and their waving tails, they swim rather clumsily.

Both the comet and the fantail goldfish come in common gold, a rare silver, orange, red, white, black, and speckled or spotted combinations of

any of these colors. When goldfish are speckled and splotched in orange, white, and black, they are called calicos.

The black Moor goldfish, with its grumpy (or sometimes sad) look, appeals to me most of all. These fat, goggle-eyed, fan-tailed creatures come only in black, but the black may look metallic and lightens to a golden gleam along the belly. In a tank of goldfish, black Moors definitely act more curious and aggressive than do other types.

There are still fancier breeds of goldfish — the bumpy-headed lionhead and the bubble-eyed celestial. Both are gargoyle grotesques, and both need heated tanks. They are fancy-looking, but not especially hardy.

Unless a fish is nearly dying, it's difficult to tell whether or not it is healthy. When you go to buy fish, look first at the condition of the tank as a whole. If dead fish are floating about, or if the tank looks dirty, don't buy fish from that tank.

After the tank checkup, pick out the individual fish you like. Larger fish are hardier than smaller fish. Look at the fins and tail for signs of

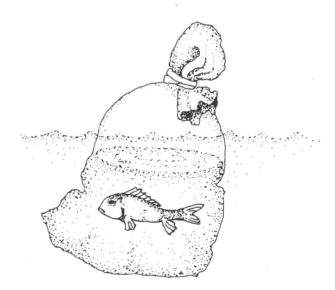

Floating the fish in its bag lets it adjust to the water temperature in the tank.

ROUND BOWL
Small water surface compared to water volume

FLAT-SIDED BOWL
More water surface, but hard to see fish

splitting or shredding. Check that the scales look smooth — no injuries, no junky white patches. Watch how it swims — not tilted, not head downward, not noticeably slower than other fish. Memorize how the fish looks so that when the clerk is standing by, net in hand, you don't have to go through the choosing all over again.

Your fish will be handed to you in a plastic bag, usually about one-third filled with water, and either tied at the top or held with a rubber band. The air in the bag will last the fish only about an hour, after which it will slowly start to suffocate. If you are buying several fish, ask for separate bags so each gets more air. Get home within a half hour.

Do not dump your fish into the prepared tank immediately upon arriving at home. Instead, place the whole sealed bag in the tank and let it float there for a half hour. There is always some temperature difference between the water in the bag and the water in your tank. Floating the bag brings the water in it to the same temperature as the water in the tank, giving the fish time to get used to it. After the half hour, cut open the bag and let the fish swim out.

Housing

Before you bring home a fish, you'll have to set up a tank for it to live in. Find a place for the tank that doesn't vary much in temperature — no sun, no drafts from cold windows, no air-conditioning that will be turned on and off, no nearby heaters or radiators. If you don't already have a tank set up, get it ready two days before you bring home any fish so that the water can get to room temperature. Although goldfish can deal with warm or cool water, like all fish they are cold-blooded. They have no way to regulate their internal temperature. As the water around them warms up or cools down, their body takes awhile to adjust to the change. If the change is fast, they can't keep up. Fast temperature changes have killed millions of pet goldfish.

Fishbowls, the traditional home of fictional and cartoon fish, can be fish killers. The round shape, with its narrow top and small opening, provides very little water surface. It is at the surface that the water comes into contact with the air and where oxygen from the air dissolves into the water. The greater the water surface in relation to the total amount of water, the more dissolved oxygen is available for fish to breathe. Even though stagnant-water fish like goldfish are able to gulp air directly at the water surface, this method of breathing is designed to be an emergency measure, not a way of life. Fish in round fishbowls slowly suffocate. One good type of fishbowl is flat and circular with a surface broad enough to provide oxygen, but it is hard to see the fish in this bowl except from directly overhead. Ordinary tanks may not be as appealing as bowls, but they are best for viewing, and for fish health.

The basic aquarium setup on page 317 is fine for goldfish. A 5½-gallon tank is too small for more than one or two baby (two- to three-inch) goldfish. A 10-gallon tank can hold a half-dozen small fish, but none of them will grow much. To grow a nice big healthy pet, plan to have only one or two fish for a 10-gallon tank. When they are between four and five inches long, they should go into an 18- or 20-gallon tank. True, the fish will look rather small in there at first, but the extra swimming will increase their appetite and the fish can grow to their dramatic maximum of seven inches — not counting the tail.

Do not use glass gravel in your aquarium. Goldfish pick up gravel as they search for leftover food. The glass gravel cuts their mouths.

How to Net a Fish

There are times you'll need to move your fish. You may want to move it into a larger tank, take it to school for a day, or get it out of the way while you clean the tank or change the landscape.

Before you net a fish, transfer water from the fish's tank into a jar until it is one-third full. Use a square-shaped net to catch the fish. Don't chase the fish with it. It swims faster than you can maneuver the net. It also gets panicky and can hit its head on the tank wall. Fish react less nervously to a potential enemy approaching from underneath rather than from behind, so move the net slowly until it is under the fish. Then just raise it to the surface. As you lift the net from the water, close it above the fish with your other hand so it can't leap out. Turn the net upside down over the mouth of the jar and let go so the fish drops out.

Before you release your fish back into the tank, float the jar in the tank for a half hour to allow it to adjust to the temperature difference.

To get a fish from a net into a jar:
(A) Hold the net closed above the fish.
(B) Turn the net upside down over the jar.
(C) Let the fish drop into the jar.

(A)

(B)

(C)

The only other adjustment that needs to be made to the basic aquarium setup is to not include the more tender plants (see page 318). Goldfish eat plants. The most common water plants, anacharis and cabomba, are tender and will be a total loss. Tough varieties such as creeping Charlie, Brazilian sword, and banana plant are not so delicious and will last longer.

To keep your tank in top condition, follow the cleaning procedures described on page 322.

Food

Goldfish eat both meat and vegetables. Dried goldfish food, sold in pet stores as either grains or flakes, contains such goodies as shrimp and flies, along with dried vegetables, grains, and the same soybean additive that has worked its way into so many human foods. For goldfish over four inches, the same food comes in small pellets. The pellets make bigger mouthfuls for bigger mouths.

Nutritionally, dried food is adequate, but it's rather a bore. Not being fish ourselves, we don't know for sure that they feel emotions, but a goldfish encountering live prey seems to act idiotically happy. The most convenient live prey are brine shrimp. They are tiny saltwater crustaceans sold live in pet stores (they come in a cup of salty water). To feed brine shrimp to your fish, catch a few shrimp in a fishnet, then dump them in the tank. This avoids getting salt water in a fresh-

fact

Allow one inch of fish per gallon of water in your tank. If you have a 10-gallon tank, that means you can keep ten tiny (1-inch) fish, five medium (2-inch) fish, or one really big fish!

water tank, which can be dangerous. The rest of the brine shrimp can be kept in their container of salt water in the refrigerator, where they will live for a week or longer.

Another live food available in pet stores is the tubifex worm, which also lives in salt water but is an inch or more long. A three- or four-inch goldfish would relish a whole worm. You may have to cut up the worm for baby fish.

In the summer, experiment with insects you find. A fly, ant, or inchworm can be placed on top of the water. Try spiders too, and small earthworms or big ones cut to suit. Once you have a goldfish eating from your fingers like our Big Al (see page 92), you could try bits of raw hamburger. But keep an eye on these treats; less reliable eaters might leave the meat to rot in the bottom of the tank.

As for vegetables, buy tender anacharis plants; they are an all-time goldfish favorite. Keep them growing in a big jar full of water. Feed your goldfish a sprig a week. Take the stem from the water after the goldfish has nibbled off its leaves. Your goldfish may also eat lettuce, but try to remove any bits it doesn't eat before they start to decay.

Since a pet goldfish acts so enthusiastic about its dinner, you'll tend to feed it too much and too often. Overfeeding kills goldfish, but not because they overeat. Although goldfish scrounge about looking for in-between-meal leftovers, any stomach has its limits. The food your fish can't eat sinks to the bottom of the tank and begins to decay. The decaying process requires oxygen, the same oxygen your fish needs to breathe. If your

Meet Big Al

Big Al is our six-inch comet goldfish. We trained him to eat from our fingers. How? We simply fed Big Al at the same times and in the same spot every day. Before dropping the food, we tickled the water with our fingers. Within a week, the tickle brought him dashing to the surface, mouth gaping. It was only another week until we could drop a food pellet directly into his greedy maw.

Then Al made up his own trick. His small fish brain made the connection between the humans on the other side of the glass and mealtime. As he became hungry, he moved to a front corner of his tank. There he did an agitated dance, made up of jerking, grouchy-looking dashes back and forth. The constant motion drove us crazy, so of course we fed him. He is no longer a mere fish; Big Al is a family pet.

fish doesn't die from bacteria that reproduce in decaying matter, it may slowly die of suffocation.

Put only a few flakes or grains of food in the tank at a time. Watch to see that they are all eaten, then add a few more. When your fish isn't eating anymore, it's had enough. This is the best way to tell how much to feed your fish. If you decide to feed your fish twice a day, judge the amounts needed at each mealtime the same way.

Illnesses

Fish sicknesses tend to be unpleasant to see. Two common ones are tail rot, in which the fish's tail and fins begin to shred and fall apart, and ich, which sounds like what it is: icky white fungal patches that form on the fish's body. Both of these, and many other fish diseases, are cured by patent medicines sold in pet stores.

Unfortunately, many other fish disorders are not visible. By the time the fish begins to keel over on its side, skulk at the bottom, or trail long threads of excreta behind, it may be too late to save it. When it is obvious that a fish is sick, get it out of the tank and into a jar fast. That just might save your other fish, if you have any, from infection. Then find out what you can from the pet store or from someone you know who collects tropical fish. Do whatever is suggested, but be prepared for the fish to die.

Once something is wrong with a fish, be hard on yourself about the condition of the tank. Check to see that it is clean and the filter is working properly. Test the water temperature and quality: When did you last add some fresh water? As a last resort, empty the whole tank, wash it with salt, rinse it, and leave it to dry for a week. Then begin all over.

Guppies

Guppies are my only concession to tropical fish — but I'm not going to go into the fancy guppies that need heated tanks. Tropical fish are usually beautiful, but I consider them collector's items, not pets.

Common guppies are fun to have around because they are forever mating and having babies. Fish babies are called fry, as in "small fry." With the proper setup, you can achieve a self-regulating guppy population that will survive for many generations. Guppies can live in the same tank with any of the creatures in this chapter except for larger goldfish, which occasionally might eat them.

Choosing Guppies

A single guppy is too inconspicuous to bother with. Neither the male nor the female grows to much longer than an inch and a half. Start with a pair. The female has a plump belly, with a small black spot toward its rear. The black spot (a "gravid" spot) is actually a bunch of eggs and will eventually be a bunch of babies (see "Breeding" on page 94). The male's body is slimmer and smaller, longer in the tail, and often marked with very bright spots of orange, red, green, or blue. In a typical tank of mature guppies, many of the females are already pregnant. To speed things up, choose a large female with a large gravid spot. Obviously, choose the prettiest male you can.

Housing

Guppies are less tolerant of low temperatures than goldfish are. It might be helpful to keep a thermometer in the basic aquarium (page 320) so you can check that the water doesn't get below 60 degrees on winter nights. If your house gets

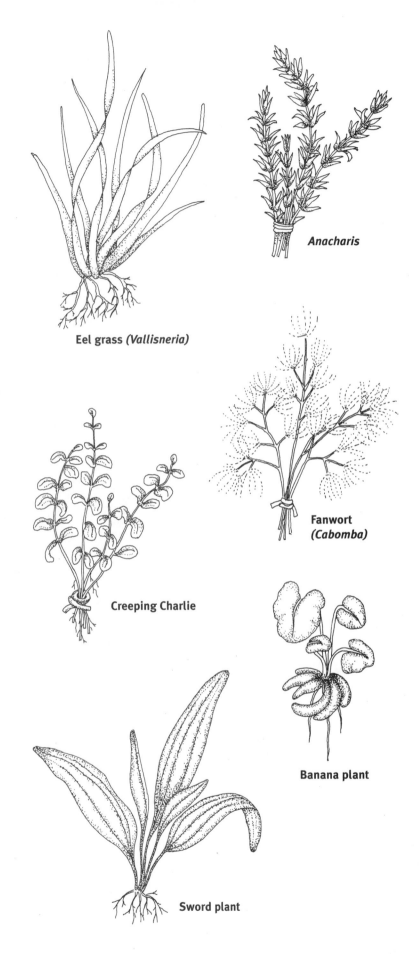

Eel grass (*Vallisneria*)

Anacharis

Fanwort (*Cabomba*)

Creeping Charlie

Banana plant

Sword plant

cooler than that, use the incandescent lamp suggested for desert vivariums on page 306. If the extra light seems to encourage algae to grow, take it out and heat the tank with an aquarium heater and thermostat from a pet store (see page 320).

To establish a natural environment in which a proportion of guppy fry survive to adulthood, you have to provide hiding places. An area of thickly planted grass like eel grass *(Vallisneria)* should do the trick. A few rocks surrounding the planted area will darken it for even better hiding.

Food

Feed guppies once or twice a day, using the same technique suggested for goldfish to avoid overfeeding (see page 91). Guppies eat a mostly meat diet, so you can't use the same food you give goldfish. Guppy food contains dried insects, shrimp, and so on, plus some cereals. It comes in flakes or grains, both sized smaller than goldfish food. When fry are born, an even finer, almost powdery food must be fed to them until their mouths grow large enough for adult food. You can try giving newly hatched brine shrimp or cut-up tubifex worms to your guppies. Both are appreciated and nutritious. Guppies don't bother much with vegetables.

Breeding

Male guppies pursue female guppies relentlessly. They vibrate their bodies to get attention and even back up toward the female to show off their pretty tail spots. When the female allows it, mating is achieved through the long male organ called the gonopodium. You can see a male guppy's gonopodium trailing along under his body, an almost transparent tube one-half inch long or longer. The guppy ejects sperm (male reproductive cells) through the gonopodium.

Unlike many other fish that fertilize (unite their sperm with) the female's eggs after they are laid in the water, guppies fertilize the eggs inside the female's body. She doesn't use all the sperm the male has put inside her at once. Once she is fertilized, she stores the sperm, and she can produce a batch of fry every month for the next four months, doling out sperm as needed.

Over the course of a single month, the fertilized eggs develop into fry completely inside the female's body. As a female's gravid spot grows larger, look at it carefully through her transparent belly. You can see the tiny gleaming eyes of the fry staring out at you.

By the last day or so of her pregnancy, the female begins to spend much of her time looking for areas in which to give birth. She will prefer a planted area of the tank for the big event.

Each fry is expelled within its own transparent, bubblelike membrane. The bubble seems to pop out of the mother's belly. Within seconds, the fry has stretched its body, broken the bubble, and swum off among the plants.

fact

Guppies are among the best fish for beginners. They can survive in foul water and in a wide temperature range (65° to 100°F), although 74° to 82° is best. They are beautiful (no two males are alike) and inexpensive, and they do not fight.

Depositing her fry in a reasonably safe area is the mother guppy's last responsibility toward the next generation. Once they are born, the fry are considered food by adult guppies, including their parents. The adult guppies will gulp down fry for breakfast, lunch, and dinner. Nevertheless, in a heavily planted aquarium, enough fry will survive to ensure future generations.

If guppy cannibalism is too much for you, net the adults and get them into another tank within minutes of the fry birth in order to save all the fry. Of course, with guppies you will face this same predicament over and over again. The chore of separating the sexes is difficult and the fry may mate before you can tell male from female. Soon enough you'll have more fry to deal with and more cannibalism to prevent. It may be better simply to leave their fate to nature.

As time goes on, the females will have fewer babies (see the box below). Smaller fry will be eaten, larger ones will survive. In general, the guppies will be smaller as adults and will take longer to become sexually mature. In time you will have a natural fish population that can go on and on.

Make Room for Guppies

Nature has devised automatic birth control for guppies. It is possible for the first group of guppy fry to be as many as 50 or 60. As normal crowding occurs, the number of fry per birth will be reduced to a couple of dozen. As the environment changes with crowding — less food, less oxygen, fewer private places to give birth — hormones in many fish cause fewer eggs to ripen or cause the female to reabsorb eggs or even to abort.

In guppies, another effect of crowding is that most — even all — the babies will be female. The scarcity of males is still another form of natural birth control. How the sex of babies is controlled is a mystery science will answer some day.

Beyond Goldfish and Guppies

Many other species of small freshwater fish are easy to care for and make great aquarium pets. As with guppies and goldfish, make sure that each new fish is healthy before bringing it home.

Barbs are colorful fish that should be kept in schools of at least six. They are highly active, but beware: They may leap out of an aquarium if startled. Keep a cover on yours.

Betta splendens are also known as Siamese fighting fish, because males (and females, to a lesser extent) fight with each other. For this reason, you shouldn't keep more than one of these fish in your tank. In fact, some people recommend that bettas be raised individually, without other fish. They have beautiful flowing tails and are gorgeously colored.

Catfish are a diverse group of fish that have "barbels" on the sides of their mouths, which look like cat whiskers. Corydoras are the most popular aquarium variety.

Mollies are peaceful fish that can grow to be nearly five inches long, so keep them in a 30-gallon (or larger) tank. They need plenty of plants in their tank and will feed off algae on the tank walls. To keep your mollies healthy, add to the tank at least 1 tablespoon of specially formulated aquarium salt per gallon of water.

Neon tetras are bright, iridescent fish that are beautiful to watch. They need plenty of friends and hiding places to feel secure. Add plants, rocks, and driftwood for a more natural environment, and keep a school of 20 or so in the tank.

Platys (also known as moonfish) come in a variety of brilliant colors, the most common being red. They do best with other fish that are not aggressive. Keep them in lushly planted tanks of at least 15 gallons.

Swordtails have a long "sword" that extends from the tails of males. These active fish love to chase each other and to jump, so keep them in schools of at least five and cover your tank. They do best when you add 1 tablespoon of specially formulated aquarium salt per gallon of water; also add lots of plants to their home.

Zebra danios are small, slender, striped fish. They should be kept in schools of six to ten, with lots of fine-leaved plants. They are very active fish and need plenty of space (at least a couple of gallons of water per fish).

Water Turtles

Scientists don't distinguish between turtles and tortoises, but other people say that tortoises are land animals, whereas turtles must live where they can get into water. Like the land tortoises in the previous chapter, water turtles can be carriers of salmonella, an intestinal illness that causes diarrhea. Hatchling turtles found in pet shops are checked by the Department of Health.

Turtles in pet shops are most likely to be red-eared turtles (so called because of red markings on either side of their heads), bred on turtle farms for the pet market. Other turtles you might find in a pet store are the painted turtle (with a red to yellow stripe down its black carapace), the more rough-shelled green-backed cooter turtle, and the brown mud or musk turtle. These common American turtles live primarily in water.

In the spring and summer you occasionally find turtles ambling across a road near water. They are usually water turtles out for a walk or sunning themselves on the hot black pavement of

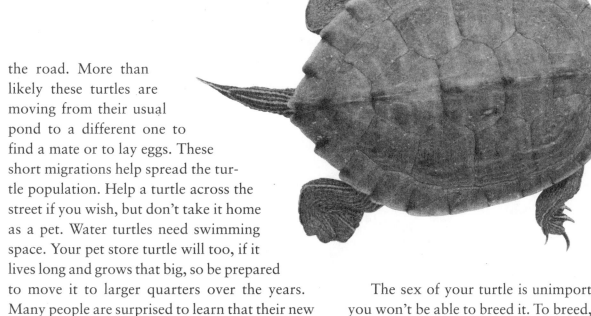

the road. More than likely these turtles are moving from their usual pond to a different one to find a mate or to lay eggs. These short migrations help spread the turtle population. Help a turtle across the street if you wish, but don't take it home as a pet. Water turtles need swimming space. Your pet store turtle will too, if it lives long and grows that big, so be prepared to move it to larger quarters over the years. Many people are surprised to learn that their new "baby" turtle, if it is one of the larger species, can grow to be as big as a dinner plate.

Choosing a Turtle

Turtle hatchlings that are less than a month old are usually only one to two inches in length. These young hatchlings have an incredibly high mortality rate in captivity, so the bigger the baby you can find, the better off you are. Turtles that have been caught in the wild are subject to a great deal of stress and exposed to a variety of diseases, so try to buy one that was born in captivity.

Squeeze the turtle's shell, especially the rear portion, between your thumb and finger. If the shell is soft, the baby is already suffering from malnutrition. Look at the turtle's eyes. Puffy eyelids, which are quite easy to notice because they are pale and partly or completely cover the turtle's otherwise round eyes, are a signal of an eye infection. Look at the skin on the turtle's legs and neck. White patches are a fungal infection.

Look for a turtle that is moving about quickly and swimming well. Turtles who have been kept too cool are sluggish, and sluggish turtles can't digest their food. Buying a pet that suffers from indigestion is at the least a bad start, and in some cases the turtle could die.

The sex of your turtle is unimportant, since you won't be able to breed it. To breed, the turtle would have to be kept outdoors, on a pond with either sandy or leafy shores and plenty of good nesting sites.

Housing

You can adapt the basic aquarium on page 317 for a turtle home by adding a dry-land area to the water environment. Lower the water level a few inches so the turtle can't climb out of the tank, and float a raft on the water for the turtle to climb up on. You can make a raft from a piece of thick cork or cork bark. Some florists keep cork bark around for training plants on; some home-decorating centers might give you a sample of the thick rough cork used to cover walls. If you can't get cork, look for a fireplace log. A rounded section of log with the bark left on can be cut to the tank's width for an adequate land area. Logs don't float as well as cork, so you'll have to cut the log carefully to size and jam it against the sides of the tank to hold it in place.

Another way to make a land area involves using shallow water and the smallest-size corner filter you can find. Fill the tank to just above the top of the filter. Set in the water a large smooth stone with sloping sides that will stick out above the water surface. The smoothness is important.

Aquaria Planaria

If you have too little space for an aquarium but still want a water pet, you can keep planaria. Planaria are tiny flatworms that live in ponds and streams everywhere. Look for them on the undersides of rocks.

When you look closely, planaria seem to be cross-eyed. The outside edge of the "eye" is really only a slight depression in the worm's head. The cross-eyed "pupils" are small spots of light-sensitive pigment — too simple an arrangement to be called an eye at all.

Keep planaria in fresh water in any sort of jar lid or in a glass cup. Be sure not to let the water evaporate entirely. Feed the worms a few times a week with a crumb of raw hamburger or other raw meat.

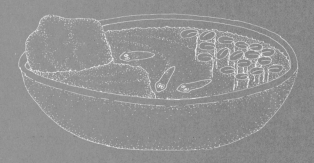

The actual size of a planarium is ¼ inch or less. These three are at home in a glass preserving jar top decorated with a stone and the tiny leaves of duckweed. Duckweed grows wild on ponds in most of the country.

Turtle shells are more tender than they look, and turtles can develop sores from scraping against rough stones or bricks. The slope is important too, because turtles are rather clumsy climbers.

Other part-land, part-water environments suitable for turtles are the semiaquatic vivariums on page 312.

Whatever land area you devise, it should be dry and must be big enough to let the turtle get all the way out of the water. Turtles may love the water, but they must dry off completely between swims to kill fungus growth. Turtles will come up onto the land area for hours to dry, warm up, and bask in artificial sunlight.

Use a fluorescent Vita-Lite bulb (page 306) to provide both heat and basking light. Turtles need ultraviolet rays for manufacturing vitamin D, and they also need heat. Like many reptiles, they are too slowed down by temperatures under 75 degrees to either eat or digest well. Keep the light on all day. During the night, you can let temperatures drop to 60 degrees or lower with no trouble.

The tank filter will keep the water reasonably clean. If the water does begin to smell or if you can see debris collecting at the bottom, siphon off the water (see page 322), wipe the tank well, and refill. Though not as effective as a filter, a bubble stone can be used if your water level is too low for a filter.

To save on tank space and to make a more lively environment, you may want your turtle to share a tank with goldfish. The deep-water tank arrangements won't bother the fish, and the light won't either. Be on the lookout for fish chasing by your turtle — yours might enjoy teasing its tank mates. Also, the calcium-containing materials necessary to your turtle's diet will kill goldfish. To solve this problem, feed your turtle separately in a shallow bowl outside the tank. It takes only five to ten minutes for a turtle to finish its meal.

Food

Turtles are more or less scavengers. In ponds they eat water weeds, dead fish, live water snails, live insects, and whatever else comes along. In spite of the fact that pet stores may sell ant "eggs" (really pupae) or dried flies as turtle food, turtles can't survive on either.

Feed your pet turtle a dried or pellet food made of many different ingredients. Also offer it vegetables in the form of water plants, like anacharis, romaine lettuce, raw spinach, or watercress. Try bits of fruit to see what happens. Chopped-up apple may work well. When you buy fish, cut off a shred or two and offer it raw to your turtle. Do the same with raw chicken and raw beef, all in bite-sized bits. Turtles think earthworms are delicious too. You must feed all these goodies to the turtle in the water; it is unable to swallow food on land.

Along with this delicatessen approach to mealtimes, turtles need additional calcium. Calcium deficiency is among the causes of soft shell, a killer disease of thousands of baby turtles. A turtle also needs extra calcium to continue growing its shell as its body gets larger.

Calcium comes in lots of forms: crushed oyster shell, sold at pet stores; powdered calcium

fact

You can train a turtle to come for its dinner by tapping on the edge of its tank every day, at the same time, and at the same spot, just before you give it its dinner.

carbonate, sold at drugstores; bonemeal, sold at garden stores; and eggshells, rescued from the garbage pail and crushed with a hammer. Sprinkle calcium on the water surface once a week.

Turtles are as intelligent as fish — which is to say not very. The limit of their learning capacity may be the old come-for-your-dinner trick. A turtle is not shocked by aquarium tapping the way a fish is, so if your turtle doesn't share a tank with fish, you can rap on the tank edge to teach it to come for its food. Teach the trick by feeding at the same time and in the same place each day. First signal with a tap, then feed.

Illnesses

Most turtle health problems arise because there's something wrong with food or housing.

Eye infections are caused by bacteria that grow in dirty water. The eyelids swell, sometimes so much that the turtle may not even be able to open them. If this happens to your turtle, ask a vet for an antibiotic eye ointment. Use the flat end of a toothpick to swab some ointment on the turtle's eyes three times a day. Carefully lift the upper lid first with the same dull end of the toothpick, because the ointment can't help if it's outside the eye. Don't expect the turtle to cooperate with this treatment. Grasp its head firmly from underneath with your thumb and forefinger so it can't withdraw it into its shell. If it pops in its head the minute you touch it, turn it upside down. This often makes a turtle put its head out in an effort to push itself upright again.

Fungal infections, which look like white patches on the skin, happen when a turtle can't

Painted turtles can grow up to seven inches long and will eat lettuce, earthworms, and raw fish or meat. They feed in the water, not on land.

get itself dry. Perhaps its basking area is not really out of the water, or you have not used a Vita-Lite bulb, or you have not been keeping it on all day. Mend your ways. Then buy an ich remedy from the pet store. It should be the kind that contains a dye called malachite green, the most effective fungal remedy in this case. Fill a big bowl with three cups of water, add several drops of ich remedy and a teaspoon of salt, mix well, and add the turtle. Let it soak there for 10 or 15 minutes twice a day. Make the bath solution fresh each time.

Respiratory infections look about the same in turtles as they do in us — runny or bubbly nose, noisy breathing (put your ear close to listen), no appetite, lots of snoozing. Even though you don't know whether your turtle has a virus cold that antibiotics won't help or a bacterial pneumonia that antibiotics will help, use antibiotics. The antibiotic tablets sold for birds work well on reptiles. Dissolve a tablet in water according to the proportions recommended for birds on the package. The turtle has to live in the medicated water for the next week, or until he gets better. But once the antibiotic is dissolved in water, it stays active for only about a day. You'll have to make the solution fresh each morning. You'll waste less antibiotic if you set up a small bowl to use as a hospital, complete with a land area and a light.

The "hospital" should be kept at 80 or 85 degrees. The same tank light you've been using should keep an ordinary kitchen mixing bowl that warm. Just lay it across the top.

Like all reptiles and most birds, turtles do not heal or recover from illnesses easily. If your turtle dies even though you have done everything you can to help it, don't blame yourself.

Plaster of Paris Molds

Another form of calcium you can give to turtles is a mold of plaster of paris. Mix the plaster with the amount of water recommended on the package label. Let the mixture harden in some sort of mold, such as an ice-cream carton, a plastic bag, or even a hole you have scooped out of damp sand, as in the illustration. When it is hardened, sink the plaster in the aquarium. Your turtle will nibble it as he wishes. (If your turtle is sharing an aquarium with goldfish, don't use this method as a calcium supply.)

MOLDING A PLASTER BLOCK IN SAND

1. Mix plaster according to directions on package. Pour into a hole scooped in sand.

2. When plaster is cool and hard, lift from sand. Rinse before putting in turtle tank.

Crayfish

Crayfish are crustaceans; they are relatives of lobsters, crabs, and shrimp. Interestingly enough, one crayfish relative, the giant spider crab, measures 12 feet from tip of toe to tip of toe, while another relative, a water flea, measures only one one-hundredth of an inch.

The eyes of a crayfish are mounted on stalks. It can see in any direction. The pinch of its claw is something to avoid — in relation to the crayfish's size (it's only a few inches in length), its pinch is close to 30 times more powerful than the squeeze of a human hand.

Trying to catch a crayfish, even in a small tank, can be an unnerving experience. When going about its daily business, the creature walks rather sedately; when faced with a net, however, it jerks its abdomen into a tight loop, propels itself backward at eye-blurring speed, and usually winds up squeezed into an inaccessible crevice between rocks.

We have not included any information about crayfish illnesses because there is really so little known about them that an entry would not be very helpful.

In many areas, and especially in the South, larger varieties of crayfish are eaten.

Choosing a Crayfish

Freshwater crayfish are sold in pet stores during the spring and summer, or you can look for one yourself in local ponds and slow-moving streams (page 26). Crayfish living in rushing streams often need more oxygen than you can provide.

Crayfish have a special value in an aquarium: They scavenge garbage. A couple of crayfish in a tank with any of the other creatures described in this chapter will clean up and eat most of the leftovers. However, they will also eat aquatic plants and small fish. Also, a big crayfish might eat a smaller one, so make sure your crayfish are about equal in size. The sex of your crayfish is unimportant, since they don't breed in captivity.

Housing

Crayfish like to lurk — behind rocks, in the weeds, and in hollows in the sand — so it would be a pity not to provide lurking places for these miniature monsters. Any aquarium setup fitted with good hiding spots is fine; having an inch of gravel on the bottom of the tank is a good idea. Crayfish aren't fussy about either temperature or light.

Food

If natural garbage like leftover (raw) fish or turtle food is not available, crayfish appreciate a bone to pick clean from time to time. An inch of chicken wing tip has just enough meat on it.

People who enjoy monster movies will no doubt love to watch crayfish tearing at the flesh with their sharp claws. If you find a dead fish or a tadpole, it will make one more ghoulish meal for the crayfish.

If your crayfish isn't able to keep up with its meals, remove the leftovers after three days so they don't rot and foul the tank.

Water Snails

To have a snail or not to have a snail is a bigger question than you might think. Just as land snails sit around and eat your tomatoes and lettuce, so water snails sit around and eat your aquarium plants. If they could be trained to eat just the algae that form on the sides of the tank, they would be the most useful of aquarium occupants. But snails are no more trainable than bugs. But like goldfish, they are less likely to bother the plants that have tough leaves. We suggest trying one or two water snails in the aquarium with any of the other creatures described in this chapter. No housing adjustments need be made for them, and no feeding is required.

As to the types of snail you might be able to get, pet stores may offer everything from tiny round brown snails about ¼ inch across to giant snails 1½ inches across. Choose a snail that you can see is moving rather than one lying about looking dead. Snails you find yourself in fresh water can be added to an aquarium too. Unfortunately, the more attractive saltwater snails would die in a freshwater tank.

An interesting type of snail you might find is the apple snail, which has an attractive golden shell and is often sold in pet shops as a "golden," "mystery," or "ivory" snail. Some species grow as big as five or six inches! Larger snails might eat everything in your aquarium, but a smaller type will happily feed on algae and fish food. As a reminder, turtles will eat small snails, so buy a large type if it will live with a turtle.

Rather frequently, adult snails produce baby snails. It's thrilling, but remember to watch out for your plants. Should baby snails arrive, move them to a separate tank.

Never release baby snails back into the wild, as they can carry parasites that would kill native species.

fact

Apple snails can eat surface food by forming a funnel with their muscular foot and siphoning water across it to catch the food particles in their mouth.

Tadpoles

Tadpoles are among those animals we humans call "cute." But guess what tadpoles are used for in laboratories? To pick bones clean so scientists can mount them as skeletons. When frog tadpoles grow up, they are frogs. Frogs are kind of cute too. Guess what's been found in bullfrog stomachs? Mice, birds, and even snakes. Oh well, cute animals can be deceiving.

Some tadpoles grow up to be salamanders instead of frogs. Salamander tadpoles are rather longer and slimmer in shape than frog tadpoles, and they grow four small legs very soon after hatching. They have feathery external gills at either side of the head — a dead giveaway, as no frog tadpole has external gills.

Choosing a Tadpole

Bullfrog tadpoles make superior pets. You can start them as eggs if you find some (page 26) in spring on a pond. Bullfrog eggs are larger than other frog eggs; they grow into big tadpoles, too.

And the tadpoles eat greedily for as long as two years before they become big bullfrogs.

Large tadpoles can share their home with any of the water animals described in this chapter, except perhaps the turtle. Small tadpoles may be in danger of becoming dinner for a large goldfish.

Housing

No adjustments of any sort need be made in the basic aquarium (page 317) for a group of tadpoles. If you can, fill the tank with water from the pond where you found the eggs or tadpoles. If you use tap water, it should sit for 24 hours to let the chlorine and excess oxygen dissolve. Keep fresh water, either from the pond or tap water that has "aged" properly, available to change the water in the tank as it gets dirty. Adding a few plants and cleaning out old food will help as well.

Food

There is a myth that tadpoles don't eat but live off their tails. The tails do in fact become absorbed as the tadpole undergoes metamorphosis into a frog. And like some other amphibians, tadpoles can go a long time without food. Tadpoles, however, will starve to death if you don't feed them. On the other hand, no matter how much you feed one, the resulting frog will always be smaller than the tadpole was.

Tadpoles eat voraciously. They like salad greens (chopped up and frozen to make them mushy), the algae that plague tanks, and chicken bones with raw meat still clinging. You can also try feeding them a pinch of goldfish food. Hungry tadpoles will even eat each other, so make sure you don't have too many in your aquarium and that they have enough to eat.

Good-bye

It's hard to predict how long a tadpole will stay a tadpole before it begins to turn into a frog. Even assuming you started with unhatched frog's eggs, the period of time could be from a month and a half to two years. Up to the time of the big change, the tadpole merely eats and grows bigger. Then the change called metamorphosis begins.

Metamorphosis is triggered by a body chemical produced in the thyroid gland, which is located at the front of the neck or, on a nearly neckless frog, on the front of the throat. A tadpole with its thyroid gland removed grows bigger and bigger. It becomes a super-giant tadpole but never a frog at all.

The first thing you'll notice when metamorphosis begins is a tiny hind leg emerging from the tadpole. Within days, the second hind leg comes along. Next

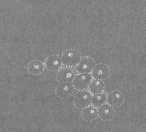

Tadpole, Hello Frog

you can see a bulge just behind the tadpole's jaw — the front legs forming under the skin.

By the time the front legs emerge, the rear legs are beginning to grow longer and more froglike, while the tail is beginning to shrink. As soon as the legs grow large enough to allow walking and hopping, the tadpole can climb out of the water and now consider itself a frog, in spite of the fact that it still carries its tail about. Within the next few weeks the rest of the tail is absorbed until no trace of it remains.

Amphibians, salamanders as well as frogs, are in decline all over the world. There may be many reasons for this, from chemicals sprayed on fields and lawns to excess ultraviolet radiation due to shrinkage of the ozone layer. But amphibians have also suffered terribly from loss of habitat as humans have drained the water from natural ponds and marshes. Most vulnerable of all are those species that breed in what are called "vernal pools," large woodland puddles that fill up

with water in spring but dry up within just a few weeks. In nature, frogs and salamanders smell their way to home waters, where they breed and lay their eggs. Consider a whole generation of spotted salamanders or common toads that, after years of life on land, return to their vernal pool only to find it is a lawn. Those generations will never reproduce.

If you raise tadpoles from eggs, collect just a few and leave the rest to hatch where you found them. When the tadpoles you've raised become adults, let them go back to their home wetland. Even then, I worry that tadpoles raised in aquariums may not recognize their birthplace as "home." The water from your faucet doesn't smell the same as that from their pond. Your ex-pets may survive, but no one knows if they really can lead normal lives in what has become foreign territory to them. But that's a risk you have to take: You won't be able to gather a proper live insect diet to keep a frog as a permanent pet.

Serpentarium Pets

Snakes are reptiles. Their ancestors, like other reptiles, had four legs. Today what remains of snake hips can still be seen on the skeleton of the python and the boa. Snakes have developed several ways of getting about without limbs. The most common is called serpentine movement, in which each loop the snake forms with its long body pushes backward against uneven terrain, propelling the snake forward. A snake using serpentine movement can't get anywhere on a smooth surface like glass.

Less common is straight-line movement, typical of boas. Boas have rather loose skin and wide, raisable scales along their bellies. They raise up a group of scales, press the edges against the ground, and push themselves forward. Groups of belly scales act in waves, so the boa appears to glide along smoothly with no visible effort. Our boa can straight-line himself along glass.

The rarest way for snakes to get around is by a method called sidewinding, and here the rattlesnake is the expert. It loops its body as though it were going to move in a serpentine pattern, but instead it moves sideways. It is actually stepping. Sidewinding is used in traveling across shifting sand where other forms of locomotion would be slow and arduous.

Snakes are cold-blooded, which doesn't mean their blood is cold but rather that they do not have a good mechanism for temperature control. Their bodies are no more than a few degrees warmer or colder than the air around them. In nature, snakes control their body temperature by seeking sun, warm rocks, or cool burrows. Northern snakes hibernate in cold weather and almost all snakes go through periods of decreased activity during the year. Pet snakes that come from the tropics catch cold easily if they are not kept in heated cages. Even northern snakes need heat to be active enough to eat.

Many people have a particular horror of the snake's typically forked and flicking tongue. Some

Serpentarium Pets *at a glance*

Snakes That Make Good Pets

FAVORITES:

Common boa

Rosy boa

Corn snake

Rat snake

Indigo snake

HOUSING: For snakes up to three feet — 15- or 20-gallon tank with mesh top, incandescent light fixture, six-inch crockery water dish. For snakes over three feet — commercial or homemade wood-and-Plexiglas cage, light fixture, eight-inch crockery water dish.

SPECIAL REQUIREMENTS: Extra heat, extreme cleanliness.

DIET: Live mice or other small rodents (available at pet stores or raise your own).

CARE: Clean and refill water dish daily. Feed once or twice a week, depending on size, age, and species. Clean floor of cage when soiled, usually once a week. Disinfect cage with chlorine bleach four times a year.

TAMABILITY: Become calm with handling. Enjoy warmth of skin. Not affectionate.

LIFE SPAN: Up to 30 years, depending on the species, but many snakes die sooner for lack of proper care.

even confuse it with fangs and think a snake is attacking when it flicks its tongue. A snake's tongue is a sense organ similar to our nose. As it flicks in and out, the tongue picks up scent molecules from the air or from solid surfaces and deposits them along a chemically sensitive area inside the mouth. A snake at rest doesn't flick its tongue; an exploring snake samples both the air and objects it comes upon in its travels. True, an aroused snake might flick its tongue in and out more frequently than a relaxed snake, but this is only the same sort of vigilance that a dog might exhibit as it sniffs the breeze. Neither dog nor snake sniffs as a first sign of attack.

A snake's vision is quite good, but its hearing is not so good. It used to be thought that snakes were deaf (in other words, they couldn't detect air vibrations like humans can). However, research now shows that snakes can hear some sounds through certain bones in their skulls. Regardless of what they can hear, snakes are acutely sensitive to vibrations in the ground. Your snake might not hear you shout but can easily feel you sneaking about in stocking feet.

Perhaps as compensation for lack of well-developed ears, snakes have a special apparatus for heat detection. The rattlesnake, for example, has two pit-shaped heat-detection organs on its face. A blinded rattlesnake can

Rosy boa

A snake that is ready to strike pulls its body into a tight configuration, with its head facing the target.

locate a mouse six feet away simply by sensing the infrared (heat) rays emanating from its prey.

Snakes shed their skins periodically. The next time you have a chance to look carefully at a snake skin, notice in particular the head section. You'll see that each eye area is covered with a special sort of scale. The scale protects the snake's eyes from damage, making both tears and eyelids unnecessary.

By saving and comparing skins each time a pet snake sheds, you can keep track of how much it has grown. It isn't true that a snake sheds when its skin becomes too tight. Body chemicals called hormones control shedding. A snake can shed as often as once a month or as seldom as once a year. Young snakes shed more frequently than older ones do.

Like birds, snakes have a hole at their rear ends called a cloaca. This hole is for urine, bowel movements, and reproductive purposes (see "Breeding," page 123). The urine doesn't remain a liquid but solidifies when it hits the air into the same white stuff that you see in bird droppings. The dark matter is undigested animal remains, occasionally complete with teeth and bones and tufts of hair.

All the poisonous snakes have venom glands in the front of their mouth. They pump venom through grooved or hollowed fangs into their prey as they strike. Many snakes that we don't consider dangerous are in fact venom-producing.

The venom glands of these snakes are located far back in the mouth, where the poison is squirted into the snake's mouth and must be mixed with saliva and chewed into well-torn prey before it can have any effect.

The major poisonous snakes in America are the rattlesnake, the copperhead, the cottonmouth, and the coral snake. If you are ever in doubt about whether a snake you see in the wild is poisonous, don't pick it up, even if it is tiny. Baby poisonous snakes are venomous from the very moment they are born.

More varieties of snakes are now offered in pet stores than ever before. Unfortunately, many snakes you find for sale are difficult to take care

Some poisonous snakes pump venom through hollow fangs into their prey as they strike.

A Little Light on the Subject

Our corn snake's tongue clued us in on an extraordinary fact about cold-blooded creatures. One winter day the lightbulb in the snake cage blew out and the temperature dropped rapidly. By the time we discovered what had happened, the corn snake was cold. His movements were slowed and weak, much as your hands would be if they got very cold. But even more dramatic, his tongue was flicking in slow motion. We could actually count the up-and-down flicks each time his tongue crept slowly out. We brought the snake into a warmer room and held him against our bodies to warm him gradually. As the snake warmed up, his tongue speeded up. It was like watching a thermometer rise. The full impact of cold-bloodedness hit us: A snake without heat is totally helpless. He can't even sniff.

of. For instance, I've seen several varieties of water snakes for sale, as well as the common garter snakes. Water snakes must have water to swim in, necessitating a semiaquatic tank, which is much too large to be practical in the home. Garter snakes emit a stinky smell when they're excited. Both water snakes and garter snakes can live on a diet of frogs, but frogs are hard to find in the winter. Many other snakes I have seen for sale require such foods as lizards, birds' eggs, and even other snakes.

The best snakes for pets are boas, corn snakes, rat snakes, and indigos. They are all rodent eaters and eat either live or pre-killed mice. Make sure you buy a snake that was born in captivity, as it will have experienced far less stress, will almost certainly be healthier, and will be a better pet.

If your family feels only lukewarm to the idea of a snake as a pet, here is some information that might calm their fears.

All the snakes this book recommends tame easily. Snakes can bite and some can constrict hard enough to kill prey, but once they are accustomed to handling, these particular snakes rarely bite and won't tighten their coils around you.

The snakes suggested are neither terribly active nor terribly fast. Their movements are deliberate and their pace leisurely. A snake is not likely to slither from your grasp.

Snakes are not slimy. They are dry and pleasant to touch, though cool rather than warm and cuddly.

Snakes can and do escape from their cages; in fact, they are very proficient at finding the smallest gaps. They are not trying to go back to nature but, rather, feel physically restless in cramped quarters. If you provide your snake with sufficient room and take care in building and

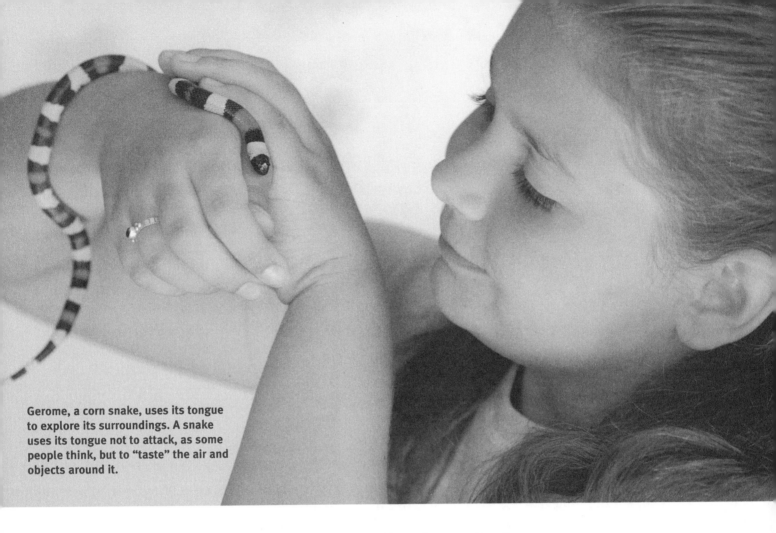

Gerome, a corn snake, uses its tongue to explore its surroundings. A snake uses its tongue not to attack, as some people think, but to "taste" the air and objects around it.

fastening the cage, you can avoid snake escapes. If your snake does escape, you will usually find it within a few yards of the cage. Escapees generally seek out warm, dark places.

Snakes are in some ways among the easiest pets to keep. They need to be fed only once a week, and adult animals can go without food for a month (but they do need water to drink). Their cage has to be cleaned only once a week, and the bedding can be plain old newspaper, though the ink may discolor scales. You can also use orchid bark or a piece of indoor/outdoor carpet. Snakes do need extra heat in captivity, but an aquarium light is usually sufficient. However, be aware that many snakes eat live prey, including things that are cute and furry. If properly cared for, they can live for many years (the rosy boa, for instance, can live to age 18), so a snake is a big commitment.

Now you are ready to pick the snake that will be best for you.

Choosing a Snake

Snakes sold in pet stores seem rather high priced in relation to how common they are in nature. It's tempting to simply scout around for a free wild snake during the summer while they are not in winter hiding. However, most snakes (and other animals) that are caught in the wild never really settle down to domestic life. The problem with most snakes is twofold: aggressive dispositions that you won't like and the need for prey that you can't provide. Wild snakes can be very difficult to feed. Certain snakes are protected by law, which is another good reason to leave them in the wild. If you can't resist a baby ring-neck snake or a beautiful black snake, keep it as a temporary guest (see page 45).

Boa constrictors, either the common boa or the lovely rosy boa, are calm, rather slow snakes that adjust well to captivity. Of the other, somewhat faster snakes, a good choice for a first-time

Bull nose snake

All snakes can travel quite fast in serpentine zigzags.

owner is the corn snake. Its more active nature is offset by the ease with which it adjusts to handling and its reliability once it has become calm.

In nature, some of these snakes are active by day and others by night. In captivity, it doesn't seem to matter much either way. Our snakes eat whenever a mouse is available, no matter what time of day it is. Although they sleep (eyes open, body coiled), they awaken easily and become active with handling at any time.

The most important thing to find out about a snake is whether or not it is eating readily. Ask your pet dealer to keep the snake you have chosen without food for a week. When you return, ask the dealer to give the snake a mouse; it should strike within 10 minutes. A snake that is not eating may not have adjusted to captivity, and perhaps never will. Or it may be sick. Breathing through the mouth can be a sign of respiratory illness, but more commonly indicates mouth infection. Don't try to examine the mouth of a snake you don't know, especially the inside. Remember, the best proof of good health is a hearty appetite.

The next most important thing to find out is the snake's attitude toward people. Snakes, like other pets, have individual temperaments. Ask the pet dealer to take the snake out of its cage. Watch while he does it. The job should be as easy as picking up a piece of rope. Once out, a calm snake won't try to get away but will explore the dealer rather slowly, winding along his arms and shoulders, "sniffing" with its tongue.

Snakes ready to strike pull their bodies into a tense, tight configuration, with their head facing the target. Many snakes also vibrate their tails, a behavior the rattlers improved upon by keeping sections of shed skin on their tail ends. As a hand comes closer to it, an aggressive snake will strike out in a springing action, mouth open. If the dealer has the courage to pick up such a snake, it will thrash about and attempt to escape.

We bought a corn snake who acted that way. The pet store owner first explained that the snake must be hungry. So he threw it a mouse. The snake ate the mouse, and then struck at the pet dealer's hand again. The man said it was all very strange, as he handled the snake often and it had always been calm in the past. Disregarding common sense, I picked up the corn snake with a towel (a trick learned from handling ornery parrots) and

They form S-shaped curves and push off from the back of each curve.

took it home. To this day, we darn well wait until that crotchety snake is in a decent mood before trying to pick it up. The rule is: If you want to be sure of a tame snake at home, choose a calm snake in the store.

Housing

The 10-gallon serpentarium suggested on page 326 is large enough for a 2½-foot snake. Boas are tropical snakes and need a daytime temperature of 80 degrees with a basking spot up to 95 degrees; nighttime temperatures should not drop below 70 degrees. Snakes from northern climates do best with daytime temperatures of between 70 and 80 degrees, but you can let the thermometer fall to 65 or even 60 degrees at night. To provide heat, use the aquarium light suggested on page 320, and monitor the temperature with a thermometer taped inside the tank.

Newspaper makes a fine floor covering for a serpentarium. Tear it to the right size by placing the top of the tank onto four or five layers of the paper. Cut or tear the paper against the edges of the tank's top. You can also use a fake grass mat, which is available at most large discount stores.

Snakes can go for long periods without food, but fresh clean water must always be available. The water dish has to be heavy enough so the snake won't tip it over when it goes to drink, and big enough for it to soak in. Many snakes like to climb in their water dishes, especially around shedding time. A crockery dog-food dish works well and is available at pet stores.

Provide a branch for your snake to climb on and a cardboard box with a hole cut out for it to hide in. We supply a rock to aid in shedding but both our snakes seem able to shed perfectly well without it. Don't forget to line the edges of the mesh top with masking tape so your snake won't get a sore nose from rubbing against the wire. And don't forget to weight the top of the serpentarium with a rock to prevent escape.

Snakes are known to be escape artists, which is one reason parents might be reluctant to allow them as pets. However, snakes usually take it upon themselves to leave their cage simply because they object to close confinement. Restlessness can be a sign that a snake needs larger quarters. The large wooden serpentarium on page 323 is big enough to contain two four-foot snakes.

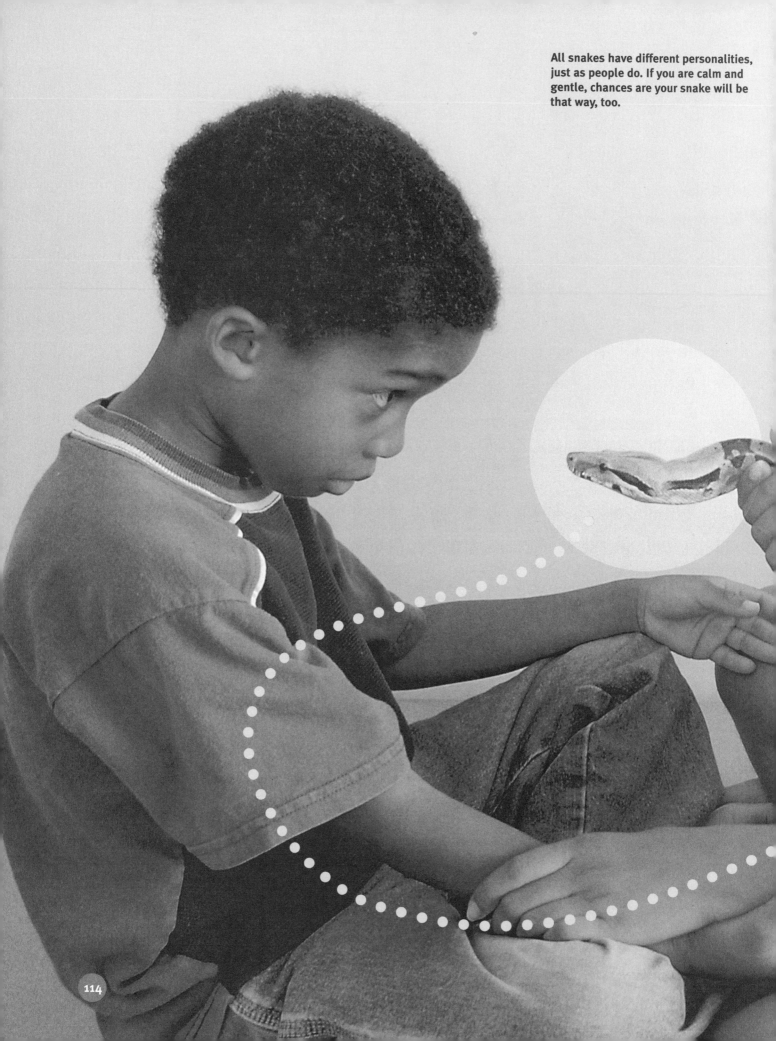

All snakes have different personalities, just as people do. If you are calm and gentle, chances are your snake will be that way, too.

114

If you get two snakes very different in size, house them separately. This reduces the risk of spreading infection or parasites. Also, some snakes eat other snakes: We know of a nine-foot indigo that ate its five-foot boa companion. That's probably the record for the long swallow!

Serpentarium Care

Temperature control is the only frequent attention you have to pay to the environment in a serpentarium. Get in the habit of glancing at the thermometer in the tank from time to time during the day. In a smaller, 10-gallon tank, you're in more danger of the temperature zooming up above 90 than dipping down below 60 degrees. After a while, you'll learn what conditions make it climb, so you can turn off the bulb before it gets too hot. In our large serpentarium we keep the light on most of the time, and we rely on the snakes' judgment to know when they should move closer to the heat or farther away.

The only daily care, other than checking the temperature, is washing the water dish to prevent funguses and bacteria from growing there. Use soap or detergent and very hot water. Rinse the dish thoroughly before refilling it with fresh water.

Your snake will probably dirty its paper or fake grass two or three days after eating, and that's the time to change the newspaper or wash the grass mat. At the same time, wash the serpentarium itself with water to which Clorox or another chlorine disinfectant has been added. Follow the disinfecting solution instructions on the package. Don't use disinfectants containing phenol or pine tar — both are toxic to snakes.

Your family will want to know where you are going to keep the snake while you clean its cage — a sensible question. Keep it in a pillowcase with the top closed with a rubber band. Plenty of air comes in through the cloth. If you ever have to take your snake anywhere — to school, on vacation, to the pet store to be boarded — carry it the

Looking for Lloyd

As our boa, Lloyd, began to grow out of his tank, he spent nights restlessly rubbing his nose against the top until he learned to lift it. From then on he was more often escaped than confined. No problem. We always found him in the stereo amplifier. He has a larger cage now but we give him freedom too, for weeks at a time.

A clumsy snake, he has fallen off rafters, knocked over plants, singed himself on light-bulbs, and gotten his head stuck in a hole in a cigar box. But snakes do learn. Now Lloyd knows the hazards of his territory, explores without mishap, and, when the adventure's over, inevitably winds up curled up in his amplifier.

same way so that it doesn't get injured. Putting the pillowcase in an appropriately sized insulated cooler offers even better protection against both injury and sudden temperature changes.

Food and Water

A snake needs little more than its own weight in food each year. It can be fed once a week, twice a week, or not at all for as long as a month if you go on vacation, but it must have fresh water daily. In nature, snakes eat many kinds of prey, from birds' eggs, insects, and frogs to other snakes. Mice are suggested for all the snakes we recommend as pets. They are a complete, nutritious diet.

The size of your snake will determine the size of the mouse you feed it. Start with small mice (very small snakes can eat "pinkies," or baby mice that are still blind, hairless, and pink), and move on to larger ones as the snake grows. Your snake will prefer its meat alive, but it is much easier (and more pleasant for the mouse) if you train your pet to eat pre-killed food. It is also easier to keep a supply of dead mice in the freezer than to go out to a pet store every time your snake needs dinner. If you do feed your snake live food, you must face how you feel about this. Watching the kill is fascinating, but not without an element of horror.

There's another problem with feeding live mice, which is that mice don't seem to be afraid of snakes. Because the mouse is unafraid, he may sooner or later take a curious nibble from the snake, and you wouldn't want your three-foot snake to be bitten by a two-inch mouse. A mouse bite can get infected and cause real trouble, even death; it's always best to stay around until your snake strikes at the mouse. A mouse will cheerfully walk along the snake's back, sniff at its nose, and sit right in front of its face, happily grooming itself. But if the snake is hungry, you will see that it is poised to strike, waiting for the right moment. Although it doesn't move a muscle in its body, it will keep its head turned toward the mouse, watching it constantly. Then, so fast that you can't really follow what is happening, the snake darts its whole body forward and strikes at the mouse. If the snake is a constrictor, at the same time it will loop its body around the mouse and squeeze. The mouse is dead within 10 seconds.

When the mouse has stopped moving, the snake begins to ingest it, usually head first. If you look at the size of the snake's head and the size of the mouse, you can see that it is clearly impossible for the snake to get that mouse inside. But it does. The snake's jaws dislocate so there is no attached bony structure to restrict the mouth opening. Its narrow throat is enormously elastic. The teeth point backward like the barbs of a fishhook. As the snake makes swallowing movements, the mouse's body slides past the teeth but can't slide forward again. It takes

fact

If the time comes when you must keep the snake outside its cage — perhaps because you need to clean the tank or transport the snake to another location — place it in a clean pillowcase and close the top with a rubber band.

ROSY BOA

This series of photographs shows how a rosy boa goes about attacking and devouring its food.

1. It wraps its length around its prey and squeezes until the prey is dead, which takes about 10 seconds.

2. It then begins to eat the mouse, head first.

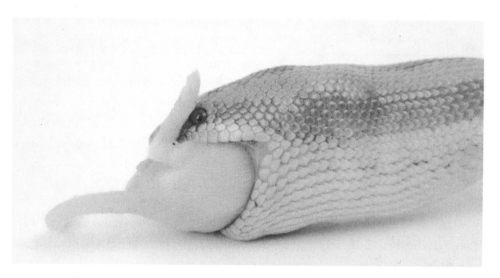

3. Its jaws separate so that he can fit the mouse past its backward-pointing teeth and down its stretchy throat.

about five minutes for the mouse to slowly disappear, head first, tail last. The bump that is the mouse then moves slowly down the long throat and comes to rest about a third of the way down the snake's body at its stomach, where it is digested over a period of days. Our boa digests it all — fur, bones, and teeth. Our corn snake digests unnervingly less. Compared to the boa's solid, simple bowel movement, the corn snake's is flecked with tiny bones, bits of teeth, and fur.

Eager eaters that share a cage may run into grotesque problems, as when two pet snakes simultaneously strike at the same mouse. Neither will let go and both begin to swallow. So if you get two snakes, take one out while you feed the other.

Remember to give your snake fresh water every day. The snake will use the same dish to soak in, especially prior to shedding, when it needs to soften its skin. As it grows, you will have to find a larger dish than the six- or seven-inch one mentioned before to fit its coiled body.

You can't tell a snake's age by its size. A snake's rate of growth depends on how much it gets to eat, as well as the temperature in its tank, its species, and its gender. Our three-year-old common boa, for example, is a mere four feet long, whereas a local naturalist's three-year-old boa measures 10 feet — about the maximum for this species. If you raise your own mice for food and if you are willing to build large quarters for your snake, you can let it grow to its natural maximum length within a few years. It won't object to frequent meals. One pet corn snake was observed to eat 13 mice in a single meal.

People who buy mice may prefer to keep their snake small, though mice and rats sold as snake food are sometimes cheaper than ones intended as pets. Once you've made the decision to grow a giant snake, there's no going back on it. Big snakes keep their big appetites.

Illnesses

If you have any concerns about your pet, take it to a vet. It's a good idea to find a vet in your area who's comfortable treating reptiles before you get a snake.

Kept in warm and clean tanks, most pet snakes do well. A healthy snake can live in captivity for a very long time, the oldest known being a ball python who lived for over 40 years. Ten years is more common. The problem is less the frequency with which they fall ill than the difficulty they have in recovering. Reptiles are incredibly slow to heal.

The biggest medical problem with snakes, usually a fatal one, is an infection called mouth rot. The infection is picked up from dirty drinking water, dirty cages, or other infected snakes. The first sign may be refusal to eat. If you examine the snake's mouth by gently pulling it open, you may see white cottony patches on the gums, foaminess at the mouth edges, or red spots. Gradually, the condition permanently destroys gum tissue. The snake's mouth hurts. It continues to refuse food and ultimately starves to death.

Mouth infections are stubborn but curable if you work hard at it. Use Sulmet, a 25 percent solution of sulfamethazine made by Lederle. Wash the snake's mouth with it daily using an eyedropper. Don't remove the white patches in the infected area, as they cushion the sore spots underneath and keep the infection from going deeper. They will fall off by themselves.

Other problems snakes can have are wounds and parasites. Thick as a snake's skin looks, it is easily injured. The most common injury is caused by a snake's nose rubbing against an unlined wire-mesh tank top or side. Treat any skin injury with an antibiotic ointment applied three or four times a day. Ask a veterinarian's advice as to the best ointment to use.

When Baby Won't Eat

Now about problem eaters. Lloyd is our boa constrictor. He was about two feet long when we got him and is four feet long now. Before we brought him home, we asked the pet store to watch and make sure he was eating readily when a mouse was put in his cage. They said he was. We brought him home with a spotted mouse. He wouldn't eat. Worried, we checked his mouth — no signs of mouth infection. We checked that the mouse was the right size. Lloyd wasn't big enough yet for full-grown mice, but this one was half grown, the size he was accustomed to eating.

We waited a few days, hoping Lloyd was just adjusting to his new quarters. Still no luck. We tried all the tricks. We waited a whole week to get him hungrier. We kept the mouse in a small box for an hour before it was to be served up so it would get nervous, sweat, and smell better. We tried feeding Lloyd late at night in total darkness, in honor of the boa's nocturnal habits. We even left the house entirely so there would be no vibrations to distract Lloyd from his dinner. Nothing worked.

Finally we took the spotted mouse back and got another one; it happened to be brown. We put it in Lloyd's cage. We came back in an hour. The mouse was gone and a telltale bulge was already about halfway down Lloyd's long digestive system. Conclusion: Some boas don't like spotted mice. Others don't like brown ones. We found out by trial and error that Lloyd didn't like white mice, light mice, or any sort of spots. Lloyd was a fussy eater.

Since Lloyd ate brown mice only and brown mice are scarce in pet stores, Lloyd's meals were few and far between. After four months, he hadn't grown enough to notice. All that changed after Lloyd's great escape.

We've said that snakes get impatient with confinement. They are also intelligent enough to follow their noses. If their noses just naturally lead over the top of the cage because someone forgot to weight it with a rock, snakes escape.

Lloyd escaped. Or rather, he seemed to vanish into thin air. We boarded up the children's rooms so Lloyd couldn't get out under the doors, and then took the place apart. We removed every book from every shelf, every baseball card from every drawer, every dirty sock from the floor. No snake. We left Lloyd's water dish out near this cage at night so he wouldn't perish of thirst.

Two weeks went by and we were into the third. Then, on a hunch, someone decided to take apart the phonograph amplifier that sits right next to Lloyd's cage. There he was; there he had lived the whole two and a half weeks. Boas aren't wanderers.

We figured Lloyd must be pretty hungry, so we offered him a mouse as soon as he was settled back into his cage. But he would not eat — he was beginning to shed. Shedding takes a week of moping around and another three or four days of soaking.

By the time he was finished, Lloyd had been without food for a month. We rushed to the pet store for a fresh mouse. There were two choices: spotted or spotted. We took

spotted. So did Lloyd. He wasn't about to starve himself for a principle. He is now cured of food fussiness. And wonder of wonders, he will even eat dead mice.

As Lloyd grew he began to eat regularly, on Tuesdays and Saturdays. And then came our next problem. Lloyd became constipated. Lloyd usually went to the bathroom after each meal: one mouse, one mess. But now, somewhere inside that long body were the remains of four mice.

We were worried. We called around. Most people said not to worry (they didn't know the answer to the question). But finally a snake lover said that snakes get constipated from lack of exercise. We should take him from his cage every day, put a few inches of lukewarm water in the bathtub, and give Lloyd a 15-minute swim. There was some bickering as it was debated whose bathtub Lloyd was going to share, but once that was decided, Lloyd started his daily five times around the pool. He loved it, and it worked. Now Lloyd is neither a fussy eater nor a constipated personality. We feel we have ironed out a few kinks.

Mites are another skin problem, as common with snakes as with birds. They are such tiny creatures, one can't tell if the snake has them or not. You suspect mites on a bird when it scratches itself, but snakes don't scratch. Our answer to the problem is to place a pest strip under the paper in the serpentarium for several weeks twice a year. Use one formulated for use with reptiles, as they are sensitive to chemicals. It effectively kills the mites, which bite at night and retire into protected places during the day. A snake who goes under the paper can also be hurt by the strip, so when you use it, secure the newspaper really well with masking tape to prevent problems. If you are dealing with a severe infestation of mites, you will need to treat the snake itself (a soapy soak should do the trick) and thoroughly clean the cage and surrounding area with disinfectant. Mites can easily spread from cage to cage, so isolate newcomers if you add to your collection.

Captive snakes are also susceptible to a variety of respiratory diseases like pneumonia and bronchitis. Take note if your snake opens its mouth to breathe. This shows that its nose is stuffy. Getting too cold is a common cause of sickness. Keep an eye on the thermometer in the serpentarium. This should certainly help prevent respiratory problems.

Once the snake is sick, the only recourse is antibiotics injected by a vet into the large muscles to either side of the snake's backbone.

Soaking in a water dish can help a snake shed its skin.

When your snake has finished shedding, you'll find the transparent outer layer of skin in its cage.

One last word. Although a snake may throw up his mouse if he is disturbed too soon after eating, we haven't heard of upset stomach problems in general. (In fact, you shouldn't handle your snake for 24 hours after it has eaten.) But snakes can become constipated. This is often due to temperatures that are too low to encourage proper digestion. Make sure your snake is warm enough. Also, a swim or a soak in a warm (not scalding) tub can often loosen things up. Overall, provide your snake with proper food and a clean, warm environment to keep him healthy.

Shedding

A snake sheds its skin at intervals controlled by hormones, diet, and rate of growth. Young snakes that are growing rapidly generally shed more frequently than older ones. Shedding, called "ecdysis," occurs from 4 to 12 times a year. The whole process usually takes one to two weeks. The outermost layer of skin becomes somewhat opaque, giving the impression that the snake's color is fading. The specialized scales that ordinarily provide a transparent covering for the snake's eyes (they are called eyecaps) become opaque too, so a snake about to shed looks like it is suffering from cataracts. It stops eating, and it may act jumpy or irritable — perhaps because it is nearly blind during this period. Shedding snakes are best left alone and shouldn't be fed until the process is over.

The actual shedding process may be preceded by a few days' soak in the water dish. You can provide a more humid environment by cutting a snake-sized hole in a plastic container and filling it with damp (not dripping) sphagnum moss for your snake to hide in. Sometimes with the help of a rock, and sometimes without, the snake then slips out of its skin. If the air is dry, the snake may not be able to shed its skin completely. Some owners gently massage the snake with a warm, wet washcloth to help the situation. If the snake cannot shed its eyecaps, you can try the same treatment. If the eyecaps still aren't coming off, consult an expert.

Both our boa and our corn snake detach their skin around the mouth and then peel it off from head to toe. It is rather like peeling off a sock. The shed skin is inside out and can be blown up like a balloon through the mouth opening. A snake's colors are at their most beautiful just after shedding.

The colors and patterns of snakes exist for a reason. They are how each species recognizes its own kind.

Breeding

Snakes in captivity are reluctant to breed. Both males and females have the same coloring, so it will be almost impossible for you to tell what sex your snake is. Like birds, snakes have no genitals outside their bodies, but the male does have a penis of sorts inside the cloaca where his tail begins. This male organ is more properly called a hemipenes, and it has two prongs. When snakes copulate they twist themselves over one another, sometimes clockwise, sometimes counterclockwise. There is no telling in advance from which side the male will have to enter the female, so nature has provided him with an ambidextrous organ.

The female is entered through her cloaca. Most of the snakes we've recommended are egg-layers, though boas bear live young. Most female snakes lay leathery-shelled eggs in shallow nests made in loose soil or rotting leaves where the sun

fact

There is a 20-year-old Indian python named Baby who is 15 feet long and weighs 227 pounds. She eats two rabbits every four to six weeks and lives in the Los Angeles Zoo.

and the heat of decay help keep them warm. The number of eggs varies from only two to over two dozen. Some snakes stay with the nest to guard the eggs and even to warm them with heat accumulated in their bodies from sunbathing. But none takes care of the babies after they hatch. All baby snakes can take care of themselves, in the wild.

To care for a baby pet snake, separate it from other snakes and keep it dry and warm. The container you keep it in should be small enough that it will find its food easily. Don't forget to include some shelter, such as a cardboard box with a hole in it, where the snake can retreat when it needs privacy. Wait until it has shed once before you offer it food, but be sure it feeds before it is a month old. Don't give it food that is too big. A newborn mouse (or pinky) that is not wider around than the snake should do.

You might unknowingly purchase a snake that is gravid, or pregnant. If eggs suddenly appear in the tank, you should remove them and keep them between damp paper towels in a warm place. Make sure the eggs stay right-side up when you move them, or the baby snakes inside will die. It's best to have an expert's help when the eggs begin to hatch. When the eggs do hatch, look for the umbilical cord that attached the baby to its nutrition, the egg yolk. Though it is less obvious in reptiles, they do have a "belly button" similar to that of mammals.

Pet Birds

Canaries, one of our most common cage birds, are similar to birds that have been kept as pets for centuries. Their close relatives, linnets, chaffinches, and the small European robins, were sold in the streets of ancient Rome and offered in the open markets of medieval towns. Canaries, as well as the mynah bird, are called "perching birds," or passerines. Passerines are the best singers, the best nest-builders, and the most numerous of all birds. (Most backyard birds are passerines.) All the passerines have one trait in common — the structure of their feet. Three unwebbed, well-developed toes stick out in front. One toe sticks out behind. The toes are connected to the bird's legs by strong ligaments. When the bird perches, the weight of its body pulls the ligaments tight, closing the toes around any perch the feet are in contact with. Because the tightening does not require a conscious muscular grip, the toes stay tightly curled around a perch even when the bird is sitting head under wing, fast asleep.

The other birds discussed in this chapter are psittacines, or members of the parrot family. They include parrots, cockatiels, parakeets, and lovebirds. Their feet are quite different, with two toes in front, two behind. Members of the parrot family can use their feet like hands to hold food, pick up objects, or climb along branches. When climbing, parrots use their beak as a third hand. Going downward, a parrot leans down, presses its beak onto a lower surface to stabilize itself, then descends one foot at a time. Going upward, it uses its beak as a hook, securing it to a higher surface and pulling up its body behind. A parrot can climb a piece of fabric with ease, gripping the cloth with its beak at every step.

Parrot beaks are different from other bird beaks. Most bird jaws are similar to ours, hinged only at the bottom. Parrot beaks are hinged both at the top and at the bottom, making a parrot yawn an impressive sight.

Pet Birds
at a glance

Canaries

PAGE 140

HOUSING: Large homemade cake-pan cage with seed and water containers and dowel perches, or small commercial birdcage.

SPECIAL REQUIREMENTS: Protection from drafts and direct sunlight. Wing clipping during taming period may be necessary.

DIET: Boxed canary seed, supplemented with fresh greens or sprouted seeds.

CARE: Feed and replenish water daily. Provide bath twice a week. Clean cage floor once or twice a week. Wash cage and perches monthly.

TAMABILITY: May become calm enough to perch on fingers and eat from hand.

LIFE SPAN: Ten to 15 years; as long as 20 to 25 with proper diet and care.

Mynah Birds *PAGE 145*

HOUSING: Large commercial birdcage.

SPECIAL REQUIREMENTS: Protection from drafts and direct sunlight. Wing clipping during taming period may be necessary.

DIET: Boxed mynah food, supplemented with fresh raw fruits, but not high-iron greens like kale and spinach. Mynahs need a low-iron diet.

CARE: Feed, replenish water, and remove leftover fresh foods daily. Clean cage floor twice a week or more often, as necessary. Provide bath twice a week. Wash cage and perches monthly.

TAMABILITY: May become calm enough to perch on hand or shoulder. Mimic sounds, whistles, and human speech.

LIFE SPAN: 40 years.

Small Parrots *PAGE 147*

FAVORITES:

Green, blue, yellow, or white parakeet

Gray cockatiel

Pied cockatiel

Albino cockatiel

Bee bee parrot (Tovi or orange-chinned parakeet)

Peach-faced lovebird

Fischer's lovebird

HOUSING: Largest homemade cake-pan cage with seed and water containers and dowel perches, or medium-sized commercial birdcage.

SPECIAL REQUIREMENTS: Protection from drafts and direct sunlight. Wing clipping during taming period. Toys.

DIET: Pelleted diet, supplemented with seed snacks and fresh raw greens and fruits. Supply bones or twigs to chew on.

CARE: Feed and replenish water daily. Provide bath twice a week. Clean cage floor once or twice a week. Wash cage and perches monthly.

TAMABILITY: Become calm and affectionate. Individuals may mimic sounds, whistles, and, more rarely, human speech.

LIFE SPAN: 15 to 18 years for parakeets, 15 to 20 years for cockatiels, 10 to 15 years for lovebirds and bee bee parrots.

Large Parrots *PAGE 151*

FAVORITES:

African gray parrot

Ringneck parakeet

Amazon parrots

HOUSING: Large commercial birdcage.

SPECIAL REQUIREMENTS: Protection from drafts and direct sunlight. Wing clipping during taming period. Exercise outside of cage. Toys.

DIET: Pelleted diet, supplemented with seed treats, fresh raw greens, and fruits. Supply bones or twigs to chew on.

CARE: Feed and replenish water daily. Provide bath once or twice a week. Clean cage floor once or twice a week. Wash cage and perches monthly.

TAMABILITY: Become calm, affectionate, and devoted to owner and family. Mimic sounds and whistles, often human speech.

LIFE SPAN: 20 years for ringneck parakeet, 25 to 50 years for other parrots.

A Word of Warning

Birds are very susceptible to a variety of common household toxins and should not be exposed to the following: Teflon or other nonstick coating on pans, irons, and ironing boards, which gives off fumes when overheated (not during regular usage); scented deodorizers and household cleaning sprays; and galvanized or zinc-coated metal (look for cage fittings, dishes, and metal toys that are made of stainless steel or other nongalvanized metal).

Officially parrots are well below passerines on the evolutionary scale. Their nests are sloppy, and their behavior simple, and they do not sing songs of their own. In my opinion, however, they are superior as pets. The bird expert, stalking the forests with field glasses, can appreciate the complex behavior of passerines, but in a cage a songbird's instincts have little outlet. Parrots, on the other hand, are driven less by instinct. They learn things you teach them and devise tricks of their own. They become so emotionally involved with their owners that affections and jealousy can become a nuisance. And just when you think you have found out everything your parrot can do, it will surprise you with a brand-new trick.

Choosing a Bird

Birds are cheap to keep but not to buy. In order of cost, from cheapest to most expensive, these are the birds commonly sold as pets: parakeets, canaries, small parrots, and large parrots. Canaries are valued for their looks and song; parakeets and the small parrots, such as cockatiels, lovebirds, and bee bee parrots, become amusing and affectionate pets. The most common of the large parrots are the Amazon (there are many varieties) and the African gray. All the large parrots are very intelligent and loving pets. All of them can learn to "talk," and the African gray parrot is considered the best mimic in the world. Though not as commonly found for sale, the mynah is also a wonderful mimic, of both sound effects and the human voice.

Problems with pet birds, and the psittacines (parrots) in particular, are how much care they need, how emotionally attached they can become, and how long they live. Many of the parrots in our family belong to one or another of our four sons and were given to them when they were eight or ten years old. The pets will live through our sons' years of junior high and high school, and then the boys will go to college, leaving the birds behind. We, the parents, may have to care for them for years unless the boys find housing that allows pets. I think that in addition to learning what you can about each species before you choose one, you should talk to the rest of the family about whether they are willing to take on the emotional as well as physical responsibility for your pet in the long future that lies ahead.

The healthiest birds are likely to be those raised in this country by breeders, rather than imported wild birds. Breeders' birds are recognized by a closed band on one leg that tells when the bird was hatched. All the smaller birds are available as breeder-raised youngsters.

Smaller birds breed well in captivity, but larger ones won't breed unless kept in very large outdoor aviaries where they can freely fly. In the past, such birds were often captured in the wild and imported into this country. The practice, which killed more birds than were delivered live, has pushed many species to the brink of extinction, and it is no longer legal to import them.

Sadly, many pet wholesalers do not take good care of either the birds they import or those they buy and sell to pet stores. Of the wild birds that survive the crowded and careless process of capture and shipment and a quarantine period, many more become sick in the equally crowded and careless conditions at the wholesalers'.

Really, you should not buy wild-caught birds. Serious breeders of large parrots do exist; they may advertise directly or sell through pet stores. Don't be scared to ask the pet store to tell you who bred a bird you have your eye on, and ask to talk to the breeder personally. Your best bet is to buy a bird that has been hand-raised and introduced to new people and new experiences from fledgling age. An enthusiastic breeder will love to

PERCH SIZES COMPARED TO BIRDS' FEET

Ideally, a bird's feet wrap only partway around a perch. The toenails dig into the perch, rather than encircling it. Having a good grip on a perch allows the bird to better maintain its balance. Provide your bird with a perch of the appropriate size, based on the size of its foot.

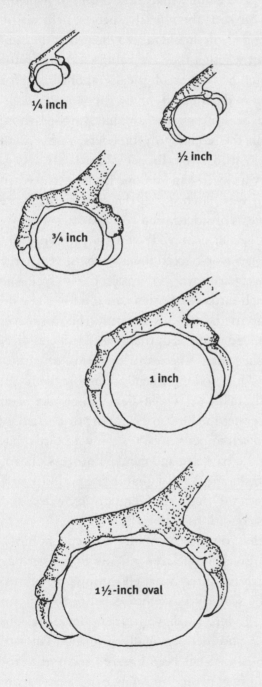

¼ inch

½ inch

¾ inch

1 inch

1½-inch oval

talk birds with you. As for the little fellows like canaries and parakeets, which are never captured in the wild these days, their health is not guaranteed just because they have been bred in captivity. Symptoms of illness are easy to misunderstand; sick birds may look cuter and tamer than the others. A sick bird feels cold, so it ruffles up its feathers. This makes it look fluffier than the other birds. Because it has no energy, it doesn't fly in panic around its cage. This makes it look more docile than the other birds. Also look closely for deformities like crooked toenails and overgrown beaks. Check that the eyes are bright and fully open. Choose a bird in good feather, with no bald spots. Look under the tail — any dirt or droppings clinging to the feathers means the bird has diarrhea and may be sick.

Any of the small birds can share a cage with one of their own kind (particularly of the opposite sex), but they may not get along with birds of different species. The larger parrots may or may not get along with one another, even if they are of the same species. Sometimes personalities clash. One cage is nearly always too small for two parrots. Some parrots, both big and small, become less fond of their owner if they can shower their affections on a friend or a mate. Unless you want to breed your parrots, a single bird makes a better pet. On the other hand, if you want a bird around but would be just as happy if it didn't get too personal with you, the bird (and you) might be happier if it had a feathered friend.

Housing

To stay healthy, a bird needs exercise. Small birds should be able to fly about their cages, large ones to flap their wings freely. The box on page 142 will give you an idea of the size to look for. Unfortunately, most cages are smaller than these ideal sizes, so under each bird's separate listing you'll find suggestions for providing extra exercise. In many cases, it's better for your bird to have a cage that is wide rather than tall, since most birds don't fly straight up and down. In all cases, your bird should be able to extend its wings fully and move about from perch to perch.

Cages come equipped with food and water dishes and with several perches made of wooden dowels. The dishes are often well designed, but the dowel perches are not always ideal. A bird's toenails grow all the time, just like yours do. In nature, wild birds are constantly landing on and walking along rough branches. Walking on bark keeps their toenails worn down to a proper length. The wooden dowels are too smooth to do this.

There are several ways you can keep your bird's toenails manicured properly with a dowel perch. You can wrap one of the dowels with fine sandpaper, using white glue to keep it in place, or you can smear white glue onto the bottom half of a perch and then dip it in fine sand. With the second method, the bird's nails will be kept worn but the tender soles of the bird's feet won't be injured. Many pet stores also sell special perches that are rough like sandpaper and may be substituted for one or more of the perches in the cage. Probably the nicest thing to do is to find a pretty branch to use instead of a dowel. It will be more interesting for you to look at and for your bird to perch on.

fact

A birdcage should be large enough to allow small birds like canaries and parakeets to fly from perch to perch, medium-sized birds like cockatiels to hop from perch to perch, and large birds like Amazon parrots at least to flap their wings.

You can wire it to the cage bars to keep it from slipping. And it's certainly easier to keep clean than sandpaper.

A branch has another advantage over a dowel. A dowel is the same diameter from one end to the other, whereas a branch is thicker at one end and thinner at the other. This lets a bird choose what thickness is most comfortable for its feet. Also, having perches of several different sizes exercises the bird's toes. The dowels that come preinstalled in cages are often too thin for the bird; its toenails wrap around them instead of hitting them, so even if the dowel is roughened, the bird's nails may grow too long and its feet become deformed. For the large birds, like parrots and mynahs, a hardwood tool handle, like those available in hardware stores for axes and grub hoes, makes an excellent perch. The oval shape is comfortable for their feet. Another advantage is that parrots, which will chew through most perches in short order, have trouble damaging these hardwood handles.

A bird's beak is covered with a thin layer of tissue similar to our fingernails. Although the bony beak underneath doesn't grow, the outside layer does. Birds manicure their beaks by either rubbing them against rough surfaces or biting on hard objects.

For small birds like canaries and parakeets, equip the cage with a piece of cuttlebone (buy it in the pet store). The birds will rub their beaks on

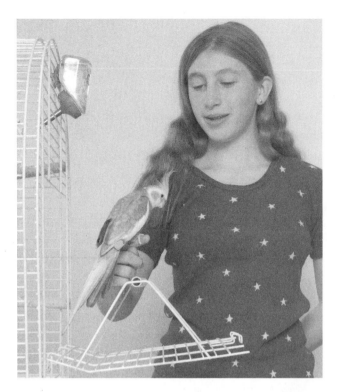

Once your bird is used to perching on your finger inside the cage, you can bring it out of the cage for some exercise and socialization.

To return your bird to its cage, have it sit on your finger, then carefully take it in through the cage door. Push your finger up against a perch; the bird will climb off.

it and peck at it. A parrot does more biting than rubbing; it will chew up a cuttlebone in about five minutes. Give parrots, instead, twigs and bones to chew on in their cages. But don't be surprised if they also chew their perches out from under themselves every few months. We gave one parrot a whetstone (knife sharpener) wired to his bars to rub his beak against. It was a good idea but it didn't work. He is an incurable perch-gnawer.

Commercial cages have a pull-out drawer bottom for easy cleaning and often come equipped with plastic side panels to prevent seeds from being scattered outside the cage. If you find the side panels inadequate, pet stores also sell vinyl buckets that fit around the bottom of the cage to catch scattered seed. Neither of these devices is foolproof, and sweeping up seed or pellet crumbs is one of a bird owner's cleanup jobs.

Newspaper is the best flooring material for covering the drawer bottom. For canaries, sprinkle medium-grit pet-store sand (gravel) over the newspaper, or offer sand in a separate dish. Because they swallow their food whole, many birds need to eat grit to grind their food inside their gizzard (stomach). Parrots crack and grind food with their powerful beaks and don't need to ingest extra grit.

Pet stores also sell cage covers to fit the various shapes and sizes of standard cages. A large towel will also work. Covers serve two purposes: They cut off drafts at night and so protect your pet's health, and they are used to quiet down a noisy bird in the daytime. A bird in a darkened cage will stop twittering, screeching, or singing. It settles down to sleep.

Cleaning birdcages. Change the newspaper (and sand if you use it) at least twice a week for all birds except the mynah. Mynahs are fruit-eaters, whereas all the other birds mentioned eat dry pellets and seeds. A mynah's droppings are more copious, mushy, and unpleasant than the droppings of seed-eaters. You may have to change the newspaper in a mynah's cage every day. Sprinkle fresh sand over the newspaper after each change. The perches should be scraped and washed, too. Dried droppings come off more easily if you wet down the perch and let the droppings loosen with moisture. A plastic scouring pad is better than a sponge for scrubbing. Wash the water dish with soap and water and rinse it well every day before refilling it. The food dish should be washed whenever it looks soiled.

When the bars of the cage begin to get dirty — the length of time depends on the bird — the whole cage has to be washed with soap and water. Birds that haven't been tamed can stay inside their cages while you sponge down the bars. Tame birds can be let out while you are cleaning.

Where to keep the cage. All the birds we recommend here as pets are tropical birds. Find a place for the cage that is warm and without drafts. Since any window creates drafts at night, find a place away from a window. (And as we just mentioned, a cover over the cage at night will help prevent drafts.) Our parrots are healthy all winter at a nighttime temperature of only 55 degrees — often the lowest setting on a home thermostat.

Sunny locations sound nice, but birds in cages can't get out of the sun when it gets too hot for them. Bright light is fine, but avoid sun.

The only other problem to consider when you find a place for the birdcage is the messy food scattering. Remember that it's easier to sweep pellet crumbs and seed shells from a bare floor than to vacuum them off a shaggy rug.

Food and Water

Canaries and the parrots we describe here are all basically seed-eaters. Canary and parakeet seed mixtures come boxed at pet stores. Parrot seed mixtures are usually custom-mixed at pet stores from bulk seed in bins, but there are several boxed brands too. Small parrots like cockatiels and lovebirds require smaller seeds, while large parrots need larger seeds. None of these mixes,

though, is made up of seeds that these non-native birds eat in their wild habitats. Some, like millet, have little nutritional value; others, like sunflower seeds and peanuts (which actually are beans), contain more fat than is healthy as a steady diet for a caged bird. Pellets, formulated to meet the nutritional needs of each species for which they are intended, are the best basic diet. What a bore, though! We've always offered our parrots seed treats like almonds, sunflower and pumpkin seeds, and popcorn on the cob. We've gathered for the little ones native grasses gone to seed; these are mostly meadow species, ones we can't always identify but that have large grains. The process of removing seeds from their shells and husks seems to interest birds more than crunching dried pellets, and such treats are valuable in making friends with a new bird.

All these birds nibble also at vegetables and fruits, though only the mynah is a true fruit-eater. Pellet food containing dried fruit and cereal is sold for mynahs in pet stores. This dry food helps somewhat to keep their droppings solid.

Whether fruit- or seed-eaters, few pet species limit their diet so completely in their natural habitat. In nature these birds occasionally need a high-protein diet that includes insects. Hard-cooked egg yolk, commercial high-protein biscuits (sometimes called conditioning food and used by breeders to bring birds into reproductive fitness), and live mealworms are all good substitutes. Conditioning food and mealworms are sold in pet stores. Offer protein foods once a week; your bird might appreciate an occasional earthworm or a beef scrap, too.

Specific feeding advice is given under the discussion of each kind of bird. In general, when offering a new food, put out only a little. New foods can cause diarrhea until the bird gets used to digesting them.

Kitchen Cautions

Experts have warned me that, of all places to keep a bird, the kitchen is most dangerous. When they overheat, nonstick cookware, irons, and other items coated with Teflon or other surfaces give off a gas called polytetrafluoroethylene (PTFE), which can be deadly. Canaries are so particularly sensitive to such chemicals that miners took them down into the mines with them — if the canaries keeled over, the miners knew to get out fast. Curious by nature, birds can also get into trouble with hot stoves, boiling kettles, and alcoholic or caffeinated drinks.

Still, kitchens are where families congregate, and in our experience there is no other place that offers such company, such comfort, running water, ready food, and such bustle and excitement as a kitchen. I don't use nonstick pans. Whenever a bird flies toward the hot kettle to land on its handle, I scream "NO! HOT!" as you might to any toddler, and I leap to deflect its flight. Birds aren't dopes; they learn. Sometimes I think that the anxious warnings of experts have not been properly weighed against loads of good. The kitchen is central to most of our family endeavors, and so it has been central to our very social birds.

Birds must be fed every day. They have a very high metabolism, which means they keep a high body temperature by burning up a great deal of food. Don't let yourself be fooled by what looks like a full dish of seeds; it may, instead, be filled with empty seed husks, and your bird may be out of food.

Fresh foods, fruit especially, rot quickly. Clean up leftovers every day. Most birds also need to eat grains of medium-grit sand, available at pet stores. Birds can bite with their beaks, but they have no teeth, and only parrots, whose hard tongues manipulate a seed or pellet in their beak, can nibble a morsel to bits. Most birds swallow grit, which stays in their gizzard (stomach) and grinds up the seeds so they can be digested. Sand can be sprinkled on the cage floor.

The cuttlebone suggested as a cage fixture under Housing is a good source of calcium. Calcium is most important to young growing birds and to breeding females, who need extra calcium to form the hard shells on their eggs. Besides cuttlebone, calcium sources include crushed oyster shells (sold at pet stores), crushed eggshells, and bonemeal, all of which can be sprinkled in with the bird's food once a week. The large parrots enjoy nibbling on small bones, which are rich in calcium as well.

Birds need fresh drinking water every day. They sprinkle seed into their water, drop their droppings into it, and even bathe in it. As their "parent," you'll have to make up for their lack of cleanliness.

Bathing

Birds will dirty their drinking water less if you give them a chance to bathe several times a week, outside of the water dish. Just among the parrots we keep, the cockatiel bathes by rolling about in wet lettuce leaves, the macaw splashes himself in a pan of water, the Amazon becomes ecstatic at the sight of a plant mister, and the ringneck will stand under the trickle of the kitchen faucet. It may take awhile to discover how your bird likes its bath. First, try a glass pie plate filled with water on the floor of its cage each morning. Since birds are nervous about a new article you put in their cage or hold near them, your bird may shy away from the dish at first or even fly about in panic. Offer the dish for a few minutes every morning for a week until the bird calms down, then put it there for a few hours each morning for another week. If it's not using it by then, try a plant mister. Again, just give the mister a moment's try each morning for the first week (not directly into the bird's face, but from above or behind). As a bird comes to enjoy a spraying, it will spread its wings and ruffle its feathers so the water can seep down to its skin. If it doesn't like the spray, it will continue to try to get away from it. The alternative for a bird dead set against dish baths or spray is wet lettuce or cabbage leaves to roll in. If the bird can have a good bath every few days (or, with larger parrots, once a week), it may give up taking baths in its water dish.

Pat down your wet bird with a towel and keep it away from drafts. Don't even think of using a hairdryer: The heat will dry up the soothing moisture the bath supplied, and you could singe your bird's skin or feathers or even endanger its health with the fumes mentioned earlier. (Come to think of it, I can't imagine a bird who would stand for the loud noise and hot wind of a hairdryer anyway.)

There is still another way that some birds like to keep themselves clean — dust baths. Unfortunately for our family, that's how our fifth parrot, an African gray, likes to bathe. If we put sand in his cage, he squats in it and kicks up the sand

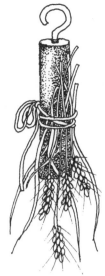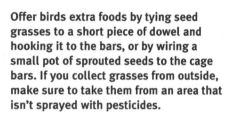

Offer birds extra foods by tying seed grasses to a short piece of dowel and hooking it to the bars, or by wiring a small pot of sprouted seeds to the cage bars. If you collect grasses from outside, make sure to take them from an area that isn't sprayed with pesticides.

under his belly and wings, and about four feet in every other direction too. So instead of sand we keep newspaper in his cage. But African gray parrots invent new ways to annoy their owners. Our fiendish bird unfastens his water dish, drops it to the floor of his cage, lets the water soak into the newspaper, chews the newspaper into a mush, and grovels in it.

Illnesses

Pet birds get sick less often and probably live longer than wild birds. The reason is simply that they don't have a lot of other birds around to catch things from. As a treat, people occasionally put a bird in its cage outdoors for a few hours in nice weather. But this is a real danger. Wild birds visit the cage, attracted by the birdseed. Diseases they harbor can be picked up by the caged bird, and often they prove fatal.

Even without exposure to wild birds, pet birds may get sick or develop other physical problems. Colds and respiratory diseases such as bronchitis and pneumonia are the most frequent problem, especially with newly imported birds. The symptoms of respiratory disease include a runny nose (a bird's "nose" is the nostrils at the top of its

Treat your pet bird to an occasional shallow bath. Most pet birds will relish the opportunity to splash around in the sink or in a small dish of water. But watch out — water will get everywhere!

beak), ruffled feathers, quietness, a squatting position, a reluctance to eat, and sometimes breathing through the mouth. Birds also cough and sneeze. When a bird is quite sick, its breathing may become rapid and even noisy.

A sick bird dies much faster than another animal might. The important thing is to act quickly. If you suspect your bird is sick, don't wait — take it to your vet. It's a good idea to find a vet in your area who knows about birds and have his or her name available before you need it. In fact, you should take in your bird for a checkup when you first bring it home.

If your bird needs medicine, the vet will explain how much to give and how often, as well as how to persuade your bird to swallow it. Sick birds need to be kept especially warm and out of drafts. You can put a blanket over the cage and put it near a heater. A smaller cage can go under a lamp for extra warmth.

Mites are a common parasite even in caged birds, but they are easily gotten rid of. If your bird

seems to be scratching itself a lot, put a white cloth over the cage at night. In the morning, check the inside surface of the cloth for tiny reddish spots. Those are mites. Buy a mite spray sold for birds in pet stores. Spray the bird thoroughly. Remove the newspaper from the cage floor and give the whole cage a good wet spraying before you put in fresh newspaper. Repeat the treatment once a week for three weeks.

Overgrown toenails and beaks seldom happen if you provide the right perch and a good beak-rubbing surface or chewing materials. But occasionally a bird has a defective beak that grows unevenly as a horny projection, or a bird might come to you with toenails or beak already overgrown. In such cases you will have to help the bird by clipping off the extra. Have your vet or an experienced bird handler show you how to do this the first time. When you're ready to do the job on your own, wrap the bird in a towel and get another person to hold it belly up. Extract one foot at a time, or the beak. Use fingernail clippers to do the clipping. Naturally, a parrot will give you a good nip if you go for its beak, but there is a simple way to do the job safely: Get a good hold on its upper beak. It can't possible bite you while you are holding on to its beak. To smooth the edges of the cut, use a nail file. Clip toenails only a little at a time to avoid hitting the blood vessel in the nail. Spread the job over several sessions so the bird doesn't get exhausted from fear. If you do hit a blood vessel and the nail begins to bleed, a styptic pencil like men use for razor nicks will stop the bleeding.

Wing Clipping

Clipping a bird's wings so that temporarily it cannot fly makes it easier to tame or train the bird. It takes two people. Use any type of scissors, but try them on cloth first to be sure they cut easily.

Wrap the bird in a soft towel. Turn it belly up, as this posture usually quiets birds. Keep a flap of towel over its face if it tries to peck. While one person holds the bird in his or her lap, the other can extract one wing from the wrapping. Spread the wing out (by straightening the "elbow") and cut straight across the long flight feathers. Cutting feathers does not hurt the bird. Like fingernails, feathers are sensitive only where they grow inside the bird's skin, and you are cutting well away from there.

You need to clip only one wing to prevent real flying. Clipped in this way, the bird will flutter along the ground but can't take to the air. The short clipped feathers will fall out during the bird's next molt, probably only a few months away. If it's tame by then, you can let its feathers grow in so it can fly again.

Two other ways to clip wings keep them looking more normal but are not as effective in preventing flight. These methods require that both wings be clipped. Either can be used with the larger birds that need nearly all their flight feathers to support their heavier weight.

The first method is to leave the first two or three flight feathers long and cut off the rest. You'll see the resulting gap when the wings are opened, but when the bird folds its wings, they will look nearly normal. The second method is to cut every other flight feather, starting with the second one. Even when the wings are fully spread, the even gaps look quite natural.

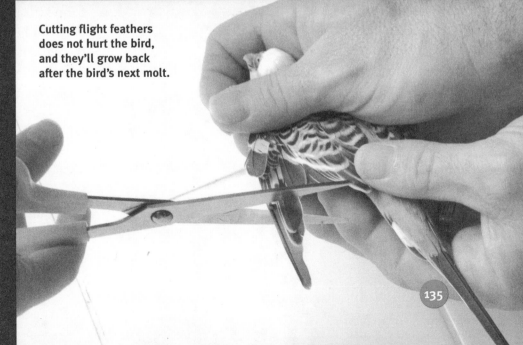

Cutting flight feathers does not hurt the bird, and they'll grow back after the bird's next molt.

At intervals during the year, every bird molts (sheds) its feathers and grows new ones. Some birds molt most of their feathers all at once, usually only once or twice a year. The molting takes a month or less. Others may molt over a longer period or may lose only a few tail feathers, flight feathers, or body feathers at a time. When a bird molts all at once, it can be a sorry sight and may worry its owners, especially because it will act rather quiet and perhaps not eat as well as usual. The larger parrots molt gradually; you will notice shed feathers on the cage floor but the bird will not look bedraggled or act dejected. Normal molting is nothing to worry about; it is the way birds replace old or damaged feathers, prepare for cold weather with a heavier plumage, or even change into bright colors for courting or for camouflage for different seasons. Your bird will be sleeker and more colorful with its new feathers.

Lovebird

Taming and Training

In general, taming a bird is mostly a matter of letting it become accustomed to you. Canaries can become calm enough to perch on a finger and eat from your palm. One canary owner I know actually seems to have won her bird's affection; the canary sits on her head and grooms her hair by pulling strands gently through its beak. Mynah friendship is probably at about the same level as canary friendship. But only with parrots can you expect insane devotion, embarrassing displays of love, and violent jealousy. Parrots are very emotional birds.

A baby bird calms down faster than an adult, but the taming method is the same. The first thing any bird has to get used to is your hand. Its idea of a hand at first might be "the thing that grabs and holds defenseless birds." You have to work on changing its mind until a hand means "the thing that is pleasant to perch on and may contain treats." It takes patience to change a bird's mind.

Beyond calmness, what you can expect from a bird depends on what sort of bird you have. Canaries and mynahs can be trained to perch on your finger and eat from your hand (pages 142 and 147) first in the cage, and then sometimes outside it. The smaller parrots may become affectionate as well as tame (page 150) and can perform little tricks like taking a sunflower seed gently from between your lips. The big parrots and the mynah birds can be trained to mimic human speech, whistles, and even short melodies (page 147). And the parrots in particular can be encouraged to perform on command tricks they themselves have devised (page 162).

Taming or training outside the bird's cage is easiest if the bird's wing feathers are temporarily clipped to prevent flying, until the bird is reliably calm. Some pet stores will clip a bird's wings for you when you buy it; vets will also clip wings.

Once you are used to handling birds, the job is easy to do yourself with the help of one other person (see the box on page 135).

Breeding

Some birds are perfectly happy to court, mate, build nests, lay eggs, and raise babies in captivity. Others are not. The mynah bird, for instance, has not been known to breed in captivity, though no one seems to know why. Most of the large parrots will breed, but only in very big outdoor aviaries. Apparently they need plenty of flight space to come into breeding condition. Canaries, parakeets, cockatiels, and lovebirds, on the other hand, have all been bred in people's homes. Each bird needs a different sort of nesting place and different treatment to breed, so we will explain canary breeding just as an example. You should be able to learn about the other species at the library or on the Internet.

First be sure that you have a male (cock) and a female (hen) canary. The cock can be distinguished by his song. The hen, which looks identical to the male, doesn't sing. Check with the bird dealer or pet store to make sure that you are not buying hybrid birds. Many of the prettier canaries sold today are actually crosses between a canary and another species of finch, a process that adds new colors and patterns to the offspring. They are pretty, but they are unable to have babies of their own.

Canaries breed during late winter or early spring, anywhere from mid-February to the beginning of April. Breeders usually start to get the birds in breeding condition by the beginning of January. Birds breed when their bodies are in peak condition. In nature, they often change their

Making Friends with a New Bird

For the first week, try to leave a new bird alone in its cage; then start becoming a part of its life. Talk to it whenever you're near. In nature, a predator doesn't announce itself, so talking means you're not stalking. Rest your hand on the cage. Open the cage door. Rest your hand on the entrance and inside the cage. As long as your bird panics (or, rarely, tries to peck or nip at you) with every intrusion, don't try to go any farther. Just getting a bird used to hands coming near it can take several weeks.

As its panic dies down, the bird will only move to avoid your hand rather than dashing about wildly. Now you can be more persistent. Put your hand next to the bird on its perch. When it moves to another perch, move your hand near again. If you play this game several times a day, most birds within a week will remain calm, even when your hand is quite near.

diet to include more fresh greens or high-protein insects before the breeding season. You can accomplish the same thing by adding special high-protein foods to the canaries' basic seed and vegetable diet mentioned earlier in this chapter. Conditioning foods (either seeds or crushed biscuits) are sold by pet stores. They have varying ingredients but are all high in protein. Offer the conditioning food every day in a separate cup. By mid-February buy yourself a special breeding cage from a pet store. This cage has two compartments separated by two removable partitions, one made of wire and the other solid. Each side has its own food and water dishes.

Put the cock in one side of the breeding cage and the hen into the other. Provide the hen with a nesting bowl, which you can either buy in a pet store or make from a kitchen strainer by cutting off its handle. Attach the bowl to a corner of the breeding cage, using wire if necessary. Be sure the nest is low enough that the canaries can perch on the edge without bumping their heads on the cage top. Both parents will feed their young by perching on the nest edge and reaching their beaks down into the waiting mouths.

Over a period of a few days to a few weeks, the male will begin to court with bursts of song. Soon both birds call back and forth in a high-pitched whistle. At this point, remove the solid partition but not the wire one. Watch how the cock and hen behave together. If they squabble through the wires, they are not ready to mate and you should replace the solid partition to give them more time. If the male feeds the female through the wires, you can remove the wire partition and expect the birds to mate.

Both male and female birds have a single opening at the base of the tail that technically is called the cloaca (the same word used for the same opening in reptiles). In common language the hole in birds is called a vent. It is used for letting out droppings, for laying eggs, and for transferring sperm. Penises are rare in birds. Ducks and geese have them, but canaries don't. The cock canary must mount the female's back while she uplifts and turns aside her tail feathers. He drops his rear end over hers until their cloacas touch. The sperm, swimming on their own, enter the hen's cloaca and move on into her oviduct, where her eggs are fertilized (joined to the sperm). This takes only a few seconds.

At this point the female's eggs are not yet covered with shell but are, instead, the pinhead-sized cells that are the actual eggs. Each egg cell has already been supplied with the yolk that will nourish it as it grows to be a baby bird, but everything else we think of as egg — the "white" (albumen), the thin membrane surrounding the white (allantois), and the shell itself — is secreted around the egg and its yolk as it travels down the female's oviduct before it is laid in the nest.

fact

Canaries, parakeets, cockatiels, and lovebirds can all be bred in captivity, unlike mynahs and some other large birds. Hybrid birds (such as a cross between a canary and another breed of finch) cannot have babies of their own.

BREEDING CAGE

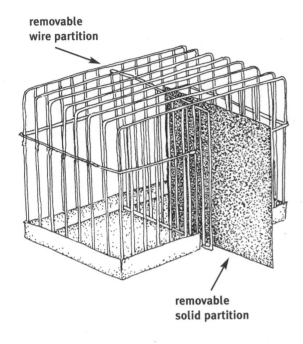

removable
wire partition

removable
solid partition

While all this is happening, the hen will want to build her nest inside the container you have provided. You may notice her picking up bits of fluff or feather from the cage floor and beginning to arrange them in the nesting bowl. At this point, supply the hen with short pieces of yarn, bits of cotton, hair from your dog or cat, or commercial nesting hair.

Once the eggshells are completed inside her body, the hen lays her eggs into her nest, one a day for three to five days. The shell is at first soft and leathery but soon turns hard and brittle. Inside the shell, the tiny fertilized egg cell begins its growth into a baby bird. Blood vessels connect the embryo to the yolk, from which it gets its nourishment. Fourteen days after it was laid, the first egg hatches. Each of the other eggs will hatch in turn, one a day and in the same order in which it was laid.

Baby passerine birds are born nearly naked and with eyes sealed shut. They have two talents:

They are usually able to back themselves up to the edge of the nest to drop their droppings over the side, and they can open their mouths and beg for food, which they do more or less continuously.

There is no reason to remove the cock canary when the babies are hatched. Both he and the hen will feed the young and keep them warm. The parents are kept quite busy filling those mouths and should still be fed a supplementary diet of conditioning food and some greens.

Nesting birds are more nervous than usual and may be too upset to feed and care for their young when you're around. Don't show off the nest, eggs, or babies frequently. Try to give the parents extra peace and quiet.

By the time they are five or six weeks old, baby canaries are covered with fledgling feathers, their eyes are wide open, and they are able to feed themselves. They should be started on soft foods — conditioning biscuit mixed with water to a mushy consistency. Your local pet store may sell a special fledgling food. As soon as you can see they have begun to eat adult canary seed, you can consider the babies grown up enough to leave their parents, either for larger quarters in your home or as pets for others.

NESTING BOWL

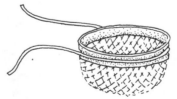

The basket from an old-fashioned strainer or a miniature wicker basket makes a good canary nesting bowl. Wire the container into a corner of the cage, and supply nesting hair (available at pet stores) or similar material for the hen to make her nest from.

Canaries

Canaries are a species of finch that have been bred as pets for almost five centuries. The canaries you see in pet stores would hardly recognize their olive-drab-colored forebears. Before Columbus discovered America, the sailors who discovered canaries in the Canary Islands brought them home for the sake of their singing. Since then, breeders have been of two minds. Some have bred canaries for their looks, so that there are brilliant yellow, slate blue, orange, red, pink, and patterned canaries that sing less varied songs. These are commonly referred to as Border canaries. Others bred the Border types with singing canar-

Once a canary is comfortable in its surroundings, it becomes a curious explorer of "strange" objects.

ies called German or Hartz Mountain Rollers, which were valued for their lovely but very soft songs. The American Singer Canary is the result of such crossbreeding.

The canaries known as choppers have a brisk, clear, high song, including elements called chops. Rollers have a much more varied but quieter song consisting of different elements called rolls, flutes, and tours. Rollers sing with their beaks closed and produce long trills of closely related notes, while choppers sing with their beaks open and make songs with distinct notes.

Male canaries do the singing. Female canaries only chirp and twitter. In nature, male birds sing at daybreak, not to express their joy but to announce their whereabouts. The song tells other male birds to keep out of their territory and invites female birds to come into their territory. (The song sparrow announces itself more often than a radio station: up to 2,305 times a day.)

Some birds vary their song somewhat in tone and intensity, so that their mate can recognize them as individuals in dense foliage where they can't see one another. Strangely, even though a canary might vary the sequence of his song — rolling first and then fluting, or vice versa — birds don't recognize different sequences as different songs. If the elements are there, it's the same song no matter the order of those elements. This is like saying you would recognize a piece of music no matter what order the individual notes were in, as long as all the notes were there.

Choosing a Canary

The only guarantee for getting a "show bird" in either looks or song is to buy directly from a breeder. You may be able to locate a canary breeder in a big-city phone directory or by asking your pet dealer, or you could do research on-line. However, show-quality canaries are expensive.

The canaries carried by most pet stores only approximate the following descriptions because they are often mixed breeds. But they are within most family's budgets.

You have to buy a male if you want to listen to birdsongs because only males sing. Because you can't tell the sexes apart by looking, pet store personnel are supposed to listen to the birds, choose the males after they have begun to sing, and guarantee the singing to you in writing. Female birds are much cheaper than males because they don't sing. When a store advertises "young unsexed canaries" at bargain prices, you can bet they are all females! Usually only breeders are interested in keeping female canaries, but they make good pets and look as pretty as the males. If the singing is not important to you, buy a female. She will at least twitter and chirp.

Of the fancy lookers, the Red Factors, Border Fancies, American Singers, and Glosters also sing passably. The Gloster canary has a round cap of feathers on its domed head that falls half over its eyes. The Red Factor was an astonishing event in bird breeding. For ages breeders have crossed canaries with other species of finch in attempts to get new markings and new colors in the offspring. They especially wanted a red or an orange bird. But although many closely related species can breed with one another, and many canaries sold are the results of such breedings, the hybrid (mixed) babies are usually sterile and can't have babies of their own. The mating of a female canary and a male red siskin (now an endangered species) produced the Red Factor — the rare case of a hybrid that can have babies.

All canaries you see for sale should be banded. The band on the leg tells you the age of the bird. A male begins developing his song at about three months of age, can be accurately identified as a male singer by six months, and has perfected his song by a year. With a bird of that age, you know what you are getting musically, and he is still young enough to become used to humans.

fact

Male canaries do the singing. Female canaries look just like males but only chirp and twitter. A male canary begins to sing when he is about three months old. He should have perfected his song by one year.

Housing

Canaries require no special alterations to a standard birdcage. However, if you want to control the times at which your canary sings, you may wish to use a cage cover.

Because male canaries sing at the break of day to announce themselves, canary fanciers can use cage covers to trick them into conveniently timed bursts of song. The cage is covered: nighttime and silence. The cage is uncovered: Daybreak and song. If you have a lightproof cover to fit your cage, you can even convince your canary to entertain you in the evening by covering its cage in the daytime and turning on some lights and uncovering it at night.

Canaries like to bathe and need to do so often to stay healthy, so the cage should be large enough to accommodate a shallow dish of water that the canary can splash around in every other day or so.

The Best Cage

This is such an important topic that it's worth emphasizing. Even if you are very conscientious about taking your bird out for play and exercise, he will have to spend a lot of time in his cage while you are at school or away from home. Think how you'd feel if you were locked in your room for your whole life!

The most important thing is to make sure the cage is the right size. Small birds like canaries and parakeets should be able to fly from one perch to another. A mynah likes to hop and should have several perches at different heights. Larger parrots must be able to stretch their wings out fully without hitting the bars. If you have room, a wide cage will probably encourage more movement than a tall one, since birds prefer to fly across a space rather than up and down.

The cage should be made of stainless steel or a non-galvanized metal. Powdered coatings that adhere to the metal are fine, but paint will chip right into a curious beak. Make sure all the joints are welded smoothly, with no sharp edges. The bars should be spaced so that your bird's head can't get through the spaces. Look for doors that are easy to open with one hand, large enough to accommodate your hand with the bird on it, and lock securely. Larger parrots especially can be very clever escape artists. Other convenient features are food and water boxes that are easily removed for filling and cleaning and that are designed to prevent birds from scattering seed out of them or messing in them.

The easier the cage is to clean, the more often you are likely to clean it. Look for bottom trays that collect scattered seed and give easy access for changing newspapers or other coverings.

Food and Water

Boxed canary food is usually a mixture of canary and rapeseed. Thistle seeds and millet make good treats beyond the basic boxed diet, but canaries ought to have fresh greens in their diet, too. Plant some millet seeds in a small flowerpot. When they sprout, wire the pot to the cage bars so your canary can eat the fresh greens. In the summer you can gather seed heads from grasses, dandelion greens, or even lawn grass. Wash them well to get rid of insecticide sprays. Hang the greens in bunches tied with string inside the cage. In winter, offer bits of broccoli, watercress, parsley, lettuce, or orange in your bird's food dish. The cuttlebone suggested for beak rubbing is also a valuable source of salts and minerals. Canaries won't bite chunks off like the parrots do, but they will peck at it. Don't forget grit on the cage floor or in a separate dish, and fresh water every day.

Taming and Training

After your canary is calm enough to sit near your hand (page 136), you can finger-train it inside its cage. Put your finger up under the bird's chest, just above its legs. Push slightly back against it. Your canary has three choices of what to do next: fall backwards off its perch, something any bird would try to avoid; fly away, something most birds do at first; or climb onto your finger, which it will ultimately do. Keep at it until it climbs onto your finger every time you push against its chest. Some people say you can couple the action with the command "Hop," so the canary learns to hop onto your finger on command. I don't believe it.

Unless a bird's wings are clipped, it is in real danger the first few times you let it out of the cage. All pet birds see both mirrors and glass as holes, similar to the gaps in foliage through which they fly in nature. Plenty of pets have killed themselves by crashing head-on into windows and mirrors. On top of that, caged birds have so little exercise and so little flying practice that they are inaccurate, have trouble landing, and get very out of breath.

Don't feed your bird before you let it out. A hungry bird will be more likely to come to you for food when it's time to get it back into the cage. Choose a small room that has curtains on the windows. The kitchen is a bad choice for canaries because they cannot learn not to land on hot pots and burners. Close the curtains; either take down mirrors or put sheets of newspaper over them. Close all the doors too. Put down the cage in the middle of the room. Put the seed box next to it.

Now you're ready; but you can't just let a bird out of a cage. Its cage is the only territory it knows, and it's not all that eager to leave safe ground. If you reach in and grab your bird, you're only ruining all that patient hand training. So put your finger in, let it perch, and see if you can very slowly move the bird out the door. This may not work; the manufacturers make those doors very small. A better alternative is to remove the tray of the cage and the metal sheet that's under it, and the food and water dishes. Then slowly turn the cage upside down. The canary will come out.

fact

Caged birds are not skillful flyers, because they get little exercise and have had no practice. Therefore, you must bird-proof the room in which you will let your pet fly, covering mirrors and windows and removing other hazards.

As the canary flies, you'll notice it may be having difficulties. It doesn't really know where to land, and it may get tired quickly. Pretend you are a bird-feeder. Sit next to the cage, pour some seeds into your hand, and hold your hand out. The idea is for the bird to recognize your finger as a safe perch, see the food it's so hungry for, and eventually land on you, the birdfeeder. After a few minutes see if you can put the cage over your bird, and then slide the metal sheet back in to close it.

If the bird never comes to you, you face the problem of catching it to get it back in the cage. Its exhaustion now may prove helpful. Get a dish towel. Each time it lands, shoo it into the air again. When you see the canary panting for breath and low enough for you to reach, just drop the dish towel over it. Hold it gently through the towel with your hands; extricate it from its wrappings as you put it through the cage door. If you've had this much trouble, it means you should probably go back to more hand feeding and finger perching in the cage before you let out the bird again. Remember that wild birds learn easily to come to a birdfeeder; your canary will too.

The other way to let a canary loose is to first clip one wing so it can't fly (see the box on page 135). Either way, a canary given liberty ultimately has to learn to get about a particular room without bumping into everything, and to come to its human birdfeeder when it's time to go back in the cage. Practice makes perfect.

Mynahs

The mynah is one of the best pet talking birds. It can repeat a large variety of phrases and sound effects, as well as making astonishing and peculiar noises of its own. It can meow like a cat, gurgle like water poured from a jug, click like a metal cricket toy, or plip-plop like pebbles tossed in a pool. Joe-Joe, the mynah who lives in our local pet shop, speaks with the clockwork sound of a cuckoo bird, which is so comical it causes the best mimic of all, the human race, to imitate him back. As a result, all the salespeople in the store sound like windup mynah birds.

The only mynahs commonly available on the market are the Greater Indian Hill mynah and the Java Hill mynah. Both are medium-sized (somewhat larger than a robin), very glossy black birds with a bright yellow beak and white eye markings. The mynah is a relative of the common starling. It is not as calm in temperament as a parrot and will spend much of its time hopping back and forth from perch to perch. Calming and finger training are possible, though individual birds will have preferences about being handled. Some owners report that their birds have a definite preference for one person in the family, while others say their mynahs love everyone equally and readily go to strangers.

You may wonder why some birds mimic sounds. It is certainly not meant simply to amuse humans. I've wondered, and have come up with an idea. Many birds are territorial animals. They stake out their own place, then announce themselves to rival birds with a special song. The song is a warning only to their own kind and doesn't mean a thing to other species. The song of the robin doesn't keep out the titmice or the nuthatches — only other robins. But suppose a mynah came along who learned to mimic the robin, the titmouse, and the nuthatch. Instead of keeping out only other mynahs, it might warn off three other species as well. Naturally, it would get that much more food and living space for itself. Logical as this idea sounds, I haven't been able to find out if it's true.

For a long time, people thought that talking birds don't really talk or have the vaguest idea what they are saying. People have been fooled by birds who hear the telephone ring and say, "Hello," or who hear the dog scratching at the door and say, "Do you want to go out?" This "finishing out" a noise (telephone ring, "hello"; dog scratch, "do you want to go out?") is similar to duetting, in which a pair of birds alternate parts of the same song so cleverly that they sound like a single bird. Duetting keeps a pair of birds in contact where dense foliage prevents them from seeing one another. I have a parrot who performs the first or last part of a wolf whistle and expects me to fill in the missing part. I'm a disappointment to her. I can't whistle.

However, recent research done with an African Gray parrot named Alex has shown some interesting things. Alex really does appear to have learned many words. When asked, he can pick objects by color, shape, and texture, and he must request specific treats by name before he receives them. You might want to read more about this very interesting topic — see the appendix for a related Web site.

Choosing a Mynah

Theoretically, male birds should be the better talkers. In nature they are the guardians of territory and the singers of songs. Both the male and female mynahs do talk, however. No one seems to know if the male learns more readily, and anyhow you're not going to be able to tell a cock from a hen mynah. If you want to be sure of a good talker, buy a bird that already talks.

As far as taming goes, a baby bird in pin-feathers is the best bet, but very hard to find. You can find breeders who will ship a very young bird, but you will have to be prepared to hand-feed it at first and give it lots of attention. The best compromise may be a bird who has begun to talk and who doesn't panic when you move your hand toward its cage. Getting a calm talker several years old is fine — they live a long life, the record being 30 years in captivity.

Housing

Though they generally prefer hopping around to flying, mynahs need to be taken out regularly for exercise. Inside the cage, perches should be set horizontally parallel so the bird can hop from one perch to another. The cage should be large, but its height is less important than its width. Place the perches in the cage wide apart to accommodate the mynah's surprisingly long hops. Standard perches that come with cages may be too small for the mynah. See page 129 for information on how to install larger perches.

Because of the mynah's messy droppings, you'll have to change the newspapers on the cage floor every day. Some of the larger cages come with a wire floor through which droppings fall onto the paper-covered bottom drawer. This keeps the bird's feet out of its own mess if it walks on the bottom, but mynahs prefer to stay on their perches and the extra wire floor is just one more thing to clean.

Food and Water

Mynahs are primarily fruit-eaters, but they'll also eat insects when they can. The dry mynah foods sold in pet stores are claimed to be a balanced diet, and they definitely cut down on the moisture and messiness of the droppings. Fill your bird's food dish with dry mynah pellets daily so food is always available. But be skeptical of the nutritional claims of this and most other packaged foods; your bird also needs fresh food. Offer small bits of oranges, apples, melons, peaches, and bananas, but give your bird no more than a heaping tea-spoonful once a day. Offer grapes and berries as treats, but not as part of your pet's regular diet.

Mynahs fed too much iron can't get rid of it, and the accumulated iron causes fatal damage to their liver. This means that high-iron greens like spinach and kale, although they may be good for other birds, are bad for mynahs. Stick with fruits.

Mynahs drink a good deal of water and bathe frequently. Remember to change the water in your pet's dish daily.

To avoid having to clean up the mess mynahs make trying to get their too-big bodies into the water dish, try giving your bird a plant-mister spray bath. Even better, once your bird is tame enough, let it get in the kitchen sink and putter around under a trickling faucet.

fact

Mynah birds are among the best sound mimics in the animal world. They not only can reproduce the songs of other birds but can also meow like a cat, gurgle like water poured from a jug, ring like a cell phone, and speak like a human.

Taming and Training

Calming and finger training a mynah can be done in the same manner you would calm and finger-train a canary (see page 142). If your bird becomes so nervous that it bats its wings or bangs its head against the bars when you reach into the cage, you might consider clipping wings (page 135) and proceeding with the training outside the cage, as you would for a parakeet, which you will read about later in this chapter (see page 150). During the out-of-the-cage training, sit in the middle of an uncluttered room so that there are fewer obstacles for your bird to bump into. Because of the mynah's nervousness and active nature, you'll need time (10 to 15 minutes every day) and patience to calm it. But it's worthwhile; mynahs are very intelligent birds and will respond enthusiastically to your attention.

Some talking birds seem to learn new words and phrases best when the house is quiet and when their owners are not within view. Mynahs tend to imitate people with high-pitched voices (women and children) more readily than people with deep voices (men), and training proceeds better if only one person is doing it. A method often recommended is to cover the cage at night, then repeat the new word or phrase on and off for 15 minutes in the morning before you take the cover off. The method sounds logical — it comes closest to a bird in nature concentrating on the high-pitched birdsong of a single species out of sight in the forest at dawn. However, other trainers say you should teach a bird to talk almost the way you would a baby — by lots of repetition and word association. If you greet your bird consistently with an enthusiastic "Hello!" and give him the names for his favorite treats as you feed him, he will eventually make the connection between the word and the object or action and begin repeating it.

Small Parrots

Parakeets, lovebirds, and cockatiels are all in the parrot family and they all make good pets. Many are bred in this country and therefore are more reasonable in price than the larger parrots that are caught in the wild. When people ask for a parakeet, they are usually thinking of only one particular kind of parakeet: the Australian budgerigar, or "budgie." There are other kinds of parakeets, some nearly as big as an Amazon parrot.

If you want any of these small parrots to become very attached to you, buy only one. Although two birds are fun to watch, they will be more affectionate with each other than they will be with you. Young budgies will be easiest to tame. Look at the forehead to help determine a bird's age; babies have a scalloped pattern on the feathers of the forehead above the beak. The scallop markings will give way to solid-colored feathers by the time the bird is 10 to 12 weeks old. Your best chance of having a very tame pet is to acquire it from a breeder who hand-rears the babies to socialize them from birth.

Choosing a Little Parrot

Budgerigars. We call them parakeets, but they're more properly known as budgerigars, or budgies. Parakeets make calm and trustworthy pets. They like to play, and like all the parrots they can get very attached to a human. They are smart for small birds, but not as smart as the larger parrots. Most of them really can't learn to talk. There's no way of telling whether the budgie you have chosen will happen to be one of the unusual ones that will learn or one of the usual ones that will never say a word. Whistling is a better bet, and if you set your sights on a wolf whistle or something equally easy, you may be pleasantly surprised.

Cockatiel

Cockatiels. Cockatiels are from Australia. They are perky, crested birds with a long tail and graceful wings. The most common cockatiels are gray. Less common are "pied" cockatiels, which have white bars and dots. The rarest is a white albino shading to yellow on the crest. Cockatiels have rosy cheeks; sometimes the orange spot on their cheeks is so perfectly round and bright it looks as though someone had painted it there. Males have a brighter cheek patch than females. The albino shows off the orange cheek and shoe-button eyes best, making it one of the prettiest birds you can buy, but it is more expensive. There are reports of talking cockatiels, but this is most uncommon.

Bee bee parrots. Of the miniature parrots, the gray-cheek parrot, sometimes called a bee bee parrot, is among the best to keep as a pet. Many birds — especially lovebirds — are prettier, but the bee bee is calm and loving, and it may become charmingly eccentric. Once you tame a bee bee, it will do things like say *bee beee beeee* at you all

Bee bee parrots

through breakfast unless you share your toast, or develop a liking for pockets and creep into them, or steal tissues, or do something else no one has thought of yet.

Lovebirds. The lovebirds come in soft rich colors. Some of the more common lovebirds you're likely to see are the peach-faced and Fischer's. Lovebirds get their name from the way a devoted pair carry on with each other. Stores may try to convince you that a lovebird can be happy only if it has a mate. This advice is great for their profits, but if you want a bird to love you, groom you, and attempt to feed you regurgitated sunflower seeds, buy only one.

Don't expect either the bee bee parrot or the lovebird to talk; both have a rather shrill screech on occasion and chirp somewhat noisily.

Housing

A small parrot has enough room to fly a little in a canary-sized cage, though a larger one is preferable. But all of them, and the cockatiel especially, need some flying time outside their cage. Follow the advice given at the beginning of this chapter for setting up a cage home for your small parrot. Provide it with the largest cage you have room and money for.

Food and Water

These small parrots should have pellets as their basic diet, with seeds as treats. Like children who prefer dessert, small parrots may eat only favorite but fattening seeds like peanuts and corn if they are available all the time. Offer fresh snacks of dark greens like spinach, romaine lettuce, parsley, and watercress, plus fruits like oranges and apples. Since the small parrots can give a nasty bite for their size, use sunflower seeds for hand feeding. They're big enough so the bird can take them from your fingers without nipping fingertips.

Cuttlebone will give the small parrots something rough to nibble on to keep their beaks in shape, and also supply minerals not found in seeds. The cuttlebone won't last as long as it does with canaries. You might have to replace it every other week. Chicken bones serve just as well, and come free off the family dinner plates. A bit of meat left on the bones or an occasional mealworm will no doubt be appreciated too.

Drinking water can be served in a dish, but some of these parrots can learn to drink from a water bottle. The kind to try has a metal spout with a ball bearing just inside the tip. Don't trust that your bird can use it until you see it drinking. The advantage to a water bottle is that you won't have to change it every day.

Once you're fed up with your little parrot's messy attempts to bathe in the water dish, experiment with the three other bathing methods: wet leaves, a plant mister, and a shallow bath dish.

Taming and Training

People who tame their small parrot tend to stop short of achieving the singular devotion and real affection these birds are capable of. You must inflict yourself on your bird several times a day, every day, to get beyond mere calmness and finger perching. For a while it won't look like you're getting anywhere. But when love happens, it happens fast, and from then on the bird will be your friend for life.

fact

Once a small parrot has accepted you, the two of you will be friends for life. Like sailors of old, you can teach it to sit on your shoulder. To express its affection, the bird will preen or groom you, just as it would another bird.

Because much more handling is involved in taming a parrot than in taming a canary, you'll have to get your bird's wings clipped or do it yourself (page 135). With clipped wings, a bird can walk or flutter only a short distance. You can train it outside the cage and yet easily retrieve it each time it tries to get away from you.

Proceed with the training as you would for a canary, resting your hand on the cage, then reaching your hand in. At first your bird will flutter and screech at you, but after a week or so it should calm down. When the fussing stops, try bringing one finger up under its chest and lifting it slightly. Your bird will step on your finger or nip it.

If it steps onto your finger, you can start taking it out of the cage this way and sitting with it at a table or on the floor. Every time the bird hops off, put your finger in front of it again. It should soon learn that nothing awful happens when it sits on this new perch. Talk to the bird in a running stream. Offer it food from your fingers. As the bird gets used to you, try transferring it from your finger to your shoulder by holding your whole arm at a downward slant. The bird's response to the downhill position should be to walk upward to your shoulder. You can take it down from your shoulder by putting a finger in front of its chest. The first sign of affection will be a gentle nibbling and pulling of the hairs at the nape of your neck.

Small parrots will perch just about anywhere, as long as you're willing to train them to do it. Just be sure you don't accidentally train them to perch in a spot you'd rather have left unoccupied!

If your parrot bites you, there is another method of taming that may at first alarm the bird more but actually seems to work faster. Put on leather gloves. They may frighten the bird because it may have been roughly handled by gloved hands in the past. Take your bird out of the cage and sit on the floor with it. Put it on one gloved finger. The bird will get off right away. Pick it up (just put your whole hand around it) and try again. Keep doing it. Talk gently as you work with it, and each time the bird hops off, put it back on as gently as you can. With this method you may be able to train your bird to sit on your hand in a single afternoon, but you will still have to win its love over weeks of talking, hand feeding, finger perching, and shoulder climbing.

Large Parrots

A large parrot is a very permanent pet. A large parrot lives so long that the bird you buy now may be your children's pet 20 years from now. The record life span for a pet parrot is held by an African Gray that lived to be 80, having been handed down through three generations of the same family. A cockatoo who lived in a zoo died at 120 years of age. A large parrot becomes so attached to the family it lives with that being given away to strangers would be a tragedy in its life. And since a parrot can cost more than a purebred dog, it makes sense to be cautious in deciding to keep one and then in choosing a bird.

No More Bored Birds

Scratching, screeching, feather plucking, or pacing can be a symptom of nervousness in caged birds or can point to another common problem — boredom. Boredom is more likely to afflict the intelligent parrot family than the less curious songbirds.

A sure sign of boredom is a bird that sits around looking stupid. In other words, if you find your bird bores you, this is because it's bored. After all, when you have to sit in school too much, you chew pencils, tip chairs, fiddle with your hair, and doodle in your books. You can't expect any more of your parrot.

So give your small parrot something to interest it. Pet stores sell all sorts of cage toys for small birds. The toys are made in bright colors or of sparkly materials. They may jingle or jiggle. Some of them are climbable or swingable.

Many bird toys have mirrors, but I don't think that's a good idea. Birds react to mirrors because they think their image is actually another bird. Upon seeing this "other bird," they ruffle up, bob their heads up and down, and carry on a lot. If they think it's a rival, it will upset them. What's more likely is that they'll think it's their best friend, which means that you will come second. If you want your bird to bond more closely with you, you might want to think twice about putting a mirror in the cage. Or, you can try a mirror as an experiment and wait and see what happens. If your bird seems too focused on its "friend," you can always remove the mirror — if, that is, you are willing to take its place. Parrots are very social animals, and they really need company.

It might be fun to make toys for your bird yourself. Here are some ideas: jingle bells on a wire loop; split rings attached to one another; split rings holding nuts and washers; paper-clip chain with buttons on the last clip; fancy dime-store "jeweled" rings; plastic Christmas-tree balls on a metal bead chain; and ladders made from two lengths of wooden lattice strip with thin wooden dowel rings glued between. Pet stores sell swings, or you can rig up your own with wire and a short piece of dowel. Just make sure the metals you use aren't galvanized or zinc-coated, as some kinds of nails, eye hooks, wire, or chain from hardware stores might be. Also avoid any objects with lead in them, which may include sinkers for fishing, weights for curtains, and soldering wire.

Toys are a real problem with bigger parrots. They can bite through strong metals. They can untwist a paper clip in a moment and undo even the largest-sized snap ring. We've found only a few toys that last: padlocks locked on to the bars of the cage; large jingle bells attached to the split rings (not snap rings) sold as key holders (or attach old keys instead of the jingle bells); the iron Indian bells available in some gift stores; and carabiner-type links. Toys less sturdy are a waste of time and money.

HOMEMADE TOYS FOR PARROTS

For small parrots, string paper clips, buttons, washers, rings, jingle bells, plastic Christmas balls, and other items on wire loops.

For larger parrots, use large bells or old keys on strong key rings or padlocks.

Use heavy, stiff wire and a dowel to make a swing.

Choosing a Big Parrot

The best of all choices is a baby parrot, because it is the easiest to tame. As with other kinds of birds, you should find a reputable breeder who hand feeds his or her baby birds and carefully raises them to be social with people. A pet store parrot is almost never that young. A real baby parrot looks like a baby — it is smaller than an adult, with fizz and pinfeathers on top of its head the same as any fledgling. A young parrot, though full grown and fully feathered, tends to have smooth flat scales on its legs and feet. As a parrot gets older, the scales become larger and coarser. Since a parrot lives so long, it doesn't really matter whether it is one or five years old so long as it is tame or tamable.

If you are buying a bird from a pet store and none of the store staff is sure how old the parrot is, you will have to decide whether to buy it based on its behavior. Come up close to its cage and watch how it acts. If it screams and growls at you, you'll have a rough time. If it just backs to the other side of the cage or climbs up higher on the bars, try putting your arm up next to it (no fingers through the bars, please!). If your parrot acts terribly frightened and bats about in a panic all over the cage, you are still going to have a hard time. If it simply acts nervous but a bit curious, you can probably tame it with little trouble.

If the dealer claims a parrot is already hand tamed, ask to be shown. The dealer should be able to feed the bird by hand and get it to climb on an arm if it is actually tame. A really tame parrot will lower its head to be scratched by the people it is used to, although it may act fearful or aggressive toward strangers until it has known them several weeks or longer.

Sometimes things happen the other way around. We once found a parrot in a pet store that the dealer claimed had never been touched. He was sure the bird was wild and dangerous. But when we approached the cage and held our arms up, it seemed calm and curious. We believed our own eyes, and bought it. Sure enough, when we let it out of the cage, it climbed right to our shoulders and preened the hair on our necks lovingly. It probably had been hand raised as a baby.

It is harder to judge a parrot's health by its plumage than it is with other birds. Feathers can look broken and dull even on a healthy bird if it has just come through immigration and quarantine, or if it's been batting its feathers against the bars of a small cage. You can see, however, any of the signs of illness described at the beginning of the chapter. Some people say that if a parrot perches on one foot, it means the bird is sick. That isn't true; you might check that its feet aren't injured, but most likely it is just perching on one foot. Don't take a parrot that has bald spots unless it's been caged with another parrot, and it's the other parrot that has been plucking the feathers. A bird that plucks itself has psychological problems. Other nervous symptoms are pacing and screaming. These emotional ills may be incurable; it's wise to avoid such birds.

fact

Among the large parrots, African grays are the best talkers. Amazons and ringneck parakeets are colorful and make good pets. Macaws and cockatoos are not easy pets, because they require so much attention and space.

The personality of parrots seems to vary as much as the personality of dogs and cats, depending more on individual inheritance and personal experience than on species. The only exception is the African Gray, which most people agree is more aggressive and more eccentric than other parrots. Since the African Gray is also a better talker than any other parrot, however, it's worth extra patience in taming.

Amazon parrots are plentiful and make good pets. All Amazons are basically a parrot green with various brightly colored heads, facial markings, and wing tips. The large Amazon family constitutes the bulk of the parrots you'll find available in pet stores. If you can find one of the larger parakeets, like the Indian ringneck, it makes an excellent pet as well.

When examining a selection of potential pets, you might find yourself very attracted to a gorgeous macaw or to a fluffy cockatoo and its wonderful crest of feathers and bright-eyed expression. But these exotic birds not only are extremely expensive, they also are not easy pets. They need an enormous amount of attention and a lot of space, and they are capable of producing a great deal of noise at top volume.

Before you take home an untamed parrot, be absolutely sure its wings are clipped. This is not a job for you to do on a large parrot until you are friends with the bird. The job should be done at the pet store and considered part of the purchase price. I emphasize it because you'll have an awful time taming a parrot that can fly.

Housing

The larger the bird, the more space it needs. If you're going to spend a lot of money on a parrot (and this might be the place to repeat that, with the exception of certain smaller species, a bird is not a cheap pet!), you should be prepared to spend just as much on a suitable cage. However, unless you can provide a real flight cage (which would take up half your living room), you'll need to let your bird out of its cage every day for exercise and companionship. A parrot confined to its cage becomes as resentful as you would be if you were locked in your room day and night. Most parrots will chew on the perches in their cages. See the housing information at the beginning of this chapter (page 129) for suggestions about replacing perches as they are damaged.

Cages that are made with wire bottoms over the solid tray floor don't really have to be cleaned more than once or twice a week. You might want to use a half inch of sand in the drawer instead of newspaper. The wire floor prevents the bird from kicking out the sand. Each week, rake seed and droppings from the sand with a fork, remove the pile, and add some fresh sand to the cage bottom. If the cage has no protective wire over the bottom, you'll need to use newspaper and change it more frequently, especially if your bird likes to walk about on the bottom.

The Cageless Parrot

If you keep your parrot's wings clipped, and if it has a reasonable personality (which most of them do), you don't have to keep it in a cage at all. Instead, you can give it a simple branch as its home (see page 129 for instructions). Our own Amazon parrot Sparrow lived on a branch in our kitchen. If you keep the branch rather high, the parrot won't want to jump down off it. It knows it can't fly well with its wings clipped; the plunge is too much like

falling. But we can't guarantee that every parrot will feel as comfortable on a branch as Sparrow did. Ringo, our Indian ringneck parakeet, felt unsafe up on a branch with clipped wings. Until his feathers grew back, he made his home under our stove. Every time we used the oven he would come out and scold us. The stove is not recommended as a parrot hole, in spite of Ringo. For a parrot that can fly, the kitchen is okay for its daily playtime only if nothing's cooking on the stove and the burners are cool.

Both Sparrow and Ringo prove a little-known point about captive parrots: They become attached to their own place. Sparrow was pleased to explore about the kitchen, but even when his wings grew back, he rarely ventured from his branch for more than an hour or so. Ringo, when he could fly again, exchanged his hideaway under the oven for a perch above the stove. Luckily, both avoided pots and burners when we were cooking, though I always worried that they might singe their feet.

Now all our parrots live in an aviary off the kitchen. When the doors are opened, it may take as long as an hour before anyone decides to come out. And in all the years since we've had parrots, with all the liberty we give them, no bird has ever explored farther than the kitchen unless first given a free ride to other areas on a friendly (and safe) shoulder.

Food and Water

Parrot food comes in boxes like other pet foods, mixed specially from various sorts of seed and grain. While parrots love peanuts and sunflower seeds, these are far too fatty to provide the bulk of their diet.

A caged bird that is not allowed to fly can get too fat and develop the same kind of health problems that might plague an overweight dog or cat (or person!). You can buy special parrot chow that is formulated to be balanced and nutritious.

In the wild, parrots eat a variety of foods, so in addition to the pellets, give the large parrots daily portions of dark green leaves like spinach, watercress, and romaine lettuce and slices of

Although a parrot will enjoy the freedom of movement cageless living allows, the bird won't often venture very far from what it considers its home base.

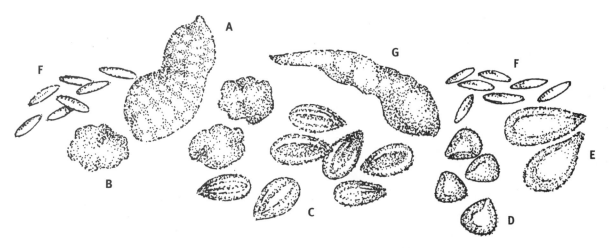

A mixture of parrot seed could include: (a) raw peanuts, (b) kibbled dog biscuit, (c) sunflower seeds, (d) whole dried corn, (e) pumpkin seeds, (f) wheat, and (g) dried chili peppers.

apple or orange. Supply either green twigs or small bones for chewing. Cuttlebone won't last long enough to bother with, but bones supply the same minerals, as do eggshells. Pet stores may sell crushed oyster shell for minerals too. A parrot may be suspicious of foods inside its cage that it has not seen before. I once made the mistake of shoving a piece of pomegranate into a parrot's cage and leaving for the day. The bird was still cowering in the corner farthest from the innocent fruit when I got home hours later. If the bird is free to investigate on its own outside the cage, it is likely to sample any food that's around, including coffee, beer, spaghetti, scrambled eggs, lamb stew, and pizza. Experts advise, though, that avocado, raw onion, rhubarb, and caffeine can make birds seriously sick.

Water requirements are no different from those of any other bird, except that I swear parrots dump newspaper scraps and apple skins into the water dish on purpose. Be sure to change that water daily. Or try training your parrot to drink from a hanging bottle with a metal spout.

Because of a parrot's size, it has trouble bathing in the water dish. A cake pan of water is fine, as is a good misting, but both are rather wet propositions for a cage. It is less sloppy to get the bird used to taking a bath outside its cage. It can perch at the kitchen sink for a mist spray or splash in a pan on the kitchen floor. If you always give a parrot a bath on a certain day of the week, it might learn to tell the day. One of our birds perches on a certain chair and spreads his wings every Saturday morning to tell us it is spray time. Another paces up and down the kitchen counter flapping and clucking until his water pan appears. That parrots so insist on a weekly bath shows that they really need the bathing to keep their skin and feathers healthy.

Taming and Training

Let me explain parrot taming by explaining some of our experiences. Looney Bird is really a parrot, an African gray parrot. But he was such a crazy baby that the name landed on him, and stuck. A mad parrot is a very frightening critter. In spite of the fact that this one was still small, with fledgling fuzz and feathers sticking from his head like a lady in curlers, a beak too big for his puny wings, and clumsy feet to match, he could nevertheless hold off the bunch of us. He growled, he screamed, he snapped. We kept our distance. But the idea of having a vicious parrot isn't appealing; Looney Bird had to be tamed. Looney couldn't be a better example of how to tame a parrot — if the method worked with him, it should work with any parrot.

Looney's cage was kept smack in the middle of the kitchen floor so he could get used to the bumps and yells of family life (luckily, Teflon fumes were not an issue; we have no nonstick cookware). We casually rested hands and feet on the cage and talked to him sweetly. He screamed. We opened the door of his cage. He growled and snapped. We offered him the end of a very long carrot with our fingers. He screamed, growled, snapped off a chunk of carrot, and tossed it away. We offered it again. Scream. Growl. Snap. Toss.

We kept up this sweet-talk-and-long-carrot regimen for a good month. Things began to get better. Once in a while, Looney would nibble on his piece of carrot for a moment before he threw it away. He screamed less often, but he still growled. In just another couple of weeks, he was eating the carrot, and the carrot stick we offered him grew shorter and shorter until he was taking it from very close to our fingers. Finally, we began to offer Looney small slices of carrot, apple, and banana from our fingers. No screams, no growls, no snaps — as long as there was food between his beak and our fingers. When we had worked our way through peanuts, and finally to sunflower seeds, we knew we faced the big question — what next?

fact

Although you can train little birds inside their cage, for parrots, the cage is home, the only place where they feel safe. To tame a parrot but still allow it a refuge, you should do the training outside its cage.

At this point some books say to put on heavy leather gloves, put your hand under the chest of the bird while it is still in its cage, and encourage it to climb onto your hand. In the case of the big parrots, the books are wrong, and this is why: When a parrot is caught in the wild, the catcher wears heavy leather gloves. When a parrot is handled — mostly mishandled — in shipment, the mishandlers wear heavy leather gloves. When the parrot is removed from its cage and shoved into another cage for you to take home, the shover wears heavy leather gloves. All of these experiences have terrified the parrot. Big parrots have long memories. Heavy leather gloves terrify parrots forever and ever.

The books also say to do all the taming inside the bird's cage. They are wrong again. The parrot's cage is its home, the place it feels safe — the place it will defend like a pioneer with a shotgun. Little birds may let you finger-train them inside their cages, but if you want to tame a large parrot, you have to do it outside the cage, on your territory. The catch is, the parrot may have become attached to its place; it may not want to come out.

Now is the time to start leaving the parrot's cage door open. Offer it food very close to the door so it gets used to coming to the door when you open it. Sooner or later, the parrot's intelligent curiosity will get the better of its fears, and it will venture out — probably to sit on top of the

Love a Parrot

You have to have several parrots to really appreciate parrot passion. Our most affectionate parrot is named Sparrow. (The name reflects the mood in which my husband greets any new animal in the house — the name is similar, for instance, to the cat he named Temporary.)

Sparrow has taught us all we know about loving parrots. He has shown us that to pet him well we must pretend our fingers are beaks. As beaks, they can scratch between his ruffled feathers but they can't smooth his head the way a flat hand can pat a dog. And they can lightly pluck at individual feathers as a parrot's beak would do if he were grooming. If Sparrow wants his head groomed, he lowers it and ruffles; if he wants to be groomed under a wing, he lifts the wing. He enjoys being scratched behind his jaw, but one must be careful of the delicate eardrum, which is on the side of his head.

Sparrow grooms us back when we groom him. At his best, he will groom the hair at the nape of your neck gently, in a tickly fashion, or remove a breakfast crumb from your lip. At his worst, he will try to remove foreign bumps that you, as a bird, ought not to have. The bumps include buttons, glasses, earrings, and ears.

On several occasions, Sparrow has gone into paroxysms of affection, leaning down from my shoulder, falling in a rolling fashion onto my chest, nudging around under my hands like a feathered pig in a mud wallow.

Since Sparrow was my first parrot, I didn't know much about them then. Because he was so tame, it seemed safe to let him loose outside so he could fly about a bit. What I didn't know is that parrots that aren't used to flying will fly up but won't fly down. Also, parrots have little sense of direction. They get lost. Sparrow flew to a tree, then to a higher tree, then to a higher one. Each was farther away, and soon we lost sight of him in the woods behind our house. Thinking he would surely come back, we gave up the search after an hour.

It had been a warm June day, but that evening the weather turned raw and it began to rain. We sent word out through the neighborhood for people to keep their eyes open for a lost parrot. A week of awful, cold wet weather passed and no one reported him. At last the milkman, our best-traveled news carrier, reported that a family on his route had been "taking care of" a stray parrot for several days. We rushed over, only to find that the "care" had been to leave poor Sparrow unprotected on the lawn with a soggy piece of bread in front of him. He could no longer eat; he could no longer move. He lay soaking wet, wings out flat, unable even to lift his head from the cold grass. We figured he would die within the hour.

We drove home with Sparrow lying limply in my lap, bravely muttering the sweet things parrots mutter to the people they love. We wrapped him in towels and held him next to a radiator. We thought of brandy, something people sometimes use to warm up. We had only vodka. We took a plastic dropper and squirted a shot of vodka down Sparrow's throat. He choked, gasped, picked up his head, took a few unsteady steps into my lap, and rolled about in ecstasy. It was either gratitude or drunkenness.

The African Gray parrot is more aggressive and more eccentric than other parrots. It is also the best talker of all the parrots.

cage. (Since its wings are clipped, the only way it can get anywhere but to the top of its cage is to waddle pigeon-toed across the floor — a vulnerable position that parrots prefer to avoid.)

Sweet-talk your parrot a lot and give it nice bits of food. After a while, it will climb back in through the door again to eat dinner and you can shut it in. When it is used to coming out of the cage and used to being fed by hand there, buy yourself a dowel stick the same thickness as the perch in the cage. Cut it in half so it isn't clumsy to use. Leave it on top of the cage.

Your parrot will be suspicious of the stick at first — it may start to scream again when it sees the stick there, or it may pick it up and angrily toss it. Persist, with patience. Pick up the stick and lay it on the cage again. Lay your hand on the stick innocently. Move it around a little. Keep it up for however many days it takes the parrot to decide the stick isn't going to attack. When your bird doesn't mind the stick and your moving it about, pick it up gently and rest it against the bird's chest just above its legs. If the parrot stays calm, lift the stick slightly and see if it will transfer its feet from the cage onto the stick. If your parrot doesn't the first time, it will sooner or later, and then you will be the proud possessor of a stick-trained parrot.

By now you may discover, as we did with Looney, that your parrot likes to be out of the cage, and is perfectly happy to live on top of it. The stick will become a great help because you can get the bird on its stick and transfer it in through the cage door to its own perch. When you try this, be careful to hold the stick so it is tilted upward. A parrot will always tend to climb up rather than down. If you tilt the stick down, "up" will be toward your hand and you may find your parrot sitting on your arm somewhat earlier in the game than you would have liked.

If your bird panics, refuses the stick, and won't go into the cage, there are two other methods. Get a bath towel. Corner the bird and throw the large towel over it. Wrap the parrot in the towel; take it to the cage door and carefully manipulate it into the cage as you unwrap the towel. Or remove the bottom drawer and wire floor from the cage, and put the cage over the parrot. When it climbs up inside, you can slide the bottom parts back into the cage.

From now on the taming is largely up to your parrot. All you can do is feed it a snack by hand every time you come to its cage, let it sit on the stick you are holding, talk to it a lot while it is on the stick, and feed it more snacks. Believe it or not, eventually your parrot will begin to like you. And when it does, the following will happen. One day Looney Bird was sitting on his stick, and we held out a sunflower seed for him to eat. He reached out his head to get the seed, but instead of taking it in his beak he made a little muttering noise, lowered his head, and ruffled the feathers on his scalp. We tried offering the seed again, but he wouldn't take it. He just kept muttering, ruffling, lowering his head. At last we understood. It was an invitation — he wanted to be groomed. Looney was tame.

From that point on, the only problem with a parrot is how to get away from it. Once friendly, you can substitute your forearm for the stick, but then your bird will want to sit on you all the time; it will groom your hair and clean your fingernails; it will mutter and make eyes at you (by contracting them and dilating them in a provocative way — at least it is provocative to other parrots); it will enjoy being gently petted more than being fed; and, most loving of all, it will bob its head up and down, then regurgitate seeds into any available opening, usually your open hand, but occasionally your open ear. If it could figure out your strange anatomy better, or if you behaved properly and opened your mouth, your parrot would feed its regurgitated seeds to you. This is a mark of great love and devotion among parrots.

The tamer your parrot is, the more interesting and eccentric it is likely to become. Looney Bird himself has reached the height of eccentricity. He now sleeps upside down, hanging from his toes like a bat.

Sometimes an eccentricity can be turned into a trick. Looney used to hang onto one side of his opened cage and, holding the door in his beak, bang it noisily against the cage side. We began to say "Bang your door" each time he did it, and soon he learned to do his trick on command. One day, when Looney was making a nuisance of himself on the kitchen table, someone said, "Oh, Looney! Go bang your door," at which command that brilliant parrot picked up the nearest spoon and proceeded to bang it against the tabletop. These days, Looney stays mostly in the aviary off the kitchen. Deprived of loose objects with which to bang, he has come up with still another way to satisfy the command. He stands at the glass and knocks against it with his beak — surely the most literal way to bang his door.

Looney so enjoys attention that just getting everyone to look his way is enough reward for a trick. Rewards of food, especially favorites like peanuts and bits of apple, might work better in training parrots in general to perform their natural tricks on command.

As your parrot becomes tame and loving, you can let it out of its cage every day. But you must be prepared to keep careful watch on it. Parrots chew everything in sight, including electrical wires and the kitchen chairs. Looney likes to drop coffee cups off the edge of the table. Sparrow takes buttons off shirts. Ringo chews up pencils, dismembers ballpoint pens, and leaves footprints in the butter. They all plop droppings on the floor. We know it's not their fault, so we try to clean up cheerfully. You should, too.

Sometime after you have tamed your parrot and it is accustomed to walking about outside its cage, those clipped wing feathers will molt and new flight feathers will grow in. At this point, your bird will learn to fly across the room, scattering homework from the table, knocking over knickknacks on the shelf, and landing on your head when you least expect it. For your pet's safety and your own sanity, you might want to retreat to the every-other-flight-feather kind of clipping mentioned earlier (see page 135). This style of wing clipping will allow your bird to flutter for short distances but will discourage headlong dive bombing. By now your parrot should be tame enough for you to manage this clipping on your own, with the assistance of a friend.

Don't be tempted, just because your parrot is so tame, to let it loose outdoors. This is especially important if you've let your bird grow back all its flight feathers.

Yellow-faced Amazon parrot

Pocket Pets

This chapter is called "Pocket Pets" because it is about a group of animals that not only are small enough to hide in a pocket but even seem to love to do so. What are these animals? They are mice, rats, hamsters, and gerbils — and they are all rodents.

The word *rodent* makes many people think of pointy snouts, sharp teeth, beady eyes, and germs. Rodents such as hamsters and gerbils aren't very pointy-snouted, but all rodents have sharp teeth; they need them to gnaw the hard foods that are their basic diet. Their eyes may gleam like beads, but I prefer *bright-eyed* as a description. For small animals, rodents are particularly smart. As for germs, rodents get them mostly from us. Well adjusted as they are to sharing human food — in the form of both stored food and leftover garbage — wild rodents pick up and carry about the germs our discards provide. But that is accidental, not vicious. Pet rodents don't get a chance to sample the local dump or live near sewers, so they are perfectly clean.

The rodents now sold as pets have come to us by way of the laboratory. These animals have helped scientists to understand, to treat, and even to help prevent disorders as varied as cancer, diabetes, and burns. They are very useful as lab animals for several reasons. Both rats and mice have dietary needs nearly identical to humans and so have helped us with all sorts of nutritional studies. All rodents breed early and often, so there is never a shortage. And they are easy to care for and to handle.

No doubt rodents are much easier to handle now than when the first ones were captured in the wild and bred for research. Natural selection has been at work. Annoyed by nips and exasperated by panicky coworkers, scientists probably bred their gentlest rodent specimens and ignored the wilder ones. The result over many generations is a rodent population gentle enough to find its way into the pet stores — and into your pocket.

Pocket Pets
at a glance

Hamsters *PAGE 172*

HOUSING: Medium homemade cake-pan cage, plastic hamster Habitrail-type cage, commercial wire rodent cage, or 5½-gallon tank with mesh top, water bottle. Wood (not cedar) shavings for bedding.

SPECIAL REQUIREMENTS: Prefer to live alone, though two females from the same litter may be compatible.

DIET: Boxed hamster food. Supplement with fresh raw vegetables.

CARE: Feed, check level of water in water bottle, and remove leftover fresh foods daily. Clean cage once a week. Provide twigs or bone for gnawing once a month.

TAMABILITY: Become calm with handling, but tend to nip when sleepy or frightened.

LIFE SPAN: Two to four years.

Gerbils *PAGE 174*

HOUSING: Small homemade cake-pan cage, commercial wire rodent cage, or 5½-gallon tank with mesh top, water bottle. Wood (not cedar) shavings for bedding.

SPECIAL REQUIREMENTS: None.

DIET: Boxed gerbil food. Supplement with fresh vegetables and dried cereals.

CARE: Feed, check level of water in water bottle, remove leftover fresh foods daily. Clean cage once a month. Provide twigs or bone for gnawing once a month.

TAMABILITY: Become calm with handling.

LIFE SPAN: Two to three years.

Mice *PAGE 177*

HOUSING: Small homemade cake-pan cage or 5½-gallon tank, mesh top, water bottle. Wood (not cedar) shavings for bedding

SPECIAL REQUIREMENTS: Baby mice can squeeze through bars of commercial wire rodent cages. Females can be kept in pairs, but two males will fight. Only have a male and female together if you want many more mice very quickly.

DIET: Lab chow sold in bulk or boxed parrot seed or gerbil food. Supplement with fresh raw vegetables, meat, and cheese.

CARE: Feed, check level of water in water bottle, remove leftover fresh foods daily. Clean cage once or twice a week. Provide twigs or bone for gnawing once a month.

TAMABILITY: Calm down somewhat with handling, but remain nervous.

LIFE SPAN: Two to four years.

Rats *PAGE 179*

HOUSING: Medium homemade cake-pan cage, commercial wire rodent cage, or 10-gallon tank with mesh top, water bottle. Wood (not cedar) shavings for bedding.

SPECIAL REQUIREMENTS: Rats are very social and intelligent animals and require more attention than other small rodents. Two or three can live together (males can be neutered if you want to prevent babies).

DIET: Lab chow, sold in bulk, or gerbil food. Supplement with fresh raw vegetables, meat, and cheese.

CARE: Feed, check water level in water bottle, remove leftover fresh foods daily. Clean cage once a week. Provide twigs or bone for gnawing once a month.

TAMABILITY: Become very calm with handling. Enjoy exploring and being carried around outside of cage.

LIFE SPAN: Two to four years.

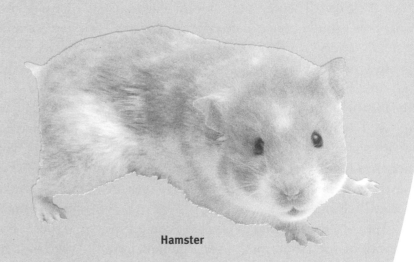

Hamster

As for pockets, the reason rodents like them so much has to do with their normal way of life. Mice, rats, hamsters, and gerbils are all nocturnal (night creatures) and dwell in holes and burrows. Pockets are simply snug, dark holes — obviously safe places for short naps.

Choosing a Pocket Pet

Much as all rodents may seem alike to people who dislike them, as pets they are quite different from one another. Read each of the separate sections following before you decide which would be best for you. Gerbils, for instance, are the easiest to care for, but rats are the most intelligent and social. Mice are perhaps the sweetest-looking, but they are rather smelly; and hamsters are a bit more difficult to handle than their plump cuteness would imply.

Buy any rodent as young as you possibly can. Full-grown rodents will be hard to tame, whereas a rodent bought just after it has been weaned (about a month old) will become very reliable if handled often. As for health, look for plumpness, a sheen to the coat, and check under the tail for signs of diarrhea. Individual animals will have differences in temperament, but it can be difficult to evaluate personality at the time you buy your pet. A good, calm, curious baby rat should certainly come to investigate your hand when you reach into the cage, but mice, gerbils, and hamsters will all scramble away.

Before picking up any pocket pet, make sure it's thoroughly awake, as a sleepy one might become alarmed and bite in self-defense. Talking as you approach the cage, taking off the lid, nudging a sleeping box, or pulling off some nesting material should rouse even the heaviest snoozer. When you have your pet's attention, use both hands to scoop it up, approaching from the rear so it doesn't feel threatened.

Housing

A pocket pet should live in a metal or hard plastic cage or a covered aquarium tank. Rodents chew through any other sort of home. Commercial hard plastic cages are not engineered to fit together or come apart easily. They are attractive but frustrating. Most commercial metal cages are not well made either. The floor trays that hold shavings for your pet's bedding are too shallow and have sharp edges. Wire bars are too far apart for baby mice, who escape the first time you're not looking. All the commercial cages I've seen have only one small door through which you're supposed to reach for your pet and drag it out to play. This is a good way to get bitten. A 10-gallon tank makes a better home, big enough for a mouse family, a twosome of gerbils or hamsters, or a single rat. Pet stores sell mesh tops to fit the tank. The easiest cage to clean, however, is the homemade cake-pan cage described on page 330. It also is good housing for your pocket pet.

fact

Pocket pets are bright, curious, and nocturnal creatures. In other words, they'll play in their cage at night. That's why you should keep the cage in a place where the noise of a small pet scampering about won't disturb anyone's sleep.

Replace wet shavings in your pet's cage with dry shavings once a week.

You will need a water bottle mounted on the side of the cage unless you want to change a water dish every day. You don't really need a food dish. A rodent is happy to find its food in the same corner every day, and the only advantage to a dish is that you will be able to tell more easily when it is getting short on rations. Both crockery and hard plastic dishes are sold in rodent size.

You'll need bedding to absorb urine on the floor of the cage. Individual rodents may be allergic to cedar shavings (you'll know because they sneeze a lot). Pine chips and chlorophyll-treated pine shavings are both good, or use bedding made of recycled paper.

Any of these rodents feel more comfortable if they can make a nest to sleep in. You don't have to buy anything. Just put in an old sock, tissues, paper towels, a washcloth, or any other soft material. The pet will do the rest. Mice and rats love to have a box to hide in — shoe boxes with a small door cut in one side are perfect and easy to replace when they get soiled.

The best exercise your pet can get is being let out to play. For more exercise, especially at night, you can buy an exercise wheel to fit its cage. Commercial cages often come equipped with a wheel, but freestanding ones are available for tanks and homemade cages. However, be aware that a squeaking or rattling wheel going full speed at midnight can make it difficult for the human occupant of the room to sleep! Your pet may need to spend its nights in the bathroom or hallway.

Cage cleaning. How often you clean depends on which of these pets you choose, but don't just let your nose be the guide. Urine-soaked shavings cause first a sort of diaper rash and then infection. Ammonia fumes can build up quickly in glass tanks, so be especially vigilant if you use this type of cage. Every week you should scoop out wet shavings (there is often a particular corner that gets used as a bathroom) and replace with a handful of clean ones. All but gerbils, because they urinate so little, can go a month between complete changes.

Before you clean your pet's cage, take out the animal; put it in the bathtub with the drain closed. Gerbils, mice, hamsters, and rats cannot get out of a bathtub. You might also invest in a plastic storage bin with a lid to use as a temporary home or carrying cage; make sure you punch air holes in the lid. Empty the bedding into the garbage, then wipe up any you have just spilled on the floor. Keep the nest unless it smells. Wash out the cage with dish detergent and water, rinse it well, and dry it. Wash the water bottle and the food dish. Put in fresh bedding about an inch and a half deep. Add new nest materials if you have had to throw out the old nest. Put the cage back together. Don't forget to refill the water bottle and fill the food dish. For complete satisfaction at a job well done, add some of the snacks and toys that are recommended for each pet.

Food and Water

Mice, rats, gerbils, and hamsters are basically seed- and grain-eaters — the historical scourge, in fact, of barns and granaries from the time agriculture was invented. But any old seeds and grains won't do as a diet for caged pets. In the wild, these animals eat from nature's remarkable delicatessen, which in addition to the basic seeds and grains may include fresh vegetables, bark, and assorted gleanings from garbage pails. The only balanced diet you can depend on for rats and mice is called lab chow, which consists of pellets that are specially formulated for these rodents. Unfortunately, it's difficult to find lab chow. It is sold in bulk to science laboratories but is seldom commercially packaged for pet stores. The packaged food that is available in pet stores is intended for hamsters and gerbils only, and even for these rodents it is not likely to be the complete diet the packages claim.

The problem is easily solved by offering your pet a delicatessen similar to nature's — but from the leavings of your family dinners. Your pet's own body will influence its choices, just as it would have in the wild. You'll find details of what snacks to use to supplement the basic grain diet in the discussion of each kind of pet.

Good water bottles have a ball bearing inside the metal spout. When the animal licks at the spout, it joggles the ball bearing and water seeps out.

ball bearing

If a rodent does suffer from malnutrition, an early sign is hair loss. If your pocket pet starts losing its hair, add rodent vitamin drops (available at pet stores) to its drinking water, following the instructions on the bottle. But start offering the suggested variety of snacks, too. By watching what your pet prefers to eat and continuing to feed it those snacks, you can keep it on a balanced diet. Of course, the opposite problem can happen as well — don't let your pet get too fat!

A water bottle is the best way to keep drinking water available. A water bottle has a slightly bent nozzle, and the best ones have a ball bearing behind the opening on the drinking tube. The ball bearing closes the hole so water can't leak out. When the rodent licks at the end of the nozzle, it joggles the ball bearing and water seeps around it for the rodent to drink. If your pet lives in a wire or hard plastic cage, secure the bottle on the outside of the cage with a U-shaped holder. If your pet lives in a tank, secure the bottle to an inside wall with a metal bracket (sold separately). Rodents may chew out the rubber stopper used in some types of bottles; there are metal containers that hold the water bottle and prevent nibbling.

Check the food supplies daily and don't be fooled by what looks like a full dish — often it is only empty shells and there is really no food left. Rodents eat a high percentage of their body weight every day because their hot bodies and active nature require that much fuel. This means that a rodent can starve to death much faster than a larger animal can.

Illnesses

Besides malnutrition, rodents can come down with various viral and bacterial diseases. They can catch germs from people, so if you've got a cold, wash your hands before handling your pet. Rats are prone to respiratory illnesses. If your pet does get sick, pet stores sell antibiotics that might help. They are usually in tablet form, to be crushed and added to drinking water or sprinkled on food. However, don't be afraid to check with your vet about treatment. Many practices these days have exotic pet specialists who will care for rodents, reptiles, and birds. Some will even do surgery, such as removing tumors or even neutering a male rat so he can live with a female and not become a dad.

Recapturing Escaped Pets

The easiest way to recapture a lost pocket pet is with a Havahart trap. The device is a wire tunnel with a trapdoor at each end. Bait (your pet's favorite food) is placed on the platform in the middle. The trap is placed in a corner or under a piece of furniture near where your pet escaped. When it comes for food, the platform triggers the two trapdoors, which fall shut without harming the animal at all.

Put the trap, animal and all, into your pet's cage. Then lift the trapdoors and let it come out in to its cage.

You can buy the smallest-size No. O Havahart trap in a hardware store.

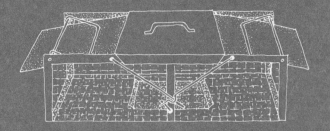

Hamsters

Hamsters have a fat and fuzzy look. They smell less than mice, move more slowly, and act less nervous. They can, however, be grouchy, especially when they are woken from a sound sleep. Both of the hamsters that lived with us would nip our fingers if they were handled roughly, if they were busy eating, or if they were sleepy. They bared their teeth and squealed at us in warning if they had time.

Waking up a hamster sounds easier than it is. They are stubbornly nocturnal, but worse than that, their daytime sleep is best described as similar to a coma. We were once sure our hamster was dead, belly-up, on the floor of his cage. We picked up his limp body and laid it on a table. He came to life about as slowly as a parent on a Sunday morning. Hamsters don't often sleep in that dead-looking posture but usually curl into a ball so tight you can't tell nose from rear. I've been told that if you get a hamster young enough and handle it a lot during the day, you can get it to switch to your schedule. The person who told me has a nursery school where the hamsters are played with constantly during school hours.

fact

Hamsters, like squirrels, carry extra food by packing it — as much as half its own body weight — into the pouches of skin along their jaws. A hamster with full pouches looks like it's wearing big shoulder pads.

The original pet hamster, the one that still lives in the wilds of Europe and the Middle East, is tobacco colored, with darker markings about the shoulders and pale grayish white underneath. All the millions of pet hamsters in the world are descended from one male and three females that were captured in the wild early in this century: They produced 150 babies by the end of their first year in captivity. Breeders have since developed albino strains, spotted hamsters, beautiful apricot ones, silver grays, and a long-haired variety called a teddy bear hamster, which can come in any of these colors.

Housing

Many hamsters live in cages made of transparent plastic rooms and tunnels that interconnect in lots of ways. Since the hamster is a burrowing animal, it is very pleased with these plastic burrows and is active, acrobatic, and fun to watch, especially in the middle of the night. But this kind of cage can be a nuisance to clean and handle.

A hamster's plumpness is deceiving. Hamsters can flatten themselves to slide through astonishingly small openings. You'll have to check any cage you buy to be sure it doesn't offer escape hatches. One way hamsters often escape is by pushing out the tray that holds shavings in wire cages. Once the tray is pushed out an inch, there is a gap left beneath the wire that a curious hamster could squeeze through. For this reason alone, if not also for the expense of commercial hamster cages, I suggest the wire cage on page 330. It is foolproof. Or, if you prefer, try the 5½-gallon tank with a mesh top.

You can improvise your own playground for your pet hamster for much less money than the plastic tunnels cost. You could, for example, lean a branch diagonally across the cage, screw a small eye screw into it near the top, and hang from this screw a big metal curtain ring attached with wire to act as a swing. Use a small milk carton with a hole cut in it for a room, and make a ladder out of ice-cream sticks for the hamster to use to climb up to the top of the house.

Hamsters also appreciate old socks to burrow into and hide inside, as well as cardboard tubes and small boxes. Provide your hamster with shredded paper towels, tissues, or newspaper to nest in. Avoid cotton batting and other fibrous types of nesting material, as they can wind around tiny paws and cut off circulation. Also, they're totally indigestible and can cause blockages. Hamsters, like mice, chew to keep their teeth down, so many of the things you make won't last too long. But they are easy to make again, and you may get better ideas than these as you go along.

Hamsters have a habit of following their noses no matter where they lead — probably because they have an instinct to follow tunnels and tunnels don't require too many left-turn, right-turn, straight-ahead decisions. So you will find that if you keep putting one hand in front of the other, the hamster will keep running from hand to hand in the most senseless way. It doesn't seem to bother it at all that it is getting nowhere fast.

For this same reason, hamsters are tireless users of exercise wheels. Exercise wheels always seem to squeak, so use a stick of graphite to keep them running silently — except for the pitter-patter of tiny hamster feet.

Hamsters have been known to fall off tabletops and human shoulders rather easily. They are not climbers in nature, are not accustomed to heights, lack a sturdy tail with which to balance

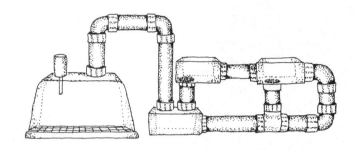

A transparent plastic hamster cage

A milk-carton house and a popsicle-stick ladder

A curtain ring swing

An exercise wheel

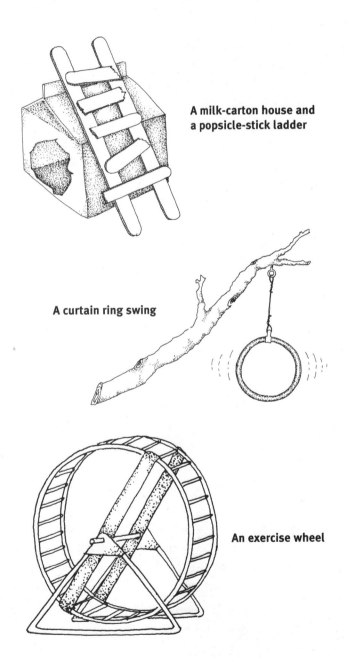

themselves, and are supposedly nearsighted as well. Since one bad fall can kill a hamster, keep careful watch over it when it is out of the cage. You can purchase a special plastic hamster-exercising ball, which keeps the hamster safe inside while it manipulates the ball around the floor. Again, be very careful to keep an eye on your pet — it could get stuck in a corner or tumble down a flight of stairs.

Food and Water

Hamsters, like squirrels, store their food. They have pouches inside their cheeks that stretch to hold an amazing number of seeds. The pouches can hold half the hamster's own weight in food. The instinct to store is so strong that one common hamster, a guinea-pig-sized relative of the Syrian pet-store variety, was found to have stored 190 pounds of corn and potatoes in its burrow over a single summer.

Of course, hamsters don't need to store food in their cages, where they are fed regularly, but they do it anyway. They will stuff their pouches and then empty them out, eat some of the seeds, and stash the rest in a hidey-hole. To prevent decay, you will have to clean out the caches of stored foods every day.

Any pet store carries hamster food, a good basic combination of seeds and cereals with some dried vegetables added. A good diet for a hamster also includes snacks of fresh raw vegetables and fruits. Try spinach, lettuce, carrots, and apples in very tiny amounts. Withhold fresh foods for a few days if your pet gets diarrhea and call the vet if it doesn't go away. Make sure your hamster has fresh water, preferably in a bottle with a sipper tube, attached to the side of the cage. Keep an eye on your hamster to be sure it is drinking when it needs to. You can adjust the height of the sipper tube if your hamster can't reach it.

Gerbils

Gerbils were first brought into pet stores in this country about 40 years ago and were such a rarity that they sold for $15 each. People soon found out that gerbils breed prolifically just like any other rodent, and so the price came down, though some fancier versions may cost more. Gerbils are about the size of hamsters, but their fur is grayish brown and has a slight layer of oil on it, which keeps them from looking fluffy. Their long tails are furred and have a tuft on the end.

When they're not sleeping, gerbils are almost as hyperactive as mice, but they don't seem to be as easily startled. I've seen panicky mice, but never a panicky gerbil. They aren't quick to bite, either. Our gerbil takes readily to daytime hours and calmly rides in a pocket for a full afternoon, peeking out at the world from time to time.

Housing

Gerbils are the easiest rodent to keep. They are desert animals that have developed the ability to use almost almost every drop of water they take in at the front end, so there's very little left to come out the other end.

Gerbils have no smell (to people), and the cage has to be cleaned only once a month if it has a thick (1½ inches) layer of bedding. It should be at least the size of the homemade cage described on page 330, or, if you prefer, substitute a 5½-gallon tank. Gerbils are diggers, and in a metal cage their constant attempts to dig holes will throw bedding all over the place. A tank solves that problem. If you are using a mesh cage, cut down a cardboard box and place the cage inside it.

Like hamsters, gerbils enjoy running on an exercise wheel, but buy one that doesn't have open bars for tails to get caught in. If you can't

find one, cover the metal bars with stiff paper to keep your gerbil's tail unbroken and be prepared to replace the paper as needed.

We had a problem with our gerbil that may or may not be typical. He used his whole cage as a nest, rather than the neater corner arrangement our hamsters, rats, and mice have built. The nest always grew to water-bottle height. Then the drops from the bottle would soak the whole nest and we'd start all over again. It was as though because he was unable to dig through the floor into a burrow, he was making himself a whole underground world instead. Finally it dawned on us to give him a burrow to make his nest in. We cut off both ends of a dog-food can for the burrow. Sure enough, it took him only a couple of nights to move his shredded papers into the can, leaving the cage floor clean. When he goes into his burrow to sleep, he pushes his nest around inside the can until he has sealed up both entrances.

Food and Water

Gerbils eat commercial gerbil food, available at pet stores, plus snacks like raw oatmeal, peanut butter, dry breakfast cereal, and popcorn. They should have small amounts of leafy greens, broccoli, carrots, and apples as well. Give gerbils things like twigs and bones to chew on too.

In the wild, gerbils get all the water they need from the vegetables they eat, but caged gerbils should have a water bottle to make up for the dryness of their diet.

Photographing a Pocket Pet

The propensity of a gerbil to sit in a pocket for so long got us to thinking one day about snapshots. Obviously, a pocket's a good place to put a gerbil if you want it to stay in one place long enough to take its picture. You need a close-up attachment if your camera won't focus at less than three feet, and you need a flash to take the pictures indoors. Focus the camera and wait until your gerbil pokes its head out. Then snap its portrait.

What else works? Well, a toilet paper tube, for one thing. A gerbil can't leave a tube alone.

It simply must go inside! Once in, it must poke a nose out. There's your picture. For the same reason, a small cardboard box with a hole torn in it makes a likable snapshot.

We found that the height technique works not only for gerbils but also for mice, hamsters, and rats. None of the pocket pets likes to climb down from heights, all of them love tubes and pockets, and they're all so curious that they must stick their cute noses out of holes so you can snap their picture.

Mice

Mice, being the smallest of these pocket pets, are the cutest. White mice are most common but black, brown, apricot, gray, and spots of all those colors are available too. At their tamest, mice are nervous, fidgety animals. They slip easily from hands or even jump. Once lost, they remain hidden and may be very difficult to find.

Housing

The mouse cage can be the smaller homemade cage on page 330 or a 5½-gallon tank.

Of all the small rodents, mice leave the worst odor. It is more their urine than their droppings that smell, and males smell worse than females. Chlorophyll-treated shavings work rather well. You may get by with a weekly cleaning if your nose isn't too sensitive. The mouse itself will not smell because it grooms itself.

Give your mouse tissues, toilet paper, torn-up newspaper, or scraps of fabric for nesting material. It will chew up everything and form a round ball to sleep in. It will add to the nest from time to time until it gets quite big. After a while you may not like the smell of the nest anymore, so remove it and give the mouse new materials. Another nest will appear in a single night.

Food and Water

Mice can survive very well on lab chow if your pet store carries it. If you can't find lab chow for mice anywhere, feed your pet gerbil food or even cereal (not the sugary kind; plain oats will do) instead, but supplement with very small snacks of cheese, raw vegetable, peanut butter, meat or fat from meat, uncooked oatmeal, and nuts. If you always offer a snack with your fingers, your mouse will learn to come to your hand to see what tasty treat you might have for it. It's an easy way to encourage it not to scramble away when you want to lift it from the cage.

Mice, like all rodents, have front teeth that continue to grow all through their lives. To prevent their teeth from getting so long that they can't close their mouths, mice have to gnaw. A lot. If you don't give your mouse any choice, it will spend most of the night gnawing at the bars or mesh of its cage. That upsets nearby people: Not only do they think your mouse is trying to escape (which it isn't), but it makes an awful racket as well. Give your mouse leftover bones and green twigs, which it will prefer to wire anytime. Both the bone and the green bark serve as food, too.

Be sure to keep your mouse's cage securely locked down, because mice are escape artists. They are so small that they can slip through the tiniest cracks and hide just about anywhere — even right under your nose!

Intelligent and friendly, rats are
the best pets of all small rodents.

Rats

In my opinion, rats make by far the best pets of any of the small furry rodents. They are calmer, friendlier, and more intelligent; they don't make a cage smelly like mice do; they don't kick their shavings around like gerbils do; and they don't slither out of your hands like hamsters do.

Wild albino Norway rats were domesticated long ago for use as laboratory animals. Their descendants, sold in pet stores today, are smaller, far less aggressive, and probably not as bright as the original wild rats. Besides the albino, pet stores often carry solid brown or gray rats, as well as a particularly nice black, gray or tan and white combination called a hooded rat. Some breeders are interested in "fancy rats," ones with a wide range of coat colors and textures. (There are even some that hardly have any hair at all!) If you're interested in one of these less common types, look for a breeder near you.

Not all pet stores carry rats, though they are easier to find than they used to be. Too many people think of rats as horrid dirty things. This is true of wild rats, which can be vicious, large, scurrying, and as germ-laden as the garbage they eat. But laboratory rats represent hundreds and hundreds of generations of mild-mannered cage-contented pets. They have forgotten their beginnings. Many people also object to the rat's long tail. There is nothing you can do about that but keep the rat to yourself.

Many people think of rats as only larger mice. Anatomically that's close to the truth, but their behavior is very different. Compared to the more timid mouse, the rat is a brave, curious, friendly giant. If your pet store does not carry them, the manager might be able to get one for you from a distributor, but make sure you get a young one so you have a better chance of taming it. If you have a choice, a female rat is more alert and less lazy than a male. She is also prettier.

You can give a pet rat baths and let it swim in the bathtub (caution: not all rats like to swim, so be sure this is a treat, not a torture). You can carry it with you in the sleeve of your sweater; it will not be jumpy. It will be contented in a plain cage; it will be curious about a new environment. It is a good acrobat; it is the only rodent you can really play with. For example, the rat I had as a child went to school with me almost every day, happily riding in a sweater sleeve or calmly staying in my gym locker or a school desk. The teachers never even knew. The same rat went to camp with me in the summer and took a morning swim with me in the lake each day. Running loose in my room in the evenings, she would explore about, climbing up on the bed from time to time to sit on her hind legs and beg for a snack.

Housing

Most of the cages sold in pet stores are too small for a rat. You'll be better off with the larger homemade cake-pan cage shown on page 330 or a 10-gallon tank. The cage needs nothing extra in it but the water bottle and food dish, some bones to gnaw on, and some paper towels for your rat to chew up for nest building. If you choose a tank instead, weight down the wire-mesh top with a rock or two.

You can let a tame rat out of its cage to wander around your room for hours at a time — it won't escape because it doesn't want to. But you do have to watch what the rat is up to, since it can disappear into holes in walls and under low furniture. Wild rats have been known to eat through lead pipes and gnaw through concrete. I know from experience that a pet rat can bite a good-sized hole in a one-inch-thick wooden desk drawer, and neatly sever every lamp cord in sight. Rat-chewing damage in the United States alone amounts to billions of dollars each year. That's not eating; that's just chewing.

Give your rat some exercise by allowing it out to explore your room a few times a week, or build a playground for it to play in.

Food and Water

Lab chow is a totally balanced diet for rats. If it's not available in your pet store, feed your rat gerbil food or birdseed mixed equally (in equal amounts) with rabbit or guinea pig pellets. Offer plenty of snacks from the same food groups humans need. Given a choice, a rat knows what to eat to avoid malnutrition. We give our rats, whom we have named Eliza and Marjorie, meat, cheese, and raw spinach, along with a mixture of seeds and dog chow that they share with the parrots. On top of all this, the rats are forever begging for food as we walk by their cages. So they get bits of peanut-butter sandwiches, potato chips, grapes, and just about everything else. One rat owner I know says her rats are crazy about bananas.

The Breeding and Birth of Rats

In nature rodents are the major food of a horde of animals from cats and snakes to hawks and coyotes. So rodents have to have plenty of babies if they are to escape extermination. Theoretically, one pair of rats can multiply to 800 within a single year; they have babies, their babies have babies, and so on. The number of mice and rats alone, never mind all the other rodents, is greater than the human population of the world.

So if you want to breed your pocket pet, think very carefully about where all those babies are going to go. Find out if those friends who say they want one are going to be allowed to actually keep it, and ask your local pet store if it takes surplus

Rats are curious, and they seem to love exploring this easy-to-construct playground. It's fun to design and build using a cardboard box, the tube from a paper-towel roll, branches, rope, and whatever else you dream up. You can make mazes and climbing structures for your rat out of cardboard boxes, old crates, almost anything. This one has twigs glued to a ramp to make a ladder.

babies from individual breeders. Be aware that any babies you sell or give to a pet store might wind up as snake food.

Breeding rats is very similar to the breeding of any of the pocket pets, so you can use this step-by-step description to help you if you'd like to breed hamsters, gerbils, or mice.

If one of the reasons you want to have a rat is to see it have babies, be sure you are getting a female. You can tell the sex of a rat after it is six weeks old. Lift up the rat by its tail and look for testicles. If you don't see any, you have a female. Of course you will then have to buy a male rat too, unless you can find someone who will lend you one. If you don't want to buy one, perhaps you can board your female rat with a male at the local pet store when she is old enough to breed. It's worth asking.

A rat is grown up and able to breed when she is only three months old. From then on she has eggs ready to be fertilized every four days. It takes only 21 days of pregnancy until the babies are ready to be born. The mother can mate again the following evening.

As the time of birth grows near, the mother will want to build a particularly fine nest, so give her lots of materials to work with. Rats tend to give birth between midnight and 4:00 A.M. It takes only an hour or so for a rat to give birth to a litter of six or more babies. If your rat goes into labor while you are watching, you will notice that she is stretching out her body and that her sides are heaving. But she will go inside her nest to give birth, so open the nest roof to get a good view. She'll repair the roof later. But don't invite a bunch of people to join you, and keep very quiet and still so you disturb her as little as possible.

Boost Your Pet Rat's Life Span

On average, a pet rat lives two to four years. But there are things you can do to extend your pet's life span.

First — and this will sound obvious — make sure your rat came from healthy parents. Next, keep your rat in a clean, healthy environment. Do not put pine or cedar shavings in your rat's cage, because the oils from these woods can cause a host of health problems for a rat, including liver damage. And remember to feed your rat good food such as laboratory pellets and fresh fruit and vegetables. An occasional treat such as a bit of chocolate is fine, but don't make junk food a staple of your pet's diet.

Finally, love and affection play an important role in any pet's life span. By paying attention to your rat, you can add months to his or her life.

If you follow this advice, who knows but that your rat may set the new world record? According to *The Guinness Book of World Records*, the world's current longest-lived rat, named Rodney, lived for seven years and four months.

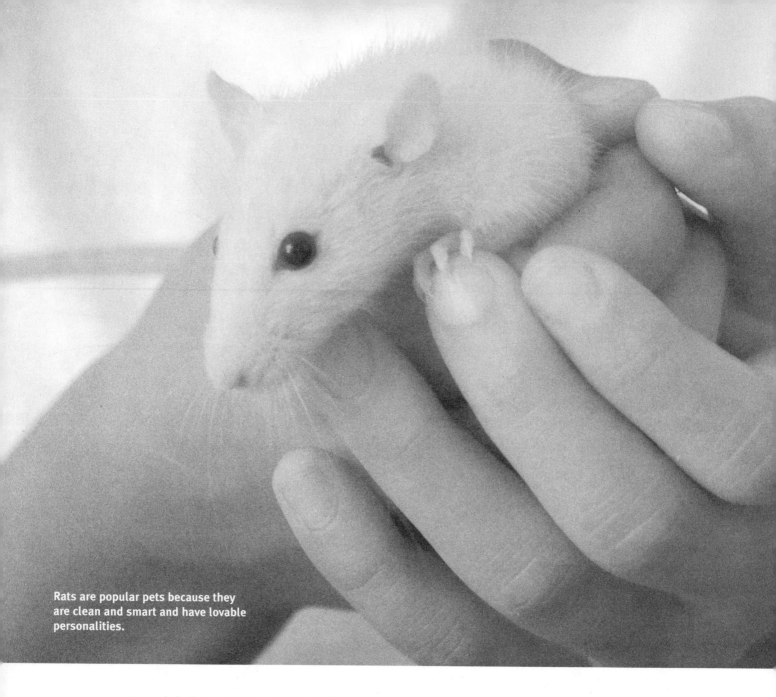

Rats are popular pets because they are clean and smart and have lovable personalities.

As each baby is born, the mother first removes the transparent wrapping (amniotic sac) that is around the baby. Then she bites off the umbilical cord, which connected the baby to her placenta and through which the baby was fed when inside the mother's womb. She eats it and the placenta, and thoroughly licks the baby clean. The licking and handling stimulate the baby to breathe and start its blood flowing.

A few minutes pass and the next baby is born. The babies are a bluish pink with skin so transparent you will be able to see blood vessels under-neath. Their eyelids are still fused shut over their eyes and their ears are still fused flat to their heads. They are hairless and quite helpless. They can't walk yet, but they can pull themselves along with their front legs. And they squeak to call for help when they find themselves no longer touching the other babies or their mother. Much of what they say is lost to our ears, though; rats talk in ultra-sound — high squeaks only your cat can hear.

When the last baby has been born, the mother will pick up in her mouth any baby that has crept away or rolled from the nest and carry it into the baby heap inside her nest. If there is a baby that she shoves aside or ignores, you can be sure there is something wrong with it. It is either dead or will die soon. A mother rat's mind is made in such a way that if a baby does not act like a baby — move, squeak, feel warm, smell right — it is not a baby at all. Sooner or later she will eat it as she ate the other nonbaby stuff, the cords and placenta. If this is too horrifying to you, remove the dead baby and bury it, or wait for the sick one to die and bury it. You will not be able to save its life.

There is a myth that giving a rodent meat will get her in the "habit" of eating her babies. That's just plain silly. If it were true, we wouldn't have mankind's old rat and mouse problems; as both eat meat in nature, they would long since have turned cannibal and eaten themselves into extinction. The commonest reasons for cannibalism are crowding, when there are many mothers trying to nest in a small area, and nervousness, caused by disturbing the mother, the nest, or the babies. Cannibalism can also be caused by malnutrition. To be sure of a good diet, we have always fed our pregnant rats and mice extra foods like cheese, vegetables, and meat. Liverwurst is a great favorite.

The babies have only one talent at this point: sucking. They can barely get to the nipples of their own accord, pulling themselves shakily along and falling often on weak and uncoordinated legs. The mother helps. In fact, she spends a great deal of time in the nest at first, letting the babies nurse almost constantly, day and night. Within a week a sheen of fur is already sprouting from the babies' naked skin. In five more days their eyes have opened, their ears stick out from their heads, and they are furry.

Like all babies, their heads look big, their bodies small, and their feet a size too large. They are adorable. The mother weans them the easy way: By the time they are about three weeks old she just gets up and walks away whenever she is sick of nursing. The babies, disagreeing as most babies do with the need to be weaned, hang on to her teats for dear life but tumble off in the end. In their less babyish moments, though, they are getting interested in grown-up food and giving it a try. As they try to do the grown-up things — getting into the food dish, washing their backs, climbing the mesh — they totter and tumble like toddlers. At this point, be sure to lower the water bottle to their level. They have to drink too.

Now you are the happy owner of seven rats, or maybe fourteen. What next? Well, you could keep them, but even with just one male rat in the litter, you could have 100 rats in less than three months. In a well-stocked, catless granary, a rat population can double every two months. Unless you want to go into the rat business, it's best to find homes for them.

fact

Rats are very smart. They can be trained to nestle on your shoulder, use a litter box, sleep on your pillow, travel in your sweatshirt pocket or sleeve, come when called, and just about anything else you might imagine.

Unusual Apartment Pets

The four animals in this chapter — rabbits, guinea pigs, skunks, and ferrets — satisfy the description of "medium-sized furry pets that are not cats." All four need similar-sized housing and make fine apartment pets. Otherwise, they don't belong together as a group. Some people think of rabbits as big rodents, but they're not. Others don't think of guinea pigs as rodents, but they are (the biggest rodent of all, the 110-pound capybara, looks a lot like a giant guinea pig). Ferrets are carnivores who would spend their lives happily hunting rabbits and guinea pigs if they had half a chance. And who would have thought that a garbage-eating skunk is the ferret's kissing cousin?

Making up your mind about which of these pets is best for you may be difficult: They are very different from one another in both looks and behavior. And, of course, you may be limited in your choice by which is available for sale.

The least demanding of the four is a rabbit. It is easy to feed and keep clean and will even consent to live its life in a hutch, if what suits you is a pet to watch more than to cuddle with. Guinea pigs can be cuddled, but they don't respond to petting as affectionately as do rabbits, and their cage flooring has to be changed more frequently. Yet they look as cute as bunnies, and the Peruvian guinea pig is certainly more comical. Skunks appreciate affection, but on their own terms. A skunk might appeal to someone who wants a more aloof pet. As to ferrets, they are very active, demand attention and play, and would really be unhappy with someone who leaves them in a cage and doesn't care to spend hours amusing them.

Consider as well your other pets. A ferret is likely to attack a pet rat, and your dog may be a bad companion for a bunny. When you first introduce a new pet to other pets, be sure that it is protected in its cage. If a new pet arouses too much aggression in your other animals, return it, or keep them always separated.

Unusual Apartment Pets
at a glance

Rabbits *PAGE 187*

HOUSING: Homemade indoor hutch or commercial hutch or homemade outdoor hutch. Crockery food dish and large water bottle.

SPECIAL REQUIREMENTS: None.

DIET: Pet rabbit pellets, grass, and timothy hay (from feed stores and some pet stores). Supplement with discarded vegetable peelings and outside leaves of salad greens.

CARE: Feed, check level of water in water bottle daily. Change newspaper under indoor hutch twice a week. Move outdoor hutch once a month. Groom every few days during periods of heavy shedding.

TAMABILITY: Become calm with handling; may seek attention and affection. Some individuals can be housebroken.

LIFE SPAN: Six to ten years.

Guinea Pigs *PAGE 193*

HOUSING: Homemade or commercial indoor hutch or homemade outdoor hutch. Crockery food dish and large water bottle.

SPECIAL REQUIREMENTS: None.

DIET: Guinea pig pellets and vitamin supplement. Supplement with discarded raw vegetable peelings and outside leaves of salad greens, or let graze on pesticide-free grass.

CARE: Feed, check level of water in water bottle daily. Change newspaper under indoor hutch twice a week. Move outdoor hutch once a month. Groom long-haired varieties weekly.

TAMABILITY: Become calm with handling. Squeal at owner for food.

LIFE SPAN: Five to seven years.

Skunks *PAGE 198*

HOUSING: Cardboard carton with old towels inside or sleeping basket (small dog size) or homemade plywood cage. Crockery food and water dishes.

SPECIAL REQUIREMENTS: Regular veterinary examination and inoculations. There is not an approved vaccine against rabies for skunks, and it is not legal to keep them in all states.

DIET: Primarily vegetarian, with some lean meat and cereals.

CARE: Feed, replenish water dish, change newspaper or litter in "bathroom" corner daily.

TAMABILITY: Become affectionate, devoted to own family. Aloof with strangers. Easily housebroken.

LIFE SPAN: 10 to 12 years; some as long as 20.

Ferrets *PAGE 201*

HOUSING: Homemade plywood cage or commercial cage. Water bottle. Optional plastic litter box.

SPECIAL REQUIREMENTS: Regular veterinary examination and inoculations. It is not legal to keep them in all municipalities.

DIET: High-quality ferret food, which is higher in protein content and fat than cat food and can be purchased at pet stores.

CARE: Feed, check level of water in water bottle, change newspaper or pick droppings from litter box daily. Change litter in optional litter box once a week. Wash cage as necessary.

TAMABILITY: Playful and friendly, but tend to revert to wild if allowed freedom outdoors as adults.

LIFE SPAN: Six to eight years, maybe as long as ten.

Ferret

Rabbits

Rabbits are excellent pets — they are quiet, clean, and affectionate if handled regularly. They are not good pets for very young children, as they panic easily and can scratch badly when struggling. They are more fragile than you might think; their skin tears easily, and dropping a rabbit could break its back.

Rabbits can live in a cage or roam around free in a room. Their cage is constructed of wire to allow their droppings to fall through onto newspaper, and although the newspaper can get pretty messy if you forget to clean it, the cage stays healthy. Rabbits, like rodents, can drink from a water bottle, so you don't have to change the water every day. And you can buy a food dish large enough to carry your rabbit over several days if you are away.

Cute, soft, and friendly animals, rabbits raised from babyhood will follow you about the house like puppies and hop into your lap to be petted. A rabbit who has been accustomed to handling while young is not scared of humans and can be let loose in the house. It will not panic easily, run off, or try to hide. More surprising, it can be housebroken.

The small Dutch rabbit is probably the most popular because of its size. The albino Dutch rabbit is sold at Easter time, but the same small rabbit comes in black, "wild" brown (called agouti), golden tan, lovely grays, and spotted versions of all the above. But the Dutch rabbit, cute as it is, looks ordinary next to the incredible breeds rabbit breeders have developed.

Pet stores may not be able to help you much with fancy breeds. The place to learn more is a rabbit show (check the Web for information on shows near you or contact the American Rabbit Breeders Association at P.O. Box 426, Bloomington, IN 61702). Another good place to learn about rabbits is the rabbit barn at a large country fair. Once you find a rabbit show, you can expect to be treated to a view of fluffy Angoras, the huge Belgian hare (who must have been a model for Br'er Rabbit), rabbits colored and shaded like Siamese cats, and so on. The most wonderful rabbit of all is, unfortunately, too big and too expensive for most people to keep. It is the French Lop-Eared rabbit, a huge, plump bunny with great wide ears that flop down like a stuffed animal's instead of standing stiff like other rabbits'.

Many different breeds of rabbit exist. Some are big, some small, some shaggy, some short-haired. A rabbit breeder can help you pick out a healthy pet.

If handled regularly and gently, a rabbit can become affectionate, even enjoying cuddling with its owner.

The French Lop weighs in at 15 pounds, while the Dutch is more likely 4 pounds.

Although most fancy rabbits are bred for their looks, some people breed rabbits for meat and skins. The practice of breeding rabbits for meat (instead of hunting them) began as early as the first century B.C. But it took the taxonomists until the mid-20th century to identify rabbits as a unique group, called lagomorphs, that developed at least 60 million years ago. If rabbits are related to rodents, their common ancestor would have had to live in the Age of Reptiles, at the time that the dinosaurs were becoming extinct.

Wild rabbits, even if taken as babies, don't eat well and usually die in captivity. It's a pity, because it would be fun to own a western jackrabbit that can leap 20 feet at a single bound and outrun any predator except a cheetah!

Choosing a Baby Rabbit

Rabbits are weaned and ready to leave their mother at eight weeks. There are two ways you can pick up a rabbit when examining it. Grab the scruff of its neck firmly with one hand, just behind the ears, and place your other hand under its rump. Or instead, grab the scruff with one hand and the skin over its rump with the other. Neither method sounds comfortable to us, but if you try to pick up a bunny as you would a kitten or a puppy, you'll see it feels unsupported, kicks, jumps, and often falls. Never pick up a bunny by the ears.

A healthy baby should have thick, somewhat glossy fur and a solid, not too skinny feel in your hands. Look under its tail; if its rear end is messy, it probably has diarrhea. Check the baby's eyes and nose to see that neither is runny. If you notice a baby that is calmer than the others, it would be your best bet as an apartment pet. Males (bucks) and females (does) make equally good pets, but in general, adult rabbits do not get along well together. Unless you're intent on breeding, a single rabbit is advised.

Both sexes should be altered, for your sake or for theirs. Does should be spayed after six months of age to avoid the possibility of uterine cancer. Bucks should be neutered at five months to avoid the possibility of their spraying around the house (like tomcats do) and to keep them mild-mannered.

Housing

Rabbit houses are called hutches. You can buy a hutch in just about any pet store, especially at Easter time. The usual ones, and the cheapest, are made of wood and chicken wire, with a heavier hardware cloth mesh on the bottom and a sliding Masonite top. The smallest size, about two by three feet, is large enough for one Dutch rabbit, but the bigger breeds should have a hutch four by four feet unless the rabbit is using the hutch only to sleep in at night. If someone in your family is willing to help, you can make a better hutch yourself. (See the instructions on page 332.)

Rabbits are more sensitive to heat than to cold. Breeders don't heat the sheds where they keep their rabbits but do cover them with plastic sheeting or similar protection when the weather is windy or bitter. If you have an outdoor area — under a porch or in an open shed — where there is protection from rain and the hot sun, you can keep the hutch outdoors most of the year. Apartment dwellers lucky enough to have a terrace, balcony, or roof can keep the hutch outdoors too. (Remember that it's illegal to keep any obstacle on a fire escape.)

Newspapers, spread six sheets deep beneath an indoor hutch, will catch droppings and urine. Change the paper twice a week, or more often if you'd rather. Wash the whole hutch outdoors with water from a hose or indoors in the bathtub every couple of months.

Your rabbit can live outside a hutch in a small room if you wish. Keep its food and water dishes in the same place from day to day, and check the section on Taming and Housebreaking.

If your rabbit will be living in your backyard, you could make an outdoor hutch instead with a sloping roof to keep out the rain. A hutch made this way can simply be moved from spot to spot when the ground beneath gets covered with droppings. The droppings can be left to disintegrate and fertilize the lawn.

fact

A rabbit you've raised from babyhood will be an attentive pet; it will follow you around like a puppy and hop into your lap to be petted. You may even be able to train it to walk on a leash.

Food and Water

The best basic diet for a rabbit is rabbit pellets, but look for a kind that is formulated for pets. Traditional rabbit pellets were designed to produce meat rabbits and are high in fat and protein. Most pet stores carry the sort intended for pets. Use a crockery dish that the rabbit won't be able to tip over.

Rabbits, which are grazers in nature, eat all day long. Their natural diet is grass, clover, hay, and field crops such as timothy and alfalfa, and the greens in people's treasured vegetable gardens. They would love pellets, hay, and fresh greens to be strewn wall to wall in their hutch, as though it were a meadow there for the munching. Alas, caged rabbits get too fat when they're allowed to eat all day. One solution is to let out your bunny to exercise before you leave in the morning, and again after school until bedtime. Otherwise, you'll have to ration its food. Offer a small helping of pellets two or three times a day, along with a handful of nonfattening vegetables like carrot and spinach. Lawn grass that hasn't been treated with pesticides is a lo-cal snack, but if you live in an apartment, you're not likely to have a lawn. Alfalfa or timothy hay may be available in small quantities at your pet store. If you live in the suburbs, check at feed stores or see if you can get hay from a local barn.

Because their teeth grow continuously, rabbits need to gnaw on wood to keep them trimmed down. If you don't provide sticks, your rabbit may chew chair legs instead. Wild cottontail rabbits have killed most of the trees in my young apple orchard by gnawing their tender bark. Obviously, pruned twigs of apple, pear, and other fruit trees would delight them. (I might as well mention that while rabbits in the summer are primarily grazers of grass, they become browsers in the winter. Browsers, like goats, are able to chew and digest twigs and bark.)

Rabbits need to drink a lot of water. They can drink either from a water bottle or from a dish. If you use a dish, it should be crockery so it is heavy enough not to tip, and you must change the water every day. A water bottle is easier. Change it only as the water gets low. Large water bottles that hold several days' supply can be bought at pet stores. The best ones have a ball bearing inside the tip of the spout to prevent leaking.

One thing I should mention is rabbits' interesting double digestion: The first pellets they drop after a meal are soft and still contain some nourishment; the rabbit eats them. Then, after more digestion, it drops hard dry pellets devoid of further nutrition. So don't be concerned when you see your bunny eating its own feces — this is normal and indeed necessary for proper digestion.

Illnesses

Rabbit diseases are rather complicated, but fortunately pet rabbits do not get sick very often. They can get ear mites, so watch for itchy, red, sore-looking ears and seek advice on treatment from your vet. Rabbits who go outdoors can get fleas. Use a cat flea powder to kill them, following the instructions on the label. If your bunny seems to have something seriously wrong — stops eating, breathes noisily, moves jerkily — take it to your veterinarian. A common sign of illness is fewer droppings than usual — a sign that your rabbit is no longer eating well. Don't try to give antibiotics to your pet without a vet's advice — rabbits are very sensitive to some medications. A rabbit can live for 10 or even 12 years, and most pet bunnies die of old age.

Taming and Housebreaking

Rabbits need to be handled for frequent but short five- or ten-minute periods in order to grow used to humans. Handling doesn't mean hauling your rabbit all over the place and subjecting it to the kinds of play a puppy would enjoy. Pick it up, pet it for a few minutes, put it down, and let it come back to you in its own time. As the rabbit gets older and more used to you, it will become calm and even affectionate — especially if you offer it snacks from your hand when you come to see it.

Many rabbits can be housebroken, but there is no guarantee that every individual is trustworthy. This is the way to do it. Let your rabbit loose in some room that you hope will be its home — your bedroom, or your kitchen if you can keep the door shut, or a playroom, or even the whole basement if it isn't very large. You'll notice that the rabbit tends to leave its droppings in only one or two corners. Put a regular cat litter box in the corner (or each of the two corners) it uses. It will probably accept the box as its bathroom and you will have a housebroken rabbit. A rabbit loose in a room will nibble on furniture, not to mention electrical wires, houseplants, and books, so confine it if you're not around to supervise.

If you choose to let your rabbit live in a hutch all the time, you may be able to avoid the nuisance of newspapers. One family we know keeps a mixing bowl under the mesh of their rabbit's bathroom corner. It deposits its droppings there, and they clean the bowl every couple of days.

Grooming

Rabbits, like dogs and cats, have periods of shedding. The heaviest shedding starts as the weather warms up, but there is some shedding all the time.

Walking Your Rabbit

You can also take a rabbit out on a leash, not as part of the housebreaking but just for exercise and the fun of it. City streets may be too confusing for most rabbits, but a city park or the suburbs or country is fine. The kind of harness that is used for cats is just right for a rabbit. You may have to take your rabbit with you to the pet store to fit it properly.

When your rabbit is very tame and comes to you easily in the house, you can risk letting it loose for a few minutes at a time outdoors, if your yard is fenced in. It will love to nibble the grass and will not be interested in running away. Be careful of dogs, though. If a dog comes up to it suddenly, your rabbit may be startled and bolt away. Or the dog might try to kill it. If you have a fenced yard to keep dogs out, a rabbit can live free outdoors all summer long. In fact, we once had a small gray rabbit named Toby who wouldn't run away no matter what we did. We lived in a house where the landlord threw a tantrum one day and banned all pets. The house was in the country, so we figured it would be an easy thing to just let Toby go. (I didn't realize, at that early age, that domesticated animals are seldom capable of fending for themselves in the wild.) We let him go. He stayed. Perhaps he liked us — he would hoppity-hop up to us every time we went outside and stand on his hind legs pawing gently at us for a pat. Or perhaps he liked the flowers that grew in the landlord's garden — he ate them up. The landlord wasn't pleased, so we took Toby for a drive and deposited him in a less civilized area about a mile away. Two days later, Toby poked his head up from the midst of the ruined flower bed, very pleased with himself. We moved to a different house — with Toby.

The fluffy hair floating around sticks to things and is difficult to vacuum off rugs and fabrics. Some people are allergic to rabbit hair, and even nonallergic people can get an itchy nose.

Loose hair in the rabbit's coat can get matted and messy. There is also some danger that the rabbit, who grooms itself by licking, will swallow enough hair to form a mat in its intestines. A bristle dog brush will get out the loose hair easily. If that seems clumsy, try the finest-toothed metal comb for dogs or buy a grooming mitt — a mitten with short spikes in the palm that lets you pet and brush your bunny at the same time. A weekly brushing or combing should be enough during most of the year, with more frequent grooming if the rabbit is shedding heavily.

Breeding

The rate at which rabbits breed is legendary, but actually rabbit breeding is not all that easy. The babies are born extremely immature — eyes shut, bodies naked, and with poor temperature control. The mothers must keep them warm as well as nurse them. But mother rabbits with litters are nervous: If they or the babies are disturbed, they may abandon their offspring and leave them to die.

Professional rabbit breeders provide specially constructed nesting boxes and are careful of the doe's diet as well as her peace of mind. Still, it is common for several babies in a litter to die.

If you want to give breeding a try, the 4-H Club in your area can tell you where to purchase a nesting box and how to go about introducing the doe to the buck. Rabbit copulation must be one of the fastest known — breeders advise leaving the doe in the buck's hutch no more than five minutes. No one mentions rabbit courtship — there probably isn't time for any preliminaries. If you do breed your doe, have a plan for finding homes for the babies.

Guinea Pigs

Guinea pigs are not pigs — they are rodents, tailless relatives of rats and mice. They don't come from New Guinea either. They are native to the Andes Mountains of South America, mainly Peru, where they were named "guinea" because to the English the word once meant any strange, faraway land. Everyone agrees that they are called "pigs" because of the oinks, honks, snorts, and whistles they produce. If a regular pig could produce that much noise in proportion to its body size, it would be a terrifying creature. Among the more charming noises guinea pigs can make are rattling purrs that they reserve for their mates or for any human who will scratch them behind the

Guinea pigs are sturdy pets that can become very tame if handled properly.

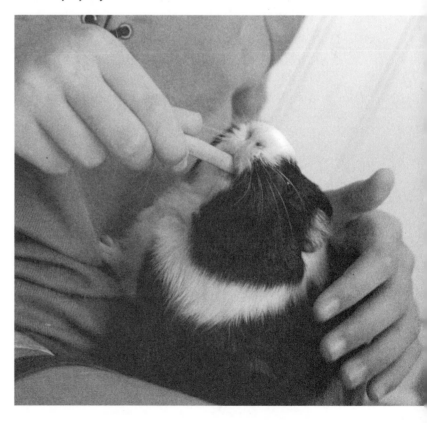

A cardboard carton serves as both a burrow and a perch.

ears. Knowledgeable people skip the nickname of guinea pig and call them by their native Peruvian Indian name: cavy.

Cavies are nearly as cute as rabbits and are certainly as tame if they are handled a lot, but they're dumber. They're far less likely to seek affection, to follow you around the house, or to come when called, but some might. Don't expect housebreaking, either.

The ordinary cavy has short glossy hair that lies flat to its body. It comes in a variety of colors including pure white, deep black, bright ginger, pale gold, and the "wild" agouti brown. Guinea pig fanciers often look for special patterns of color combinations, like tricolor stripes, a black spot over each eye, and a white "cape" over the shoulders. The next fanciest breed is the Abyssinian cavy, which has silly-looking whorled cowlicks in illogical places, like its rear end. The fanciest breed of all is the Peruvian cavy, which has some cowlicking, but since its hair ordinarily grows to five or even eight inches long, it looks like a dust mop with feet. There are reports of Peruvians growing three-foot-long coats. No doubt it gets difficult to locate the eight-inch pig underneath. The colors of the two fancy breeds are as varied as those of the smooth-haired varieties.

Choosing a Guinea Pig

Nearly every pet store carries guinea pigs from time to time. You may find both babies and adults for sale. Adult guinea pigs look so tame that many people are happy to buy them. However, though guinea pigs certainly won't bite you, they can be very skittish if they're not handled a lot while they are young. So instead of getting an adult, you may want to look for a three- to four-week-old baby, the calmest one you can find. Though all babies will scamper away as you reach for them, a baby that kicks and squeals when it's picked up may have a nervous temperament. A cavy that is well socialized purrs when you scratch behind its ears.

As you pick up each cavy to determine its temperament, examine its body too. It should feel solid and heavy, not light and skinny. Its fur should be thick and, if it is a smooth-haired variety, glossy. Check its rear end for signs of diarrhea and its front end for signs of runny eyes or nose. You may notice what look like splits or tears in the ears. These are not old, healed wounds but normal cavy ears.

If you want more than one cavy, have the sales clerk check their sex carefully by feeling for testicles under the skin at the rear of each animal. You can't keep more than one adult male in a hutch, but you can keep females together, with or without a male. If you do have both sexes, they will surely have babies.

Housing

A guinea pig can live in the same sort of hutch as a rabbit (page 332). It will drop about as many droppings as a rabbit would, usually in two or three of the four corners of the hutch. For some reason, though, guinea pigs are incredibly wetter than rabbits. Why guinea pigs must drink so much only to piddle so often is a mystery we have not been able to solve. Change the newspaper in the hutch at least twice a week, and scrub down the hutch when it starts to look messy.

Guinea pigs enjoy having a perch in their hutch. A brick will do if you don't want to go to more trouble. It would be nice, though, to get a small sturdy carton, cut the sides low enough so that your pet can climb onto it, and then cut a door in one side so it can crawl under. The cavy won't soil this perch or the home inside it.

A cavy's hutch can be kept outdoors if it is protected from wind, rain, and sun. Bring it in during the coldest winter weather. Apartment balconies are a perfect place to let a cavy loose for exercise. You can let your guinea pig loose outdoors in the country too, but only if you have an open space where you can keep an eye on it. If your yard has anything remotely resembling a burrow, your pet will be down it or under it faster than you thought its plump, short-legged body could go. If there's nothing to scramble under, your guinea pig will concentrate on munching its way through grass. An upside-down laundry basket makes a fine temporary grazing pen that will keep your pig safe (though you should never leave it unattended while it is out of its cage).

Food and Water

Guinea pigs are more interested in food than you can believe. They will eat their way in a straight line through almost any vegetation you put in front of their faces. Ours eats cabbage, apples, spinach, beets, cauliflower, corn, lettuce, bark, seaweed, flowers, grass, hay, leaves, and peanut butter sandwiches. He doesn't appreciate jelly.

The basic diet should be guinea pig pellets, left daily in a dish in the hutch to be nibbled on all day. Guinea pig pellets look exactly like rabbit pellets but are actually composed of different foods in different proportions. Pet stores usually carry rabbit pellets, insisting they are fine for guinea pigs too — but they aren't. Be insistent, or be prepared for malnutrition. If you have no way of getting the right pellets, add to your pet guinea pig's diet leafy greens like romaine lettuce and spinach, vegetables like carrots, and fruits that have high levels of vitamin C, like apples. Offer fresh foods only a little at a time to be sure you don't set off a bout of diarrhea. You can also add 500 mg of vitamin C to an eight-ounce water bottle and change it daily.

In nature a guinea pig grazes on grass and other vegetation, but it also chews on twigs along the way. The twigs help to keep its teeth short enough. In captivity a guinea pig's teeth, like those of rats and mice, will grow too long if it is given only soft foods like vegetables. The pellet food helps keep its teeth worn down, but twigs may be needed too.

In the summer, fresh grass and hay plus some green twigs for chewing is an adequate diet for a guinea pig. Like rabbits, caged guinea pigs can get overweight, but again the cause is not overeating

fact

In nature, a guinea pig chews on twigs to keep its teeth short and sharp. Long teeth can lead to poor health. If your pet guinea pig's teeth begin to grow long, give it a twig or two to chew on.

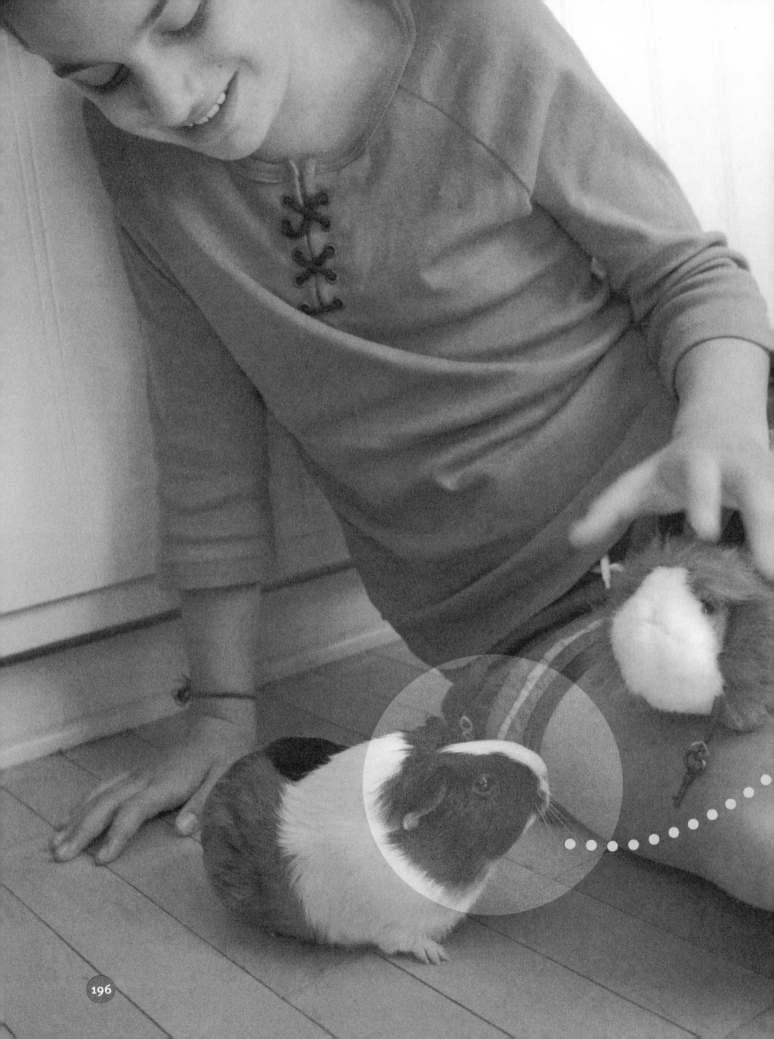

but not enough exercise. If you think your guinea pig is beginning to look a bit plump, try giving it more freedom, not less food.

Don't worry about forgetting to feed your guinea pig. It will remind you. A guinea pig feels so passionate about food that if it so much as hears your footsteps when it is hungry, it will whistle and honk at you until you bring something to fill its belly.

Provide water in a large water bottle to avoid the mush of sodden pellets and droppings that guinea pigs manage to get into water dishes.

Illnesses

The most common health problem with guinea pigs is vitamin deficiency. They are particularly apt to get scurvy, which is caused by too little vitamin C. The first symptom of malnutrition you'll notice is thinning hair along the center of the cavy's back. You'll be able to see skin under the hair. The moment you notice thinning hair, start adding vitamin drops to the guinea pig's water. The instructions on the bottle from the pet store will tell you the proportions to use. Reexamine the diet you've been giving your pet. Try to get back on a balance of guinea pig pellets, raw spinach or romaine, and carrots.

Other diseases in guinea pigs are rare when you keep them as pets, and their life span is quite long — about five years, occasionally even eight.

Grooming

Smooth-haired guinea pigs stay neat and clean, but the Abyssinians and Peruvians can get droppings stuck to their fur or knots of matted hair. They require grooming and sometimes a bath.

You can give guinea pigs a bath with warm water and mild soap if their fur has gotten messy. They don't seem to mind it. Rinse well and dry with a towel afterward.

A fine-toothed metal comb or a small-bristle brush is handy for grooming. Short-haired cavies will not need grooming often, but you may want to brush or comb out loose hairs if your pet is shedding. The shedding is never as heavy as with rabbits and the hair is not as itchy-feeling. The long-haired cavies, especially the Peruvians, need grooming. Their own licking can't get out the mats and tangles that form in the fur. If mats form that are too hard to get out, cut them out with a pair of scissors. The hair will soon grow back. It's impossible to keep long-haired guinea pigs in good coat if they are not in separate cages. Natural affection among guinea pigs is expressed in fond hair nibbling.

Breeding

Guinea pigs are easy to breed, but the females must be bred for the first time before they are about seven or eight months old. Later first pregnancies are dangerous because the females' pelvic bones fuse and do not permit delivery of the young. Guinea pig babies are born looking like miniature adults — completely furred, eyes open, able to walk about and even to eat solid foods. Because the babies are so mature at birth, their gestation period (how long it takes before they are born) is long — about three months. Usually only one to three babies are born, but there may be as many as six or eight. To breed guinea pigs, you have only to leave a boar (male) and a sow (female) together in one hutch. Sooner or later, usually by the time the sow is six months old, she will get pregnant and have her babies. Remove the boar right before the babies are born or he will breed the female again while she is still nursing her litter.

If you are breeding, it might be a good idea to put vitamins in your pet's water and to pay special attention to its diet. Even if you are very careful,

To make a mother guinea pig happy, give her a nesting box with soft bedding inside her cage.

the mother guinea pig will lose much of her hair and look pretty scrawny until some weeks after the babies have been born. In the wild, guinea pigs keep their babies in burrows. To make your sow happy, place inside the cage a box with a door cut out, and put some hay or grass inside the box as bedding for the babies. The sow may pull out some of her own hair to add to the nest.

Once the babies are born, the mother guinea pig will nurse her babies for about three weeks, even though they are eating for themselves during the same time. A three-week-old guinea pig is old enough to give or sell to someone else as a pet.

Remove the young boars before they are three weeks old or they will try to mate with their mother and sisters and could easily get them pregnant. You can tell they are males by feeling for their testicles under the skin at their rear ends. Also, they will begin a characteristic "purring" sound as they approach a female — this is a sign of interest in mating.

Think very carefully about what you're going to do with all the babies before you put a male and female together. There are plenty of guinea pigs that wind up in animal shelters because no one wants them. If you have a male and a female, you can get the male neutered and they will live quite happily together without babies.

Skunks

We have never really had a pet skunk ourselves. We had one for three days, but she was fat, sullen, sleepy, and smelly. We thought skunks didn't make good pets. Now we know Eugene, a skunk belonging to Igor, a friend of ours. Igor's father says of Eugene, "If he was a person, he'd be the sort that would hand you an exploding cigar and then laugh his fool head off." He lies in wait for their dog and their cat and then dashes up from behind and pounces on them. They don't appreciate practical jokers.

With his own human family, Eugene is likably playful and even affectionate, climbing into laps and sprawling for a good petting. He's pigeon-toed and clumsy and waddles when he walks. The fact that he tries to look dignified at the same time makes him a natural clown. Other skunk owners report that their pets are very curious and will get into all sorts of places where they shouldn't be.

Eugene, like all skunks, is shy of strangers. When guests visit, he nobly mounts the stairs, tail up in disdain, to retire to his basket. The raised-up tail is not to be feared in de-scented skunks, but you'll still get some skunk smell out of a frightened or annoyed pet even after the operation to remove scent glands.

Skunks and ferrets both belong to a family of animals called the mustelines. All the mustelines exude scent from glands in their skin when they are upset. Naturalists have observed, but not explained, how reluctant skunks are to spray. Before a skunk lets loose, it ups its tail, bows forward, and sometimes even stands on its front legs, balancing like an acrobat. The warning is usually enough for any animal that has had experience with skunks, and the encounter usually ends without spraying.

No doubt everyone you know says that skunks stink. Tell them that when scientists have performed tests in which they have people smell the skunk scent at a low concentration without telling them what it is, most people find skunk scent pleasant. Very little children rather like skunk scent, even in normal concentration. Musk, a substance taken from the anal glands of musk deer, is the "turn-on" smell in our most expensive perfumes. On a direct hit, however, the spray of a skunk can damage eyes to the point of temporary blindness.

Choosing a Skunk

Before acquiring a skunk, check with your local wildlife office to make sure it is legal to keep one in your state. Like all animals in this chapter, a skunk must be acquired when it is young in order to be socialized sufficiently. Eugene was bought as a caught-in-the-wild baby at a pet store, both descented and neutered, but we have seen only one other skunk for sale in a pet store. You can buy pet skunks from people who breed them for fur, and the wild animal farms that advertise in poultry magazines sometimes sell baby skunks.

Pet skunks can be descented, or have their musk glands removed, so that they will not spray if they become frightened.

This type of woven dog or cat bed is perfect for a skunk.

Get one that has just been weaned. Baby skunks are usually descented by the breeder, but you will need to have your pet spayed or neutered as well. Going into heat makes female skunks restless in confinement; unneutered males often become aggressive and unpleasant.

Housing

Because skunks are nocturnal, you can trust them to stick to their own quarters during the day and join the family in the evening. This makes them perfect pets for working families, since no one has to worry about what the skunk is up to when no one is at home. In the evening your pet is awake and ready for company. Skunks are not terribly active at any time, which makes them ideal for small apartments.

Eugene spends much of his time, by choice, in a small bathroom. He has not been caged and doesn't seem to need to be. He has a cavelike basket to sleep in and a piece of newspaper in a corner to use for his droppings. Skunks aren't difficult to housebreak. Just observe which corner the skunk prefers, then leave newspaper there.

Food and Water

People used to think that cat food was a good choice for skunks, but it's not. A steady diet of cat food can cause all kinds of health problems. In nature skunks are omnivorous, so they need a wide variety of foods, including fresh vegetables, fresh fruit, lean meat, grains, and cereals. Feed your skunk once each evening when it wakes up.

It's impossible to predict how large the evening meal should be. If your skunk begins to put on weight, cut down the quantity of food it gets. Wait and see if the new amount keeps it at a stable weight. When you have it right, stick to that amount.

In nature skunks, like bears, go into a very deep hibernation while it's cold. During the late summer and the fall, when the eating is good, they stuff themselves to the point of extreme obesity. During that winter nap, which lasts about four months, skunks live on the fat they've accumulated in their bodies. We've heard that you have to put pet skunks on a diet during this time of year. The theory is if they get too fat, they will try to hibernate even if they live in a warm house. Igor says this is not true of Eugene, and that he is kept on a strict diet all year long. Although Eugene is not fat, the skunk we tried to keep one November was awfully fat — and cranky. We think she was trying to hibernate.

Illnesses

We have not heard of any particular health difficulties with skunks except fatness. An improper diet can cause liver and kidney problems. Skunks should be inoculated by a veterinarian for feline and canine distemper. There is no rabies vaccine approved for skunks, as there is for cats and dogs. A strictly indoor pet, though, has little chance of getting the disease, which can be carried by raccoons and bats.

If a skunk does get sick, try seeking advice from your vet first. If she is unsure what to do, call nearby zoos or nature centers that may keep skunks. Their experience is often helpful with unusual animals.

Ferrets

Ferrets are small, weasel-like animals domesticated from the wild polecat. They hunt snakes, rodents, and other animals for food and are by nature quick, bright, aggressive, and sharp-toothed. Many people think ferrets are wild animals that can be tamed much like a skunk or a raccoon. There is one wild ferret species — the black-footed ferret of North America, which is nearly extinct — but the domestic ferret is no more a wild animal than our domestic cat. Ferrets have been domesticated for more than 2,000 years, so long that no one is sure which of the many wild polecats they were originally bred from. Domestication has made the ferret less touchy, less agile, and less nocturnal than its wild relatives.

Domesticated ferrets have been kept during all these centuries as hunting animals. Let loose from time to time around barns and homes, they can kill as many rats, mice, and snakes as can a cat. But mainly ferrets have been trained as rabbiters. Their narrow foot-long bodies are made to fit through holes. Equipped with either a tiny muzzle to prevent them from eating bunnies in their burrows or a collar of jingle bells to warn their prey, they chase the rabbits from the warren (the large underground communities European rabbits live in). The hunter then kills the rabbits and rewards the ferret with rabbit liver. A preference for livers, kidneys, and hearts is still typical of ferrets. Ours gobbles chicken hearts and beef kidneys the way kids gobble cookies.

Ferrets belong to the family of carnivores called mustelines, which are not only the most primitive of all meat-eating mammals but also the stock from which all other meat-eaters evolved. Mustelines include skunks, which have developed to a fine art the musteline trademark of musk-producing glands at the base of the tail. Male ferrets have a slight musky odor all the time, and females also smell if they are angry or frightened or in heat. Our female ferret smelled objectionable only for the first few evenings she played with our overenthusiastic 90-pound puppy and the one morning after she had accidentally gotten locked into the clothes dryer for the night. These days she smells less strong than a wet dog or a dry mouse.

Choosing a Ferret

It is illegal to keep ferrets in some states and even in some municipalities, so check with your local wildlife office before deciding to get one. As they

Pest's Place

Our ferret is named Pest and her quarters are built into a cupboard at floor level, constructed much like the drawing on page 337). Her den is just a closed-off portion of her cage entered through a corner cut out of the plywood partition.

She has a supply of rags with which she both makes her bed and plugs her hole at naptime. The plywood partition is removable so we can take out the pieces of meat she sometimes drags inside for midnight snacks.

Ferrets are lively and curious animals that need lots of attention and can be very satisfactory pets.

have increased in popularity, they are often available in pet stores, though you should find out where the store gets its babies from. You can also check the classified ads for a breeder in your area. The important thing to ask about any ferret you purchase is how much it's been handled by and exposed to humans. You want one that is used to people and comfortable being handled.

Males should definitely be neutered, which cuts down their musky odor and reduces aggression as they get older, and females will generally be healthier if they are spayed. Some people have their ferrets descented as well, but many owners find it unnecessary, as ferrets smell bad only when they are frightened or threatened.

Some domesticated ferrets are albinos with white fur and red eyes. There are also nice brown ferrets and crosses between the two. The crosses are the prettiest, having white fur on the belly and sometimes on the paws. The rest of the body is tan, tipped with brown, with an almost black tail. Our albino-brown cross turns quite pale and frosted-looking in the winter and a warm brown in summer. She has a white marking on the top of her head and white toes all year.

Housing
While ferrets can roam free for as much of the day as you're willing to supervise them, they should always be caged when you're not at home. Pet

stores sell multilevel wire cages that accommodate the ferret's desire for a separate toileting area and a place to hide while sleeping. Or you could build the cage on page 336) from wood and wire mesh, with newspapers spread on the floor. It is shown equipped with a den, a nearly closed-off area where no one can spy. The den is absolutely necessary. Ferrets sleep very heavily, sometimes requiring several minutes to wake up even with much joggling and prodding. Somehow ferrets must be aware that deep sleepers need a safe place for snoozes.

You'll find your ferret will use the darkest and most private corner of its cage for a bathroom, but never its own den. As soon as it's decided which corner to use, put a small box of kitty litter there. You can even buy specially shaped litter boxes to fit in corners.

Cage Cleaning

Change the litter in the litter box and the newspaper every few days. Ferrets have a way of backing themselves into a corner to go to the bathroom, so you may have to scrub the corner walls each week. If you don't like scrubbing, tape a folded sheet of newspaper into the corner behind the litter box. Then any mess will be on the paper, which is easily taken down and changed.

Once your ferret knows how to use its litter box, it will be easier to train it to use a litter box outside the cage when it's roaming free.

Food and Water

Ferrets should be fed a high-quality food especially formatted for them. Many pet stores or feed stores carry ferret food or you can order it on the Internet. Most commercial dog and cat foods do not have enough digestible protein for ferrets, though some higher-end cat foods may be acceptable. They do not get much nutrition from veg-etable matter, so any pelleted food must be high in animal protein. Ferrets should be allowed free access to food, as they need to eat frequently. An occasional treat of cooked meat (organ meats are a favorite) or canned cat food is fine. Dairy products generally give ferrets diarrhea.

Provide a water bottle at all times. You can also use a heavy ceramic dish for water, but many ferrets like to play in their water dishes and make a mess.

Illnesses

Ferrets are hardy, healthy animals, but should always be housed indoors. They can catch any of the diseases a cat can and should be inoculated by your vet against feline rabies and distemper. If your ferret is allowed outdoors on a leash, it should have a rabies shot as well. Take a stool sample to the vet to check for worms. Fleas can be treated with kitten flea powder or spray; apply it every three days for three or four weeks in order to kill new fleas as they hatch during treatment. Ferrets are also susceptible to human colds and viruses, so be careful not to sneeze on your pet, and wash your hands before and after handling it if you have a runny nose.

Bathing and Grooming

Our ferret enjoys bathing in water from time to time. We set out a roasting pan filled with water at room temperature. She dives in the water, head and all, and comes up shaking like a puppy. Since a ferret's bathing style requires much leaping in and out of the water, put the pan on the bathroom or kitchen floor so you can mop up afterward. Or you could put the pan right in the bathtub or the kitchen sink.

For a long time we couldn't figure out why our ferret, Pest, always looked so neat and clean. We never saw her grooming herself. Then one night she settled down to sleep under the covers of my bed. Judging from the humpy movements of her body for the next hour, I could see that she was grooming herself thoroughly. But every time I lifted the covers to watch, she stopped. I assume that ferrets, like some humans, prefer to groom themselves in private.

Taming and Housebreaking

Pest is not the first ferret we have had as a pet. Puck, a male and half grown when he arrived, came before her. He was unaccustomed to handling and had not been neutered. He was untamable and eventually ran away.

We decided to try again. This time we ordered a female and insisted she be no more than six to eight weeks old. At this age a ferret has just been weaned and has not yet formed a firm opinion as to the sort of life it will lead. Pest arrived by air from the animal farm where she was born, well crated and in good shape. She was still too young to really walk; her belly more or less followed her front paws as she pulled herself about. Her eyes, just opened, were sleepy, and in fact she could stay awake only for about 15 minutes before collapsing into a comalike snooze. She didn't bite at all, although she nibbled fingertips in a cuddly way, and she wasn't ready yet for playful antics.

We handled Pest constantly. She got her belly rubbed and her neck petted, sampled food from our fingers, and slept in our laps. Pest is now a thoroughly socialized, delightful, amusing, reliable, affectionate pet. When we leave her, she runs

fact

Ferrets were domesticated for use as hunters; they killed rats and snakes and flushed small prey like rabbits from burrows in the ground. As pets, ferrets are lively, intelligent, quick, curious, and affectionate.

after us, muttering a ferret tune that sounds strangely like a laugh. When she's tired she climbs into our laps and sleeps in the crook of an arm, sometimes rolling belly-up as though she were in a hammock on a summer afternoon. When we stop petting her, she opens her eyes and nudges for attention like a dog. When she plays, it is a dance — around and around and pop into the air. Legs stiff, back humped, eyes shining, she circles, pops, and POUNCE! She's got a toe. Her nip is not a bite but a tickly nibble (what is known to scientists as an inhibited bite), and then she's off in her dance again. The only time we could complain of her teeth is when we accept the challenge of her dance and roll her about with our hands as you do with a kitten. Then she will hang on to a finger and kick her legs against our hands in mock fierceness. But still she tries to be careful with her teeth and has never really hurt us.

Box training our ferret was quite easy. Pest goes to the bathroom after she eats and after she wakes from a nap. At first, we gave her a chance to use her box before we let her out of her cage. Then we could trust her not to mess around the house for several hours. As she began to run loose for longer and longer periods, we found she had chosen a corner of the kitchen under a projecting cabinet for a downstairs bathroom. So we put a litter box there too.

The larger the area in which a ferret runs free, the more litter boxes it will need. If you have a large house, your ferret is likely to choose more spots than you want to supply with boxes. The answer is to keep your ferret loose in a smaller area. We keep doors shut to confine our ferret to the two areas of the house that are convenient to her two litter boxes. Small-apartment dwellers may get along with only one box.

A ferret's instincts tell it to do a few things that are a nuisance in a home. Ferrets are burrowing animals and would as soon burrow in a flowerpot as elsewhere. Beware also of letting a ferret inside your pants legs or under your shirt. Their claws are sharp, and shirts and pants are like burrows to the ferret. Burrows, of course, start out as holes. A ferret will go into any hole, including wastebaskets, dog-food cans, shoes, and milk cartons. Puck escaped the house by creeping through the plastic tube that vents the clothes dryer. Sometimes there are holes under the kitchen sink where pipes come through the wall or floor; these, too, could be escape routes. Your pet might nap in a sock you've left on the floor, where you could step on it. Or it will snooze under a couch pillow and get sat on. And ferrets are thieves as well, though not on purpose. They like to make their own beds, so if you are missing socks or underpants, very likely your pet has dragged them off to a hideaway.

We take Pest out on a leash. She wears the smallest-sized cat harness and a light leash. It was a kicking scramble to get it on at first, but now she is used to it and no longer objects.

Breeding

Ferrets can have several litters of a half-dozen or so babies each year, but breeding is best left to professional breeders. Pregnant and nursing ferrets are ill-tempered, and unneutered males don't remain attached to the home.

Pup and Pest

Ferrets are known to be totally unafraid. That means they don't jump when you drop a book two inches in front of their faces, and they don't run away from anything. Unfortunately, that means a pet ferret won't run away from a dog.

You can't have a houseful of more or less free animals without letting them learn to deal with one another. But when we first got Pest, our pup was both energetic and clunky, and we figured one good bam with a paw or one excited snap at Pest and it was all over. We let them play together for only a few minutes a night until we felt the pup was calm enough to be trusted.

One evening we turned and saw that our worst fears had come true. Pest lay dangling from the puppy's whiskery mouth. But no, not quite! Pest was hanging in midair, all right, but on her own steam. She had clenched the pup's whiskers in a death grip. The puppy had no idea what to do next. She just stood there blinking, dangling a determined ferret. Within a few days, the puppy begin to carry *her* pet ferret around in her mouth. It just goes to show that ferrets can get used to anything.

Pet Cats

For such a small animal, being not much bigger than a bunny really, the cat carries a heavy load of superstition. The ancient Egyptians thought cats were gods. Anyone who killed a cat was treated like a murderer and executed. When a cat died, it was made into a mummy. Three hundred thousand cat mummies were once found in Egypt, all buried in the same place. During the Middle Ages, people thought cats were witches and burned them at the stake. The cats of Germany and England were just about wiped out by that superstition.

There are still superstitions existing today. In America, black cats are bad luck. In England, white cats are bad luck. And my mother-in-law once warned me that cats smother babies.

Of course all this is nonsense. But it makes me wonder — what is it about cats that has made so many people imagine so much for so long? I don't know the whole answer, but I can understand some of it. Cats make me uncomfortable. They stare at me. They don't let on what they're thinking. They don't let me love them when I feel like it. They rub against me when I don't feel like it. They don't seem to need human approval in the way dogs do.

The cat is the way it is because, of all our common domesticated animals, it is the only one that in the wild would live by itself. Wild dogs live in packs, geese in flocks, and cows in herds. With the exception of lions, wild cats are solitary. The cat in Kipling's "Just So" story said it straight out: "I am the cat who walks by himself . . ." No creature that lives in a group can afford to act aloof. It needs its family and friends in order to survive; it had best be nice to them. But a cat in the wild can survive with no love from anyone.

It's easy to think that domesticated cats are standoffish and unfriendly, but if you accept them on their terms, you will find that many cats are in fact very affectionate and like human companionship just as much as dogs do.

Pet Cats at a glance

Most cats are mixed breeds and come in a huge variety of colors and length of coat. There are a number of purebred cats with distinct characteristics. You can find a cat through a newspaper ad or flyer, adopt one from an animal shelter, or buy one from a breeder.

HOUSING EQUIPMENT: Food and water dishes. Litter box (one per cat) and litter. Collar with name tag; optional leash or harness. Brush and comb for long-haired cats. Carrying case for transporting to the vet.

SHORT-HAIRED

SPECIAL REQUIREMENTS: Initial veterinary examination and inoculations for kittens; males should be neutered and females spayed; annual checkups.

DIET: Kitten or cat chow and/or canned cat food.

CARE: Feed, replenish water, and clean droppings from litter box daily. Clean and replace litter in litter box once a week. Groom long-haired cats weekly. Groom any cat as necessary during heavy shedding periods. Take to veterinarian for checkup and booster shots once a year.

LONG-HAIRED

TAMABILITY: Need introduction to litter box or to outdoors, but most cats essentially train themselves. Individuals may learn a few commands and to follow their owner on walks. May become aloof or very affectionate and responsive, depending on treatment as kittens.

LIFE SPAN: On average, cats that go outdoors have shorter lives than cats that live indoors exclusively. A well-cared-for cat can live more than 20 years and some have been known to get as old as 30, though 12 to 15 years is the accepted life span.

The wild Kaffir cat of Africa was first domesticated in Egypt 4,500 years ago, much more recently than the dog or even the ox. At that time, the Egyptians had launched a program to try to domesticate and find a use for all sorts of animals. They even tried the hyena. Cats were extremely helpful in keeping rodents and snakes away from stores of grain. Another use they found for the cat was as a bird hunter and retriever. Except for the fact that I never saw a cat go hunting and retrieving for its master, our domestic cats of today have changed little in thousands of years.

Hunting is an instinct in cats and you can't teach yours not to do it. Domestic cats survive well in the wild as long as there is sufficient prey to eat. Dogs, who hunt and live in packs, have years in which to learn hunting skills from adult dogs. Cats don't. A mother cat leaves her kittens shortly after they are weaned. They are on their own as half-grown kittens, using extraordinary senses and instincts to fill their bellies.

Hunting is made up of three steps — the stalk, the pounce, and the killing bite. The steps are automatically triggered by slight movements or rustling sounds. Jiggle your toes under the blanket in bed or make a scratching sound on your sheet. Your kitten will crouch and begin to creep toward the sound and movement. That's stalking. Then it pounces, its hind feet landing first, its front paws free to sink their claws into your foot. Then comes the killing bite, if you haven't pulled your foot away.

Of the three steps, only the killing bite must be learned. The bite is given in the back of the neck. A canine tooth is used to feel out the space between two neck vertebrae through which the spinal cord can be severed. Instinct tells a kitten to aim its bite roughly where the body of an animal narrows for a short space — the neck. (That explains why kittens bite ankles.) The direction of fur or feathers may aim its mouth toward the spot too. But to learn the art of feeling out the vulnerable spot with the canine teeth and severing the cord, a kitten needs two kinds of experience.

First, it must see its mother kill prey. Second, during a critical period of early kittenhood it must be brought live prey to practice on. Mother cats that are allowed to hunt first bring home dead prey for the kittens to eat. From that experience the kittens learn what is their proper food. A kitten taught to eat only mice will be slow to bother birds, and vice versa. Then the mother begins to bring home live prey, first killing it in demonstration herself, then letting her kittens practice killing their own dinner.

Kittens raised with mice or rats will not hunt them. They have not been taught to see them as prey. Kittens raised by nonhunting mothers will go through the first two steps of hunting but may not be able to kill their prey. This is sometimes the reason for what looks like cruelty to us: the cat that seems to tease its prey. This is not the cat's fault; it is short-circuited. Lacking the last step in the sequence, it lets the prey go; but then the prey moves, makes a noise, and the first two steps are automatically triggered all over again.

Both sight and hearing in cats are specially developed for hunting. A cat's ears are tuned to

fact

Some experts believe kittens instinctively know how to stalk their prey and pounce on it, but they have to be taught how to kill it. If their mothers teach them to eat only mice, they will be less likely to catch birds.

ultrasound, like the high-frequency squeaks of mouse talk that are inaudible to human ears. Naturally it's helpful to a cat to hear the mice talking behind the baseboard. The cat's automatic reaction to rustling sounds comes from a built-in sensitivity to the faint stirrings of leaves and grass that might betray a mouse or a bird.

A cat's eyes are like colored bicycle reflectors, flashing back even small amounts of light in red, green, or yellow. The Egyptians thought that cats kept the sunlight in their eyes overnight, and it was this sunlight glowing out that explained why cats can hunt in darkness. In fact, a cat in a totally dark room — one with no light at all — could not see any better than you or I could. But nighttime darkness is not at all pitch-black, except to our poor eyes; for a cat's eyes, aided with those sensitive whiskers, the night offers plenty of light seeing its way around.

In the dark, a cat expands its large pupil so that all the light possibly available hits the extremely light-sensitive area at the back of the eye. In bright light, it contracts the pupil to a mere slit. To watch it happen, use a penlight in a dark room. With the cat in your lap, shield the light so you can just barely see its eyes, then gradually point the light at its face. The pupils will contract slowly enough for you to watch.

Cats don't use their noses to sniff along a trail as dogs do. Birds leave no trails and a mouse's trail ends in a hole the cat can't enter. Instead, a

When a cat falls, it swivels its tail for balance as it turns its body to land feetfirst.

cat stations itself in a likely spot and waits for tell-tale sounds and movements. An experienced hunter will wait three or four hours, motionless but for its twitching tail, for a mouse to venture from a hiding place.

As the cat waits, it sees but does not notice grass blades, twigs, and leaves — until they move. This is not really a strange skill. We do it all the time when we fail to hear anything that is going on around us until someone speaks our name. Our brain blocks out what is unimportant to us and notices only what we want to hear.

When cats bring home their prey — dead, alive, or mutilated — it is not a "gift" for you at all. It is only a not very hungry cat bringing its prey home for future dining. This behavior becomes appropriate when a mother cat is caring for her kittens. Lacking kittens and not allowed to hunt, one frustrated female was even in the habit of bringing her two catnip mice to her dish each night. When animals are run by instincts but don't need to use them, some of the things they do seem crazy.

There are several explanations for a cat's whiskers, all having to do with hunting. The whisker area is supplied with an abundance of nerve endings, so there's little doubt that whiskers are a sense organ of some sort. They could be wind-detectors, telling the cat which way the wind is blowing so it can locate its prey better; but since any animal can feel which way the wind blows without whiskers (and cats don't use their sense of smell much in hunting), this doesn't seem enough of an explanation. For a while the most popular theory was that whiskers warn a cat whether a hole or crevice it is trying to squeeze through as it hunts is really big enough. This made sense for cats with long whiskers that would really be able to feel out the size of a hole, but short-whiskered cats would be out of luck.

Then someone discovered that if you touch a cat's whiskers, it blinks. Try it. Whiskers acting as a trigger for a blinking reflex makes sense. A cat stalking through shrubbery at night with its eyes wide open could get some nasty pokes in the eye from twigs. But if whiskers brush the twig first and trigger a blink, such accidents would be neatly avoided.

Cats climb trees with ease by gripping the bark with hooklike claws. On the ground, long curved claws that stuck out from toes would break in no time. So cats' paws are made with sheaths into which they can retract their claws completely. When a cat's claws are retracted, its velvety pads are noiseless.

Choosing a Kitten

Cats need good mothering, play with their litter-mates, and handling by humans if they are to be friendly, happy pets. They especially need all three kinds of friendship between four and eight weeks of age. That means often an orphaned kitten will not act like a normal cat, a stray will be scared of people, and even a kitten raised without litter-mates may be neurotic when it grows up.

The healthiest kittens can be home-raised kittens. Look in the classified section of a newspaper for ads for kittens that have been home-raised. The domestic short-haired kittens (alley cats) are almost inevitably free. Purebred kittens, varying in price, are offered by ad too. Even a free kitten will have the initial cost of vet's visit, inoculations, and possible deworming. Most important is to have your kitten spayed or neutered between four and six months of age.

If you do find a kitten at a private home, make sure the mother has been tested for feline leukemia and feline acquired immune deficiency (FIV). These diseases are common in cats that are allowed outdoors and haven't been vaccinated.

CAT'S RETRACTILE CLAW

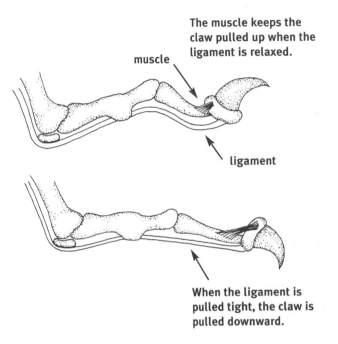

The muscle keeps the claw pulled up when the ligament is relaxed.

muscle

ligament

When the ligament is pulled tight, the claw is pulled downward.

Also find out if the mother has been regularly vaccinated and dewormed, or you might be bringing home some problems. A healthy queen (mother cat) is the best chance for a healthy kitten.

You can also buy kittens in pet stores, but be aware that they may have been taken from their mother too soon. Find out how old they are, when they were weaned, and where they came from. Kittens should not be weaned before they are six to seven weeks old. Pet store kittens may not have been properly socialized by humans — ask how much they are handled by the staff.

Another place to find kittens or older cats is your local animal shelter. During the spring and summer months, thousands of kittens are born to homeless cats and many of them are rescued by humane societies. In some cases, not much will be known about the kittens, but often the litter will have been born at the shelter or brought there right after birth. Often the mother will still be with them and they will not be released for adoption until they are properly weaned and have their first series of shots. That's why there's a fee for adopting an animal from a shelter. You will also have to promise to have your kitten spayed or neutered; sometimes the cost of the surgery is included in the adoption fee.

Wherever you decide to look for a pet, try to visit the kittens when they are six weeks old and still with their mother. Ask to pick them up. Healthy kittens have thick coats. They don't have pot bellies. They don't have runny eyes or noses. They aren't skinny. Feel a kitten's skin and look at its tummy to check for rashes, bald spots, scabs, and fleas. Look not just at your favorite but also at its littermates. There's no sense starting out with skin or other health problems.

No matter what the owner promises you a kitten's disposition is going to be, you have to do some testing of your own to choose a good kitten.

First ask to see the mother cat. If she's very shy and nervous, the kittens are likely to have inherited her timidity. Perhaps her jumpy behavior also affects the kittens. A kitten from this litter will need extra time and attention to become a friendly, relaxed cat.

If the mother is calm and friendly, here are some tests to try. Watch while the mother nurses the kittens. Some will act aggressive, pushing others out of the way to reach their accustomed nipple. (Each kitten chooses and keeps its own nipple soon after birth.) Others will be timid — the last to claim their nipple. Neither the most timid nor the most aggressive is a good choice for a house pet.

When the kittens have finished nursing, pick up the one you have your eye on. At first, it will cling to your hand with its claws out; its body will feel tense. Pet the kitten and hold it close to your

Having Temporary Kittens

If you're dying for a litter of kittens to take care of, there's a better way than letting your cat get pregnant. Ask if your local animal shelter needs foster families for pregnant and nursing cats. It's much healthier for kittens to be born and raised in a home than in a shelter with many other cats around. Kittens are weaned naturally by about eight weeks of age and will be ready then to go to new homes. If you want to keep one, you'll know exactly which one is the best for you, and you'll have the satisfaction of knowing that you've given the others a good start in the world.

Kittens can't resist curling up in small spaces. Check your drawers before closing them!

body, where it will feel safer. If it has been handled enough, it should relax in your hands, sheath its claws, and stop clinging.

Last, ask to take the kitten into a room by itself. Put it down. The kitten should attempt to explore the room a little. After you've given the kitten a chance to explore for a few minutes, go near it and clap your hands hard or slam the floor. If it is a normally curious kitten, it should recover quickly from its startled reaction and go back to exploring. Crumple a little paper and toss it a bit to see if the kitten attempts to play. A relaxed kitten will, a tense kitten won't. A kitten that has been well mothered and handled enough by people should have a strong desire to follow you.

This series of suggested tests is pretty rigid and even the sweetest, most social kitten would find it hard to get straight As. But it is important for a kitten to do well on most of them before you decide to make it your pet.

When you've chosen a kitten, arrange to bring it home when it's two months old. Bring a carrying case. Being loose in a car can be scary for the kitten and unsafe for the driver. For example, it is difficult to stop your car if there is a kitten crouching under the brake pedal.

Housing

Many cat breeders recommend keeping cats as strictly indoor pets. Although we have always allowed our house cats to come in and out at will, there is no doubt that the big outdoors is dangerous. Besides cars and dogs there is another hazard: A friendly kitten may strike a passerby as a "poor little stray" and be innocently kidnapped. To prevent that sort of "accident," provide your cat with a collar and name tag. Most cats that wind up in animal shelters do not have any identification and are not reunited with their owners. Or ask your vet about a tracking microchip that can be implanted in your pet's ear during a routine office visit.

Another concern with outdoor cats is that they kill birds and other wildlife. Not only is this bad for the birds, but also your cat is more likely to pick up parasites and diseases from eating its prey. You and your neighbors might object to having gardens or sandboxes used for bathrooms, so be very considerate if your cat is causing problems.

Always bring in your cat at night at the very least. Try letting it outside in the morning and after you feed it and bringing it back in later in the day for a meal and a nap.

Indoor cats appreciate having a variety of places where they can climb and hide. You don't have to let your cat walk all over the counters or the dining room table, but do provide a spot where it can be high up and out of the way. You can even buy or make a shelf to go in front of a sunny window where your pet can bask and watch the birds in action. Pet stores sell carpet-covered climbing perches for cats.

Even a cat that goes outside will need an indoor litter box for its droppings (one per cat is recommended). There are a variety of litter boxes available, from simple pans to ones that are enclosed to prevent the litter from being scratched out onto the floor. You can even spend a lot of money on an electronic kind that automatically sweeps droppings from the litter after each visit — you just have to tie up the plastic bag and throw it away!

There are different sorts of litter too, all based on some material that absorbs and supposedly deodorizes, like clay. Some are dusty, which can be irritating for both you and your cat. Some are scented or formulated for use by multiple cats. Some "clump up," allowing wet spots to be more easily scooped out. You might try several before finding the one that works best for you and your cat.

To control odor and keep the litter fresh for your cat, you must change the litter regularly. How often depends on how often your cat uses it and how many cats you have. At the very least, you should scoop up feces (solid waste) and whatever wet litter you can every day, and dispose of it. Replace all the litter every week. Even if you could stand the smell enough to let the litter become dirty, your cat wouldn't, and it would begin using other places. If the litter box becomes dirty or if your cat starts using other places to relieve itself, odor becomes a problem. In fact, *odor* is probably too nice a word. Like the smell of skunk, cat smell is difficult to get rid of.

Some cats are very finicky about their litter boxes, while others can tolerate a higher degree of messiness. If your cat doesn't like the location or

fact

Cats enjoy being in the room with you, but they often prefer to be in a high, out-of-the-way spot. They scale curtains, bookshelves, and other natural "ladders" on their way to the highest perch.

Too Many Kittens

Did you know that cats can have up to three litters a year? That's one reason there are so many more cats in the world than dogs, which come into heat only twice a year. Also, cats tend to be less supervised while outdoors and therefore are more likely to find opportunities to mate. Over the course of seven years, one female cat and her offspring can produce over 420,000 kittens. The Humane Society of the United States estimates that 8 to 10 million animals enter shelters in this country each year, with approximately half of them being adopted. There just aren't as many good homes as there are unwanted pets.

cleanliness of its box, you might find it using your fireplace or bathtub instead. Changes in litter box habits can indicate a health problem, so if finding a new spot or keeping the box cleaner don't work, take your cat for a checkup.

Food and Water

Mother cats wean their kittens when they are between six and eight weeks old, though the babies will begin eating adult food while still nursing. At six weeks, they need to be fed three or even four times a day. Gradually reduce the number of meals as the kitten grows. Grown cats can eat once a day but often bother you for a second meal.

There are basically three types of food available for cats: dry chow, canned food, and semimoist varieties. In many ways, dry food is preferable. It's usually cheaper, keeps longer, doesn't smell as much, and can be left out all day for free-choice feeding. It's also better for your cat's teeth. Canned foods are nutritionally complete,

and cats usually prefer them. However, canned foods spoil more readily and the smell can be nasty. Semimoist foods combine aspects of both but may be high in sugar, salt, and preservatives. The best way to find a good diet for your cat is to read the labels and talk to your vet.

Cats and kittens need a water dish left out for them all the time so they can drink as they need to. Kittens can have a little milk but weaned cats can live without it. In fact, milk gives many adult cats and kittens diarrhea. Use fresh or dried milk, or evaporated milk diluted with an equal amount of water.

If your cat gets finicky, firm steps are necessary. A healthy cat that eats its meat but won't touch its dry chow may wind up with dental problems. The same is true of pampered pets that have been led to believe that if they are stubborn enough, someone will finally offer canned salmon, raw beef, calf's liver, or fillet of flounder. The firm step for problem eaters is to offer primarily dry chow with a small amount of the preferred food mixed in and gradually offer more and more dry food. You may feel mean, and it's annoying because the cat will rub against you and meow for the two or three days of treatment. Whatever you do, don't give in or you will just reinforce your cat's behavior.

Always offer your cat some food every day — going without food at all can cause serious liver problems. If you have a fat kitty, put it on a restricted diet, not a starvation diet.

Be careful with mealtime handouts and leftovers. Cats can be allowed to chew on small bones, but not those from fish or chicken, because they tend to splinter and stick in the cat's throat. An occasional treat of turkey or bacon from your sandwich will be appreciated, but be aware that cats can become as pesky as dogs at begging for food, so don't encourage it.

Illnesses and the Vet

Every new kitten should be taken to a veterinarian after you get it home. Your vet will examine the kitten, give it the proper inoculations, and check it for worms. Roundworms are passed as larvae through the mother's placenta to even the healthiest of kittens. Tapeworms are carried by fleas and the eggs may be ingested when a kitten eats a flea. Both kinds of worms are very common.

Bring a sample of the kitten's droppings with you in a small container or a plastic sandwich bag so the vet can check it under the microscope for worm eggs. Worms are gotten rid of by a medicine that kills them without harming the kitten.

Many kittens die of influenza, feline distemper, and other diseases that could have been prevented by inoculation. Find out from the previous owner if the kittens were started on their series of shots, and if so, when. Most shelter kittens get their first shots before they are adopted. Then your vet can either start or complete the series for your kitten. Cats must also be inoculated against rabies, a fatal disease that can affect all mammals, including humans.

While you have your kitten there, talk to the vet about spaying and neutering. All pet cats should be altered so that they don't produce kittens. Females come into heat as early as seven months and continue at intervals of six weeks through most of their adult lives. Unlike dogs, which may take it in stride, a female cat in heat yowls, screams, groans, rolls, rubs, and pushes her rear end in the air. While she's inside the house driving you crazy, the howling, fighting tomcats are outside the house driving you even crazier. The operation of spaying could be done when a kitten is between four and six months old. The kitten's ovaries and uterus are removed under anesthesia and she sometimes must stay at the hospital overnight. Spaying does not make the cat lazy, fat, or stupid. Spaying often does keep her more social and friendly than she might have been.

Similarly, you should neuter a male kitten. Unneutered tomcats are propelled by their hormones to wander, to fight, and to spray urine all over your home. Scientists used to think spraying urine was a way of marking a territory. They thought each spray of urine on a tree trunk or rock was a KEEP OUT signal. But now researchers in animal behavior think spraying is more like a calling card, which states who the cat is and when he passed the spot. Since most cats in the wild are solitary creatures, these calling cards politely help them avoid the discomfort of meeting one another, or help to arrange meetings between male and female. A tom will mark his home regularly unless he is neutered as a kitten.

Unneutered tomcats can't be stopped from wandering or fighting. A tomcat regularly comes home from his prowls with split ears, nasty bite wounds, and bloody gashes. He may stay home to lick his wounds for a few days, but then he's off on the prowl again. Unneutered cats can also contract fatal contagious diseases while fighting with other male cats.

Neutering, also called castration, is less complicated than spaying. It can be done when the kitten is between four and six months. Neutering means that the vet removes the testicles, which are the glands that produce sperm and the hormone testosterone. The operation requires anesthesia, but the kitten can come home the same day.

fact

Most cats have no eyelashes, but they do have an inner eyelid, called a nictitating membrane, over each eye. This keeps the eye moist and clean. If the cat is sick, the membrane may close partially.

Housebreaking

When you read an ad for kittens in the paper that says "adorable kittens, housebroken," it's a good come-on but inaccurate. No one has to housebreak a kitten. Cats cover their feces and urine by instinct. As long as they are offered a place in which they can dig and bury, they will use it as a bathroom. Any kitten that is raised by its mother for the first few weeks of its life learns how to use a litter box from watching her. The only training involved once you get your new pet home is showing it where the litter box is and making sure the kitten can get to it.

It makes sense to keep your new kitten confined near the litter box at first or to show her where it is several times a day. Kittens tend to eliminate after eating, napping, and playing; those are good times to bring a kitten to the litter. Remember, a small kitten needs a box with lower sides than a grown cat does.

Both cats and dogs may express displeasure or depression by soiling on rugs and furniture. You should discuss any sudden change in your cat's toileting habits with your vet. The only cure I know of for purposeful soiling is to give the cat more love and attention no matter how mad you are. Cats aren't reasonable. You can lock a cat in a bathroom when you have to go out as a safety measure, but it's not guaranteed to help.

Irresistible Catnip

Catnip toys are always winners. Although the chemical in catnip that gives such pleasure to cats has been identified, no one yet knows why it makes cats behave so strangely. But it's no myth: Catnip excites cats and even fills them with ecstasy, causing them to roll, rub, and make noises of pleasure. You can buy catnip toys in pet stores or department stores or you can make them yourself.

Dried catnip is sold in many health-food stores. Cut a rectangular piece of cloth from any scrap that's around. Fold it in half and sew up two sides. Turn it inside out, stuff it with catnip, then turn in the edges of the third side and stitch the edges together. Use the illustrated pattern to make a catnip mouse toy for a special pet treat.

Even more fun for a cat than a catnip toy is a whole bed of catnip. Herb nurseries and many garden centers carry packets of catnip seeds during the spring. Choose a sunny place but one out of the way, since catnip is a member of the mint family and can be very invasive. The cat will find the catnip bed for itself and spend hours at a time rolling and sunning in it. If you have no yard or if you keep your cat confined to the house, plant a pot with catnip to keep your kitten happy. Late in the summer you can harvest the potted or outdoor catnip crop and dry it. Pull up the plants and hang them upside down in small bunches tied with string in any dry room. The dried catnip will give you a winter supply for toy stuffing.

Interestingly, not all cats get excited about catnip. Kittens aren't interested in it until they are about three months old, and approximately a third of all cats don't have any reaction to it at all. Scientists believe that there is a genetic component to catnip responsiveness.

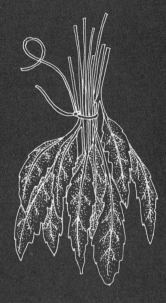

CATNIP
Hang catnip in small bunches to dry in the fall. Use it for stuffing cat toys.

TO MAKE A CATNIP MOUSE

1. Cut two mouse-shaped pieces from any scrap of cloth.

2. Cut two ear-shaped pieces from felt.

3. Cut a four-inch piece of string.

4. Lay both ears and the tail on one mouse-shaped piece as shown.

5. Lay the other mouse-shaped piece on top; pin in place; stitch along dotted line.

6. Turn inside out; stuff with dried catnip; sew up gap.

7. Draw on eyes with marking pen.

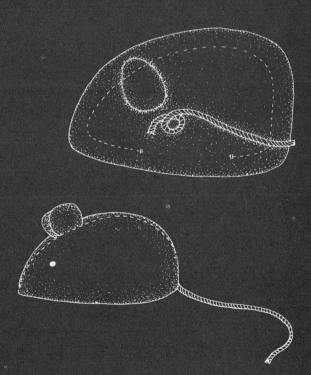

Kittens knead their mother's belly with their paws to help the milk flow. Some grown cats still do this when they are petted and feeling happy.

To get the smell of urine or feces out of rugs, clothing, or furniture, wash the area with a commercial preparation sold in pet stores. This is probably better than the traditional remedies like baking soda and vinegar.

Taming and Playing

To raise your eight-week-old kitten into a really friendly pet, you need to give it lots of affectionate attention. A puppy will demand love and attention even if you ignore it, but a kitten will probably be more independent. It will learn to ignore you if you ignore it; it will grow into an aloof cat. If that's what you want, fine. But if you want a cat that really seeks out your affection, you have to work at socializing.

Hold the kitten often so it gets used to the slight restraint of your hand. Let it sleep in your lap and on your bed too, as often as you can. Pet it while it's eating. Let other people handle and pet it too — guests, relatives, friends, and neighbors. The more people a kitten gets used to, the friendlier its attitude will be toward people in general. But a word of warning: A kitten is a baby and needs to be handled gently. If you're too rough, you'll teach it to be afraid of you. Also, all babies need plenty of sleep, so resist the temptation to wake up your kitten to play with you.

Play with your kitten at every opportunity. Crawl after and chase it and let it chase you back. Try the game called "kill the foot." It's played when you're in bed, dying to go to sleep but

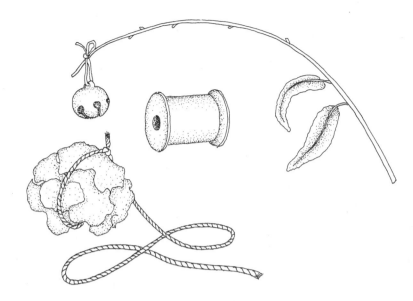

unable to keep a toe from twitching under the blanket. The kitten waits for the twitch, pounces, grabs, and bites. Another way to play this game is to lay a blanket or quilt on the floor. Tie a toy (spool, catnip mouse, baby's rattle) to a long string, put it under the quilt, and yank the string to make the toy move. As the kitten begins to attack the lump under the blanket, you can cleverly move it about by pulling the string from side to side.

You can persuade a kitten to play at hunting with any toy that jerks and rustles. A crumpled piece of paper or cellophane makes a great victim. Try tying a paper ball or a bell on to a long string; then pull the ball slowly and jerkily along, flicking it in the air sometimes for the kitten to leap at. Most kittens enjoy this game.

The branch of a weeping willow tree, sometimes called a willow whip, makes a super toy. Tie a paper ball or even a jingle bell to the end of the branch to provide the noise. As you start to play, you'll find the suppleness of the branch lets the toy bob and jump about, but you will have better control of the action than you would if you were using a string.

Any small thing that rolls is a good chasing toy. A wooden spool would be perfect, but most spools today aren't wooden, and some are Styrofoam, which will get chewed to bits in no time. Ping-pong balls are a kitten's favorite, although the small rubber balls with a jingle bell inside that are sold as cat toys are nice also. Rubber toys with a squeaker attached are fun for cats, but the squeaking can be annoying once a kitten gets over some initial caution and starts using it a lot. A little windup car is a marvelous toy too.

Still another way of involving yourself in your kitten's life is to set up adventures for it. Put it up on the kitchen counter and turn the water faucet on to a mere trickle. Put your finger in and out of the water until it can't stand your having all the

Kittens will play with nearly anything. You can make toys for them from bells, spools, and other common household objects.

fun and tries it too. The result will be a funny conflict between the kitten's curiosity about water and its dislike of having wet paws. Games like this one are not a way of teasing, since you are not frustrating it by interfering with what the kitten wants to do.

Open out a paper bag on the floor for your kitten to investigate. A cat in a bag can be pretty amusing. Pick up a cardboard carton at the grocery store and cut windows and doors into it with a sharp knife. A kitten can have fun exploring, and with the addition of a towel for a mattress, it might adopt the little house as its bed too.

A family we know got such a kick out of their kitten's exploring new structures that they now feed their cat on a constantly changing contraption out on the porch. One day their cat discovers he has to climb a ladder to his dinner, then the family adds a swinging door the cat has to get through, then a narrow catwalk, or a seesaw or a tunnel. If you have enough space and spare lumber, you can invent your own cat contraption. This kind of exploring not only keeps a cat amused and involved with you, but actually makes it more intelligent as well. Trickling water, paper bags, and swinging doors, after all, give even a kitten pause for thought.

Body Language

The result of all this playing and petting will soon be evident. The kitten will begin to follow you about the house. It will invite you to play by pouncing out from behind the drapes, stiff-legged and puffy-tailed. It will greet you with its tail up straight and its head bowed low, and rub against your ankles. It will leap into your lap and nuzzle you, contracting its eyes to mere slits as it purrs.

All of these attentions are, of course, in cat body language. Hair raising on body and tail is very common in mammals. It is meant to make the animal look very big to its enemies and scare them off. Even humans raise their hair. When you feel your scalp or the back of your neck prickling from getting "the creeps," you're experiencing a remnant of human attempts to bluff enemies by a false impression of size. Cats not only raise their fur but also hump their backs, stand on tiptoe, and turn sideways to the "enemy" to look as enormous as a smallish animal can.

Coming toward you with the tail held straight up, bowing, and rolling over on one side are all friendly greetings. The greetings started as kittens' signals to the mother cat to tell her that they needed to be cleaned and nursed. They are held on to as simple "Hello, friend" messages in adult cats.

I used to think cats rubbed people's ankles to annoy them. My own reflex makes me kick at anything that unexpectedly brushes my ankles. As it turns out, when a cat rubs its face against you or brushes its tail along you, it is marking you with a friendly-smell message. A cat has scent glands distributed along its lips, behind its ears, and at the base of the tail. When it leaves its scent on you, you are supposed to be appreciative.

Cats enjoy our smells too. Even a grown cat will sniff, nuzzle, and push its paws rhythmically against you, purring all the while, as though it were still a kitten nursing at its mother's belly.

The pupils of a cat's eyes express emotions. So do ours. When humans fall in love, they dilate their pupils at each other. Cats do the opposite. If a cat dilates its pupils at you, this means it's scared or angry. A contented, loving, purring cat contracts its pupils in pleasure.

Training

If a kitten has been socialized by plenty of petting and playing, it can be trained — slightly. People with a great deal of patience have successfully taught cats to do all sorts of amazing things — look at all those cat "actors" in the movies and television commercials. Cats are just as intelligent as dogs, but not as easy to train because they don't rely on the approval of their owners in the same way.

Start training by taking advantage of things kittens do naturally. Kittens naturally follow people they like, so some can be trained to follow you on command. When you see your kitten hold its tail straight up in the air and begin to follow you, encourage it in a high, catlike voice. You can reward it with tiny snacks along the way too, first indoors and then outside if you have a place to walk that is safe from both dogs and cars.

If your cat won't follow — and only some will, even with the most patient training — you can try leash training. Get a lightweight collar or a harness and let your kitten wear it around the house. Tie a crumpled-up piece of paper to a string two feet long and attach the other end of the string to the harness or collar when the kitten stops trying to scratch and rub it off. At first, just the slight weight of the paper will be enough for the kitten to get used to. If it plays with the paper, all the better. After the first couple of times, you can begin tugging gently at the string while you dangle the paper for it to grab. Call the kitten at the same time you tug. When the procedure

Nosing the hand that holds a yummy treat, Rumple the cat doesn't suspect that he is about to be taught to beg.

does not bother it anymore, substitute a light leash. Let the kitten drag it around and play with it. Then start the tugging and calling. After a few more days, try this outdoors for a few minutes at a time, encouraging the kitten with tidbits and calling it to follow you.

Cats have also been taught to beg for a snack and to fetch a toy. Hold a snack in your closed fist just over your kitten's nose and see if you can get it to sit up to sniff at your hand. Say "Beg" if it does. Repeated several times a day every single day, you may get to the point where you can just say "Beg" and your kitten will sit up. But you will probably always have to reward your cat with a snack to keep it doing the trick. Unlike dogs, cats don't do things just to please you.

Some kittens will chase a toy and carry it back to you, and some won't. A catnip mouse is more likely to become a good fetch toy than others. If your kitten brings a catnip mouse to you, take the mouse from the kitten, say "Fetch," and throw it for the cat to retrieve. The reward here is play rather than food, so even if your kitten learns what the word means, it will probably only fetch when it's in the mood for play.

For bad behavior like biting your hands or jumping on the dinner table, it's useful to teach your kitten the word *no*. Say "No" first, then flick the kitten on the nose with your finger. A mother cat disciplines a kitten with a cuff of her paw. Each time the bad behavior is repeated, say "No," then flick. Sooner or later the kitten will begin to pause when it hears the command "No." Then you can stop flicking and just use the word. Of course, you should never hit your kitten with your open hand or fist. For long-distance discipline, try squirting your kitten with a jet of water or startling it by shaking a can full of pebbles or coins. Any kind of discipline is only effective if it happens at the same instant as the offending behavior. Even one minute later is too late.

There are other habits cats have that can't be stopped by discipline. Scratching is one, chewing another. Kittens and cats rake their claws against rough surfaces like rugs, furniture, and drapes. Though the scratching probably does keep the tips of the claws in shape, sharpening and cleaning don't seem to be the only purposes. A wild male cat leaves his urine mark at the base of a tree, then reaches up as high as he can to claw at the bark. The scratch marks clearly tell other cats how big he is.

You can't stop a cat from scratching. Pet stores sell carpet-covered scratching posts that may or may not attract your cat's attention. Get one early in your kitten's life. When it claws at something it's not supposed to, try saying "No" and flicking its nose with your finger. Then take

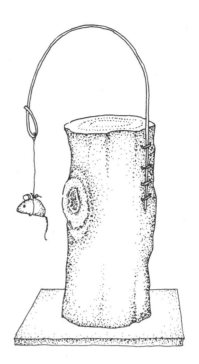

LOG SCRATCHING POST
Many cats prefer the rough texture of bark for scratching. You can attach a length of sturdy wire (such as from a coat hanger) as a springy support for hanging toys.

the kitten to the scratching post and show it what it is supposed to do by moving its front paws against the post. If the kitten won't use the post, it might prefer a rough log nailed in an upright position to a plywood stand.

It's a good idea to keep your cat's claws trimmed. Ask your vet to show you how to do this. If your cat is scratching at a good piece of furniture, you can try draping it with a blanket or towel for a while to discourage the use of that particular spot.

Some people declaw their cats to stop them from scratching furniture, but humane societies, pet advocates, and most vets discourage this practice. It is the equivalent of removing the tips of all your fingers — imagine how you'd feel if that happened to you. Declawed cats should not be allowed out outdoors since they are missing their major defensive weapon.

Most dogs chew things up only when they are puppies, but a few cats may do it all their lives. They favor wool, probably because it still smells like animal to them. Cats that hunt are seldom problem chewers. Nonhunting cats probably develop the habit out of a frustrated urge to chew up furry prey. Cats that don't get a chance to hunt should have chop bones or sparerib bones to chew on and toys made of real fur, like a rabbit-fur mitten or a bit of sheepskin. Some cats deprived of hunting animals attack and bite ankles instead; fur toys may help get rid of this bad habit too.

Some cats chew up houseplants. There's a reason for everything. Cats are frequent grass-eaters; deprived of grass, they chew up plants. You may wonder at that, since cats are supposed to be exclusively carnivores. So are dogs, but they also eat grass. Both wild dogs and wild cats eat the stomach of their prey, complete with whatever's in it. Their prey are mainly grass- and grain-eating animals like rodents, birds, and rabbits, whose stomachs are full of grass and grain. Neither cats nor dogs digest this roughage well. As you've probably noticed, they throw it up or let some of it pass all the way through their digestive system to come out in their droppings. It's possible the periodic eating of roughage helps keep the dog's or cat's digestive system clear of parasites, indigestible food, and hair it has swallowed while grooming itself.

Since there are dozens of plants that are poisonous to cats, an obvious solution to the problem of plant-eating house cats is to give them what they really want: grass. Fill a disposable aluminum pan with soil, sprinkle grass seed over it, rake in the seed lightly with a fork, and water it. If you keep the soil moist, the grass will sprout within a week or so and will grow well in a sunny window. Your cat will soon enough discover this treat all by itself and feel all the better for thinking it has discovered the best houseplant of all behind your back.

Grooming and Bathing

Grooming a cat is important. Cats shed a little hair all the time, and a lot when the seasons are changing from warm to cold or cold to warm. Long-haired cats can't get out their own tangles, and even with a short-haired cat the hair gets all over the furniture and upsets whoever has to do the vacuuming. A bristle brush is all you need to groom a short-haired cat, but a metal comb and blunt scissors may be necessary to cut and untangle mats in long-haired cats.

Start getting a kitten used to grooming right away. Keep the brush handy; wait until the kitten is drowsy and relaxed in your lap. Then use the brush as though it were your hand, gently stroking down the kitten's head, neck, back, and sides. Forget its belly for now; belly tickling sets off a clawing and wrestling response in any kitten. Stroke the brush the same way the fur lies. Brushing against the lay of the fur irritates cats and might cause them to bite the brush, a game that you may never be able to end.

A long-haired cat's fur will mat unless brushed and combed at least once a week. You will most likely need an adult's help with the job. Don't cut mats straight off, as that leaves temporary bald spots. Instead, use a blunt scissors to make several cuts straight into the mat (but not the skin!). Then gently comb the loose hair, a little at a time, from the mat. You can find special grooming tools for long-haired cats. Most cats will struggle or even try to bite or claw as you tug at the mats. When the job is finished, you might decide you never want to go through it again; your cat came to that conclusion long before you did and is probably hiding by now. When you can get hold of it again, trim the hair shorter under its legs, beneath its tail or wherever else the worst matting occurs. You will still have to groom, but the mats will take longer to form. Several short

Going to a Cat Show

Pedigreed cats are usually very expensive, and most people who are just looking for a pet will find a free kitten in the newspaper or go to the animal shelter. But it's a lot of fun to learn about different breeds of cats, and a good way to do that is to go to a cat show. You may be familiar with dog shows, but did you know that lots of people who breed cats like to show off their feline friends in much the same way?

As you might imagine, a cat show is quite different from a dog show. For one thing, you won't find the cats trotting around the ring on a leash with the judge watching from the middle. Instead, the cats in each class are brought to a judging area and put in cages near a table. The audience sits in front of the judging table to hear what the judge has to say about the individual cats. One by one, the judge brings each contestant to the table. He or she examines the cat to see how closely it conforms to the breed standard, which means what the perfect cat of that breed should look like. The judge looks at the coat for color and condition, at the shape of the head, the body proportions, and whatever else defines that particular breed. He or she might also put the cat on the table and "tease" it with a feathered toy to look for playfulness and alertness.

Your pet cat might object to such treatment and try to run away, but show cats are used to all the attention and don't seem to mind being examined, held up so the audience can see them, and carted around from judging table to judging table for different classes. When they're not being judged, the cats relax in the benching area where their owners set up cozy cages with all the amenities of home. Some of the cats you might see at a cat show will be familiar, like Siamese and Persian, but you might also see some more exotic breeds like the Sphinx, which has very large ears and very short fur. The Russian Blue has thick, smoky blue fur, while the Bengal is spotted like a wildcat. A Burmese looks like a cross between a Persian and a Siamese. Maine Coon cats can be nearly any color but all have luxuriant tails and furry feet. It's fun to go and see what breed your own beloved pet looks the most like.

grooming sessions will be easier on both of you than one long protracted struggle.

As your kitten begins to relax during grooming, gradually begin to include the belly hair. You can always take your cat to a professional groomer if necessary, but don't let a long-haired get terribly matted or it may need to be completely shaved — a sight you'd rather avoid!

Long-haired cats pick up a lot of fur on their tongues as they groom themselves. They swallow the hairs, which form into indigestible wads or strings in their stomachs and intestines. The hair wads cause vomiting (although vomiting doesn't always get up the wad) and sometimes sickness and even death. A good precaution is a half teaspoonful of mineral oil once a week, mixed directly into the cat's meal, or a commercial hairball prevention remedy available at pet stores and veterinary hospitals. The oil coats the wad and lets it slip out through the digestive system.

There are times when even the cleanest of cats needs a bath. The occasion may mark an interlude with a rotten rabbit, a close investigation of the oily underside of a car, or a naive attempt to approach a skunk. Cats don't like being wet, but if a bath is necessary, use lukewarm water (lukewarm means the same temperature as your skin — you can hardly feel the water because it is neither warmer nor cooler than your hand).

fact

Most cats have five toes on each front paw but only four toes on each back paw. In rare cases, cats have extra toes on one or more paws. This trait is genetic — passed down from one or both of the cat's parents.

Fill the kitchen sink with the lukewarm water. Put a piece of rug or towel in the bottom so your cat won't slip around and panic. Get someone else to hold it firmly while you do the bathing.

Gloves of some sort might be a good idea. Use a plastic pitcher to pour water over the cat, and baby soap, baby shampoo, or unperfumed adult soap for sudsing. Try not to get soap in its eyes. Rinse your cat very well so it doesn't feel itchy from soap afterward. Dry it with a regular bath towel.

The Older Cat

With good veterinary care and a safe, stable home, cats nowadays can live 20 or more years, although the average life span is 12 to 16 years. (Official records have cats living to age 36.) Like people, cats age at different rates. Some start acting like senior citizens at eight years old and others don't seem to age at all until they are well into their teens. Some cats go gray around their mouths and noses; all of them get thinner and their bones seem more prominent.

Other signs of aging are harder to spot. Your cat may eat less, drink more, and sleep long hours. It may seem stiff and unsteady. You may realize one day that your cat cannot hear you when you call it. You may notice that its fur is matted, because it can no longer reach far-away parts of its body to clean itself.

This is all part of a natural process. The most important thing is to make sure your cat is comfortable in its last days. Your cat will feel the cold and the heat more, so make sure its environment is kept at a moderate temperature. Because it can't groom itself, you can gently brush your cat to remove mats and tangles. Do everything you can to give your pet a peaceful life. Don't introduce a new cat or kitten (or dog!) to the home if your cat is very elderly. The arrival of a new cat in a household is a stressful event for the ones already there. If your home is going to have a temporary or permanent change (a big birthday party, some work on the house), let your elderly cat stay in a separate, safe, quiet room.

As your cat grows older, it may grow stiffer in the joints. If it has a favorite high spot, you can make it easier for your cat to reach by placing a ramp or a stepping-stone nearby. A beanbag makes a good bed for an older cat because it can mold to the cat's shape and keep it warm.

A Climbing Lesson

We once had a cat who regularly took her kittens hunting. We noticed that she would tempt the kittens into a rousing chase. Then she would leap onto a tree and climb quite high. The kittens would follow her, clawing their way up the trunk. She would let them come up only a foot or two, then she'd back down toward them, forcing them to the ground. Each time she let the kittens climb higher. Each time she forced them to back down. She was teaching those kittens how to get down out of a tree. When you think about it, it's perfectly logical. How in nature could a tree-climbing animal survive if it was not able to get down? There are no firemen in the wild.

That experience should have made me less naive during one episode with a cat. It was winter and bitter cold. The wind was howling and the trees creaking when we heard a bloodcurdling noise coming from the woods. There, high up in an oak tree, yowled a huge, lanky white cat.

Filled with admiration for his size and sympathy for his predicament, my children and I hoisted a long aluminum extension ladder a good two stories high. My eight-year-old volunteered to climb up and fetch the cat, who gratefully met him at the top of the ladder and melted into his arms.

We fed the cat and stroked him and decided we liked him a lot. We waited impatiently for my husband to get home so he could help us think up a name. He did. The name was Temporary.

That night, Temporary ate our hamster. The next morning he was gone. By afternoon he was one house down, again yowling in a tree. Rescued by our neighbors, he stayed at their house for a meal and a warm bed. Then he worked his way down the road to the next house-with-tall-tree-and-sympathetic-people. No doubt something had gone awry with his early socializing. But I'll bet you anything he knew darn well how to get down out of trees.

Pet Dogs

If you have decided you want a dog more than anything else in the whole world, you will find that the first step in getting one is to convince everyone else in your family that it is a wonderful idea. You will say, "Please, can I have a puppy?" and someone

will say, "Well, I don't know," or "Who will take it out?" or "Dogs are smelly." And then you will say, "I promise to take it out, I promise to give it a bath every week," and then someone will say again, "Well, I don't know."

Convincing everyone can take rather a long time — from months to several years. To get through it, try to remember that the adults are right: Dogs can be a nuisance and do require care; you will not do all the things you promised to do; adults will have to help you. Training and caring for a puppy is probably the hardest, most time-consuming job you have ever taken on. You will start fewer arguments and receive fewer lectures if you admit these facts in the first place and then try to settle on who can do what. The four main jobs are feeding, grooming, taking the dog out, and training it, all explained later on in the chapter.

Feeding is the easiest job, followed by taking the dog out and grooming. Training, including housebreaking, is by far the most difficult job of the dog owner. Plan to get a puppy as close to the beginning of summer as you can. In summer you will be home to do the work, and the pleasant weather will make housebreaking easier on you. Read through these sections (and get some other books about puppies) before making promises you may not be able to keep.

In deciding to adopt a dog, remember that you are making a commitment to an animal that will live 10 years or more. Dogs cannot be left alone for several days like a pet rodent or even for a day or two like a cat. They need to be fed and walked every single day. But if you take good care of your dog, your devotion will be returned and amply rewarded.

Pet Dogs at a glance

HOUSING EQUIPMENT: Food and water dishes. Brush, slicker, or metal comb. Flat or buckle collar and ID tag; leash, slip collar (for training). A crate if you are crate training your puppy and/or some kind of bed (can be made rather than purchased). A doghouse if your dog is going to spend a lot of time outdoors.

SPECIAL REQUIREMENTS: Annual veterinary examination and inoculations, probable worming, and flea and tick medication. All dogs, even purebred ones, should be altered (neutered or spayed) unless they are to be bred.

DIET: Dry puppy or dog chow; can be supplemented with canned food.

CARE: Feed and replenish water dish daily (more often for puppies). Walk at least twice a day (more often for puppies). Groom once a month to twice a week, depending on type of coat. Bathe as necessary. Take to veterinarian for checkup and booster shots once a year.

TAMABILITY: Must be housebroken. Need basic obedience training to be well behaved. Become exceptionally affectionate, devoted, and responsive. Can learn to play several games and perform tricks.

LIFE SPAN: Large dogs tend to have shorter life spans, perhaps 10 to 12 years. Smaller dogs usually live longer, up to 14 to 15 years.

SMALL DOG

MEDIUM DOG

LARGE DOG

Choosing a Puppy

Choosing a puppy that will make a good family pet means satisfying everyone at least a little. It's too much to expect different people to all love St. Bernards or chihuahuas. And people look at the same dog from different points of view too — yours may be size, your father's the food bill. You may look for cuteness, while your mother looks at the hair on the rug. Luckily, there are hundreds of breeds of dogs and millions of mongrels — all different. First decide the basics, like small, large, or in between. Then get everyone to contribute his or her reservations — small but not yappy; big but not bouncy; any size, as long as it doesn't shed! Try to build a composite picture, the kind the police make of suspects, then go to the dog books to see what fits the description. There are several good dog encyclopedias available at most libraries. Or you could log onto the American Kennel Club Web site, which tells about all 150 breeds currently recognized. In doing your research, you'll discover that there are large dogs that wouldn't think of bouncing, small dogs that wouldn't dream of yapping, and all sorts of wire-haired and woolly dogs that hardly shed at all.

By the way, you will find the descriptions quite exaggerated (they are written by the breeders). That's exactly why they are helpful. Each kind of dog breeder has a fantasy about what a "perfect" dog should be like; even if an individual dog falls short, the breed in general has probably been the breeder's wish come true. If the ideal dog described is about the same as yours, that's probably the breed you want.

Besides reading dog books, you may learn a lot by talking to dog owners — friends, a vet, breeders, and even strangers out walking their dogs in the morning. Any information you can get will help, not only in choosing a purebred dog but also in choosing a mongrel. For instance, ads in my local papers recently have advertised golden retriever crosses, Labrador crosses, spaniel crosses, collie crosses, poodle crosses, and terrier crosses. Often the owners know for sure if the mother is a purebred dog. They may or may not be sure about the father.

After you have an idea of what kind of dog you want, you are faced with choosing the puppy that will grow up to be a good pet. This is not the same as choosing an adorable puppy. All puppies are adorable. Not all puppies grow up to be good pets. My husband once lovingly hand-raised and -fed a boxer puppy whose mother could not give him enough milk. Once grown up, the dog fought other dogs and killed cats. He knocked people down when he greeted them. He pulled them down when he was on the leash. He had to be kept penned. He was not a pet.

Twice I took in stray puppies from the pound. Both grew up to chew rugs, steal food, and bark incessantly. When scolded they cringed and dribbled urine. They were pathetic dogs, but they were not good pets either. No one wants a dog that isn't well adjusted and trusting.

To be normal socially — well behaved and friendly with other dogs and humans — puppies need certain relationships during the early critical months of their lives, particularly from 6 to 14 weeks of age. They must be fed, nuzzled, and finally weaned and disciplined by their mothers. They must play with and sleep next to other puppies, and they must be handled and spoken to by humans. In practical terms, this means many puppies offered through pet stores are in some way socially damaged. Often they are weaned and taken from the mother and littermates at six weeks. They miss out on a critical period of socializing with other dogs and with humans. If you are tempted by a darling pet store puppy, ask a lot of hard questions about where the puppy came from (there are terrible places called puppy mills that produce dozens of puppies at a time with no regard for making them into good pets). Find out when the puppy was weaned and whether it has been handled frequently by the staff. Spend a lot of time with the puppy before you decide. Another thing to think about is that pet stores usually charge the highest prices.

If you don't particularly care about having a purebred dog, you can look in your newspaper for puppies at people's homes or you can go to your local animal shelter. Again, you should ask a lot of questions and really observe the puppy before making a decision. If you can examine the mother dog and you don't like the way she behaves, be wary of taking one of her pups.

Also, there are some tests you can do to learn more about a puppy's personality; see pages 235–236.

Unless you are an experienced dog owner, don't pick a puppy that is exceptionally fearful, overly aggressive, or very shy, no matter how cute it is. While many dogs can overcome a bad start in life with good, consistent training and lots of affection, you have to devote a lot of time to teaching a "damaged" dog to be confident and trusting. The same thing applies to older dogs. Many families have found wonderful companions at the pound, but you have to know what you're getting into. Sometimes the staff know quite a bit about a dog that is available for adoption, but sometimes they don't, and you could be in for an unpleasant surprise if your new pet turns out to be a barker, a furniture chewer, or a cat chaser.

This advice may be strong medicine for you to swallow. The puppies in the pound or in the pet store window look awfully cute and are certainly in need of homes. But a dog lives for 10 or even 15 years. If you are 11 years old now, you'll still have this dog when you're 21. You want to spend those years with a dog that is fun to be with. If your puppy starts off with a good personality and is raised responsibly, with consistent training and a predictable routine, you'll have a wonderful addition to your family.

If you have decided to buy a purebred dog and know which breed is right for you, contact the American Kennel Club for the names of breeders near you or look in local papers for ads. Many communities have free monthly newspapers that deal with animals — those are a great resource. You want to avoid breeders who raise litters out in the kennels. Ask if the pups were raised in the home and make sure you at least get to meet the mother. You should get to see the father as well, if he's on the premises.

You may want to decide before you look at puppies whether you want a male or female. There can be a difference in both personality and behavior, though individuals differ. Male dogs — called dogs — tend to wander more, especially if they are not neutered. Beagles and Labradors are famous for it, but other breeds wander too. Female dogs — called bitches — are more likely to stick to home territory. Dogs fight more frequently than bitches, though plenty of female dogs are aggressive with other dogs.

Male puppies should be neutered (have their testicles removed by a vet) by about six months, or whenever your vet recommends. A bitch that has not been spayed attracts a gang of dogs when she is in heat (ready to become pregnant) and can present you with an unexpected litter of puppies. Females generally have two heat cycles a year, during which they will drip blood on the carpet and may undergo some personality changes (usually not for the better). A female puppy should be spayed (have her

fact

When choosing a new puppy, look for the one that makes eye contact with you. If you're looking at a litter of puppies, the first to come toward you may be the most energetic, and perhaps not the best choice for your family.

The right dog can truly be your best friend.

ovaries and uterus removed by a vet) by the time she is six months old. It is a myth that she needs to go through her first heat cycle before being spayed. After the operation she will neither attract dogs nor become pregnant. It is not a serious operation and will not change her personality at all. Both spaying and neutering help prevent serious health problems in older dogs.

You can go look at a litter of puppies when they are about six weeks old and just getting weaned, but don't expect to take home your new friend until it is at least eight or even ten weeks old. The time it spends with its mother and littermates is very important. Go to look at several different litters if you can. Ask to see the mother and decide if you like her; her puppies might take after her. Ask what sort of mother she has been. If she hasn't had enough milk or if she's been reluctant to care for the puppies, it's a bad sign for their future temperament. Ask to handle the puppies so you can check them close up. A healthy puppy is plump, smells good, and has shiny eyes and thick fur. It should not have runny eyes, a cough, or smelly ears (the smell is from an ear infection). It should not be skinny or have scabs or a dusty, dull coat. These are not necessarily signs of fatal illnesses but they are signs of neglect. Neglect of any sort affects personality.

There are a few tests you can use to see which of the puppies are most sure of themselves. Sit on the floor. Puppies that are used to handling should come to you of their own accord. Puppies that hang back, whimper, keep their tails between their legs, or retreat when you reach for them are too shy to make good family pets. Notice if the puppies that do come to you stay upright as they approach or fall over on their backs, squirming and letting out a few drops of urine. That fall-over-and-wet signal means more fear than you want in a pup. When the pups are near you, slap the floor hard. The noise will probably startle the pups or even send them scrambling, but the bold, curious ones should recover quickly and come back to investigate the sound.

Get up and walk a short distance from the puppies. Lean over, clap your hands, and call to them in the high voice puppies seem to respond to best. They should come to you. Walk backward away from them. They should want to follow you. Again, the ones that don't show signs of following may not be sure of their relationship with humans.

Sit back now and watch the puppies at play or while they're fed. Watch for what could become annoying habits — the pup that whines a lot or yaps will usually be a whiner or a yapper when it grows up. A puppy that growls at the others at feeding time will growl and snap at you when you try to get things from its mouth.

After you have chosen a puppy, there are arrangements to make with the breeder. First, be sure the breeder understands you want that particular puppy, no other. When I was ten, my parents let me proudly go by myself to choose a pup from the litter my poodle had fathered. I knew how to choose puppies, so I chose the best one. When it came time to bring the puppy home,

The New Puppy

Before you pick up your puppy and bring it home, get ready all the things you'll need. You'll need a flat buckle collar with a name tag. Your puppy will outgrow the first collar you get, but it's better not to have one that's too big at first. Buy an inexpensive leash (it will get chewed) and two dishes, one for food and one for water. There are lots of dishes to choose from. Puppies have the least trouble with heavy dishes that don't slide along the floor. Buy a processed chow made especially for puppies and, if you choose to supplement your puppy's diet, canned dog meat.

Prepare the puppy's den and its bed. Call the vet to make an appointment for the puppy's checkup sometime during the first week.

If you have to travel in the car to pick up the puppy, get ready to deal with car sickness: Bring a roll of paper towels and a plastic bag. If the trip is long, stop often to let the puppy have a drink and go to the bathroom. Holding an unhappy puppy in your lap for anything over an hour can be tedious. A towel-lined carton may be helpful.

The bouncy puppy you chose will no doubt act bouncy until you get it in the car. At that point its eyes will roll, its tail will tuck, and it will tremble and whine. Happy as you are to get it in your arms at last, it is not about to

share your joy. A puppy that has just left its home, mother, brothers, and sisters is inconsolable. Expect a new puppy to be miserable for two days and a few more nights; expect it to cry and even howl most of the night; expect it to urinate frequently; expect it to eat poorly; expect it to have diarrhea; expect it to smell doggy. Not all these things may happen — maybe none of them will — but you should be prepared (and not worried or annoyed) if they do.

There are ways you can help your puppy through its first few nights. Make its sleeping place soft, even if it means adding a pillow under the towel. Warm the sleeping place by tucking a hot-water bottle under the towel. If it still cries all night, some people say it helps to wrap a ticking alarm clock in a towel near it — this is supposed to sound like its mother's heart beating nearby. (Make sure the alarm is turned off!)

It may help to bring the puppy from its den into your room to sleep next to you (not on the bed, or it will wet it). Keep it on the floor with plenty of newspaper, and on a leash so it can't get off the papers. Warning: Sleeping near you may be habit-forming for your puppy.

If your puppy has diarrhea that first week, feed it boiled rice and cooked hamburger instead of the diet recommended later in the chapter. If that doesn't work, call the vet and ask about giving a dose of Kaopectate. Don't ever withhold water. Keep fresh water out all the time.

If your puppy won't eat at all the first day or so, don't worry. Keep water available. At feeding time, offer only a spoonful of food and take it away if it's not eaten. Try again the next feeding time. We've never heard of a pup starving itself to death. It will eat by the third day for sure.

If the puppy dribbles urine when you approach, be as gentle as you can. Don't try to get it to play yet, and move slowly and talk quietly around it. For a bold puppy, the symptom should be temporary — a week or less. All puppies safeguard themselves when frightened by a belly-up-and-wet signal. In the wild, the act identifies them as babies that should not be hurt. Even the most vicious dog in the act of attacking is inhibited by this puppy urine signal. Watch a dogfight some day if you can stand it — the loser signals defeat by rolling belly up and, even though it's grown up, letting loose a couple of drops of urine. The attacker stops fighting and walks away.

A doggy smell is another sign of nervousness. No doubt dogs, with their far better noses, can read a whole paragraph in the message. For us it says one thing: scared pup. It, too, will pass.

During the first week, a new puppy will fare best with gentle petting, plenty of talking, and only as much playing as it initiates. Remember, puppies need lots of sleep, so resist the temptation to take your new pet all over the neighborhood with you until it gets used to its new home. Before the week is out, take your puppy to the vet for its checkup and shots. Besides the routine checkup outlined on the next pages, ask any questions that have come up (why the puppy threw up, scratches a lot, has bad breath). If no problems are found, it's polite to let the breeder know. If the vet does find problems, discuss the advisability of returning the pup.

the owner had sold him to someone else. No doubt he thought I was just a dumb kid and any pup would do.

Next, be sure you understand what the price, if there is one, includes. The price should include all vet bills for any reason (including possible ear cropping and tail docking) up to the time you bring the puppy home. You can't force a family blessed with mongrel pups to have the litter checked by a vet, but a purebred breeder should certainly have had the pups checked for worms and protected by the first shots in the inoculation series. The owner should be asked what shots remain so you understand what you will be responsible for.

With any puppy, make sure the breeder guarantees the puppy's health in writing. The piece of paper should give you one week after you take the dog home to get a checkup at the vet. If the vet finds a disease or defect, you should be able to return the pup in exchange for another or for your money back.

Last but not least, set a date to pick up the puppy. Then go home and get things ready.

Housing

Many families think they have solved the problems of the dog owner by deciding on an "outside" dog. For the small additional expense of a doghouse or a bed in the garage, they will be spared the nuisance of shedding, muddy feet, strewn garbage, and puddles on the rug. This is true, but they will not have a pet either. Outside dogs make good watchdogs and sporting dogs, but only the house dog really learns the ways of humans. A dog has to be around when you have an awful headache to understand there are times it should fade into the background. A dog has to be around when you have friends over to understand whom to welcome, whom to threaten. A

Your puppy's corner should have a box bed, hook, leash and collar, newspapers, and water dish.

dog has to be around all the members of a family most of the time to learn that different people like dogs different ways — bouncily or quietly, clownishly or with dignity. That sort of sensitivity is not learned in the doghouse.

Inside the house, a puppy needs a smaller place of its own where it can stay during most of the day while being housebroken. The reason that dogs can be housebroken at all is that they are housebroken in nature. Wild dogs do not mess their dens. The trouble is that your house is much bigger than a den and most puppies seem to think that while part of it is "home," most of it is "outside." This is an important trick in housebreaking: Give a puppy a small enough "den" of its own and it will try very hard not to soil it.

An old playpen makes a good den for a small puppy. A larger puppy might need a small bathroom to itself instead. Tying a puppy up works too, but only if you have some place that is far from table legs and chairs so the puppy doesn't get itself tangled up. A hook can be screwed into a wall about two feet from the floor to hold the leash. If your puppy chews its leash, you may have to tie it with a chain. If you're going to tie your dog, find a place near where people gather so it will not be lonely. Put layers of newspaper down everywhere the puppy can reach — not to "paper-train" it, which is an unnecessary step, but just so you can clean up easily.

A lot of dog trainers advocate crate training your puppy by providing it with a large crate for its den. When you're not home, the puppy can be left in the crate so it won't soil in the house or go crazy chewing things. There are many books and articles about crate training and they are worth reading. Whatever method you use to confine your puppy at first, you should never leave it alone for hours at a time.

Make the puppy a bed to go in its den or crate. For a small pup, cut down the side of a corrugated carton and line it with old towels to make the bed soft. For a larger dog, fold an old blanket or several towels into a bed. Place the bed to the rear of the den area — in the corner or against the wall. For now, this den is where you will feed the puppy and where you will leave its drinking water. You'll be confining it to the den whenever you can't keep an eye on it and whenever it wants to sleep.

As the puppy becomes housebroken, you can dispense with newspapers and leave only the dog's bed. By the time it is a year old, you may have to move the bed. Find a place that is not underfoot, but is on the fringe of family life. Even fast asleep, dogs like to be where they can have a sense of the comings and goings of their family.

Food and Water

You can feed a puppy dry chow moistened with water. Add a spoonful of canned dog food for flavor if you like. There are many brands of puppy chow that are specially formulated to contain all the basic nutrition — vitamins, minerals, carbohydrates, and protein — that growing dogs need. Unless your vet recommends it, supplementing the puppy chow with milk, extra calcium, extra meat, or other protein foods and powdered vitamins is not necessary and may be harmful.

Normally an eight-week-old puppy needs four meals a day, usually breakfast, lunch, afternoon snack, and dinner. If it barely touches one of these meals, it may need only three meals a day. By the time it is six months old it needs only two meals a day, and by the time it is a year old it needs only one meal a day. All these meals can be identical — chow, moistened with water and flavored with a little canned meat. The younger the dog, the moister the food should be. As it grows, it will begin to prefer its food crunchy rather than soggy.

There are all sorts of charts and measurements that tell you how much food to feed your puppy at each meal, but there's no reason this need be so complicated. Start out with a half cup

fact

Dogs will let you know if they are hungry, but it is harder to tell if they are thirsty. Make sure that fresh water is available to your puppy at all times of day. Rinse out your dog's water bowl every time you refill it, and wash it regularly.

As a safety measure, train your dog from puppyhood not to guard its food. You should be able to touch the dog while it's eating, move its bowl, and even take its food away without the dog becoming upset.

for a little puppy, a cup for a bigger one. Then let the dog judge the quantity for you. If it doesn't finish its meal, you're offering too much food. If it finishes the food, try more at the next meal. If it finishes its meal every time and is getting fat, you've gotten a dog with poor judgment and you'll have to cut down on meals. A dog is too fat when it's hard to feel any ribs or backbone, and too skinny when ribs and backbone feel sharp under the skin. Some puppies may be so active they stay skinny no matter how much they eat. They begin to put on weight at about a year old. A puppy puts on weight and loses weight quickly, so you won't have to wait long for signs that quantities need adjusting.

When your dog is a year and a half old, it can change chows from puppy to dog. An adult dog does not need any food other than the chow. It contains everything a dog needs, and it is the cheapest way to feed your dog, too. Dry chow is important for another reason: It's crunchy, and as the dog chews it, its teeth are scraped clean. A dog fed only on soft foods or on chow softened by too much liquid can develop bad tooth decay. However, there are two problems with chow. One, people think chow is boring and feel sorry for the dog. Two, dogs think chow is boring and feel sorry for themselves. You can try switching brands, or keep flavoring the chow with canned meat, or start spicing it up with healthy table scraps and gravy. Some dogs like leftover vegetables, too. But no matter how you fancy up the chow to make it delicious, remember that it should still be the basic diet. Dogs in the wild eat the same diet all the time, and over the ages their digestive systems became accustomed to not expecting surprises. If you change a dog's diet, its surprised intestines will give it diarrhea.

When you feed your dog, take away its dish as soon as it wanders off. It's best to train a dog not to eat bit by bit, since it might spend half the day growling at anyone who comes near its leftovers. By the way, if your pup does growl at you while it is eating, grab it by the scruff of its neck and give it a good shake while saying "No!" in a firm voice. Then start staying with it while it eats; touch the dog, take food away, give it back, and in general make it perfectly clear that dinner is not private. Get your puppy used to taking food gently from your fingers as well. Dogs that protect their food are dangerous to people.

Dogs learn how to inform you that they are hungry, but it is less easy to notice when they are thirsty. Keep water available to your puppy day and night, changing it regularly. As a puppy gets bigger, it will undoubtedly find its own supply of water in the toilet. Whether you allow the dog to drink from the toilet is up to you and your family; it won't hurt the dog.

Vets prefer that puppies not have bones to chew. They advise any of the nylon or rawhide substitutes sold in pet stores. If you still wish to offer your pup a bone, vets suggest only beef shin or knuckle bones (sometimes called marrow bones), which do not splinter readily.

Housebreaking

Often the first annoyance with a new puppy is the first puddle on the living room rug. Confining a puppy to its den or crate when you can't watch it is the best way to avoid messed-up rugs and floors. It is also the best way to start housebreaking. When the newspapers get wet or dirty, just fold them up, put them in a plastic bag, and put the plastic bag in an outside garbage pail. Spread several layers of fresh newspaper in the puppy's den.

When the puppy wets or messes off its paper, clean it up right away. Soak up puddles with paper towels. If the puddle is on the bare floor, wipe the spot with a damp floor sponge. If it is on a rug or fabric, soak the spot with a cup of water to which a quarter of a cup of white vinegar has been added. The vinegar prevents bleaching. Let the spot soak for a few minutes, then wipe again with paper towels. Pick up bowel movements with paper towels, and clean the spot with a damp sponge and a very little bit of liquid detergent. Diarrhea and vomit can be scooped up with an old dustpan and paper towels. The spot will need a good scrubbing; use rug shampoo if it is on carpeting, detergent if it is on bare floor. You can also buy cleaners and sprays that are specially formulated to get rid of pet stains and odors.

The best way to avoid any messes in the house, besides confining a young puppy to its den for much of the day, is to take your puppy out frequently. You can expect a puppy to need to go each time it wakes up from a nap; after every meal; very early in the morning, probably before you usually get up; and in general, every half hour all day long.

If your puppy begins to hold its head low to the ground and to circle, take it outside for a pee break.

Take your puppy outside the moment it stirs in the morning. It will have to be on the leash unless you live very far from roads or unless you have a fenced yard. Puppies have no sense at all about cars. If your puppy has already wet and messed before you get up, get an alarm clock and get up earlier. Carry the dog outside or it will let loose before you get to the door. If you possibly can, take your puppy out when it wakes up from every nap, too. After a successful half hour of play-without-mess, either take it out again or take it to its den.

When you let a new puppy loose in the house, you'll have to watch it every minute. If you catch it in the act of soiling or puddling, you can scold it by grabbing the scruff of its neck and giving it a good shake before you take it right outside. Forget anything you've heard about rolled-up newspapers, rubbing its nose in the mess, and so on. By the time you get the newspaper and roll it up and chase the pup around the house, it's not going to remember what you're scolding it about. Noses in messes make no sense at all to a dog. In fact, there's no proof that scolding a dog for messing works unless you catch it while it's making the mess. Dogs have very short memories and smaller vocabularies than a lot of people think, so yelling at your puppy after it makes a mistake just frightens and confuses it.

Try to notice how your puppy behaves just before it soils so you can get it outside in time. Some puppies pant as a sign of discomfort, some just wander off to find a private place. Almost all hold their heads low to the ground and circle a bit just before they go to the bathroom.

You can see that housebreaking is difficult. But if you confine your dog to its den when you are not with it and watch it to prevent accidents when you are, and take it out very often so it does most of its business outdoors, you will notice progress. Nature is on your side too. As your puppy grows, it has to urinate less often. And as you get to know the dog, you will be able to notice signs that it is about to go off and puddle or mess.

The biggest problem with housebreaking is that the dog often knows what's expected of it before its people understand the signals. For instance, if you find your dog has chosen a private place in the house to mess — like in an upstairs bathroom or basement laundry room — but not in the more public parts of the house like the living room and kitchen — then your dog is housebroken but you are not. The poor cuss is looking for the most "outside" place inside the house. But somehow you're failing to notice the signs that show it needs to go and you're not taking it out.

When and if you get to this stage, begin by keeping all the doors to those rooms shut so the dog can't use them as private bathrooms. And stop letting the dog loose so often. Then try to figure out what times of day you're missing the boat. Often it's during the night — are you taking your pup out for the last time late enough? Are you getting it out early enough in the morning? Have you stopped confining it during the night too soon? If it happens after the pup's after-meal walk, wait longer to walk it next time it eats. Don't bring your puppy back from its walk until it has done something.

Watch more carefully for "having-to-go" signs — walking off from you, sniffing the floor, circling around, disappearing into the next room.

No matter how hard you are working at housebreaking (and you have to be very patient with this stage of development), you can't possibly expect a dog to be housebroken until four months, and not reliably so until six months. Many dogs have lapses up until they are 10 months; this is especially true for small dogs, which can take a long time to become trustworthy.

By the time a puppy is six months old, it may get along on four walks a day — first thing in the morning, at noontime, at about three or four o'clock in the afternoon, and at about nine o'clock at night. Stick with that leash — even among adult dogs, the number one cause of death is car accidents.

Grooming

Grooming means brushing and/or combing a dog. Short-haired dogs like dachshunds need a good brisk brushing once a week to remove dust and loose hair. Woolly dogs that tangle badly — poodles, English sheepdogs — are often groomed twice a week. For other dogs, use your judgment. As long as your dog's coat looks and feels fine, don't bother. If a coat gets full of burrs or begins to tangle, it's time to groom. If a dog is shedding, groom often.

Get your dog used to grooming, if only for two minutes at a time, while it's still a baby. An older dog isn't going to like this new procedure suddenly sprung on it. Just give your pup a minute or so of brushing every once in a while in your lap as a playful introduction.

Puppies may sound like they're being murdered when you first try to brush them. Even a calm adult dog will startle and yip and begin to struggle when you pull a tangle too hard when you get to the parts that are tender — muzzle, ears, tail, belly, and feet. When a puppy yips and starts to scramble away or bite the brush, most people get mad, yell back, and hit. Don't. Instead, when the puppy first complains, act as though it wasn't you that hurt it. Say, "Oh, you poor thing, did the brush get you? Well, you good, good dog, I'll take care of you." Pat your dog as you act sorry for it and then start brushing again. Your puppy will think that you are trying hard to protect it in a situation fate has brought about.

Dogs, especially puppies, will chew on the hand that brushes them. And if they tire of that

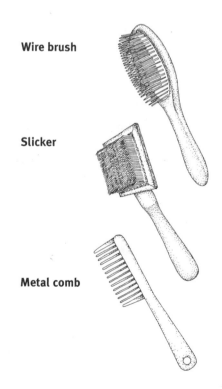

Wire brush

Slicker

Metal comb

game, they will simply leave. The trick to getting a dog brushed is to rig things so it can't turn its head and can't walk away. The requirements are met with a leash, a slip collar, and two people to do the job instead of one. You should also train your dog to "stay" when you need to groom it.

First, put a slip collar and a leash on the dog. The slip collar, which tightens on the dog's neck, will help you control it. If it's small, lift it up onto a steady table (the dog will get panicky if the table jiggles or rocks). If it's big, leave it on the floor — or you could do the job outdoors. Move the collar up until it's just behind the dog's ears. Get the second person to hold the leash straight up, with just a little pressure. This keeps the dog's head from turning and holds up its front end. It does not hold up its rear end. To do that, the person who is brushing has to keep one hand up under the dog's belly just in front of its back legs.

There are several kinds of brushes and combs sold for dogs. Which kind you get depends on the kind of dog you have. A slicker is a brush made of thin, stiff wires set into a rubber base. Each wire is bent backwards at its tip so it can grab hold of loose hair and pull it out. Use slickers for dogs like collies when they are shedding their undercoat in the spring; or poodles, to get the mats and tangles out of their fur; or Scotties, whose wiry coat is too thick for an ordinary bristle brush to get through. Slickers come in small to large sizes, just like the dogs they are intended for.

The next most useful brush is made of natural bristles, wire bristles, and sometimes both. Some have handles and some don't. You might find one with a handle easier to use. This kind of brush is good for short-haired dogs like dachshunds and beagles, which just need a vigorous brushing to get out loose hair and dirt. It is also fine for long-haired dogs if their coats are not very thick — an Irish setter, for example, or a cocker spaniel.

Brush your dog often, starting when it's a puppy. If your dog has very shaggy or silky fur, it might make sense to have its coat trimmed regularly by a professional groomer.

Most dogs don't need combs. The ones that do — poodles, woolly sheepdogs, and really long-haired dogs like the Maltese and Yorkshire terriers — will be best off with one of those steel combs that are rather sharp so that you can get all the way down to the skin. Metal combs can be bought with fine or more widely spaced teeth, depending on the coarseness of a dog's coat. This type of dog often benefits from the attentions of a professional groomer in between routine brushing from you.

Before you start grooming, get out a paper bag to empty hair into as it accumulates in the comb or brush. Start brushing or combing along your pup's back and sides, where it won't mind it much. Work down each leg. Save the tender areas — ears, belly, inside the legs, and face — until last.

As you work, feel along the dog's skin. You may find burrs. Pull apart the hair around them, then comb them out. You may feel a fingertip-sized lump, a tick filled with blood. Part the fur, take a look, and, if it is a swollen, pinkish brown tick, pull it out and get rid of it down the toilet. Dark gritty crumbs down near a dog's skin are flea droppings. Even if you can't find the fast-moving fleas themselves, a treatment with dog flea powder or dog flea spray is in order. Follow the directions on the container. (Don't use flea collars. They work, but too many dogs are allergic to them and develop a nasty rash on their

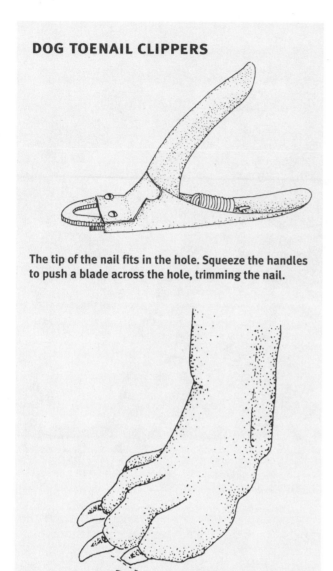

DOG TOENAIL CLIPPERS

The tip of the nail fits in the hole. Squeeze the handles to push a blade across the hole, trimming the nail.

Clip off the tip of each nail below the dark vein.

noticeable, cut the mat straight down toward the dog's skin in several places, then tease out the loosened hair with a metal comb. It may still look a bit funny but it won't be a bald spot.

If you find any other skin problems — rashy areas, sores, lumps, or cuts — it's best to ask the vet about them.

When the brushing is finished, vacuum up the hair from floor and table, put your clothes in the laundry, and, if you itch, take a shower.

The last task of grooming is toenail clipping. Dogs that walk on concrete pavements or scramble over rocks wear down their toenails by themselves. But unfortunately, dogs with dewclaws (the extra claw up high on the foot) always need the dewclaw trimmed, and dogs that walk mostly on grass need all their nails taken care of.

When a dog's toenails *clackety-clack* across the floor, they are too long. When a dewclaw begins to curve inward like the letter C, it is too long. Dewclaws can curve themselves right into the dog's skin. Long toenails push the dog's toes up and back, eventually causing sores and deformed feet.

Pet stores sell special clippers made for clipping dog toenails. You hold the dog's foot, slip the clippers over the first eighth of an inch of nail (below where you can see the vein, if your dog's nails are light in color), and snip. Many dogs don't mind the procedure. Other dogs scream, bite, jerk their paw away, and escape. Their fear may be caused by having a paw held firmly, because the cutting itself doesn't hurt. You can train your dog to hold still if you are patient and offer plenty of rewards for good behavior. I know someone whose dog always gets little bits of frankfurter during a manicure — she doesn't mind having her toenails clipped at all! If your dog makes a really big fuss, you will have to have the clipping done by a professional dog groomer or a vet.

neck. Your vet might recommend a monthly treatment with flea medication that is applied between the shoulders.)

Big lumps of fur are called mats. Look for mats between the toes, under the legs, and under the tail especially. If a mat isn't in a visible area, you can just cut it off with blunt scissors (baby nail scissors work well). If the bare spot would be

Bathing

Puppies, particularly new ones, may get messier and smellier than grown dogs. Because they have always been covered with fur, dogs have never had to develop the tough skin most humans have. Most of us can get soap on our skin every day without itching — a dog can't. Luckily for grown dogs, they don't need baths often, and some dogs don't need baths ever. Besides smelly pups, the kinds of dogs that need baths most often are white ones that live in sooty cities, dogs like Airedales with oily coats that hold on to dirt so that brushing doesn't clean them, and dogs with woolly hair that also doesn't shed dirt well. Some dogs have a doggy smell and need a bath once a month just for that reason. Too much bathing dries out the skin and can cause itching and irritation.

Use plain soap to wash a dog or a puppy. The plainest soaps are baby soaps and unscented adult soaps. Baby shampoo or castile shampoo is gentle too, or look for a special dog shampoo at the grocery or drugstore. Fill a bathtub or sink with warm water. Put an old towel or a rubber mat in the bottom so the dog won't slip and panic during the bath. Get a plastic pitcher or freezer container to pour water from. Put a slip collar and leash on your dog and find somebody who will hold the leash. If your dog is pretty big, get just about completely undressed because your clothes will get very wet. Lift up your dog by holding it under its chest and its rear end, and put it gently into the tub or sink. If you bathe your dog in the tub, sit on the edge of it with your feet inside; if in the sink, stand on a stool if you need to. Whoever is holding the leash should hold it straight over the dog's head and keep pressure on it all the time to discourage the dog from taking a step anywhere.

Start pouring water over your dog's head and then soaping all around its neck, ears, and the top of its head, avoiding the eyes. It won't like this, but neither will any fleas that happen to be around. If you don't wash your dog's head first, the fleas will scurry up its neck and into its ears to ride out the storm and will emerge happily after the bath is over.

Your dog will absolutely hate having its muzzle washed, and since it will leap and struggle, save washing this for last to keep most of the bath as calm as possible. After its head and neck are soaped, rinse carefully and try not to get any soap in your dog's eyes. Then pour water over its body and get that washed. Lift its legs one at a time to wash them. With a large dog, you'll find that you're all the way in the tub by this time. That's why you took your clothes off.

You will find the bathwater is now gray, scummy, and disgusting. It is obviously not clean enough to use for a good rinsing, so pull the plug and get rid of the water.

fact

Grown dogs don't need baths often, and some don't ever need them. But puppies, white dogs, and dogs with oily or woolly coats do need regular baths. Use warm — not hot — water and a plain, non-perfumed soap or a dog shampoo.

When the weather is warm, you can bathe your dog outside. It will certainly cut down on the mess!

Rinsing well is harder than washing well. There are several ways to accomplish it. In the kitchen sink, a hand spray is best if you have one. In the bathtub, keep the drain open, turn on the faucet, and just use your plastic pitcher to rinse the dog. This works for small dogs, but it takes rather a long time for larger ones and it's awfully difficult to rinse bellies that way anyhow. What seems to work best is to rinse as well as you can with the pitcher and then refill the tub or sink and rinse again, splashing water up onto the dog's belly and chest. We wouldn't recommend a shower; it terrifies most dogs and seldom works.

When the rinsing is finished, let the water out. Pull the shower curtain shut, shield the dog with a towel, and step out of the way, because sooner or later your dog will shake, and water will go flying everywhere. The dog should still be on the leash, and whoever is holding it should be as shielded as possible — or at least prepared to get wet. Let the dog shake a few times before proceeding. When the dog has gotten the worst of the water off, dry it with a large towel, not forgetting to dry its feet. It will still be wet, of course, but now when you at last let it out of the tub or sink, it won't soak the room from floor to ceiling. Dry it again with another towel before you let it out into the rest of the house.

No dog will consider your drying job adequate. The moment you let it free, it will scramble in circles like a maniac, rubbing its face along carpets and furniture, rolling and kicking and acting crazy. If mayhem ensues and somebody yells to let that crazy dog out, it will continue to dry itself in the dirt and you may find that you should have kept that leash on longer. (Never let a damp dog outside on a chilly day; the dampness combined with the chill will make the dog *very* cold.)

There is one more step to bathing a dog, and that is cleanup. Be sure not to forget it.

Illnesses and the Vet

During a puppy's first few months, it needs one or more inoculations to protect it from distemper, rabies, and other serious or fatal dog diseases. Vets differ as to the sort of vaccines they use, so the number and frequency of shots differ too. Every dog needs a single rabies shot at six months. And any puppy almost undoubtedly needs a deworming. Depending on the breed of dog and your own preferences, the puppy may need several visits to the veterinarian for procedures like ear cropping, neutering or spaying, and dewclaw removal. During the rest of its life, it will need booster shots annually. Count on at least another visit each year for cuts, broken bones, internal problems, infected ears, rashes and assorted illnesses. If you are the one taking the dog to the vet, it will help you to understand what is expected of you, what the doctor is doing, and why.

Always make vet appointments in advance, unless it's an emergency and you must bring your pet in immediately. Your dog must be on a leash, and should not be brought up to meet any other dog (some are sick; some are hurt and in a nasty mood about it; most are scared and don't want anyone to bother them).

If you have a new puppy, bring in a stool (bowel movement) sample on the first visit so it can be checked for the roundworms almost every puppy gets. The sample can be small — put it in an empty jar or just in a plastic sandwich bag.

The breeder should have given you inoculation information: what vaccine was used, the date it was given, and when any further shots are needed. Give this information to the vet.

In an ordinary examination, the veterinarian takes the dog's temperature — rectally, with an ordinary rectal thermometer. The normal temperature of a dog is 101 degrees. Watch how it's

A sick dog might be very quiet and unresponsive, even about going for a walk.

needle is small and barely hurts. Many dogs don't notice it.

If you have brought your dog in because you think it is sick, the doctor will ask you questions. He'll ask if the dog has been eating well and if its bowel movements have been normal; if the dog is active or has been acting unusually quiet; when you first noticed something was wrong and what you noticed.

Your dog will obviously need medical treatment for gaping wounds, collapse, or convulsions. Less obvious symptoms that require medical attention include:

Unresponsiveness. The dog stays in one place, doesn't want to move, may wag its tail quietly when you call to it but doesn't leap up enthusiastically. Often people wait a day or so to see if anything more specific develops. Don't. Dogs can be very sick and complain little. Unresponsiveness is a frequent sign of being very sick.

Smelly ears or lots of head shaking. That means the dog's ears hurt or itch and something is wrong.

Constant scratching. This may mean fleas, dry skin, or an allergy, but find out.

Chewing and licking at one particular spot. Look under the fur — you may see a wound you didn't know was there or a patch of eczema that needs treatment.

Loss of weight in spite of normal eating. This can be a sign of worms, or of something worse.

Vomiting. This is only unusual if it's over a period of hours, since dogs normally vomit up anything that isn't digestible.

Diarrhea. Dogs get diarrhea from almost any change in diet and often from any change in routine, like when you go on vacation or even on a long car ride. It is worrisome only if it occurs over a period of days or if you see blood in the diarrhea

done. You may need to check it yourself someday if your dog is acting sick. Then the doctor checks your dog's abdomen. He puts his hands on both sides and presses them up to feel if the dog's belly is tense (which would mean it hurts), if there are any lumps that should not be there, and if the liver or kidneys are too large or are sore. He'll check the puppy's eyes and inside its ears, and will run his hands over the dog's bones and joints, pressing down hard on its rear end to see if its legs are strong. He'll check teeth and gums and listen to your dog's heart. And if the puppy needs any inoculations, the vet will give the shot. Most shots are given subcutaneously, which means the needle is stuck inside a fold of skin on the dog's shoulder or rump. The

or worms or bits of mucus. Don't worry about weird colors appearing. They are not unusual.

Medical attention is also necessary if your dog refuses to eat for several days; cries in pain, even if you can't see where it hurts; cries when you touch it somewhere; or limps.

Puppies aren't usually afraid of the vet but they dislike being left alone to go through strange and painful things. So try to stay with your pet.

If your dog has been sick and hospitalized, it may still need medical treatment after being released. Ask the vet to demonstrate to you exactly how to care properly for the dog. There's a special way to give dogs pills; liquid medicines; and ear, eye, and wound medications. Most of the methods are easy, but frankly, giving pills only looks easy. If you can't do it the way the doctor does, stick the pill into the middle of a small piece of liverwurst rolled into a ball and give it to your dog for a snack.

Taming and Playing

A new puppy graduates from being pathetic to being a pain in the neck in about one week. The puppy that wouldn't eat at all is into the garbage pail. The puppy that cried those first nights now leaps at you and rips your clothes. The puppy that would not budge from behind the couch is all over the house now, chewing as it goes.

All this is bad behavior. If you think stealing, biting, leaping, and destroying belongings are just high jinks that the pup will outgrow, you'll wait forever while your puppy grows into an obnoxious dog.

A mother wolf or wild dog plays with her pups, but she doesn't stand for nonsense. When she's fed up with them, she gives a warning growl — like a low-voiced NO. When they still bother her, she cuffs them — like a slap against the nose. When you discipline your puppy with a growl or

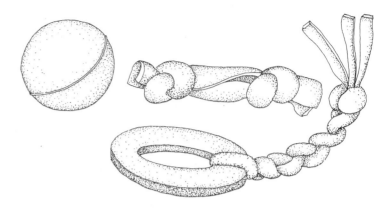

Dogs love anything they can chew or chase after.

cuff, just as when you let it kiss your ear or play its puppy games, you are speaking its own language. The better you learn your puppy's language, the better it will one day learn yours. The longer you wait, the worse it gets. Tap (or even slap) a pup with the flat of your hand right up under its chin when it bites you or your clothing. Say "No" in a deep voice and loud enough to startle. Do it every time. If the puppy jumps on you, be just as stern. For a big puppy, bring your knee up against its chest when it jumps. For a small puppy, slap your hand against its nose.

Put the garbage pail up on a counter while the puppy's around, and keep an eye on your sandwich. Keep your shoes, socks, hats, underpants, and toys where they belong. You're not just saving your family's temper with these precautions; puppies chew up and swallow just about anything — splintery chicken bones, sharp plastic objects, electrical wires, and even medicines of all sorts. An Airedale puppy of ours once ate a whole bottle of decongestant pills similar in effect to pep pills. The poor critter chased hallucinated rabbits around the house for 24 hours, in spite of a sedative injection that was supposed to knock him out. I know of another puppy that ate a pincushion, including the pins, and had to have two surgeries to remove them.

You have to exercise a certain balance in discipline. If you hit and scream at a dog all day, you're going to make a wreck of both of you. One growled "No!" when you catch it doing something is all it takes. Instantly, put on a happy smile and act like nothing happened. Pet your pup, or invite it to play. This is not being phony. It just takes account of the fact that puppies have short memories of past crimes, even five minutes past.

Try to substitute a legitimate game for a criminal action. For the pup that tugs and rips your clothes, play tug-of-war. You can buy rubber and rawhide tugging toys at pet stores, or you can knot an old rag or a piece of rope instead. Vicious as they act, most puppies aren't as strong as you, so let the dog do the pulling until you get the feel of how hard it can pull. Then pull back. This can turn into a tussle for dominance, so when you play this game, make sure the puppy learns that you get to end up with the toy. Teach it to let go on command and reward it with a treat or some more playtime.

Nature prepared pups to chew a lot so they would get enough to eat. The fact that we invented tender tidbits instead of tougher meals doesn't change the instinct. For the dog that chews everything up, provide plenty of things to chew. Rawhide bones, available at pet stores, are fine. They get nice and gushy as the dog works at them. Nylon bones are chewy in a different way. Soup bones or marrow bones, bought at supermarkets or gotten free from friendly butchers, are for hard, serious chewing. Any other kind of bone splinters and is dangerous.

For puppies that chase and pounce on you too much, try weaning them to a good game of ball. The best balls for dogs are solid, hard rubber (not sponge rubber). They don't get chewed up and swallowed. Pet stores carry solid rubber balls and other good throwing toys.

From these descriptions it sounds as though you are substituting human games for a puppy's play. Not at all. It is you who are learning to play dog. For instance, when your puppy greets you as you come home, it jumps on you. If you lean down to it, it licks your mouth — or rather your muzzle. Why? Wild dogs and wolves don't carry home prey to their young like wild cats do. Instead they regurgitate freshly swallowed meat for the pups to eat. That muzzle licking is a begging gesture — the way a pup gets an adult to regurgitate food. You don't have to allow the jumping, you don't have to get your mouth licked, and you certainly don't have to throw up. But you'll find if you turn your face to the side as you lean down to greet your puppy, it will be delighted to lick your ear: This feels good, and you're learning to play dog.

When your puppy's in the mood for play, it may let you know by bouncing about, bowing, and pawing at you. In adult wild dogs, this is an invitation not to play but to hunt. For 10 minutes or more, the hunters bow to one another, paw, muzzle-lick, bounce, and make short dashes away, only to start the procedure all over again. It's like a pep rally before a football game. Each dog is encouraged by the enthusiasm of the others until, when the cheering has reached a peak, the dashes become a headlong run and the dogs are off to the hunt. Try bowing, pawing, and making short dashes yourself. Your puppy will understand the invitation.

Puppy play is itself a training ground for the moves of hunting. The crouch, with rear end wiggling, gets the pup set to move whichever way the rabbit (or the ball) goes. Then comes the chase, the pounce, the grab. Try the same game with something limp like a knotted rag and you'll understand the tug-of-war game too. After the grab, the rag is shaken — if it were a rabbit, that

Preventing Bad Habits

Bad habits should be stopped when they start, not after everyone is having temper tantrums about "that darn dog." One of the best ways to stop unwanted behaviors is to teach acceptable ones instead. All dogs need to know how to sit and stay on command and to come when they are called. Another very useful ability is a "long down," in which the dog learns to lie quietly until released. If your dog knows these basic rules, you can ask for (and reward) good behavior instead of just yelling about the bad habits.

Jumping on people. Every single time your puppy jumps up on you, push it down and make it sit. If it's big, bring your knee up into its chest. If it's small, bring the palm of your hand up under its snout. Do both hard enough to get a whimper out of your dog. If you fool around with jumping games, there's no way in the world that pup is going to figure out that while you like jumping, other people may not. If you teach your pup to sit quietly before you greet it, you will short-circuit a lot of excited greeting behavior. Once the dog is sitting, make sure you reward it with lavish praise and attention.

Jumping on furniture. Decide early where the dog is allowed to go in the house and then be consistent about removing it from forbidden spots with a firm NO! or OFF! If it's allowed on your bed or only on the old sofa but not the new one, a dog is smart enough to learn there is a piece of furniture it can sleep on and others it is never to go on. What it can't learn is that sometimes you're in a good mood and will let it on the couch and sometimes company's coming and you won't. Since dogs long for soft beds, get a dog pillow or bed for your dog to sleep on and keep it where it most enjoys sleeping.

Taking food. Puppies are not sneaky about stealing food. They come right up to you and grab your sandwich out of your hand. The best approach here is prevention. Teach your dog to lie quietly while people are eating and never give your puppy food at the table, even if you are on a picnic and the "table" is a blanket. It's very hard to catch a dog with a contraband sandwich, but if you can, grab it by the scruff and give it a good shake. Also, extract the sandwich from its mouth so it doesn't get to eat it.

Now trick your dog. Put a treat on the chair where it can be reached. As it goes for the bait, say LEAVE IT! Now put the sandwich on the floor next to the dog. If it reaches for it, correct it again. Tempt it in every way you can (without encouraging it to take the food, because then you are sending a very mixed message), but discipline it each time it goes for the food and then reward it with a treat from your hand.

When you offer it something to eat, however, either its dinner or a snack from your hand, the floor, the chair, or anywhere, say OKAY, then let it eat. (This is where knowing how to stay on command is a very useful behavior.) The point is that the dog should take no food at all unless you say it's okay. This is not just to teach your dog politeness, but to be sure that it does not steal food out of garbage cans or off the kitchen table or pick up rotten food from the gutter or the poisonous food that is sometimes around.

There are some bad habits that are next to impossible to break. These include digging holes, wandering, and chasing cars. If a dog keeps digging a place to lie in the cool earth at the roots of its favorite bush, and the bush is dying, you can fill the hole and put a big rock on top of it. The dog will of course find another place, but you have saved that bush. A dog that wanders simply has to be tied, penned, or watched and taken out only when on a leash. Many communities have regulations about unleashed dogs, so you could get in trouble for letting your dog roam around, as well as endangering it. The same goes for a dog that chases cars.

shake would break its back. Playing dog this way is only what any pup would do to practice for the hunt with friends.

Part of learning a puppy's language is noticing when it is miserable. Signs of misery are harder to notice than signs of joy. For instance, you can't read a tail by its wagging. You have to notice where the tail is as well. When your puppy greets you, it holds its tail high as it wags. When it meets a stranger, watch the tail — it may still wag, but it is held lower. The lower the tail, the more frightened or worried a puppy is feeling. When a dog tucks its tail beneath its rear end (even though it may still be wagging!), it has probably done something for which it expects to be scolded and is very worried. It may also be apprehensive about a strange person or situation.

A dog's ears show fear, too. A dog that is unafraid holds its ears up — or pricked, if it has drooping ears. The more frightened the dog is, the lower it lays its ears back along its head.

As you play with your puppy, pay attention to what it is saying with its ears and tail. If a game gets too rough or if it is being scolded, it will tuck its tail and flatten its ears. That's the time to stop scary playing or let up on the scolding. Your puppy may also flatten its body toward the ground, turn its head sideways, or roll onto its back. Even in a grown-up dog these gestures mean "Don't hurt me, I won't hurt you." When it was a baby, our puppy "groveled" like that to its mother. In return, she licked its turned-up belly (to stimulate digestion and elimination), turned on her side, and let it nurse. If you're playing dog, keep in mind that it's against the rules of dog society to continue to scold a dog that

is groveling for you. It has already admitted it is "only a pup." At the same time, it has admitted that you are the boss. A pat or two from you will acknowledge that you understand the gesture and appreciate it.

There is one more dog meaning you should learn. When your puppy flops down, closes its eyes, and falls asleep, it means "For heaven's sake, let me sleep." Puppies need as much sleep as babies. Don't wake them up.

Training a puppy takes a long time. The secrets are patience, consistency, and many short sessions. Puppy classes are a good way to socialize your dog and learn how to work with it.

Simple Commands

Once you have become familiar with dog language by playing dog, begin to teach your dog human language by training it. You can start even a very young puppy on simple commands, though you must be very patient and not expect great results in a short time. After all, you go to school for years before people think you've learned everything you need to know. Don't expect your puppy to pick up everything right away. Even if you have put off training for years, you can still train your dog. It is not true that old dogs can't learn new tricks. But it's a lot easier to start them young!

There are many classes available for dogs at all levels of learning, and it is a good idea to take your puppy to one. Check at your local humane society, veterinary hospital, or boarding kennel for information about classes in your area. Puppy classes are a great way for both you and your puppy to learn good dog behavior and for your puppy to get socialized with other dogs. Besides, the classes are always a lot of fun.

Dogs love best the person who trains them. Sometime after it is six months old and before its first birthday, a dog will choose its master. Its master will be the person the dog has come to listen to best and who best understands it. The best way for a potential master and the dog to learn how to listen to each other is by working together. Training is that work.

The minimum obedience a dog has to learn to be likable is to walk on a leash without pulling, to sit and to lie down when it is told, to stay, and to come. There are many books available that go into more detail about training, and it's a good idea to have one or two, since we can go over only the basics here.

All the initial training is done on a leash and with a slip collar. You'll need a six-foot web lead and a slip collar that just goes over your dog's head without too much extra length. A slip collar, which is made of either webbing or chain, is often

fact

Basic training equipment includes a six-foot web lead and a slip collar that fits easily but not loosely over your dog's head. As rewards for getting something right, you might offer small treats, but praise will work just as well.

misunderstood. People think the collar chokes the dog all the time and that this is a cruel way to train. Some call it a choke chain. But the whole point of a slip collar is that you don't choke a dog with it because you never let it pull against the throat. You use it only to jerk your dog as a signal. It tightens around its neck for a moment, but then you must let it go slack. You should never pull a dog by its slip collar or let it pull you.

First, get the collar on the right way. Look at the picture on page 259. The collar has been put on the correct way for walking the dog to your left so that your right hand is free. If you're left-handed, you might want to reverse the collar and walk your dog to your right. When the collar is on correctly, it tightens as you tug the leash; when you release pressure, the weight of the collar pulls downward, making the collar slacken. Put the collar on the wrong way and see what happens. When you tug and then slacken, the collar doesn't respond. And if the collar doesn't respond, your dog isn't getting a clear signal.

Remember, when you're working with your dog, short, frequent sessions are more effective than long, tiring ones. Also, just like kids, dogs will learn more quickly and be happier pupils if they are treated with kindness and affection rather than scolding and yelling. Be firm when correcting your puppy, but praise it lavishly for the right behavior. There's nothing wrong with giving small treats when your pup gets something right — rewards of food and praise make it want to keep pleasing you.

The leash. Teaching a dog to walk on a leash without pulling you has a simple logic behind it. One dog trainer described it this way: If a dog is running headlong toward a wall and crashes into it, it will learn very quickly not to run into walls. If a dog wearing a slip collar runs headlong next to you and pulls ahead and you give it a jerk backward, it will learn very quickly not to run ahead of you.

Put your dog on the leash (check to see that the collar is on correctly). Hold the leash close enough to the dog so there is only about six inches of slack. You can hold the extra length in your other hand, or bunch up the leash and hold it all in your left hand. Don't wrap the leash around your hand. The slack allows you to jerk the dog instead of pulling. Most people are tempted to hold the leash rather close, keeping a little pull on the dog's collar all the time. But that just confuses it, because then there isn't enough difference between how its neck feels when it's walking in the right place and how it feels when it's walking into the wrong place.

For training, a slip collar (sometimes called a choke chain) is a useful tool. However, don't leave this kind of collar on your dog all the time, as it can get hooked on things and might strangle your pet. When a slip collar is on correctly, the leash is connected to the end of the chain that lies over the top of the dog's neck.

Heel. A dog should feel absolutely nothing when it's heeling (walking level with you) and a really hard jerk when it gets out of place. If the dog moves ahead, just raise your left hand a little and bring it back to your side fast. If the dog moves behind, move your hand backward and give a sharp tug forward. The dog must not be allowed to lengthen the distance between you, either; if it does, move your hand away from your side and bring it back sharply. If your dog moves into you and bumps your leg, give it a bump with your knee (or your foot, if the dog is little). Say your dog's name and then tell it what it's supposed to do — for example, "Fido, heel!" As you say "heel," start walking. If your dog pulls ahead, jerk hard as you say "Heel" again, but always

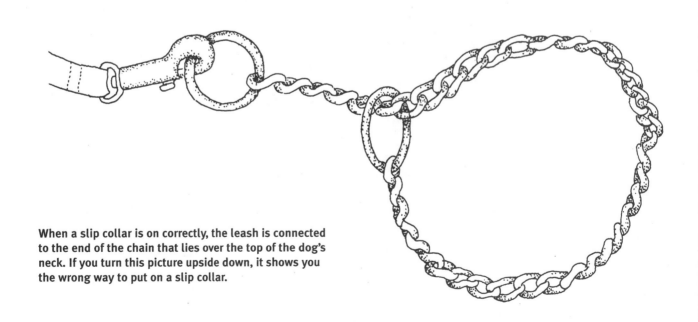

When a slip collar is on correctly, the leash is connected to the end of the chain that lies over the top of the dog's neck. If you turn this picture upside down, it shows you the wrong way to put on a slip collar.

slacken the leash right away. If it pulls to the side, do the same thing. And if it trails behind, do the same thing. You are never pulling on that leash. You are only giving a quick, firm tug to tell the dog where you want it and then letting the leash go slack again. Reward the proper position with a small treat or words of praise — this will get your dog looking at you and eager to keep doing the right thing.

When your dog has learned that there's only one place it can walk comfortably (because it gets a big jerk when it walks anywhere else), show it that the pace can be fast or slow. Walk at a normal speed, then start to trot. Jerk the dog up if it lags behind. Then suddenly slow down. Jerk if your dog gets ahead. This may seem too hard on the dog, but it isn't at all. It can see to the side of its head better than you can, so it always has a glimpse of what you're up to, unless it isn't paying attention.

When your dog can heel passably well, it's time to teach it how to turn while heeling. Walk in a straight line, holding the leash tightly and keeping your left arm stiff and straight at your side. Then suddenly make a right U-turn. (If the dog is walking on your right, make a left U-turn.)

Next try a turn in the opposite direction, turning toward the dog. There's no way you can give your dog a jerk with the leash when you're turning toward it, so you'll have to use a different method. Walk along normally, and then, without warning, make a sharp left turn, pivoting on your left foot. As you pivot, unless your dog has been paying attention to your leg, your right foot will bump into the dog. If the dog wasn't paying attention the first time, it will be soon.

All the time you're training your dog, keep bending down to pat it and tell it how good it is. There is never need to scold it for a mistake. If you keep up the training, your dog will learn that

HEEL
This dog has its slip collar on correctly for walking on the left side.

if it doesn't pay attention when it's out walking with you, uncomfortable things happen. When it is alert, it is pleasantly rewarded.

You can't expect your dog to walk at heel every minute it's on a leash, but it should learn that it may never tug and pull at the leash. Start with short sessions and then say "Dog, [your dog's name], okay," and give it a push on the rump to get it out of the heel position, then relax your hold on the leash. It won't take it long to learn it can wander to the leash's end when you say "Okay."

SIT, STEP 1
A firm push on a dog's rear end will help it learn the command "sit." Praise your dog as soon as it sits.

SIT, STEP 2
At first you may have to keep your hand in place to reinforce the idea of sitting.

Sit. This is probably the most important thing you can teach your dog, other than to come reliably. If your dog can sit when asked, you can stop it from jumping on people or chasing after other animals or begging at the table. To start, hold the leash straight upward (not jerking it now, just firmly taut) or hold the collar and say, "Dog [your dog's name], sit!" At the same time, push down on its rump with your left hand. You may have to lean awfully hard on a big dog, by the way. When you've managed to wrestle it into a sitting position, tell it how wonderful it is. Now walk with it a few steps and say "Sit" again. Sooner or later, your dog will catch on.

Stay. When it will sit on command, you can teach your dog to stay. Get it sitting first. Or try this after your dog knows how to lie down, as it's easier for it to move out of a sitting position than a lying down one. Then hold the palm of your hand in front of its face and tell it, "Dog [your dog's name], stay!" If it gets up, bring your palm up quickly for a good tap under the chin. Get it sitting again, repeat the words "Dog, stay," and try again. Chances are sooner or later the dog will figure out that that hand just happens to come up to slap its chin every time it makes a move forward. It will begin to stay. At first, reward it with praise or a treat after just a few seconds, increasing the time gradually. When it will stay for a while (maybe 30 seconds or so), try backing off, standing a few feet away, and then coming back to praise. After a while, you can begin circling around behind the dog while it sits (still holding the leash, of course). Every time the dog gets up,

STAY
Once your dog has learned to stay when you're right in front of it, holding up your hand as a signal, you can try slowly backing away, until your dog learns to stay no matter how near or far away you are from it.

go through the whole deal again. Keep increasing the length of time you ask the dog to stay, and always give a positive release command, like "Okay," so that it knows when it can move.

Come. Your six-foot leash will be important for teaching your dog to come — you can get six feet away from your dog without it getting away from you. When your dog will sit and stay even when you back off the whole six feet of leash, you can teach it to come. Walk ahead of it the full six feet. Face it and say, "Dog [your dog's name], come!" Many puppies will run right over to you, especially if you bend over a little to encourage them, and they should get lavish praise. If your dog does not come, pull the leash in, hand over hand, as fast as you can to drag your dog to you. Act as though the dog came to you of its own free

will and congratulate it. Sooner or later, it will leap to you before you get a chance to pull it in.

Down. To teach a dog to lie down, you have to get it to lie down in the first place. This can be very hard. A big dog has muscles superior to yours. Even a small dog resists pressure to force it down. Any dog tends to panic when it feels someone tackle it to the ground, and so would you. You have to gently trick a dog into a lying-down position so that it is lying down before it knows what is happening. First get your dog to sit. Then say, "Dog [your dog's name], down!" as you pull its front feet slowly out from under it and to one side, so as not to cause alarm. The dog will now be lying on its side. Pat it calmly while it is lying down and say how good it is. Then let it get up before it panics. Needless to say, wait until your

Shaggy Dog Stories

The stunts — good ones and bad ones — a dog thinks up all by itself can be quite eccentric. Because I've never figured out whether dogs are awfully dumb or awfully bright, I leave you with these four stories to figure out for yourself.

Sheevra, an Airedale who learned everything in this chapter and more, was terrified of thunderstorms. At the first rumble, she would dash into the bathroom, leap into the tub, and frantically try to dig herself into the only hole in our city apartment: the bathtub drain. After 10 years and 200 thunderstorms she never saw the ridiculousness of the situation.

My old French sheepdog, Amber, loved the water. She could be found in the summertime stretched full-length in a roaring brook, her head supported on a rock. In the winter, every time I drew myself a hot bath she stepped sedately into the tub and sat there, grinning, panting, snuffling up the steam as it curled about her whiskers.

I was certainly surprised to have that sweet old dear accused by neighbors of being a thief. They complained she stole their garden tools, their children's toys, and their husbands' dungarees fresh off the clothesline. Of course I didn't believe them. Then came spring, and the snow at the bottom of the yard melted. Gaily waving her plumed tail, Amber took me to her cache: 30 feet of garden hose, a rake, a child's truck and bulldozer, and the dungarees.

Most starling is a greeting ceremony invented by my wolflike, one-eyed mongrel bitch, Greta. Greta's fierce devotion pushed her to unusual feats — like jumping a seven-foot fence to escape from the vet's exercise yard and trekking home cross-country over five miles of completely unfamiliar terrain. In Greta's early years, an impolite brown poodle lived next door to us. Each morning at 7 A.M. he appeared at the ridge of a rock that separated our boundaries, trotted down the slope, and deposited a bowel movement on our front-door step — a shocking disgrace to dogdom. Greta took to chasing the crude fellow away with a nip on the butt, egged on by me and the whispered command "Get 'im!" As the months passed, nipping the poodle's rear end became such a roundly applauded stunt that Greta lived with her eye to the boundary ridge. The moment the poodle appeared, she was off up the rocks to try to get in a nip before he made it to the safety of his own territory. Gradually the ceremony became a way of greeting me when I returned from work. Whether the poodle was there or not, Greta would dash up the rock, make a show of investigating for poodle intruders, and then dash back to me to say hello.

More years passed and the poodle died. But the ceremony had become a ritual. As Greta grew old, we got an Airedale pup. The pup learned the ritual. Greta died, but the dash up the ridge and back did not. The poodle dash, performed as our car pulls in the drive, is a dog-to-dog tradition in the family, unbroken now for several generations of pups to whom it can make no sense at all.

dog is in a relaxed mood to start teaching it to lie down. Another method is to hold a treat in your closed fist and place it on the ground near the dog's feet while you give the command "Down." Your dog will bend its head down to get the treat and usually will wind up lying down in order to get closer to it. The instant it does, say "Good dog," and give it the treat.

By the way, dogs have trouble learning that *down* means one thing one time and another thing another time. Or that two different people use different words to mean the same thing. For instance, if you use the word *down* to mean "Get off the couch" and also to mean "Stop jumping up on me" and also to mean "Lie down," you're going to get nowhere fast. If you like, you can use "Lie down" so the dog won't get confused, or "Off" for getting off furniture.

Dogs also have trouble finding a key word they're supposed to listen to if you have surrounded it with a bunch of other words. If you say, "Now listen, dum-dum, I said *down* and I mean it," your puppy will wag its tail and wonder what is going on. Limit commands to one or two words. Remember the training order: dog's name first, command second, firm jerks only on the leash, no scolding, lots of patting. Also, don't keep repeating a command over and over or your dog will learn that it can ignore you. If it doesn't respond, correct it and show it what you want. Don't move to off-leash commands until you're sure your dog is reliable on a leash.

Consider training an everyday, all-day thing rather than a special lesson. That is, your dog should heel when you ask it to, except when you say "Okay." It should sit anytime during the day when you'd like it to sit. It should stay when it's convenient for you to have it stay — indoors or out. You have to do these things all the time with your dog, anytime you think of them, and not just in a quiet place. After your puppy has learned the basics, take it to different places to reinforce the lessons while there are distractions around. You want a dog that behaves itself everywhere, not just in your living room. Training isn't a thing you do once. It's a relationship developed between dog and master.

Fancy Tricks

The principle behind any trick from fetching to begging is to manipulate your dog into the right action as you say the words, and then pat it enthusiastically as though it had done the action all by itself. Scolding only confuses the dog. Since it doesn't know yet what it is that it's supposed to be doing right, it certainly doesn't know what it did wrong. If you use food as a reward, don't give it every time. Occasional treats reinforce good behavior more effectively than constant ones, and patting works almost as well. When training is done, you want your dog to behave with or without food rewards.

Begging. Get your dog into a corner and get it sitting down with its rear snugly into the corner. Say "Dog [your dog's name], beg!" as you lift its front end up into the right position. Hold it for a moment and then tell it how wonderful it is. Dogs get upset when they think they are falling over backward, so try not to push it too far. If you have a very floppy sort of dog and its bottom seems to be coming out from under it whenever you try to get it sitting up, you may not be able to teach this trick.

You'll have to roll your dog over yourself the first few times you give the "roll" command, but soon enough it will understand what you want it to do.

Shaking hands. Most dogs sooner or later paw at you for attention, so the gesture of shaking hands is half done for you by nature. Get your dog to sit. Pick up a front paw while saying, "Dog [your dog's name], shake hands"; then pat it a lot. If your dog learns this without too much trouble, it may be the sort that can learn to astonish your friends. Hold your hand slightly to its left side. Say, "Shake your *left* hand," and pick up that paw. Do the same with its right paw, holding your hand more to that side. People will think your dog is highly intelligent to know left from right. The fact is it doesn't — the position of your hand tells the dog which paw to give you.

Playing dead. Playing dead means the dog must roll onto its back, belly up, and stay there for a while. Dogs will do this trick quite enthusiastically if they get their bellies rubbed in the bargain. Like other tricks, you have to manage to get the dog into the play-dead position while you say "Dog [your dog's name], play dead." It has to be

lying down first — then just roll it over. Rub its belly right away. Later, when the dog is more or less doing what you want, wait before you rub. It will learn to stay waiting belly-up for the rubbing it knows is coming.

Rolling over. This trick is hard to teach big dogs because they're so heavy and clumsy to roll. If you can roll your dog over, then you can teach the trick in the same way as all the others. Say "Dog [your dog's name], roll over" as you roll it; then give it a cuddle.

Dancing. Big dogs must feel as silly as they look when they try to stand on their hind legs. Trying to teach them this trick usually makes them suffer. Smaller dogs often prance around on two legs naturally (possibly they are trying to reach up to where the action is), so they are much easier to teach. There is no doubt that food is the best reward for this trick. If you don't use food, you will have to get your dog up on its hind legs by holding its paws, and any dog will pull away from anything holding its paws. If your dog will stand or jump up on its hind legs for even a moment for a bit of food, however, you can then stick the front part of your arm under its foreleg for support, to give it the idea that you would like it to stay in that position for a while when you say "Dog [your dog's name], dance." Don't hold the food up above its nose, because it will jump all over. Close your hand over the food and hold it right next to its nose while you hold it up for a few seconds. Let the dog down again before you give it the food. When it stands with good balance for 10 seconds or more, you can teach the dog to actually dance (even though this is the word you've been using all along, so far it's really just been balancing). Just move the hand holding the food slightly forward so the dog takes a step or two. Even later, you can teach it to dance around in a circle by moving your hand in a circle.

Saying please. A dog that never barks to get your attention is not a good candidate for the "saying please" trick. But if your dog even occasionally makes noises when it wants a bit of your sandwich, it can be taught this trick. Tempt it with a piece of food. (Liverwurst throws most dogs into a frenzy of excitement.) Keep saying "Dog [your dog's name], say please," and follow the command with your best rendition of a small bark — *wruff!* The moment any sound comes from your dog's throat, give it the snack and praise its intelligence. As soon as it says "Please" every time you ask, you can teach it to surprise people even more. Tell it to say a "little please" (and use a soft voice); give it the snack no matter how loud it is. Then tell your dog to say a "big please" (use a big voice). Don't give it the snack until it gets very exited and gives a good loud impatient bark. Before long it will take its clue from your voice and finally from the actual words you use (at which point you can give the command in a perfectly normal voice).

Fetch and drop it. Luckily, all puppies run after and pick up a favorite toy if you throw it. Sooner or later, all puppies come up to you with the toy in their mouth. Take advantage of the situation by saying "Dog [your dog's name], fetch" every time you toss something to your pup. After you toss a toy, do not move a muscle! If you go after your dog, you will be teaching it a game of tag, not a game of fetch. Just sitting doesn't look like a promising romp to your puppy and chances are it will flirt with you and the toy for a few minutes, then carry the toy back to you in its mouth. Now, tell it it's terrific, but don't play around. As you pat your dog and make a fuss, manage to get a good hold on it, and as you say "Dog, drop it," extract the toy calmly from its mouth. Wait a minute before throwing the toy again as you say "Dog, fetch." (If your dog does not calmly give things up, keep smiling; stick your finger down behind what it's holding, pull it from its mouth, and then say how wonderful it is to be so generous about giving up its toys.) Since this is not a fun game for your dog until it brings the toy back to you and drops it, it will probably learn to fetch and drop pretty fast. When your dog loves the game and does it well, you can encourage it to swim by playing fetch near water. At first throw the ball just to the edge of the water, then a little farther out.

Incidental tricks. Most dogs, in their efforts to communicate with you, develop their own ways to express themselves. A pup, in its enthusiasm for dinner, might once pick up its dish in its mouth. Or a dog might drag its leash around, hoping someone will take it out. Or stand up at the window and look out because someone it likes has just left the house. If you reward the dog right away and put words to what it is doing, it will soon have another trick in its collection. Say what comes to your mind, like "Dog [your dog's name], dinnertime!" if it picks up its dish (and feed it right away), or "Dog, bring your leash" (and take it out right away), or "Dog, see who's there" (and go and look with it and pat it a lot). It seems to be a rule that the more a dog has been trained to understand words, the easier it can learn new words and the actions that go with them. It still doesn't speak your language, but it has generalized the principle that your sounds have meaning.

Backyard Pets

Domesticated animals, like a farm cow, and pet animals, like a pet cow, are two entirely different things. A farm cow will remain aloof and dignified, while a pet cow will trot after you mooing for a glug of soda from the bottle you are carrying. A farm goat will lower its horns to a stranger, while a pet goat will check the stranger's pockets for a goodie to munch. A farm rooster will cock-a-doodle-doo at sunrise and then go about its own business, while a pet rooster will be into your business, sometimes from the vantage point of your shoulder, all day long. When you consider keeping a backyard animal, better consider whether you want a farm temperament or a pet temperament. The difference is in how you raise it. If you take a partially grown animal and simply care for its creature needs, it will think you are a kind human and leave it at that. Such a relationship is appropriate for those who want goats for goat milk or geese for dinner. But if you take a really young animal and fuss over it, feed it by hand, and carry it about, it will think you are the same kind of animal it is — or that it is the same kind of animal

you are. Either way, you may be in for a more intense relationship than you bargained for.

Before you decide to keep any of these animals, check your local zoning laws. In many areas, they are considered livestock, not pets. Also keep in mind that many neighbors will not be tolerant of a noisy rooster that wakes up early every morning or a pair of geese that raise a ruckus whenever someone comes up the driveway (and you might grow tired of that as well!).

You can learn a lot about backyard pets from your local 4-H Club or county extension office. Agricultural supply stores often have brochures as well. At country fairs you can see lots of different animals and talk to their owners about the ups and downs of keeping outdoor pets. These are also good places to find out where you can buy geese, goats, and chickens in your area.

Backyard Pets
at a glance

Geese PAGE 269

HOUSING: Natural shrubbery shelter or other shade in hot weather. Or homemade plywood poultry shed. Optional mesh door and floor. Water bucket. Bedding hay or litter for shed.

SPECIAL REQUIREMENTS: None, though they will enjoy a small pond (even a plastic wading pool).

DIET: For goslings, gosling or duck mash or starter pellets for the first six weeks. For geese, during the summer, mainly grass with some pellets; during the winter, whole mixed grains (corn alone is too fattening) or poultry pellets. Supplement if you like with discarded outside leaves of salad greens, vegetable peelings, and stale bread or leftover cereals.

CARE: Feed, or allow to graze, refill water bucket daily.

TAMABILITY: Follow owner about, enjoy human company, defend family from strangers.

LIFE SPAN: 15 to 25 years, but can be even longer with excellent care.

Chickens PAGE 272

HOUSING: Natural shrubbery shelter or homemade plywood poultry shed. Optional mesh door and floor. Optional homemade nesting baskets. Water pan. Hay for bedding and nesting in shed.

SPECIAL REQUIREMENTS: Newborn chicks require extra heat for the first three weeks of life.

DIET: Chicks, chick mash. Older chickens, chicken feed. Supplement with discarded outside leaves of salad greens, vegetable peelings, stale bread or other leftover cereals, and bonemeal.

CARE: Feed, refill water pan daily. Gather eggs daily if they are to be eaten. Rake bedding from shed floor weekly and replace with fresh bedding. Or, for mesh floor, rake droppings from under floor monthly.

TAMABILITY: Come for food at signal. A single chicken can become devoted to its owner.

LIFE SPAN: Can live up to 15 years with good care.

Pigeons PAGE 278

HOUSING: Homemade plywood coop. Water and feed dishes. Gravel, sand, or sawdust for coop floor.

SPECIAL REQUIREMENTS: Confinement of new pair for first few weeks. Dusting with bird insecticide to prevent lice during hot weather.

DIET: Pigeon feed. Supplement with bonemeal.

CARE: Feed, refill water dish daily. Rake and replenish flooring material weekly. Provide bathing water twice a week. Scrape and wash inside of coop three or four times a year.

TAMABILITY: Learn to come for food at signal, and eat from owner's hand. Learn to fly free and return home each day. Individual birds can become devoted pets.

LIFE SPAN: 10 to 20 years.

Goats PAGE 284

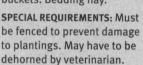

HOUSING: Stall in garage or other existing building. Or homemade goat shed. Optional goat yard attached to shed. Feed and water buckets. Bedding hay.

SPECIAL REQUIREMENTS: Must be fenced to prevent damage to plantings. May have to be dehorned by veterinarian.

DIET: For kids under three months, cow's milk, calf-starter grain, green hay. For goats over three months, goat grain or chow, green forage, and grass hay.

CARE: Feed and water daily. Spread fresh bedding hay daily. Stake or fence outside shed or stall daily in good weather. Clean stall or shed as needed.

TAMABILITY: Extremely friendly, devoted, and affectionate. Difficult to train, but have been taught to pull small carts and walk on a leash.

LIFE SPAN: 12 to 15 years.

Rhode Island Red

Geese

Geese are all-around wonderful backyard pets. They look terrific, keep the lawn clipped, chase off strangers, companionably join the family at picnics and ball games, and require next to no care. They can live to the ripe old age of 50 years, though most have a life span of about 25 years. Geese are considered to be the most intelligent of the barnyard fowl, and are certainly the most emotional. Geese fall in love — suddenly and often at first sight — long before they are old enough to mate and raise families. A female goose is called a goose, but a male is called a gander. Their babies are goslings. A mated goose and gander stay together faithfully until one or the other dies. A widowed gander or goose will search long and sadly for his or her lost love, mourning for months or even years before he or she recovers sufficiently to choose another mate. Both mother and father take care of eggs, nest, and goslings. In fact, a goose family is aware that it is a family. All through life adult brothers, sisters, and parents greet one another enthusiastically with stretched necks and noisy gabbling.

Around the yard, one pair of geese — gander walking boldly in front, modest goose behind — will follow you about for sheer company. When you sit down, they'll settle down next to you. When a stranger comes along, the gander will stretch his neck threateningly, hiss, and even nip if his threat is not taken seriously. Quite sensibly, however, geese learn to recognize routine visitors, and though they may hiss and threaten, they seldom nip people they know. However, an angry or threatened goose can inflict a nasty bruise, so keep that in mind if you want yours to roam freely.

fact

Domestic geese sometimes squawk and honk at wild geese flying high above them on their journey south in the fall and north in the autumn. Wild geese migrate not because of the cold weather but because they can no longer find food to eat.

Choosing Geese

It's cruel to buy only one gosling. Geese are social animals and must have at least one friend to share their lives with. The friend need not be of the opposite sex, since two males or two females will become just as devoted to each other as a male and a female. This is fortunate, because you can't tell a boy from a girl gosling, and you can tell a goose from a gander only by watching who takes the lead when they walk along or who is courting whom. The gander both leads and courts.

To find geese, you can look in poultry magazines for mail-order goslings or check with your local 4-H Club, a county extension office, or an agricultural supply store.

A "married" pair of geese will be more likely to mate and raise goslings of their own if they live in a group rather than if they live by themselves. But there are no hard-and-fast rules and you may well get a batch of babies every year from a lone pair.

The most typical "old gray goose" you'll see is either a Graylag goose or its larger, plumper descendant, the Toulouse goose. Another common variety is the white Embden.

Housing

If predators aren't a danger, geese need no housing at all. They can find all the shelter they need at the base of whatever shrubbery or hedges you have. Covered as they are in goose down, geese are perfectly comfortable in the coldest weather. They're fine in the summer, too, as long as they can settle in the shade when they wish. Their outer feathers serve as waterproofing in the rain.

In spite of their bold temperament, a pair of geese can still fall prey to dogs. (But a flock of six could probably defend itself.) Sleeping geese are easy prey for night-hunting foxes and coyotes. Raccoons eat goose eggs and goslings, and hawks may pick off youngsters in broad daylight. A fenced yard will keep out dogs and coyotes. The small shed on page 338 will keep out nocturnal predators if it is fitted with a chicken-wire door; just shoo the geese inside for the night. The shelter will also serve to keep goslings safe from chilling rain before their weatherproof adult feathers grow in. Provide a layer of clean hay to cover the floor. If your geese are a "married" pair, give them a nesting box inside their shelter.

The best protection you can offer geese is a fenced-in poultry yard (see the plans on page 339). If you fence in your geese, however, they will not have enough grazing space to feed themselves, and every day you'll have to feed them either whole dried grain or pellets and leftover household greens or grass.

Food and Water

Feed newly hatched goslings either commercial gosling food or duck mash bought at a feed store. Within a few weeks, goslings will be eating grass on their own. From then on, lawn grass is a perfect diet (but not if it is sprayed with pesticides) and you have no more feeding problems until winter. Keep in mind, however, that if you let them loose in your yard, you will have to watch where you walk. Geese

Chinese goose

produce large droppings, and lots of them. During the winter, the geese will still eat dry grass until it becomes covered with snow, but their diet should be supplemented every day with whole dried grains. Corn alone is fine for adult birds (buy it at a feed or pet store) and leftover raw greens from your dinner. Stale bread, particularly whole wheat, is healthy, too. It is no myth that geese will weed your garden; it's true, but they will eat the newly sprouting vegetables as well. A fenced garden is suggested.

Geese need a deep container from which to drink, because they plunge their whole head in to fill their bills. Use an ordinary bucket; rinse and refill it daily.

Geese don't have to have water to swim in. The varieties suggested here all live happily out on the lawn, just with the bucket to drink from. That doesn't mean a goose doesn't want to have water to swim in. Our geese met their end at a neighbor's pond, where they had traveled, I believe, to investigate a lakeside nesting area. The neighbor's dog had long since given up on catching wild geese, which simply fly away. But our two fat Embden geese, unable to fly and accustomed to our dogs, hadn't a chance on a strange dog's turf. It's best not to allow your geese to wander.

If you do provide them with a pond (a plastic wading pool will do), you'll have to empty and clean it often. Geese can be quite messy. If they have a real pond for their own, they will be in heaven.

A shed will encourage geese to nest. If your geese do nest there (or in some other spot of their choice) and lay eggs in the spring, don't bother the couple while they are incubating (keeping warm) their eggs. If they are disturbed, they may decide they have chosen a dangerous spot and

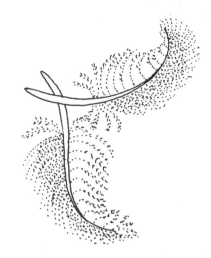

Warm feathers and down allow geese to thrive in the coldest and wettest climates. They can tolerate warm summers, too, as long as they have some shade.

abandon the nest, eggs and all. Once the half-dozen or more goslings hatch, you will see them in a matter of hours following their parents about the lawn in single file. Give them their own lower water dish to drink from, as they won't be tall enough to reach into the bucket. A large crockery dish is fine. Give them gosling feed for about six weeks, though they will be eating grass soon after hatching.

Illnesses

Geese are among the hardiest of birds. They seldom get sick and quite frequently live to be 25 to 50 years old. If your geese do get sick, country vets, trained to care for farm animals, or an avian specialist will probably be more helpful than a regular small-animal vet. However, the 4-H Club, which has chapters all over the country, is very helpful in locating someone who can tell you what to do. If you can't get help right away, confine the sick goose in a closed bathroom or in a large carton indoors. Put bird antibiotics (available at pet stores) into its drinking water daily, following the instructions on the label.

If your goose is injured by a dog or breaks a wing or leg, any vet, city or country, can treat it.

Chickens

It was not until this century that chickens (adult females are called hens and adult males are called cocks or roosters) were mass-produced as food. For 4,000 years prior, chickens were bred for just about everything except meat. The Egyptians first learned how to incubate the eggs of the jungle fowl, ancestor of all our chickens, in nests of heated brick. Necessity was the mother of this invention: All those men working on the pyramids created the need for mass-produced food. So from that time until this century, chickens were raised for their eggs. Of course, any excess cocks and old hens (whose laying days were over) were stewed down for food. But what we know today as tender fryers and succulent roasting chickens, both of which are mere babies (or pullets), were rarely eaten.

The roosters of many breeds of chickens were used through all those centuries for cockfighting, the most universal sport known to man. In spite of the fact that cockfighting is against the law in most of the United States, there are still cockfights every day, even in the most unlikely places — for instance, in New York City apartments.

After egg production had been perfected, chicken breeders veered off in an exotic direction: show birds. The Japanese, for example, bred a

The Henpecked Rooster

To be henpecked was the fate of a chicken I once raised from a hatchling. It was one of those Easter chicks sometimes sold in pet stores in the spring. Not knowing that poultry of any sort was against the law in the city where I lived, I raised the chick in a cardboard pen in an apartment. He grew up to be a large, white, insanely devoted rooster who followed my every move from either under my feet or on top of my head. Besides that, he crowed every morning at dawn and was not a good pet for a city apartment.

We decided that during his first summer we would ease him into a more natural life on a farm in the country. But — and this is what I mean about the difference between a pet and a farm animal — he had only lived with people, so he thought he was a human. That poor rooster knew nothing of chicken life. He was attacked by everyone, rooster or hen. Even adolescent pullets pecked him. He would have been killed if we had not found him another human family to live with in the country.

rooster with such long tail feathers he had to be kept on the top of a flagpole-high roost so his 30-foot-long plumes stayed neat. State fairs still give an opportunity to see chickens with extraordinary fluffy hats, chickens decorated with perfectly round white polka dots, chickens of metallic gold or silver hues and scalloped patterns, chickens with fuzzy pantaloons, chickens covered in curls, and chickens whose feathers are so fine they look like hair.

Hens seem to be quarrelsome creatures. When you watch a group of hens choosing a place to roost in the henhouse or deciding who gets to eat first, it appears as though everyone is pecking at someone. Actually, a group of hens arranges itself socially in very strict ways. The bossiest, strongest hen (the most dominant) can and does peck at all the other hens. She pecks them out of her way at mealtime, at the water dish, and in the roosting area. The second bossiest hen may not peck her, but can and does peck all the others under her. And so it goes to the bottom-most, weakest (most subordinate) hen, who is pecked by everybody but may peck no one in return. This social structure is called, logically, a "pecking order."

Roosters don't behave quite the same way as hens. The dominant rooster chooses a big area that belongs to him (his territory) and surrounds himself with the hens of his choice (his harem). He fights off any rooster that enters his territory or bothers his hens. The boldest rooster has the biggest territory and the most hens. He advertises himself and his possessions by crowing. The least of the roosters has no territory and no hens. In fact, his status is so low that he is that most pitiful of barnyard sights: the henpecked rooster. You can see why it is difficult to keep more than one rooster with your flock of hens. The roosters will fight and will probably refuse to share the small winter quarters you have provided.

fact

Chickens have very particular social rules. Hens establish a very strict "pecking order." The strongest one always goes first and pecks at all the others. Also, a flock cannot have more than one rooster, or they will fight constantly.

Choosing a Chicken

An incredible number of chicken breeds are advertised and sold through poultry magazines like *Poultry Journal*. You can even buy the real genuine original — the beautiful jungle fowl, with its rust-red feathers and metallic green and blue tail and neck feathers. Going to a country fair is a great way to see all kinds of poultry and to learn all about keeping them. Most poultry breeders recommend the pygmy chickens called bantams as pets. They're small, they're cute, they come in many colors, and they lay a lot of eggs.

Housing

Day-old chicks must be kept warm for at least three weeks before they can be allowed outdoors. Keep them in an uncovered cardboard carton with newspaper or paper towels on the bottom. Big cartons for toilet tissue or paper towels from

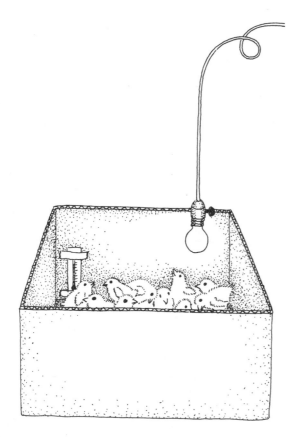

THERMOMETER
Keep day-old chicks warm in a corrugated carton heated with a 40-watt lightbulb. Be sure to hang the light from a chair back or table edge, or by any other method that will keep the hot bulb several inches away from the cardboard.

the supermarket are large enough. Cut the sides down to about 18 inches. Provide a shallow pan for chick feed and another dish for water. Small glass pie plates work well. Sprinkle grit (coarse sand) on the paper. Change the paper, grit, food, and water every day.

The box should be kept at 95 degrees the first week, 90 degrees and then 85 degrees the second week, and 80 degrees and then 75 degrees the third week. In this way the chicks are gradually accustomed to outdoor temperatures of about 70 degrees. The easiest way to adjust heat is with either the clamp-type light that is used by auto mechanics or a gooseneck lamp. Tape a household thermometer two inches from the floor inside the carton. Adjust the amount of heat by moving the clamp light up or down the side of a

chair or table leg near the box or by bending the gooseneck light up or down. If a regular 40-watt lightbulb doesn't give the box enough heat, use an infrared heat bulb instead. The chicks will tell you when they are in distress from either too much heat or too much cold. A contented chick chirps quietly. Distressed chicks peep loudly and shrilly. If they're peeping because they're too cold, you'll probably find them crowding toward the heat source. If they're too hot, you'll find them crowding away from the heat source.

After they are a few weeks old, the chicks may be left loose outdoors in both winter and summer. They have enough sense to seek shelter from rain under shrubbery and to stay close to home, where the eating is good. In winter, a simple shelter like the one described on page 338 is sufficient for a dozen bantam hens. Keep the floor covered with dry hay. Rake it out once a week and lay down a layer of fresh hay. Or use the wire floor described on page 339 and rake droppings out from under it every month.

Dogs, cats, and wild animals like foxes and coyotes are more danger to chickens than rain and snow. If you suspect you will have trouble with these animals, build a small poultry yard of four-foot-high chicken-wire netting. The yard doesn't need to be larger than six feet by six feet for a flock of a dozen chickens. It can be portable so that your chickens can forage in different areas of your yard, where they will eat all sorts of garden pests.

Food and Water

I've seen chickens raised in the rural South without benefit of any commercial food at all. They call them scavenger chickens. Besides the worms, insects, seeds, weeds, and grass these chickens find for themselves during the summer, they are given the family's leftovers, including meat scraps, bread,

When they're just hatched, chicks often look nothing like the bird they will eventually become.

and vegetables, both cooked and raw. Chickens even eat eggs — cooked and not in the shell.

To be certain of giving your birds a balanced diet, however, feed chicks daily with commercial chick mash, available at feed stores and some pet stores, until they are a month and a half old. Then switch to adult chicken feed, still feeding every day. Once in a while, sprinkle bonemeal in with the feed to give extra calcium. Offer fresh raw greens like lettuce when you have them available. None of the food needs to go in a pan once the chickens are outdoors. Chickens really prefer to peck their food out of the dust and dirt, and this lets them peck up some natural grit too. The grit

is kept in their gizzard (stomach) to help them grind up hard bits of food.

Keep out a shallow pan of water for the chickens. If they are loose in the yard, the easiest place to keep the pan is next to the garden hose, so you can simply rinse it out and refill it every day without troubling yourself too much.

Chickens do take baths, but not in water. They bathe in dust. If you don't provide your chickens with a nice dust patch, they're quite likely to make one for themselves in a flower bed. An ideal bathing area would be a shallow depression about three feet in diameter and filled with fine sand from a pet store or a lumberyard. The bathing place won't prevent chickens from pecking about in the garden for juicy worms and beetle grubs, but it may stop them from scooping out bathtubs there.

Egg Laying

Hens generally begin laying at around five or six months of age and may continue for three or four years. Some breeds lay year-round; others are seasonal layers. If you build the small shelter on page 338), you could add two or three wooden boxes to serve as nesting areas. The boxes should be filled with hay. Otherwise, look for eggs under porches, shrubs, or any other protected area around your house. Egg hunting is the more exciting way to get your breakfast.

Hens lay eggs whether or not a rooster is available. But without the rooster, the eggs can't hatch into chickens. If you have kept a rooster, all the eggs are likely to be fertile. Kept warm by the broody hens, they will hatch into chickens. If the eggs are to be eaten, you have to get to them fast before the chicks begin to form. A fertilized egg will develop a small red spot on the yolk within 24 hours. The spot is the beginning of the network of blood vessels that will bring nourishment from the yolk to the chick, and the beginning of the chick itself.

A nesting box can be built of eight-inch board cut just long enough to make a snug box for the hen. The box doesn't need a floor, but you should line the bottom with hay.

Eggs hatch into chickens only if a rooster fertilizes them. No rooster means no chicks, but still plenty of eggs!

If you are interested in raising a small flock of chickens for eggs or meat, get in touch with a local chapter of the 4-H Club, your county or state extension service, or a state agricultural college.

Illnesses

Chickens are subject to a large variety of diseases, but these are troublesome mostly to commercial chicken farmers who keep hundreds or thousands of chickens under rather crowded, often indoor, conditions. To prevent disease, farmers include daily doses of antibiotics in the chicken feed — a practice that the medical profession is beginning to doubt the wisdom of (it forces bacteria to develop antibiotic-resistant strains, not only in the chickens but eventually also in the humans who consume traces of the antibiotics along with the chicken meat they eat). A few chickens living outdoors are less likely to get sick. If one of your chickens does seem ill, seek advice from your vet or from a local chicken farmer or feed store. You can also give treatment as you would for geese (see page 271).

An Internal Homing Device

All pigeons can find their way home from at least several miles away, and in the case of homing pigeons from hundreds of miles. A pigeon close to home probably finds its way by landmarks, but landmarks are no help when a pigeon is released 300 miles from home in an area it has never seen before.

The mystery of homing seems to depend on the pigeon's remarkable sense of time, an internal clock more accurate than most watches. In its home area, at a particular time of year and at a particular time of day, the sun is always at a certain spot in the sky. When a pigeon is released away from its home area, its internal clock tells it the right time but its eyes tell it the sun is in the "wrong" place. The pigeon sets its course in a direction that will take it to where the sun "looks right" for that time of day.

Pigeons

No doubt pigeons found man before man had bothered to find pigeons. Wherever grain is scattered, whether as bread crusts in the park or oats in the barnyard, flocks of pigeons gather to feed. If there is a loft, a ledge, or even a fair-sized windowsill nearby, pigeons move in to stay. Each morning the flock gathers itself together from its night's roosting. A pigeon takes flight, wheeling in circles about the roosting area. Another joins it, and another, until the whole flock — a handful or a hundred — is wheeling in larger and larger, higher and higher circles in the sky. Within a few minutes they choose a direction to a known feeding ground and are on their way to breakfast. The flock spends the morning eating, the noontime resting, and the early afternoon eating some more. At around midafternoon, the wheeling flight begins again. When all the members of the flock have joined, they all fly home.

Pigeons have been used by mankind for food for centuries but have also been important as carriers of messages during times of both war and peace. Enthusiasts breed them for racing, for meat (the baby pigeons, called squabs, are considered a delicacy all over the world), and as fancy specimens.

Choosing Pigeons

Pigeons are usually bought as young mated pairs. They choose mates at four or five months and shouldn't be over a year old when you get them. Each pigeon should have a leg band that will tell you the date it was hatched. To make it easier for you to train pigeons to come home, buy only one pair at a time.

Pigeon breeders advertise in poultry magazines such as *The Poultry Journal* and *Game Bird Gazette*. You might also be able to locate breeders through your local 4-H Club. It's a good idea to find a breeder close by, so you can look at the actual birds you're considering. A healthy pigeon is active and its feathers look smooth, clean, and solid. Signs of illness are ruffled feathers, runny nose or eyes, and inactivity.

There are dozens of breeds of domestic pigeons, all originally descended from the blue rock dove. If you want your pigeons to fly free in a flock during the day and come home again in the afternoon, the best breeds for you are flights, rollers, and tumblers. The names describe the birds on the wing: Flights fly a lot, rollers roll over and over as they fly, and tumblers tumble downward in flight — all apparently for the fun of it.

The highest flying pigeons are logically called high flyers. They wheel higher and higher in the sky until they look no bigger than specks. The best homers are, of course, called homers. Each of these pigeon breeds looks somewhat different from the others; some have slimmer bodies, longer necks, smaller heads, shorter beaks, or different markings of black or gray on their bodies. Pigeons come in many shades, from white through grays and tawny colors.

If you are looking for a fancier breed, you can also buy pigeons with feathery leggings, curled plumage, and crests on their heads. You can leave many of these fancy pigeons loose too, not because they always come home, but because they seldom leave home. Most of them have wings that are too small for long-distance flying. Before you buy, however, check with the dealer as to whether he or she recommends leaving a particular fancy breed free.

Any of the varieties of pigeons can share the same quarters.

Housing

The coop on page 340 is large enough for six pairs of pigeons. But pigeons don't roost on the ground like chickens. They will roost and nest only up off the ground, so the shed must be mounted up five or six feet and the bottom covered with a wooden floor. The illustration on page 341 shows how to mount the shed onto the side wall of a garage or house, with the door facing south. You could also mount a pigeon coop on a tree, like a small treehouse, or even up on a post, like a large birdhouse. Some people keep pigeons on the roof of their apartment building or even in the attic of their house.

For transporting your pigeons, you can buy or build a simple, sturdy cage with a wire-mesh top.

Cold temperatures will not hurt pigeons, but drafts will. Face the coop opening toward the south to get the sun and avoid the wind. If the weather turns windy or bitter in the winter, the wire door should be temporarily covered with burlap, canvas, or plastic sheeting. Use a staple gun to attach it.

The inside of the coop has to be fitted with shelves for roosting and for nesting. Pigeon breeders have rather fancy ways of fixing up the inside of a coop with separate roosting shelves, special nesting boxes, and nest bowls. But pigeons can manage with a plain 10-inch board shelf, to which is glued a lattice strip so eggs can't roll off (page 340). If you have more than one pair of birds, provide several shelves to cut down on squabbles over nesting sites.

Cover the floor of the coop with a layer of sand. Each week, rake off the droppings and sprinkle fresh sand over the floor. Three or four times a year, scrape droppings from the shelves with a paint scraper or a pancake turner. In the spring, brush all the old sand from the coop and completely replace it.

Food and Water

Pigeon feed, available at feed stores, makes a good diet for pigeons. It is a mixture of whole dried peas, whole dried corn, and an assortment of other grains. Like any other bird, pigeons need grit in their gizzards to grind the grain. If you let your birds loose, they'll find their own sand or gravel. You should still sprinkle crushed oyster shell, bonemeal, or eggshell in with their food once a week to supply minerals.

Serve the pigeon feed in a shallow pan once a day. Usually pigeon owners open the coop and let their birds fly loose early in the morning without feeding them breakfast. Pigeons tend to come home more faithfully if they are a little hungry.

The daily meal can be at three or four o'clock in the afternoon, when pigeons naturally settle back at their roosting area. Experiment with the amount, starting with only a handful, until you find a quantity that is finished in about 15 minutes. When the pigeons have young to feed, increase the amount of food.

Instead of filling their beaks and then tilting their heads back to swallow like most other birds, pigeons actually suck up water like horses. Keep a pan of water two inches deep so they can stick their beaks in far enough. Wash and refill the water pan every day. A loaf cake pan is a good shape, because it can be kept under a roosting shelf, where it is least likely to be soiled with droppings.

Except when the weather is very cold, put out a roasting pan filled with bathing water in front of the coop several times a week. Pigeons that can't bathe are miserable. Bathing is important for another reason too. When the birds are sitting on their eggs, the moisture from their feathers after a bath moistens the eggshells and softens them somewhat. Without the moisture, the babies can't peck their way out of the hard shell.

Illnesses

Pigeons, while subject to a range of germ-caused diseases, are more likely to be troubled by them in overcrowded conditions rather than in a small flock. Check the illness information given for geese (page 271) for treatment.

In warm weather pigeons routinely get lice, which live both on their bodies and in their nests. To check a pigeon for lice, pick it up and turn it over, belly up. Stretch out one wing; this is quite easy to do after you've had a little practice with it. Lice tend to gather on the undersides of the long wing feathers. They are very small and white. Kill the lice by dusting the pigeon with an insecticide dust intended for birds and available at pet stores,

sprinkling the powder on its belly and under its wings, then ruffling the feathers to work the powder down to the skin. Sprinkle the powder in the nesting areas as well.

Flies may become a nuisance in the coop and can really bother newly hatched babies. Hang a Shell No-Pest insect strip in the highest portion of the coop where pigeons will not peck it.

Another fact of pigeon life is hawks. No matter where you live, even in suburbs or cities, from time to time a hawk may dive down and grab one of your birds as it emerges from the coop, even if you happen to be standing right there. You can't do a thing about it.

In this country, smaller hawks — chicken hawks and sparrow hawks — are common birds. And even though pigeons will cock their heads to scan the sky for hawks before they take off, they are still caught unaware by the sudden, swift dive. Once in the air they are safe, as pigeons can outfly hawks in ordinary flight.

Breeding Pigeons

Pigeons can (and sometimes do) lay eggs and rear their young throughout the year. But sensible pairs, perhaps understanding that cold temperatures kill pigeon squabs, are most likely in colder climates to lay their eggs during the spring — from March to about June or July. This doesn't mean they court only in the spring. Among the many birds that mate early and remain faithful to each other for life, courtship behavior serves as a bond to remind them they are paired. It's about the same as reminder kisses, compliments, and candy between human husbands and wives.

Before nesting time the male will find a roost for himself in the coop. He may have to battle other cocks for the right to his own roost, but once he has it, his property rights are respected. Only his hen can share his roost with him.

As nesting season approaches, the cock looks for a suitable nest site. Owners of large coops often provide separate nesting boxes on a different wall from the roosts. In your simple coop, the cock will have to settle for an area of the same shelf on which he has roosted. He and his hen mate only after they have agreed on the nest site. You can usually tell that mating is about to take place when the birds "bill." Billing describes how the hen puts her bill inside the cock's bill to receive a snack of regurgitated grain.

After mating the cock goes out in search of twigs and straw to build the nest. He drives his hen to the nest site, where she squats to receive each twig he brings and arranges it to form a circle around her body. Pigeon nests are not works of art. They are only a crude gathering of twigs or grass, but they serve to keep the eggs from rolling around.

When the nest is ready, the hen lays exactly two — no more, no less — eggs in her nest. Both parents take turns sitting on the eggs for the two

fact

Homing pigeons have a remarkable ability to find their way home, even from hundreds of miles away. Before telephones and e-mail, even before the postal service, these pigeons were used to carry messages from one location to another.

and a half weeks it takes them to hatch. The pair of squabs that hatch are very ugly and very hungry. They will double their weight in 48 hours. Unlike any other birds, pigeons feed their young on "milk," a mixture of partially digested grain and nutritious secretions manufactured in their crops (a swollen part of a bird's throat that acts as a sort of stomach). Both hen and cock produce pigeon milk for the first few days, after which both gradually substitute a higher and higher proportion of regurgitated grain. The squabs greedily beg for food by jamming their heads down their parents' throats.

As the squabs grow, the cock takes over more and more of their care, while the hen lays another set of eggs in a second nest and begins to sit on them. She can repeat the whole process several times during the warm seasons of the year, and sometimes into cold weather as well.

By the time the first babies are six weeks old, fully feathered, and following their father about the coop, old Dad decides he's had enough of the greedy beggars and begins to fly away from them as they approach. Surprised, the squabs watch him, wondering what to do next. He drinks, he eats; they watch and catch on. Within days the babies are eating and drinking for themselves.

As you can see, young healthy pigeon flocks can grow by doubling, tripling, or more each year. This small coop of yours will run out of roosting and nesting space quickly, and the result will be fights, trampled eggs, and fallen squabs. What can you do to prevent this? You can either build larger quarters for your birds or give the young pigeons to friends or a pet store. You might even be able to sell them.

Training Pigeons

Each new pair of pigeons has to learn that the coop you built is home. When you buy a new pair, keep them in the coop together for a month. If you already have other birds flying free, you'll have to confine the new pair in the coop inside a temporary cage. The cardboard cage illustrated here is strong enough, and is set up with food and water dishes of its own.

Male and female pigeons, like most birds, are called cocks and hens. You can't tell them apart by their colors; you can tell only by their behavior. The male puffs his throat, coos, and struts.

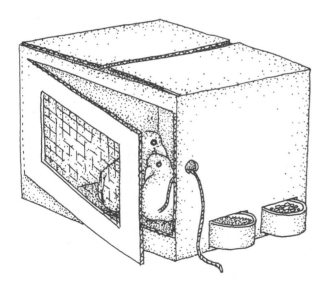

A TEMPORARY CARDBOARD PIGEON BOX

1. Glue the flaps closed. Cut the door in one side of the box. Staple hardware cloth over the cut-out portion. Tie the door shut with string as shown.

2. Cut snug slots for food and water dishes and slide them partway through so they don't tip over.

3. Cover the floor with newspaper or sand.

4. To make this box last longer, spray or brush on three coats of polyurethane inside and outside.

He eats and drinks more aggressively than the female. He may be larger, and his neck looks thicker (because he is puffing it) than the female's.

Supply yourself with a commercial wire cage, a plastic milk crate, or even a large wire bicycle basket. After the month of confinement, reach in the temporary cage and grab the hen. Grab fast, using both hands to wrap around the hen's whole body. As long as your hands are around her wings, she can't hurt herself by struggling. Put the hen under the wire basket or in the wire cage on the open ground in front of the coop. Let the cock fly out of the coop. A cock pigeon is very reluctant to lose sight of his hen. He's not likely to go far — he'll probably sit on a tree or roof nearby or even on the coop, so he can keep his eye on his hen. When you want him to come back into the coop, just put the hen back inside, and he'll fly in to join her. After a week of repeating this routine every day, you can let both the cock and the hen loose to fly, because by now their attachment to home is very strong, and the cock has had a chance to learn some local landmarks.

Pigeons easily learn to recognize you and even to come to your whistle. As often as you have the time, feed your pigeons by hand instead of putting their grain into the grain pan. To train the birds to hand-feed, first sprinkle the food on the coop floor near you. Gradually sprinkle less and less on the floor and keep more and more in your open hand. The bolder cocks will probably be the first to come to your hand, but the hens will soon follow. Each time you feed your birds, whether from your hand or in the pan, whistle to them as you arrive with dinner. They will learn to associate the whistle with feeding time, and eventually you will be able to call your flock from the sky to you with just a whistle. They will all swoop down and settle about you and on you, eating without fear from your open palm.

Goats

Smaller goats are better for backyards than larger ones. Even a small goat is very strong and can leap high. But goats are not that easy to find, and you may not have much choice as to breeds, depending on where you live. If you do, most people find the prettiest goat to be the Nubian, the only breed with long pendulous ears and a delicate Roman nose. The Alpine and the Toggenburg are both rather large goats with upright ears and dish faces (curved in instead of out). The Saanan is a white goat with a dished face and erect ears. These goats are often raised for milk production. A wonderful pet goat is the African pygmy, a dwarf breed that comes in shades of warm brown and beige, as well as spotted black and white.

Choosing a Goat

If state fairs are held near you, by all means go to see these breeds and others. Breeders at the fair will be happy to talk to you about buying a baby goat. Another way to get in touch with breeders is through a local 4-H chapter, an agricultural college, or the American Dairy Goat Association. (See the appendix for this organization's Web site and others.) Local farms or petting zoos may sell extra baby goats in the spring. Many of them raise the African pygmy.

Goats are ready to be weaned onto grass and grain by about one month old. A nanny goat or doe is a nice pet and will give milk for most of the year if she is bred each winter. The doe is taken to the buck to be "served" — most likely at the farm where you purchased her. Make sure you have a plan for the babies that are produced!

Far cheaper is the billy goat or buck that no one wants. Goat farmers keep only one or two billy goats for breeding purposes. They have a pronounced odor and are generally more difficult to handle than does. Those that aren't kept are usually killed for meat. Once castrated, however, these otherwise doomed babies make excellent pets and can be had for little more than the cost of the operation. Although castrating ensures they won't be aggressive adults, there will still be some billy goat smell.

If you're able to spend a lot of time with a pet goat, it's all right to have just one. But goats so crave companionship that you may discover that you cannot bear to live with one lonely goat's plaintive bleating. Better to have two, so they can keep each other company when you're too busy for them. Sex doesn't matter — two castrated bucks, two does, or one of each will be friends.

Housing

People have kept goats in everything from over-sized doghouses to basements. Goats need a minimum indoor space of 10 square feet each. An unused horse stall in a barn is a good goat home. You can also build a simple stall in a corner of your garage or a freestanding shed in a corner of your house lot (see pages 342–43). Goats also need to spend time outdoors. Make sure your goat has access to an outdoor yard.

Goats have a thing about getting wet — they hate it. Put the shed on a high and dry bit of land. The open front faces south for sun, the closed back protects the goat from wind. No heat is necessary. The floor can be concrete, dirt, gravel, or sand.

Spread straw on the floor for bedding. The straw will trap and absorb urine, and the small,

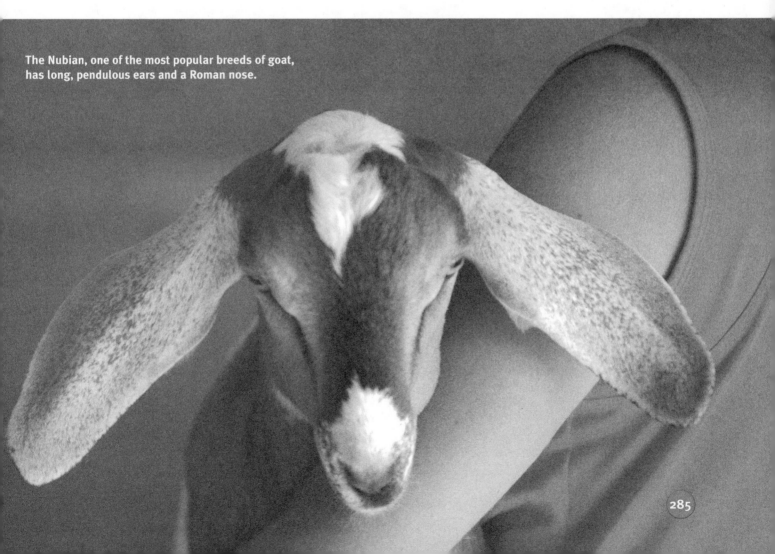

The Nubian, one of the most popular breeds of goat, has long, pendulous ears and a Roman nose.

dry goat droppings will work their way down under the bedding. Each day, cover the old bedding with a fresh layer. As time goes by and you keep adding layers of dry straw, the floor will get higher and higher, providing insulation and padding for sleeping goats. You can sometimes get straw or salt hay from a local nursery or you can ask at a nearby stable or agricultural supply store for sources of hay and straw.

Depending on the type of floor you have, you'll have to clean all the old bedding out at regular intervals. A dirt floor will allow urine to drain away, while a concrete floor will need to be cleaned more frequently. Rake out all the old bedding until you're down to dirt or sand or the garage floor again. The old bedding, left outside in a heap to finish decaying, will make good compost for the garden next season. Spread a layer of dry hay over the shed floor and begin the process over again. You can also use sawdust or wood shavings as bedding, making sure you scoop out wet spots frequently and replace all the old bedding regularly.

Confining a goat is more difficult than housing one. A goat can't live in a shed all the time. It needs exercise. But when on the loose, goats are destructive eaters. The best solution is to fence in a goat yard and let your goats have free access to it from their shed. However, the fence must be both sturdy and high. Some goats are excellent jumpers, and all goats are curious creatures that will work at a weak spot in a fence or nibble at the latch on a gate until they have — accidentally or on purpose — let themselves loose. Staking or tying a goat is not advisable, as the goat can become tangled up and injure itself. It will also be vulnerable to passing dogs and to bad weather if it's not within reach of shelter.

Food and Water

When a kid is a month old — the time you are likely to buy one as a pet — it may still be drinking milk. The milk can be cow's milk, and two pints of milk a day are enough. Heat the milk in a saucepan to 103 degrees (use a household cooking thermometer to check the temperature) and serve it to the kid in a dog's dish, in a bowl, or from a baby's bottle equipped with a crosscut nipple. A bottle is really not necessary, but it's fun to feed a kid that way. The rest of the kid's diet can be a calf-starter grain, sold at feed stores, and hays like timothy and alfalfa, too. A kid's stomach is still very small, so offer three or four small meals a day to be sure that it eats enough.

When the kid is three months old, it doesn't need milk anymore. Now it can go on to a steady diet of grain mixes (formulated for goats) and hay. Good nutritious hay is greenish in color and has a variety of leaves in it. In other words, it's not just dry yellow stalks, such as bedding straw, which goats won't even bother to eat. The best

Backyard Pet Blues

Madeline was a three-week-old Nubian nanny goat, still drinking from a bottle, still small enough to carry in our arms. Who could resist her? Not us. And the fact that she was adorable was, we were told, nothing compared to her utilitarian virtues. She would mow our lawn for us; she would decimate our poison ivy; her droppings, we were advised, made excellent fertilizer.

We took Madeline home in the car. Collar and leash weren't necessary. She followed us eagerly into the car, onto the front seat. She followed us out of the car, in the front door, up the stairs, and onto my bed. Madeline was home.

We told Madeline that she had gotten it wrong: Indoors was our home; outdoors was her home. She never did get that straight. All of us learned to sidle snakewise in through the door and slam it fast behind us. If we weren't quick enough, she'd be inside and bounding from chair to table to bed to sink. No one had told us how well goats leap and climb.

We felt we could adjust to the situation — after all, who can fail to love so loving a baby? We weaned Madeline from the bottle (well, sort of — she never did grow out of grabbing baby bottles from unwary toddlers) and introduced her to grass and leaves. Then we settled down to await the disappearance of our poison ivy, the neat cropping of our lawn. Madeline started on the flowers.

That was our first lesson — devoted baby goats don't run away from home, but they do eat everything in sight, so they have to be confined. We staked Madeline out on a chain during the day for those times when we couldn't supervise her eating. At other times, however, she was free to follow us on walks along the road and into town for shopping. She never needed a leash. She followed us so reliably, in fact, that we came up with a bad idea.

By now it was fall, and Madeline, true to her Nubian background, had grown small straight horns in her forehead. Jet black, goatlike, horned, and cloven-hoofed. Remind you of something? The Devil! Aha! Halloween! The children decided costumes were not necessary this year. All they had to do was wait until it was very dark, let Madeline follow them on their rounds of the neighborhood, ring doorbells, hide to one side, push the goat devil to the foreground, and laugh their heads off.

They rang the first bell. They hid to the side of the door. They heard footsteps coming. The hand on the knob. NOW! Madeline leaped into the house, bounded onto a table, snatched what candy she could, and disappeared off into the rest of the house.

That was Madeline's last trick-or-treat. Now we settled down to the serious business of how to keep a pet goat happy outside of family and neighborhood life. We built a six-foot fence around her shed. She leaped it. We put her back on a chain. She broke it. We got a stronger chain and sunk an iron stake far into the ground. She cried — *baa baa baaaaaa* — to be with us. And that was how we came to know the awful responsibility we are trying to explain to you now: If you

take a farm animal and make a pet of it, you become its family. Like a child, it will want to hang around you all the time.

And it isn't only goats. A woman who raised a baby pig in her kitchen has to replace the screen door every time the by now full-grown, milk-cow-sized sow walks through it to visit her home and family. A tiny Easter chick who grew into a rooster tried to spend all his waking hours on his owner's shoulder. A goose and gander, when they grew up, protected their "family" by hissing and making threatening gestures at postmen, meter readers, garbagemen, and guests.

If a backyard animal as part of the family doesn't appeal to you, avoid the emotional strain by getting an animal that has been raised in an ordinary farm situation, in an animal family of its own; and get one that you consider a young adult rather than a little baby. The physical care of these animals is the same whether you choose to raise them as pets or as farm animals. As for Madeline, she will always need human company.

hays are legume crops like clover, alfalfa, and soybean. Roughage (greenery) is necessary to a goat's digestion, so good-quality hay becomes the staple diet of goats when they can't browse in a meadow.

Goats prefer to nibble their food from high places, like the upper leaves of a bush. They are not grazers and won't mow your lawn the way sheep would. They do a more thorough job of eating their hay if it's kept high up off the floor of their shed. A simple way to manage this if you don't want to build a fancy manger (hay feeder) is to buy a big wire or plastic basket (one with large openings, like an old-fashioned bicycle basket), mount it on the shed wall, and put an armful of fresh hay into it every morning. Goat chow or a goat grain mixture — about a pound or a coffee can full each day — can be served in a small bucket hung from a hook screwed into the wall. Goats don't like to eat from the floor.

A hanging bucket is also a convenient way to provide water. If you just set the bucket on the floor of the shed, the goat will promptly knock it over. Instead, put a stout hook into the wall to hold the bucket handle. The hook should be just high enough from the floor so that the bucket rests on the floor but can't tip.

If you let them, goats will eat anything that is basically vegetable in origin. That includes paper (made from trees) and cigarettes (made from leaves). They don't eat tin cans, but they do nibble the paper labels from them. They adore roses and other flowers, as well as any ornamental shrubbery, fruit trees, and garden vegetables they can find a way to get to. And if these temptations were not misfortune enough, they also haven't the sense to keep away from an array of poisonous plants, any of which can make them sick or even kill them if they eat enough of them. A partial list of poisonous plants goats will eat includes buttercup, cowslip, lily of the valley, foxglove, laurel, rhododendron, bracken fern, dry or wilted wild cherry and oak leaves, delphinium, and yew. Feel free, however, to let your goat eat up all the poison ivy and poison oak around. They won't hurt the goats and if the goats eat them, they won't be around for you to stumble into and develop an awful itchy rash. In fact, we used to lend our goat Madeline out to friends for a day's nibbling on their ivy patches. But beware of touching your goat after it's had a poison ivy or poison oak snack: The poison oils left on your goat's skin are enough to cause a rash on your skin.

You may be interested in getting milk from your doe. Goat's milk really is delicious, and you can get about two quarts a day from one goat for about nine months of the year, for far less than you pay for cow's milk. From goat's milk you can make several cheeses, especially a soft pot cheese, quite easily. Of course, neither cows nor goats produce milk unless they have babies every year. For more information about this practical side of goat ownership, including both breeding and caring for newborns, write to your own state or county extension service, your state agricultural college, or a local 4-H Club.

Illnesses

A vet who has been trained to care for farm animals can recommend appropriate vaccinations for your goat and help you if anything goes wrong. The 4-H chapter in your area can usually give you the contact information for local vets that have had experience with farm animals.

Worms are fairly common in goats. They can be detected and treated by any vet if you give him some fresh goat droppings; the vet will examine them under a microscope.

Flies are a nuisance to goats in warm weather, but using an insecticide to get rid of them is worse. As you've learned, goats will nibble on anything, even flypaper and insecticide-soaked wood. These insecticides are poisonous and can make your goat ill. If the flies become unbearable in the summer, you and your goat will be better off if you clean out the goat shed or stall weekly.

Some goats are naturally hornless, but most have to be dehorned. Madeline was able to keep her horns with no disasters, except that her playful butting was occasionally misinterpreted by nervous mothers. Even in play a horn could hurt, and two horned goats kept together might hurt each other. Dehorning is not a job for the amateur. Instead, purchase only a dehorned goat, or find a vet who knows how to do dehorning. The operation is done with the most success and the least pain during the kid's first weeks.

fact

Goats are great climbers and leapers, and they are extremely curious. If you keep your goat penned in a yard, make sure the yard has no objects that could become a leaping-off point for an adventurous goat looking to jump the fence.

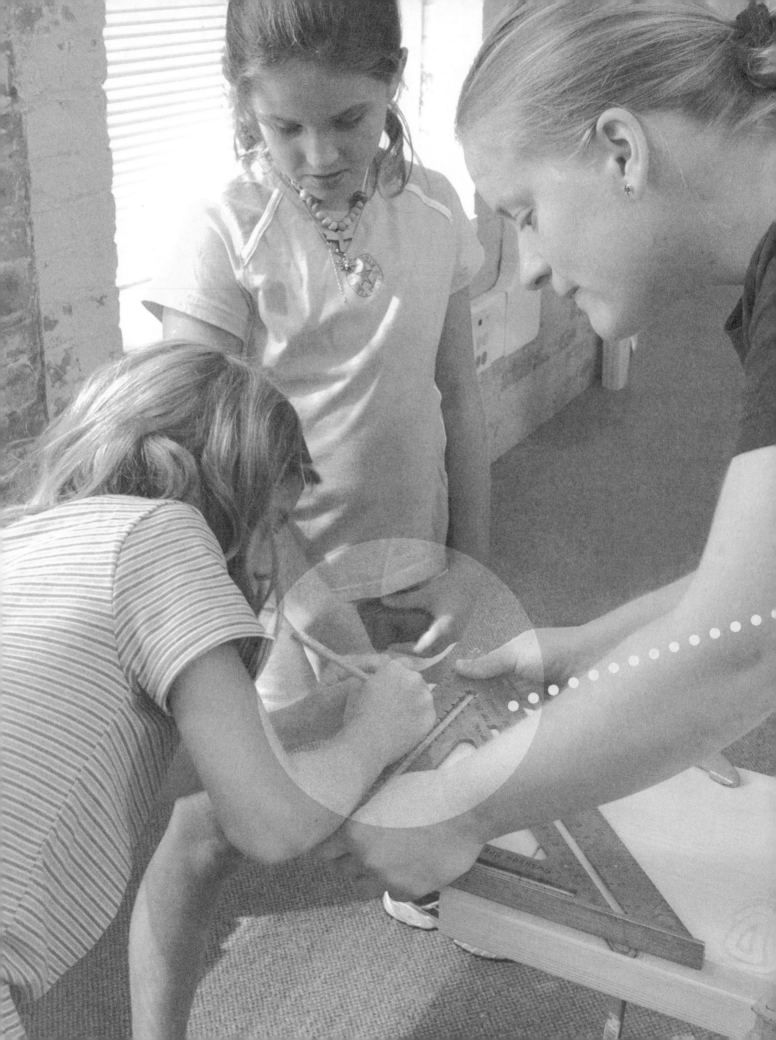

Ready-Homes Construction

Often the obstacle to owning a pet is not how to get the animal but what to keep it in. In some cases, excellent commercial cages are available in pet stores. This chapter will tell you how to set them up with all the comforts of home. In other cases, the basic

containers are available — glass-walled tanks, for instance — but you will need to know how to transform them into suitable environments for the many different needs of the pets they can house. In still other cases, there are no commercial cages available, or the ones that are could stand great improvement. This chapter gives instructions for a variety of homemade cages that are as inexpensive, simple, and practical as possible.

The simplest homes are ones that house pets only temporarily. They are an assortment of containers that can be kept on hand to take care of pets you will keep for a night or so and then let go.

Permanent homes for pets with few special needs are cheap and easy to make. These include cake-pan homes for rodents, hutches for guinea pigs and rabbits, and some tank homes. Other permanent pets have special needs that require

rather expensive lighting and heating equipment, though the setting up or construction is still easy.

A few homes require both expensive materials or equipment and hard, sometimes skilled work. Homes for backyard pets in particular need accurate construction and may run up a substantial bill at the lumberyard.

Stay with the simple projects until you get used to measuring accurately and handling tools. Before you get to homes that require carpentry skills, there is much to learn. Be sure to ask an experienced adult for instruction and/or assistance in using saws and drills.

The illustrations that follow are very basic. It won't matter if you change the dimensions a little to suit the materials you find, as long as you meet the requirements of space, environmental controls, and ease of cleaning.

Measuring

Accurate construction with lumber requires special measuring techniques. You can't precut all the pieces before you start to build. Instead, cut and build only the outside frame or basic shape of the house. When that's done, any pieces of lumber that are to be added — such as shelves, floors, bracing pieces, and doors — must be held against the place where they are to fit and marked with a pencil. Then they can be sawed along the pencil line and nailed in place.

There are two reasons for using this method. One is that no matter how well you measure the basic pieces that make up the frame of your construction, you will never saw absolutely accurately. Sawing just a hair to one side or another of your pencil line will change the overall dimensions of your building. If, for instance, you had precut a shelf that was to fit inside that building, the shelf could easily turn out either too long or too short to fit snugly.

The other reason is that the dimensions of lumber vary from one part of the country to another, from one lumberyard to another, and even from one shipment to another. The nominal dimension of a piece of lumber — a 2 by 4 (two by four inches), for example — is not the same as the actual dimension, which may be 1⅝ by 3⅝ inches, or slightly less, or slightly more.

Another note on measuring and marking lumber: If you are using a yardstick to measure and to draw straight lines, check it first along the edge of a sheet of plywood or some other surface you are sure is straight. Many yardsticks are warped and will give you a curved pencil line instead of a straight one. Long steel rulers are more accurate than wooden yardsticks. If anyone in your family knows how to use a chalk line, ask him or her for help; a chalk line is the most reliable tool of all for marking long, perfectly straight lines.

Cutting

A few projects, like birdhouses and hutches, may be made from scraps of lumber to save the cost of buying large sheets of plywood or long boards. If you can't find large enough scraps around your home, ask at lumberyards. Some keep a scrap bin of pieces that could be used for these projects. You may be able to find just what you need and not have to cut at all. Also, most lumberyards will cut lumber for you at an extra cost of only a few cents per cut.

If you do your own cutting, narrow lumber — shelving or 2 by 4s — is not too hard to cut along a pencil line with a handsaw. It is very difficult to cut plywood straight with a handsaw, no matter how well you have marked it. The job should be done with an electric circular saw, but only by someone who has experience using this dangerous tool. If no one in your family feels comfortable with the work, or if you have no saw, a neighbor might help. Once the measuring is done, the sawing itself goes quickly.

Nailing

To be sure pieces fit before they are permanently attached, tack them together with nails that are hammered only part of the way in. Then check the tacked-together piece against the basic construction. If the fit is good, hammer the nails all

Nail through the thinner piece of wood into the thicker piece.

the way in; or if the instructions call for gluing, remove the nails and apply the glue before renailing. If the fit isn't right, you can make adjustments before you glue and nail permanently.

Use nails that are two and a half to three times longer than the thickness of the wood you will be hammering through. All the following animal homes use what are called common nails, unless otherwise specified. Common nails are sold by the pound: There are 150 2¼-inch nails in a pound, fewer longer nails, and more shorter nails. A quarter of a pound of nails is enough for a birdhouse, about half a pound for any of the small sheds, and a whole pound for the goat shed.

Materials

The plywood for any outdoor housing must be what is called *exterior grade*. The layers (laminations) of interior-grade plywood will become unglued and split apart after a few rains. Shellac your buildings before you paint them, both to protect the wood and to seal it so the paint covers it more easily.

Some of the animal housing calls for hardware cloth (wire mesh) attached to wood. The easiest way to attach it is with a stapling gun, which is inexpensive to purchase or can be rented by the day from many lumberyards. An adult should do the stapling, as these guns force out the staples under great pressure and can be quite dangerous if not carefully used. Before starting on a project requiring a staple gun, make sure you can rent or borrow one easily.

Hardware cloth is sold by the foot from rolls 36 inches wide or wider. It is available in hardware stores and lumberyards. For small projects like the ones in this chapter, you must be sure the cloth is not warped before you ask the clerk to cut it. Many home tool chests don't contain the big wire shears needed to cut hardware cloth. Since

shears are expensive, try to borrow some, or ask the clerk to cut the piece you are buying to the right dimensions for your project with his or her shears while you are in the store.

Hardware

Some of the roofs and all of the doors in these projects are attached with hinges. Be sure to leave enough space between the two pieces of wood so the hinge works freely. Take your time installing

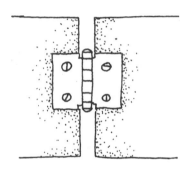

Leave space between the two pieces of wood when installing hinges.

hinges, because any crookedness at all makes the hinge bind instead of swing easily. The screws are much easier to put in if you first use a drill or a nail to make a hole smaller than the screw. The same is true when installing hooks and screw eyes, which are used to close all the cage or house doors in these projects.

Posts

Some of the projects call for putting posts or stakes into the ground. This is a difficult job. For wood posts, use 4-by-4-inch lumber or round fence posts. Paint the bottom two feet with creosote, a natural tarry substance that protects the wood from moisture and kills the bacteria that might otherwise rot the post bottoms. Common steel posts come prepainted for weather

**The carpenter's rule:
Measure twice, cut once.**

protection and have hooklike protrusions for attaching wire fencing. For any post, dig the hole two feet deep. While a friend holds the post upright in the hole, you wedge it firmly in place with rocks. Then fill in soil around the post and stamp it in hard with the heel of your shoe. Some parts of the country have no rocks. Instead, mix a bucket or more of thick ready-mix concrete to fill the hole around the post. Keep the post level until the concrete begins to set.

Quantities

We have tried to give you accurate estimates of how much lumber, hardware cloth, and other materials you will need to complete a job. For some of the smaller projects, like a birdhouse or a bug house, it would be wasteful to buy whole sheets of plywood or long lengths of lumber or window screening. Instead, try to find scraps that will fit the pattern. Many lumberyards keep a box

full of small leftover pieces of lumber, or often neighbors who are building something in their home will have scraps of materials they really don't want. Bigger projects list the materials you will need in terms of standard dimensions — 4-by-8-foot plywood sheets, for example, or 8- or 10-foot lengths of board and lumber, or standard roll widths of hardware cloth. In these projects, there will be some unavoidable waste of materials.

Costs

It is impossible for us to give you an accurate idea of what each project will cost. Prices may be higher or lower where you live, and they may differ from month to month. Also, we don't know if you have on hand many of the common materials that are needed — masking tape, wire, white glue, nails, and so on. Many of these animal homes can be made of scrap wood or old containers and parts found in thrift stores.

Attracting Birds

The best way to attract pets in the wild is with food. But for the most part there is no reason to build shelters or feeding stations for wild animals — a garbage can or a garden suits them fine. The exceptions are some songbirds, which appreciate the shelter of a birdhouse during nesting time and the convenience of a feeding station during winter.

Birdhouse

Wild birds will enthusiastically nest in a homemade birdhouse. They don't see the building as a house, only as a safe, dry nook (much like a hollow tree) in which to build a nest. Birds live in nests only during the few springtime weeks when they are laying eggs and raising their young. But a birdhouse looks pretty even when it is unoccupied.

You can design a birdhouse in any shape you want as long as the entrance hole is the right size, a perch is provided, and the house is located properly. Parent birds will be too disturbed to care for their young if the house is placed where people are always coming and going. You can put a birdhouse close by or even attached to a human home, but don't put it near a doorway, path, or gate.

This plan is for a basic pitch-roofed house that is the right size for many common songbirds. You can probably get large enough scraps of wood to fit the pattern from the scrap bin at a lumberyard.

A birdhouse is usually set up on a post six feet off the ground, but you can also nail a birdhouse onto a house or garage wall, if you check with your parents first. Before you cut out any pieces, decide which way you will mount the house, as the patterns are a little different. Then follow the illustrations to construct the house.

Some people so enjoy the coming and going of nesting birds, or so love to make birdhouses, that they end up with a bird village of a half-dozen or more houses, each different. The richer birds live in colonnaded mansions, the bird minister in his church, and others may inhabit barns, schools, firehouses, or chalets. You can add a porch to countrify a house or add a steeple to make it look like a church. You can nail in balconies and paint on windows, tack on chimneys, or even attach a weather vane. None of these additions bothers the birds, and all of them tickle humans.

Maintaining a birdhouse is simple enough. Each spring, remove the screws that hold the birdhouse in place, lift the house from its base, and

POST-MOUNTED BIRDHOUSE

Materials

- Exterior-grade plywood or board scraps to fit the pattern
- ½-inch dowel, 3 inches long
- White glue
- Common nails (the length depends on how thick your scrap lumber is)
- 1 pint of shellac
- Exterior enamel paint (you don't need much, so leftovers are fine)
- Fence post, either a 4-by-4-inch or a round post, 8 feet high (or you could mount the birdhouse on an existing post or a building wall)
- 1 quart of creosote, if you are sinking a post
- Screws

Tools

- Yardstick
- Handsaw
- Drill with 2-inch and ½-inch drill bits
- Hammer
- Paintbrush
- Shovel or spade, if you are sinking a post

remove last year's nest by hooking it through the door with a bent piece of wire coat hanger. After you've removed the nest, check the house for wear and tear. Remove or sand off splinters, replace loose screws or nails, and shore up the post, if necessary. Then set the house back on its base and screw it back into place.

MAKING A BIRDHOUSE

1. From the plywood, cut out the four walls to the dimensions shown in the illustration below.
2. Drill two holes in the front, one for an entrance and one for a perch. Check a birding guide to determine the right-size entrance hole for wild birds in your area. For the perch, hold the 3-inch dowel to the front wall and trace its circumference with a pencil. Then drill a hole exactly that size. Coat one end of the dowel with glue and push it into the hole, using a hammer to gently knock it into place if necessary.
3. Glue and nail the four walls together.
4. Use the top edges of the four walls as a guide to measure and cut the two roof pieces. Glue and nail the two roof pieces together. Then glue and nail the roof to the house.
5. Use the bottom edges of the house as a guide to measure and cut floor and base pieces. The floor should stick out 2 inches farther than the birdhouse walls all around. The base should stick out 1 inch farther than the floor on all sides. Glue the house to the floor, and nail from underneath.
6. Shellac and then paint the house, floor, and base.

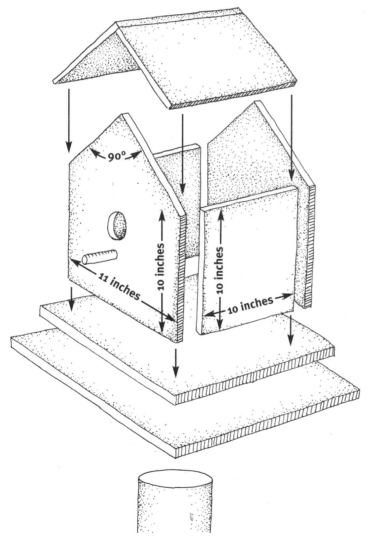

7. If you're installing a new post to set the birdhouse on, dig a hole 2 feet deep in the site you've selected.
8. Paint the bottom 2½ feet of the post with creosote.
9. Set the post upright in the hole you've dug. Wedge rocks around the post to hold it in place. Then fill the hole with dirt, tamping it down firmly with your feet.
10. Hammer the base into the top of the post with 4-inch nails. Then screw the house to the base at each corner.

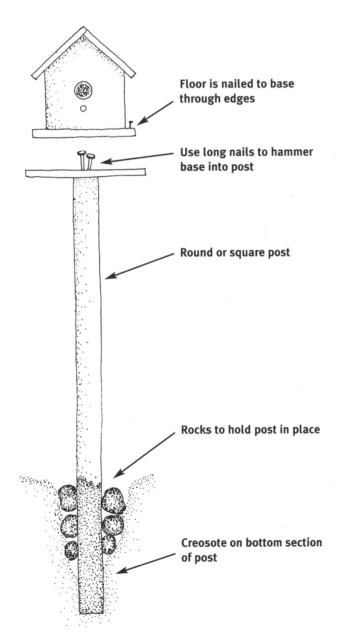

Floor is nailed to base through edges

Use long nails to hammer base into post

Round or square post

Rocks to hold post in place

Creosote on bottom section of post

To make a birdhouse that can be mounted on a wall, cut the back wall 8 inches higher than the front wall. Cut the floor to fit even with the walls instead of sticking out. The roof can stick out in the front but is even with the back wall. Nail the back wall to a fence or a building wall.

To make your birdhouse look like a church, cut a steeple from a piece of 4-by-4-inch lumber and paint on the rest of the decorations.

To make a mansion for your wild friends, cut the roof pieces 6 inches longer to overhang the porch and cut a triangle for the front. The floor piece is 6 inches longer too. Use ¾-inch dowels for columns at the front and lattice strip to make shutters for false windows. Paint on the rest of the decorations.

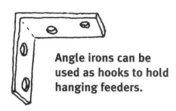

Angle irons can be used as hooks to hold hanging feeders.

Masonry nails are thick and grooved.

Hang bird feeder through this hole.

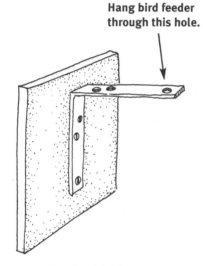

To mount a hanging bird feeder to a wall, first attach a bracket to the wall, using nails (if the wall is wood) or masonry nails (if the wall is brick or concrete).

Bird Feeders

Since birds live in houses only during the spring, the way to keep them around in other seasons is to feed them. Feeding attracts the most birds during the winter, when wild foods are scarce.

Feeding stations that contain seed will attract many kinds of birds. The feeders don't have to be any fancier than a flat tray that you sprinkle the seed on every morning. If you want something fancier, you can make a coffee-can feeder that you won't have to refill too often or, even nicer, a plastic milk jug feeder. Filled with sunflower seeds — which most birds eat like candy — these feeders become bird magnets.

During the cold winter months, many birds seek high-energy fatty foods such as larvae and grubs. To attract these birds to your backyard, you can set out similar high-energy fatty foods, such as suet and peanut butter. Suet is the crackly dry fat from beef. You may be able to get it free from a butcher, but if not, it is inexpensive even in supermarkets. Peanut butter is more expensive than suet, but birds love it, especially when it's mixed with birdseed. You can scoop suet or peanut butter into any

SEED FEEDERS

Cut holes at the bottom of the coffee can, so that as birds eat seed, more spills out. Set the coffee can on a pie plate to contain the seeds.

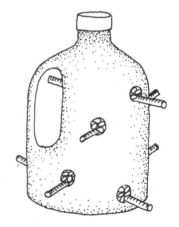

Fill a milk jug with sunflower seeds. Cut ¾-inch holes on opposite sides of the jug. Stick dowels through for perches. You can hang the jug by its handle.

simple container that birds can perch on and reach into to get at the goodies. Even a pint-sized ice-cream container makes a good fat feeder; just fill it with suet or peanut butter, poke holes in the walls so the birds can reach through to get at the fat, and stick twigs through so the birds can perch to eat. A nylon net bag, such as the type onions are sold in, also makes a good feeder.

Be sure to place your bird feeder within sight of a window in your house, so you can watch the birds feeding at it. People who live in the country don't usually have much trouble figuring out how to attach a bird feeder somewhere. It can be hung with string from a tree branch, nailed into a wooden window frame or fence post, or simply placed on a terrace wall. People who live in apartment houses in the city may have more trouble, however, particularly if they don't live at ground level and the only outdoor surface near their windows is brick or concrete. If this is your situation, you'll have to make a special bracket for your feeder to hang from. Just attach a large, sturdy angle iron to a small piece of board and attach the board to the masonry wall with masonry nails (sold at hardware stores). Of course, be sure to check with your parents before you fasten anything to a wall of your house or apartment.

HOMEMADE SUET
Any sort of leftover fat from cooking can be transformed to bird food with little work. Use grease that hardens at room temperature, like bacon fat. Wait until the fat has cooled a little bit so it won't melt the container you're going to put it in. Mix some birdseed in with the liquid fat, then pour it into the container you've selected. After the fat hardens, cut holes in the container with a sharp knife, stick twigs or dowels through to serve as perches, and tie three strings to the top so you can hang up the feeder (see the illustration on page 311).

FAT FEEDERS

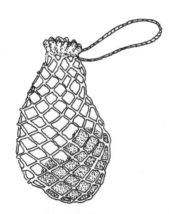

A nylon net bag can hold lumps of suet. Birds can perch on the netting easily and peck at the suet through the mesh.

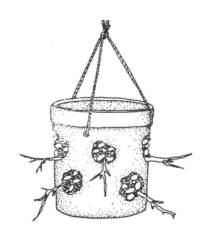

An ice-cream carton can be packed with birdseed in bacon grease. The holes are cut after the grease has hardened, and twigs are stuck in for birds to perch on.

Overnight Pet Houses

TANK HOME

Materials

- 5½-gallon tank. The tank can be a leaky one bought cheaply at a thrift shop or garage sale.
- Wire-mesh top, made according to the instructions given for the desert vivarium (see page 304)
- Rock to weight the top
- Several layers of newspaper to cover the tank floor
- Two small crockery dishes
- Empty can

Overnight pets — the ones you keep for only a day or so — tend to turn up unexpectedly before you have a home ready for them. It rains, and suddenly you find an adorable salamander walking on the lawn, but you have no cage to keep it in. At last a baby deer mouse is discovered in the bottom of the dog-food bag, but no home is ready for it. Rather than miss these opportunities, keep on hand the following ready homes, each of which costs from nothing at all to only a few dollars.

Tank Home

Without the can or dishes, this tank can house temporary pets like large toads, large lizards, snakes, and land or water turtles. For an overnight rodent like a mouse or a chipmunk, provide water and birdseed in the two small crockery dishes. Add the empty can to serve as a hiding place.

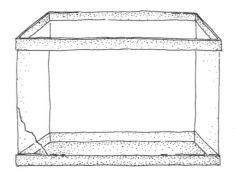

A tank with a crack in it or a leak in the seams may cost only a few dollars.

BUG CAGE

Materials

- Wire window screening, cut with scissors to 9 by 14 inches
- Two empty, clean tuna fish cans, 12 ounces each with one lid removed
- Soft wire, about a foot long

Tools

- Ruler
- Scissors
- Wire cutters

Bug Cage

This cage is good for larger insects like grass-hoppers, crickets, katydids, walking sticks, cater-pillars, moths, fireflies, and beetles. It is easy to make. Just stand the screen on one of its 9-inch ends and curve it into a cylinder that fits snugly inside the tuna cans. Then weave the overlap together with the soft wire.

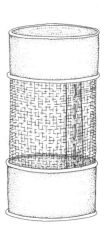

Jar House

Cut a square of cheesecloth to fit over the mouth of each of your jars. Hold it in place with a rubber band. Use the small jar as is for land snails, cocoons, insect and spider eggs, small toads, small lizards, and baby snakes. To keep moisture-loving pets like salamanders and tree frogs overnight, place a layer of moist paper towels on the bottom of the small jar. (And make sure it stays moist through the duration of your pet's stay in the jar.) Use the large jar filled with the right kind of water as temporary quarters for water pets — saltwater ones like starfish and crabs, or freshwater ones like frogs, baby water turtles, and crayfish. Don't leave the jar in the sun; it acts like a greenhouse, heating up and killing the animals inside it very quickly.

Use a rubber band to keep the cheesecloth in place.

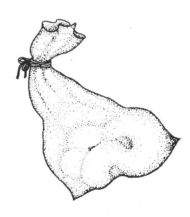

A snake can live temporarily in a pillowcase.

JAR HOUSE

Materials

- Cheesecloth
- One-quart widemouthed jar
- One-gallon- widemouthed jar (pickle and mayonnaise jars come in gallons)
- Wide rubber bands to fit jar mouths
- Paper towels

Emergency Homes

If, in spite of all warnings to the contrary, you still find yourself with a temporary pet and no place to keep it, these emergency measures should tide you over the time it takes to build a more substantial home.

For insects, small snakes, toads, and salamanders, use a jar house, as described above. If you don't have cheesecloth, any type of cloth will do for a cover. Do *not* use a metal lid, even one with holes punched in it.

For snakes, use a pillowcase, closed at the top with a rubber band.

For water animals like crayfish and tadpoles, use the largest container you can get, like a plastic pail, filled with water from the pond or stream where you found the animal. Again, don't leave it in the sun to heat up.

In an emergency, turtles, snakes, mice and other small rodents, large beetles, salamanders, toads, frogs (except tree frogs, which can cling to the sides), and most other animals can be put in the bathtub, with or without water, depending on what sort of animal you have. The sides are too steep and slippery for them to escape. Be sure to close the drain first, and be sure to clean the bathtub afterward.

Desert Vivariums

A vivarium is a special enclosure designed to mimic the unique environment a variety of small creatures live in. These animals would usually not survive in the environment of a human house; it would be too cold, too dry, or too humid for them. Although a vivarium is basically nothing more than a tank, the accessories you need vary so much from one animal to another that there is no such thing as a "normal" vivarium.

A hot, dry desert vivarium creates a home for creatures that come from hot climates, such as land tortoises, desert iguanas, anoles, and tarantulas. The common iguana needs a similar environment but with more humidity, which can be supplied by equipping the dry desert vivarium with a large dish of water set into the sand. The tank should be at least 10 gallons to provide enough room for these creatures; for desert iguanas, you will need an 18-gallon tank. In either case, you can save money by purchasing a secondhand or leaky tank.

Sand

Wash the sand by putting it all in a pail and running water into it, letting the water overflow until it looks clear. (The reason for this is to get rid of dust that might bother pets when they breathe.) Pour out the water

A HOT, DRY ENVIRONMENT

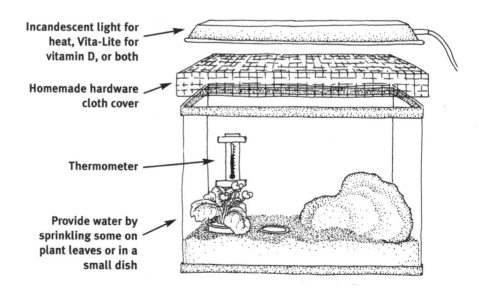

Incandescent light for heat, Vita-Lite for vitamin D, or both

Homemade hardware cloth cover

Thermometer

Provide water by sprinkling some on plant leaves or in a small dish

slowly. The sand will remain on the bottom of the pail. Spread the sand out on newspaper and let it dry for a day or two in the sun. Or dry it for a few hours in a roasting pan in the oven at the lowest setting. When it is dry, spread the sand in the bottom of the tank.

Lid

Lizards, spiders, and other creatures that like to climb must have a lid on the top of their vivarium. Even creatures that don't climb, such as tortoises, will benefit from having a lid, as much to keep other things out as to keep them in. You can make a lid from hardware cloth (see page 294) or buy a commercial screen top for your tank.

MAKING A TANK LID

1. Measure the top of the tank. Trim a piece of ¼-inch mesh hardware cloth 2 inches larger than the top of the tank on all sides.

2. Snip 2 inches into all four corners as shown below to form four flaps.

4. Take the top off the tank and weave the flaps closed with soft wire. If the edges of the top are sharp, snip the wire ends and fold a 1-inch-wide strip of tape over the edges. Use freezer, adhesive, or friction tape.

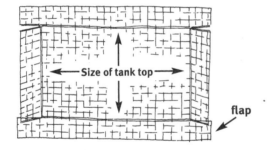

Size of tank top

flap

3. Put the hardware cloth on the tank and bend the edges over so the top fits snugly. Bend the flaps around the corners.

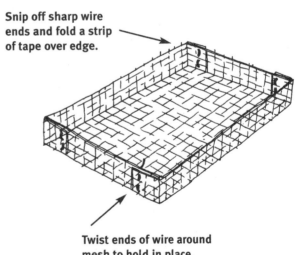

Snip off sharp wire ends and fold a strip of tape over edge.

Twist ends of wire around mesh to hold in place.

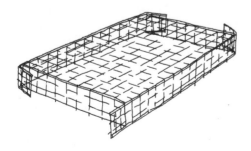

Heat

Any local lizard, spider, or tortoise can no doubt do without special heat in this vivarium. If your home or apartment is air-conditioned in the summer, however, even a locally captured pet will need daytime heat. The least expensive way to heat the tank is to let a 40-watt lightbulb (screwed into a socket on an extension cord) hang over the side of the tank or lie on the wire top.

Pets imported from desert areas will need a better heat source, and in some cases ultraviolet light as well. Heat alone is best provided by an incandescent tank fixture designed to fit the top of your tank and sold in pet stores. More expensive, but necessary for tortoises and lizards that must bask in sunlight to manufacture vitamin D, is a fluorescent tank fixture outfitted with a special kind of bulb called a Vita-Lite. Sunlight shining through windows or glass tank walls is of no use to basking animals. The ultraviolet rays they need are filtered out by glass. The fluorescent fixture may come with a plastic tank lid, but this lid prevents adequate ventilation and shouldn't be used. Both light fixtures can sit on top of the tank itself or on the hardware-cloth top.

A HOT, HUMID ENVIRONMENT

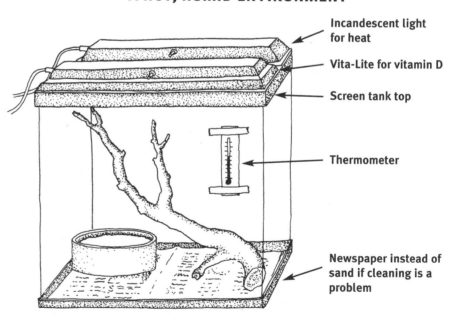

Incandescent light for heat

Vita-Lite for vitamin D

Screen tank top

Thermometer

Newspaper instead of sand if cleaning is a problem

This is an 18-gallon "tall" tank — good for an iguana. The dish is large enough for bathing. Plants could be added too.

It's useful to tape an aquarium thermometer to the inside of the tank so you can check on the temperature. They come bent over at the top to hang on the tank edge, but measuring the temperature so close to the source of heat won't tell you how hot or cold your pet is down at the bottom of the tank. Straighten out the bend and tape the thermometer inside the tank close to the bottom. The Vita-Lite will keep a 10-gallon tank over 80 degrees during the daytime, and over 65 degrees at night, even in the winter. Incandescent lights are hotter, so they should be checked often to prevent overheating (over 90 degrees for most animals). When a tank overheats, snap off the light. Sunlight may also overheat a tank. If your vivarium is temporarily empty, by all means keep it in the sun for the benefit of the plants. But while it is occupied, keep the tank away from sunlight. The plants will manage on artificial light.

Water

Every pet except the anole needs a water dish. The common iguana needs one 6 to 8 inches across for bathing; a 3-inch dish is fine for all the others. Bury the dish so that its top is level with the surface of the sand.

Accessories

If the vivarium is to be used for small lizards, you might want to plant cacti and succulents. Most of them come in 2-inch plastic pots, which can simply be sunk into the sand wherever they look right. Anoles need a leafy plant rather than a cactus type, because they drink water droplets from its leaves. Water cacti and succulents every two weeks; spray the leafy plant with a mister every day, water once a week. Don't bother with plants for tarantulas or tortoises. Spider webs are hard to remove from the plants, and tortoises knock plants over.

A piece of driftwood or an interesting rock will help make this vivarium a convincing desert as well as provide shade and hiding for pets. Add a branch for climbing pets like lizards. A rock that leans against a corner forms a good cave.

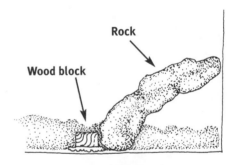

Wedge a leaning rock in place with a small block of wood glued to the tank floor with epoxy glue. Cover the block with sand so it is not visible.

Cleaning

A dry desert vivarium is easy to clean. With a fork, rake the surface of the sand so all the debris is in a pile. Pick up the pile with a spoon, and dump it in the trash. From time to time, sprinkle on more sand.

The moist woodland vivarium can be home to pets like the tree frog.

Moist Woodland Vivarium

A vivarium can be kept as a moist, humid environment by planting it with moisture-loving (usually woodland) plants. This vivarium looks pretty all the time, even when you're not housing pets in it. It stays damp enough for small salamanders, tree frogs, and land snails.

Soil

Wash the container well. Put a 2-inch layer of bone carbon charcoal in the bottom and a thinner layer of well-rinsed pebbles over the charcoal. The charcoal keeps stagnant moisture in the bottom clean and fresh smelling, and the pebbles provide a drainage area so soil doesn't get soggy.

Planting

The next step is to plant your vivarium with small plants and mosses. You can buy potting soil and moisture-loving plants like baby's tears, ferns, and African violets. Baby's tears will spread nicely to form a woodland floor. Spread 3 inches of soil over the pebble layer. Transplant the plants into the soil, or bury the pots in the soil so only the plants are exposed.

You can also collect your own plants and mosses from the woods and plant them in soil collected from the same area. Since this vivarium is to be a moist woodland environment, find a moist woodland for your plant collecting. Be sure to ask permission from the landowner. Start collecting what you need in this order: Collect soil first, then some mosses, then a stone or a bit of bark or twig with an interesting fungus or lichen on it, and then the plants, last of all. Don't try to just pull out a plant; instead, dig around it first to loosen the soil so that the roots are injured as little as possible. As soon as you have a plant, put it in its own plastic bag to keep it moist. When you get home, put the plants, roots and all, to soak in a bowl of water, while you put 3 inches of soil in your container. Then dig holes, spread the plant roots well in them, and tamp soil firmly around them. Water the plants once they are in the soil. Put the moss down to make a pretty forest floor, and set the rock or twig anywhere you like. Clean the sides of the terrarium with a paper towel.

Do not obtain babies of plants that will grow larger — they would quickly grow too big for your vivarium. Look instead for naturally miniature plants like the ones shown on page 331.

MOIST WOODLAND VIVARIUM

Materials

- Large glass container (a gallon-size jar or a round fishbowl) or a tank. The smallest tank is the 5½-gallon size. The most useful for permanent pets is the 10-gallon size. The tank can be secondhand and even leaky.
- Bone carbon charcoal, available in pet stores (check the label, as other, cheaper kinds are ineffective in preventing decay)
- No. 5–grade gravel (pebble-size), available in pet stores; or you can use clean driveway gravel
- Soil, either the smallest bag of potting soil or soil you collect from the same place you find your plants
- Plants, bought or collected
- Stones or twigs
- Plant mister
- Paper towels or sponge

Accessories

- Trowel and plastic bags, if you are collecting your own native plants
- Lid for vivarium. The lid can be glass, screen, or cheesecloth, depending on the type of container and the pet you are keeping. A glass lid to fit a tank can be cut by a glazier or lumberyard.

Light and Water

Keep a woodland vivarium in bright light but not in the sun. Extra heat isn't necessary. Watering is best done with a plant mister. How often you mist depends on the size of the container and on whether or not it is covered. A mayonnaise jar, for instance, has a relatively narrow mouth, which cuts down on evaporation, and won't need misting more than once a week. An open tank would probably need misting once a day, but if you fit the tank with a glass cover, once every other week is sufficient.

Lid

To contain pets, the vivarium may need a top to prevent escape. Glass cut to size makes a fine lid, provided you lift it once a day and ventilate the vivarium by fanning in fresh air with a piece of cardboard. Better ventilation is provided by a cheesecloth top for a jar or a commercial screen top for a tank. (The homemade mesh top on page 305 has holes too large to contain small creatures like tree frogs.)

Cleaning

The animals that live here are too small to make a noticeable mess, so no cleaning is necessary. The exception is the land snail, which can leave mucous trails on the glass walls. Clean these off with paper towels moistened with water (not cleaning solution).

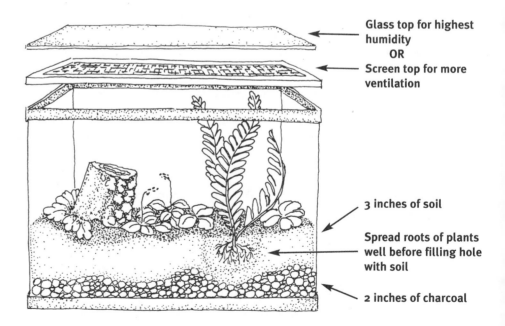

Glass top for highest humidity
OR
Screen top for more ventilation

3 inches of soil

Spread roots of plants well before filling hole with soil

2 inches of charcoal

SMALL PLANTS FOR THE MOIST WOODLAND VIVARIUM

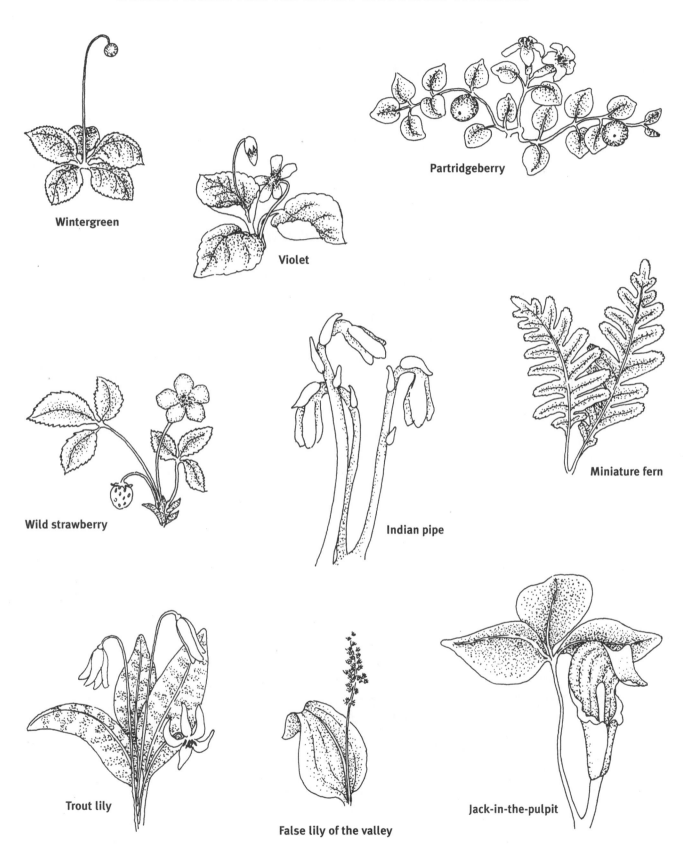

Wintergreen

Violet

Partridgeberry

Wild strawberry

Indian pipe

Miniature fern

Trout lily

False lily of the valley

Jack-in-the-pulpit

Semiaquatic Vivariums

A few animals require both land and water to simulate their natural environment. Water turtles may spend much of their time on land but must eat in the water. The large salamanders and most frogs need to have a swimming or soaking pool. There are three ways to set up a semiaquatic vivarium; at least a 10-gallon tank must be used for each of them.

Sunken-Dish Semiaquatic Vivarium

This is by far the easiest semiaquatic vivarium to set up, as well as the easiest to keep clean. But because the water area is rather small, it is only appropriate for a large salamander, small frog, or very small water turtle. The dish has to be removed at least once a week for washing and refilling (more often for a turtle), but otherwise this vivarium is no different in maintenance from a woodland one.

  If you are keeping a small water turtle in this vivarium, you will not need a lid, but you must have a fluorescent light fixture with a Vita-Lite bulb resting on the top of the tank

1. Create a moist woodland vivarium.
2. Sink a water dish in the soil up to its rim.

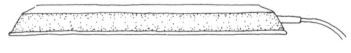

Use a shallow water dish with sloping sides. Lift it out to clean it.

A sunken-dish semiaquatic vivarium can be planted in any way you wish.

Sloped-Incline Semiaquatic Vivarium

This arrangement is not hard to set up, but it does require a tank without leaks. It is more work to keep clean than the sunken-dish arrangement, but it supplies far more water. It is a good setup for a water turtle.

1. Wash the stones, or scrub the log with a brush under fresh water.

2. In the tank, build up the stones into a gradually sloping 8-inch hill. Or fit the bark or log into the tank at about the same incline.

3. Add fresh water to a height of 6 inches. It is important that the last 2 inches of land area be perfectly dry, especially for turtles, which may suffer from fungus infections if they cannot dry off completely between swims.

4. Add whichever top is needed by your pet — or no top at all for turtles. The fluorescent light for turtles rests on top of the tank.

5. Connect the bubble stone to the pump with the plastic tubing and let the stone rest in the deep end of the water. The bubble stone, while it doesn't actually clean your tank, will help to slow down decay of leftover food or droppings. It does this simply by bubbling air into the water. Aerated water, rich in oxygen, is a discouraging environment to bacteria.

This tank must be taken apart and cleaned thoroughly once a month. Even if you pick up leftover foods as you notice them, bits will accumulate under the wood or between the stones — and you will begin to smell the results. As soon as the tank begins to smell or the water looks murky, take everything out of the tank, wash the tank and everything in it with salt and water, rinse well, and replace.

SLOPED-INCLINE SEMIAQUATIC VIVARIUM

Materials

- Smooth rocks or a small log or piece of bark cut to fit diagonally across the length of the tank
- Scrub brush
- 10-gallon leakproof tank
- Bubble stone and a pump to run it (both available at pet stores)
- Several feet of plastic tubing to connect bubble stone to pump

Accessories

- Glass or commercial screen top
- Fluorescent light fixture and Vita-Lite bulb

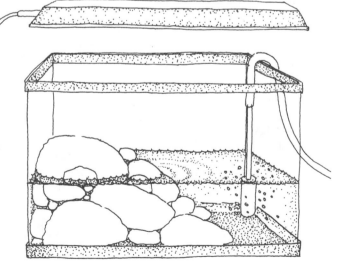

The resident of this semi-aquatic vivarium has plenty of swimming space and can climb up on top of the rocks to dry off.

- Piece of Plexiglas (the height and width will depend on the height of the filter and the width of your tank)
- Shortest possible inside-tank filter, a pump to run it, filter fluff, and filter charcoal
- 10-gallon leakproof tank
- Silicone glue
- Bone carbon charcoal
- No. 5–grade gravel (pebble-size) or clean driveway gravel
- Soil
- Moss, grasses, or other plants

Accessories

- Sloping rock
- Glass or commercial screen top
- Fluorescent light fixture and Vita-Lite bulb

Split-Tank Semiaquatic Vivarium

Because it provides plenty of water space, this is a very practical setup for water turtles and large salamanders, but some construction is required. Take care of this tank according to directions for aquariums (page 322).

1. The Plexiglas will separate the water from the land in the tank. Measure the height of the thicker tube that juts out the top of the filter. The filter will not work unless the water level in the tank is higher than this tube — which means the Plexiglas partition must be higher, too. (The filter we measured would need a 7-inch-high partition to keep the water level high enough.) Have the Plexiglas cut for you at a lumberyard or glazier's; if necessary, bring the tank with you to be sure the piece fits well.

2. Using plenty of silicone glue so you're sure there's no leakage from the water to the land side of the tank, glue the partition into place about one third of the way across the tank.

3. Prepare and plant the larger area just as you would a moist woodland vivarium.

4. Fill the smaller area with water nearly up to the height of the partition.

5. Prepare the filter according to directions on the package, connect it to the pump with the plastic tubing, and place it in a corner of the water area.

6. If a turtle is going to live in the tank, add the sloping rock so it can climb ashore.

7. Add a top for large salamanders or a light for turtles.

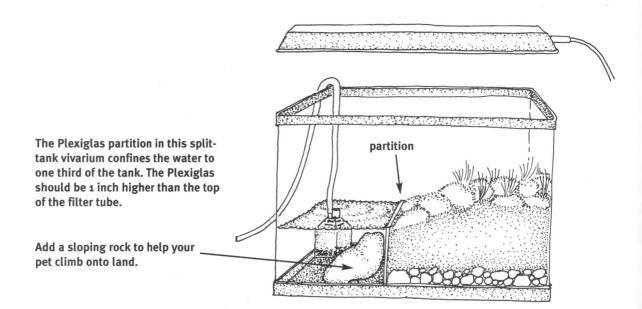

The Plexiglas partition in this split-tank vivarium confines the water to one third of the tank. The Plexiglas should be 1 inch higher than the top of the filter tube.

Add a sloping rock to help your pet climb onto land.

partition

Ant Vivarium

Ants need a very special type of vivarium if you want to enjoy watching them at work underground. Commercial plastic ones are available. This homemade one is built of wood and glass. The narrowness of the structure lets you see the whole complicated network of tunnels and rooms that are ordinarily hidden in the soil beneath an ant hill.

1. Precut all the pieces of this vivarium before you being construction. This is how to measure them accurately: Mark two 10-inch-long side pieces on the 1-by-2-inch lumber, using the side of the glass as a guide. Cut the two side pieces. Then lay the two side pieces on the edges of the glass with the 1-inch side against the glass. The top and bottom pieces will run across the top and bottom edges of the glass, connecting one side piece to the other. Mark the top and bottom pieces on the 1-by-2-inch lumber, using the space between the side pieces as a guide. Cut the top and bottom pieces. Check that all the pieces fit well by laying them out on the glass. They should form a neat frame that just comes to the edge of the glass all the way around. If the pieces fit, assemble the ant vivarium according to the illustrations. If the fit is not good, make adjustments before you start to glue.

ANT VIVARIUM

Materials

- 1-by-2-inch lumber, 4 feet long
- Two pieces of window glass, each 10 by 12 inches
- Scrap of plywood or board, about 6 by 16 inches
- Common nails, 1½ inches long
- Small eye screw
- Masking, friction, or adhesive tape, 1 inch wide
- Paper towels
- Loose, dry soil from the area in which you collect ants

Tools

- Handsaw
- Epoxy glue

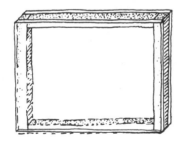

Vivarium frame

2. Glue the bottom piece along the center of the plywood or board base, 2 inches in from each end. Nail the two pieces together, hammering in the nails from underneath the base.

ANT VIVARIUM (CONTINUED)

3. Glue one side piece to one piece of glass.

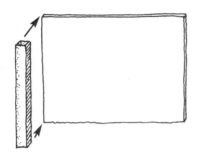

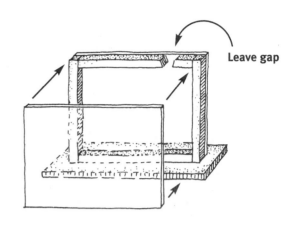

Leave gap

4. Glue the glass with the side piece to the bottom piece, so that the bottom piece now butts up against the side piece.

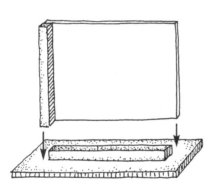

6. Glue the other side piece and both top pieces in place. You will find it is easiest to assemble this vivarium if you now lay it out on a table, with the base sticking over the edge so the glass lies flat. Do not glue the wedge in place.

7. Clean the inside of both pieces of glass with plain water and a paper towel.

8. Glue the second piece of glass in place.

5. Cut a 2-inch wedge from the top piece near one end. Put an eye screw in the wedge to serve as a handle.

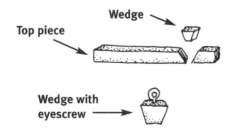

Wedge

Top piece

Wedge with eyescrew

9. Fold 1-inch friction tape over all the edges except where the wedge fits in.

10. Use the funnel to pour the soil you collected into the space between the two panes of glass. Fill the vivarium to within 2 inches of the top. Close with the wedge.

Aquariums

An aquatic vivarium, usually called an aquarium, is not just a tank of water, but an environment no less complicated than any other vivarium. A good aquarium must supply oxygen for the animals and light for the plants and must filter out waste materials produced by both.

A filled tank is terribly heavy to move, so decide where you're going to keep the tank, and put it there, before you fill it with water. Avoid places that get direct sunlight, that have air-conditioning, or where the windows are left open on cold nights, because temperatures in these locations are likely to change quickly. The creatures that will live in your aquarium can get as cold as 60 degrees and as hot as 85 degrees, but rapid temperature changes can kill them.

Setting Up Your Aquarium

1. Rinse the tank so it is free of dust.
2. The most basic aquarium setup calls for a tank, gravel for the bottom, and a filter and air pump to aerate and clean the water. Put the gravel in a pail and run fresh tap water (it doesn't have to be dechlorinated) into it. As you let the water run and overflow, stir the gravel with your hands. When the water looks clear, the gravel is clean. Pour off the extra water and spread the gravel in your tank. (Don't use glass gravel, because the sharp edges can cut the mouths of pets like goldfish, who pick it up in their search for leftover food. Avoid fine terrarium sand too; pretty as it is, it is difficult to keep clean.)
3. Fill the tank with tap water. In many places, water is chlorinated to kill bacteria. Chlorine is a lethal poison to water creatures. Pet stores sell a liquid chlorine remover that works instantly and makes chlorinated water perfectly safe. A few drops to a gallon is all it takes. Read the instructions on the bottle to be sure you are accurate. Other chemicals are equally lethal. Copper, which seeps into the water from new copper plumbing pipes, kills many water animals. If new plumbing work has been done in your house, get your water from a neighbor until the pipes have been in use for six months.
4. Install the filter and air pump, following the directions on their packaging. The filter instructions may neglect to say that you have to rinse the charcoal to remove its black dust before you use it. It's easiest to rinse it in a kitchen strainer under running water.

AQUARIUM

Materials

- 10-gallon tank, preferably new
- 10 pounds of No. 3–grade gravel, natural or colored
- Inside- or outside-tank filter, charcoal, and filter fluff
- Air pump
- Large pail
- Kitchen strainer
- Several feet of plastic tubing to connect filter to pump
- Several gallon plastic jugs for storing extra water

Accessories

- Chlorine remover, if your water is chlorinated
- Decorative rocks or other decorations
- Water plants
- Fluorescent light fixture and Gro-Lite bulb (if you have plants)
- Heater (optional; to keep water temperature constant)
- Siphon and bucket for occasional cleaning

First, cut the stems at an angle above the rubber band marks.

Then twist lead plant weight loosely around the stems and plant bunch sideways under rock.

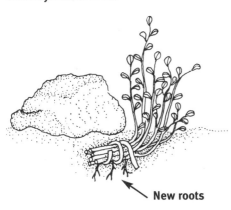

← **New roots**

Some bunch plants, like cabomba and anacharis, are bought mostly as food for hungry goldfish, turtles, and tadpoles. They are slow to root and quick to break and decay. You can keep bunch plants like this in a jar of water and put a sprig at a time into the tank for snacks.

Water Plants

Aquatic environments need nothing more than the basic elements we've just described, but decorating a tank is almost irresistible. There are dozens and dozens of water plants with which to decorate an aquarium, but few of them do well at room temperature. Before you buy, ask whether the plant you like is a tropical plant that will grow only in a heated tank. Plants come two ways: in bunches without roots and as individually rooted plants.

Bunch plants are cuttings — pieces of stem cut from a "mother" plant. Eventually, almost all of them will sprout roots near the bottom of their stem and can be established as rooted plants. If you want to root a bunchy plant, take off the rubber band that holds the stems together. With a razor blade, slice each stem above where the band probably crushed it. Put the cuttings into a jar of water and keep them in a sunny window. Change the water daily, and cut off any portions of the stems or leaves that begin to rot. When roots appear, you can plant the cuttings, following the suggestions below for rooted plants.

If this method of rooting plants sounds like too much trouble, you can just remove the rubber band, slice the stems above the crushed area, hold the bunch together with a lead plant weight (bought at the pet store), and shove the stems down into the gravel. If the weight isn't enough to keep the plants from floating upward, plant the bunch with the roots bent sideways and put a rock on top. The tops of the stems will soon turn upward, and at least some of the stems will root into the gravel.

Some of the plants that come with roots are ones that grow in sand or soil at the bottom of the tank. A native water plant of this type that you may be able to collect yourself is wild watercress. Others, though they may send roots to the bottom eventually, are floating plants that don't need to be anchored in soil. Among the floaters is a funny plant called a banana plant, which floats on bladders that look like a tiny bunch of bananas. Another is a native temperate-zone plant called duckweed, which you can collect yourself. You may see it nearly covering ponds with its tiny green leaves during the summer. Duckweed will probably do so well in your tank that you'll have to keep removing it by the handful.

Rooted plants get some nutrition from animal wastes at the bottom of a tank, but most will do better if they have a nutrient soil to grow in rather than the sterile gravel you are using as a floor. No one wants mud on the bottom of a tank, so here's a trick: Buy tiny plastic flower pots, the kind baby cacti often come in. Fill them halfway up with a good potting soil. Spread the plant roots over the soil. Sprinkle a little more soil over the roots. Fill the container to the top with coarse gravel or small pebbles to hold the soil in place and match the ground in your tank. Soak the pots thoroughly. Now sink the potted plants (very slowly) into the gravel in your tank bottom. The pots will not be visible, the plants will get good nutrition, and when you change your mind about where the plants should go, moving the pots is easy.

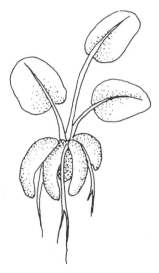

FLOATING PLANT
This doesn't need to be planted at all.

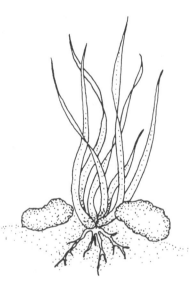

ROOTED PLANT
Mound gravel around the base of the plant. Hold down with rocks, as shown at left.

Or plant in a 2-inch plastic pot sunk to its rim in the gravel, as shown at right.

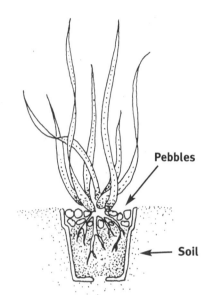

Pebbles

Soil

Tank Decorations

You can also buy any of the hundreds of commercial tank decorations available at pet stores or you can collect some from nature. Watch out for tank decorations that may contain harmful chemicals, though. Shells, coral, and some rocks contain lime. Lime makes water too alkaline (the opposite of acidic) for freshwater creatures. Copper minerals, of course, act the same way as new copper pipes. Stones from the seashore and artistic driftwood make water too salty. To be safe, stick to petrified wood, freshwater driftwood, slate, quartz, granite, or basalt.

If your school, your community, or an artistic neighbor has a kiln, you can make your own tank decorations. Use moist clay, either terracotta or boneware — the kind you have to fire, not the kind that is self-hardening or that is baked in a home oven. Caves are fun, especially for

To keep track of the water temperature, attach a stainless-steel tank thermometer to one of the tank walls.

A thermostatic tank heater is set to a particular temperature. When the water temperature falls below that point, the heater comes on.

crayfish, which will lurk appropriately. Tall thin clay pieces can look like coral. Of course, you can make monsters and mermaids, too. The pieces can be left plain or glazed. Lead glazes, which can be lethal to humans, don't hurt water creatures at all.

Light

The pets that are going to live in this aquatic vivarium don't need light, but the plants do. They would all love some sun, but any sun at all will encourage algae — green plants that bedevil the tank owner by covering everything with green fuzz. There is no perfect solution for getting healthy plants and no algae, but the closest thing to it is to use a fluorescent lighting fixture that fits snugly on top of the tank. The fixture should be equipped with a special Gro-Lite bulb, available to fit 5½- or 10-gallon tank fixtures in either pet or garden stores. The Gro-Lite is a balanced fluorescent lamp that provides the ultraviolet light plants need without the intense light algae love and the heat many water creatures hate. Experts recommend that you leave the light on for six to eight hours every day. If algae nevertheless get a foothold, compromise. Cut the light hours down to four, and see what happens.

Temperature

Temperature is maintained in a tank either by just keeping it in a room that stays about the same temperature all the time (no air-conditioning, open windows on freezing winter nights, or direct sunlight) or by a thermostatically controlled heating system. The heater and its controlling thermostat are available in pet stores. A thermostatic tank heater looks complicated, but it is not difficult to use. Hang the heater on the tank rim with the glass tube inside the tank. Turn it on. Keep checking the tank thermometer until it reaches the desired temperature. Turn the thermostat dial slowly until you hear the heater click off. From now on the thermostat will click on again whenever the water temperature falls below that point.

Heated tanks are necessary only for tropical fish. Tropical fish are complicated to keep, so the aquatic animals we suggest in this book are all ones that remain healthy without a heating system.

The Filter System

Theoretically you could keep an aquarium clean by siphoning off a third of the water from the bottom every week and replacing it with fresh water. In practice, siphoning is a long, messy, inefficient job, and is not recommended. You could also theoretically establish a balanced environment of plants and scavenger animals, which would function much like that of a stagnant but livable pond. In practice, this is best left to ecologists who know exactly what they're doing. For most people, a filter system is definitely the best way to cope with keeping a tank clean.

The filter system performs various functions: It traps particles of algae (tiny green water plants), waste products, and leftover food in the fluff, keeping the water clear. It filters the water through charcoal, which removes some chemical waste products. And it provides oxygen by bubbling air through the water.

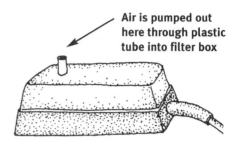

Air is pumped out here through plastic tube into filter box

An air pump is a simple electric motor

OUTSIDE TANK FILTER

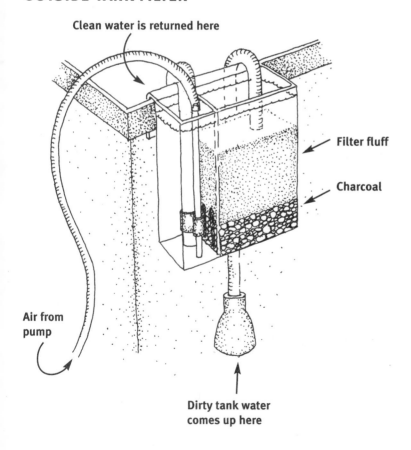

Clean water is returned here

Filter fluff

Charcoal

Air from pump

Dirty tank water comes up here

INSIDE TANK FILTER

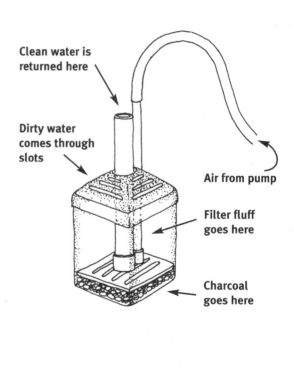

Clean water is returned here

Dirty water comes through slots

Air from pump

Filter fluff goes here

Charcoal goes here

Aquarium Maintenance

The filter must be cleaned every week. Read the instructions that come with the filter to see how much charcoal and filter fluff your filter needs. Unplug the pump and pull the filter up out of the water. Detach the plastic tube from the filter box. Take the filter to the sink, take off the top, and throw out the dirty filter fluff balls. Rinse the charcoal at the bottom under running water, and replace the dirty fluff with new fluff. Every other week, replace the old charcoal with fresh, well-rinsed charcoal. When a filter box feels slimy or looks dirty, wash it out with salt and rinse it well. Never use soap or detergent, because the residue you don't notice can kill your pets.

Each week, replace the water that has evaporated with fresh water, dechlorinated if necessary and left to sit at least two days earlier so it is the same temperature as the tank water. Keeping two-gallon jugs (milk bottles) of prepared water on hand all the time makes the job easy.

Three times a year, siphon off a third of the water in the tank and replace it with new water. This helps remove accumulated wastes that the filter can't handle. Prepare the new water two days beforehand and set it aside so it's the same temperature as the water in the tank. You'll need almost 4 gallons for a 10-gallon tank.

Siphons these days are made with a bulb device at one end. The bulb may be rubber (the best kind) or molded right along with the tube itself (not very good). The principle behind siphoning is that any continuous stream of water will flow toward its lowest point. Gravity sees to that. A siphon is simply a way of connecting the water in your tank in a continuous stream with a lower point so that it will flow downward. This sounds easy, but there is a catch to it. First you have to get water up into the tube. That's what the bulb is for. Stick the bulb end down into a pail on the floor. Put one finger over the bulb end and squeeze the bulb; that forces air from the tube. Still holding your finger over the bulb end, release the bulb. Water flows into the tube. Now you can take your finger off the end, and water will start flowing from tank to pail in a continuous stream.

If you ever have to empty and clean a tank — because it's been neglected or is full of algae — use salt to scrub it, not soap or detergent, and rinse well.

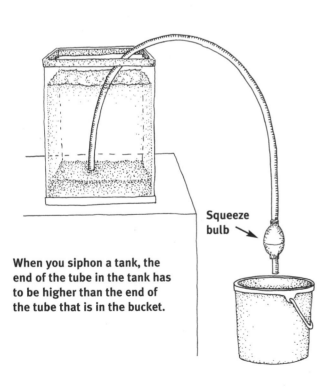

Squeeze bulb →

When you siphon a tank, the end of the tube in the tank has to be higher than the end of the tube that is in the bucket.

Serpentariums

Baby snakes up to two and a half or three feet long can live in a serpentarium that is nothing more than a tank with a screen or mesh top. Large snakes over three feet long need larger quarters. Restless nibbling against the top of a tank may be a sign that a snake is seeking more space. You can either buy a larger tank — they come up to about five feet long — or build a wood and Plexiglas serpentarium yourself. Neither is cheap.

Wood Serpentarium

A wood serpentarium is basically a plywood box, opening at the front. The opening is fitted with two sliding Plexiglas doors that move along a standard aluminum track. Wire mesh is not a good substitute for the Plexiglas, as you will not be able to protect so large a surface with masking tape. Don't buy either the track or the Plexiglas until you have finished building the rest of the serpentarium. Once you know the exact dimensions of the front opening, a glazing company can cut the track and Plexiglas for you and tell you how to install the doors.

A determined snake will force its way out where the two sliding doors overlap in the middle. There's probably a sophisticated method of preventing this, but we just use a piece of masking tape. If your snake learns to slide open a door by pushing against it with his nose, a piece of dowel can be cut to the right size and wedged between the door and the side of cage, as shown in the illustration on page 325.

Interior fixings might include a branch for the snake to rest on, a large crockery water dish for drinking and soaking, and a rock for shedding. A cardboard box with a hole in it serves as a burrow — a luxury that most tanks are too small to hold. This cage is sized so that you can easily cover the floor with standard newspapers (not opened out but overlapped, as shown below).

Overlap newspapers to cover the serpentarium floor.

Fake grass is sold by the foot. It can be used instead of newspaper for flooring.

WOOD SERPENTARIUM
Materials

- ½ inch interior-grade plywood, one 4-by-8-foot sheet
- White glue
- Common nails, 1¼ inches long
- 8-inch shelving board, 3 feet long
- Porcelain light fixture
- Electrical cord, plug, cord switch, and 40-watt lightbulb
- Double aluminum sliding tracks, cut to fit top and bottom of front opening by glazier or lumberyard
- Two Plexiglas sliding doors, cut to fit front opening by glazier or lumberyard
- 1 pint of shellac
- ½-inch dowel, 36 inches long

Tools

- Yardstick or long ruler
- Circular saw
- Handsaw
- Hammer
- Drill with 1-inch bit
- Screwdriver
- Paintbrush

Accessories

- Hardware-cloth bulb guard
- Tank thermometer
- Newspaper or plastic grass matting to cover floor of cage
- Crockery water dish
- Climbing branch and rock

WOOD SERPENTARIUM (CONTINUED)

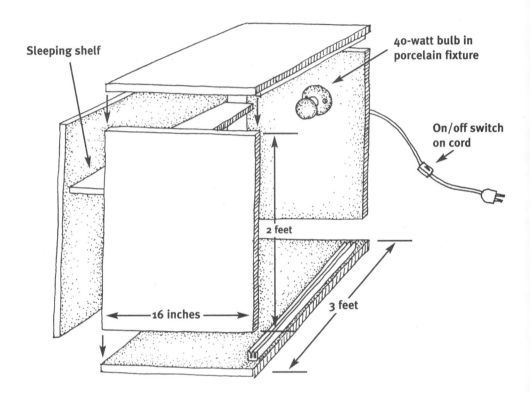

Sleeping shelf

40-watt bulb in porcelain fixture

On/off switch on cord

2 feet

16 inches

3 feet

1. From the ½-inch plywood, cut two side pieces that measure 2 feet by 16 inches. Then cut a top piece and a bottom piece that each measure 3 feet by 16 inches. Glue and nail the top, bottom, and side pieces together to form a box, as shown above.

2. Use the assembled box as a guide to mark the dimensions of the back wall on ½-inch plywood. Cut out the back wall, then glue and nail it in place.

3. Measure across the inside of the box for the sleeping shelf, which will stretch from one side wall to the other. From the 8-inch shelving board, cut the shelf to the right length. Glue and nail it in place, toward the top of the back wall. The snake will enjoy snoozing on this shelf, basking in the heat of the light fixture.

4. Drill a 1-inch hold for the light cord two thirds of the way up the middle of one side. Screw the fixture in place, with the cord emerging through the hole.

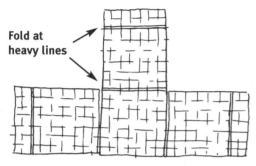

Fold at heavy lines

A hardware cloth guard protects the snake from a hot lightbulb. Cut and fold as shown. Staple in place.

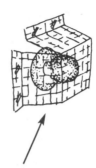

Change the bulb through the bottom opening

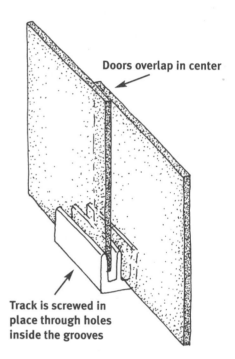

Doors overlap in center

Track is screwed in place through holes inside the grooves

5. To protect the snake from the hot bulb, cut a piece of hardware cloth in the pattern shown above, with the three sides of the cloth long enough to enclose the bulb. Fold over the bulb and staple in place.

6. Measure the front opening of the box carefully. Bring those dimensions — if not the box itself — to a glazier or lumberyard and ask to have Plexiglas and aluminum track cut to fit the opening. Ask the glazier or lumberyard how to install the track, because installation differs depending on the type of track you're buying. Follow those instructions to install the track and Plexiglas.

7. Shellac the inside of the serpentarium.

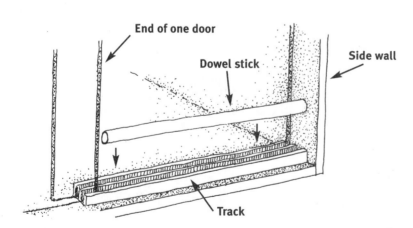

End of one door

Dowel stick

Side wall

Track

8. A smart or curious snake will learn to slide a door open by pushing against it with his nose. To prevent this, cut a piece of dowel to size so you can wedge it between the door and the side of the cage, as shown.

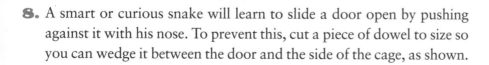

Tank Serpentarium

Before you acquire a snake, have a tank ready to house it. To prevent escape, the tank must have a top. If you're using a commercial screen top, line the inside perimeter with masking tape to protect the skin on your snake's nose when it rubs against it. You can also build the home-made mesh top pictured on page 305; just cut the hardware cloth 3 inches longer on all sides than the top of the tank, make 1½-inch slits in the corners, and, after you've wired the corners together, line the inside perimeter with tape, as shown.

Lay an incandescent light fixture across the top for warmth; you should turn it on when temperatures drop below 70 degrees. Tape a thermometer to the inside of the tank. (If you don't want the tape to show, fold it into a ring, sticky-side out; it will hold to both the tank and the back of the thermometer.)

Serpentariums must be kept very clean. Gravel may look pretty, but it invites bacteria and can't be washed well enough. Use newspaper or plastic grass matting for flooring material. The newspaper can be changed each time it gets soiled, and the plastic grass can be washed off.

Add the crockery water dish. Your snake will use it for both drinking and soaking, so the dish should be large enough for the snake to submerge all but its nose in it. A rock to hide behind and to rub against at shedding time is welcomed. Another nice addition is a branch propped diagonally from one side of the tank to the other, for resting and climbing.

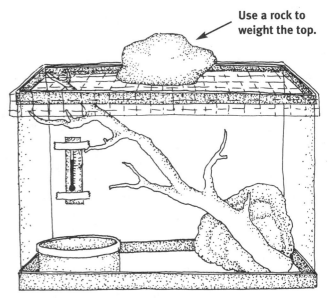

Use a rock to weight the top.

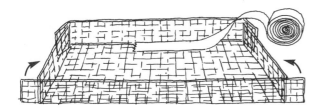

Line the inside margin of the top with wide tape.

Birdcages and Perches

It is very difficult to make a birdcage as well designed and practical as a commercial cage. However, the cake-pan cage assembled on page 330 can be made larger to serve small birds like canaries or parakeets.

1. Follow the illustrations on page 330 to construct the basic cage.

2. Stick branches through the mesh from one side of the cage to the other to serve as perches, prying open holes if necessary so the branches fit through.

3. To insert the tube-shaped seed and water dispensers, use wire clippers to cut out whatever area of wire is necessary to make a hole large enough to accommodate the dish part of the containers.

4. Spread sand or newspaper for flooring.

To clean this cage, simply lift the cage off the bottom pan. The bird will perch inside the rest of the cage while you empty and wash the bottom pan with soap and water and change the newspaper or sand.

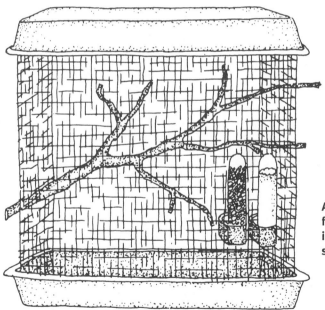

A cake-pan cage made from tall hardware cloth is suitable for housing small birds.

BIRDCAGE

Materials

- Two roasting pans, each 12 by 18 inches
- ½-inch-mesh hardware cloth, 19 by 66 inches
- Several feet of soft wire

Tools

- Wire shears
- File
- Pocketknife for cutting perches
- Wire clippers or pliers that cut wire

Accessories

- Small branches for perches
- Tube-shaped water and seed dispensers, available at pet stores
- Several layers of newspaper or sand for flooring

Parrot Perch

If you wish to keep a parrot outside a cage, here is a perch setup that works for one that has had its wings clipped. You will need an adult to help you choose the spot to hang the perch, because it must be secured to a ceiling beam, which may be hidden behind the ceiling. (If you happen to try to attach the perch to a part of the ceiling that doesn't back up to a beam, you could pull down part of the ceiling.) Your adult will also need to help you install the metal utility shelf, because it must be secured to studs behind the wall or secured with expansion bolts.

You should be able to figure out from the illustration how to put this perch together. Of course, your branch may look different from the one shown here, and you'll have to make adjustments to suit it. Just be sure that the perch hangs steadily and parallel to the floor. Locate the utility shelf within reach of the perch so your bird can get to its food and water dishes. A sheet of newspaper on the floor under the perch catches droppings and seed; you should replace it every day.

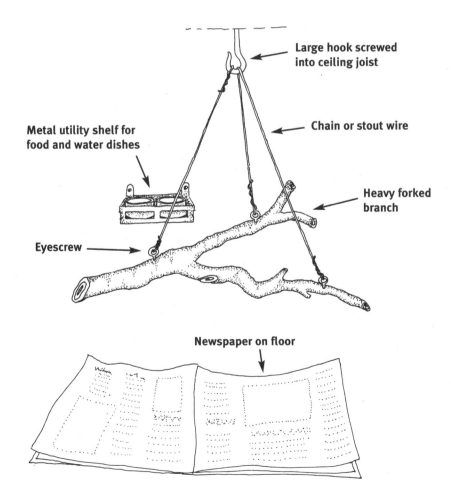

Large hook screwed into ceiling joist

Metal utility shelf for food and water dishes

Chain or stout wire

Heavy forked branch

Eyescrew

Newspaper on floor

Mynah Perch

A mynah can be kept outside a cage on an easy-to-make wooden perch setup, which includes a tray to catch drippings and seed. The bird will stay there simply because, with its wings clipped, the floor looks very far way.

1. Try to find scraps of plywood at the lumberyard the right size to make this perch. Glue and nail the two plywood pieces together in an L-shape, as shown in the illustration, and reinforce them with angle irons screwed to the inside corners.

2. Measure, mark, and cut the lattice strip so it fits the edge of the shelf as shown. Glue and nail it in place, using the smaller nails.

3. Drill three ¾-inch holes in the back wall of the perch to accept the dowels. Space them with your mynah bird's hopping distance in mind. Cut the dowel into three equal pieces for perches, and glue the perches into the holes.

4. To attach the perch to a wall, you will have to have an adult locate studs to nail into. Hammer two 4-inch nails into the studs about 5 feet above the floor. Measure the distance between them, and then drill ½-inch holes that distance apart in the back wall of the perch so you can hang it.

5. Give the wood several coats of shellac.

6. Cover the shelf area with folded newspaper, and put the food and water dishes in place.

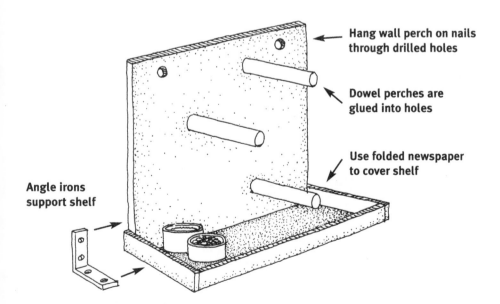

Angle irons support shelf

Hang wall perch on nails through drilled holes

Dowel perches are glued into holes

Use folded newspaper to cover shelf

MYNAH PERCH

Materials

- ¾-inch interior-grade plywood, two pieces
- White glue
- Common nails, 1½ inches long and 4 inches long
- Two angle irons, 2 or 3 inches long and enough screws, ⅝ inch long
- 2-inch lattice strip, 4 feet long
- ¾-inch dowel, 36 inches long
- Pint of shellac

Tools

- Hammer
- Screwdriver
- Yardstick
- Handsaw
- Drill with ¾-inch and ½-inch bits
- Paintbrush

Accessories

- Crockery food and water dishes
- Newspaper

Materials

- ½-inch-mesh (for mice, ¼-inch mesh) hardware cloth; 36 by 10½ inches for the small cage, 42 by 13½ inches for a medium-sized cage
- Two aluminum baking pans: 9 by 9 inches for a small cage; 8 by 12 inches for a medium-sized cage
- Several feet of soft wire
- Rock to weight the top

Tools

- Wire shears
- Wire clippers

Accessories

- Newspaper or wood shavings
- Nesting materials (toilet paper, yarn, cloth)
- Water bottle and wire bracket

Cake-Pan Rodent Homes

Gerbils, hamsters, mice, and rats are all rodents — and also all gnawing animals. Gnaw-proof commercial metal cages are available, but this cake-pan cage serves very well. Because the top removes for getting at the animal and the bottom removes for washing, it is a more convenient cage than the commercial ones. And it is just as gnaw-proof.

Examine the roll of hardware cloth before the salesperson in the hardware store cuts it. If the mesh is warped, don't buy it. Warped mesh will make it impossible to construct anything but a jiggly cage.

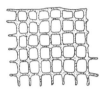

The corners of straight hardware cloth are square

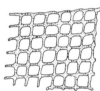

Warped hardware cloth is slanted

1. The hardest part of making this cage is cutting the hardware cloth. The clerk in the hardware store may do the rough cutting for you, but he or she will leave the cloth with sharp ends sticking up from it. You will have to trim these off. You can use either wire shears or a wire clipper.

2. When all the spikes are trimmed, put one end of your piece of hardware cloth in the pan, and give it a bend where it meets the first corner. Take it out again and crease the corner up to the top edge. Repeat the process of bending and creasing for each corner, as shown in the illustrations.

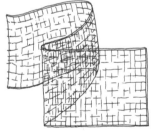

First bend

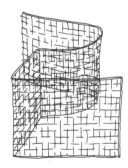

Second bend

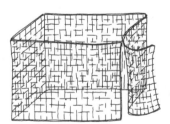

Third bend

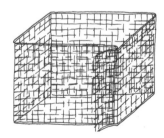

Fourth bend

3. Your piece of hardware cloth is long enough to form a 2-inch over-lap. Check that the creases fit neatly into the corners of the pan, and then weave the overlap together with soft wire.

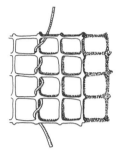

Use soft wire to lace together both edges, from the top to the bottom of the cage.

4. Set 1½ inches of wood shavings on the floor as bedding material. Add soft materials like toilet paper, cotton batting, yarn, and cloth for nesting materials (the rodent will make its own nest from it).

5. Attach a water bottle to the side of the cage, as shown. If your water bottle didn't come with a wire bracket, the illustration here shows you how to shape a bracket out of heavy wire.

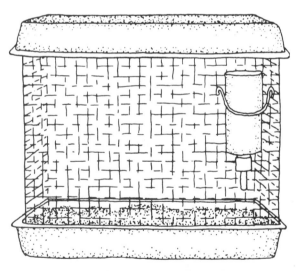

In ¼-inch mesh, you'll have to pry open space for the water bottle spout to fit through.

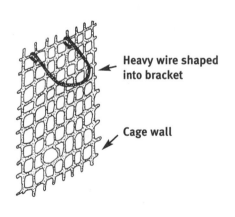

Heavy wire shaped into bracket

Cage wall

6. Put the other pan on top, and weight it with a heavy rock or book.

Rabbit or Guinea Pig Hutches

Around Eastertime, pet stores may sell hutches. Since they are neither cheap nor well made, you're probably better off with a homemade hutch. A hutch is a wire and wood cage with a mesh floor that is raised a few inches from the ground. Your rabbit or guinea pig's droppings will fall through the holes in the mesh onto a sheet of newspaper indoors (or the ground outdoors). Instructions are included here for both an indoor and an outdoor hutch.

Indoor Hutch

This indoor hutch is mostly mesh, allowing you to keep an eye on your pet from both front and back. It is easy to make and easy to clean.

1. Trim the 36-inch-wide hardware cloth to 30 inches before you start. It's a good idea to carefully trim the spikes off the cut edge so you don't scratch yourself as you work.

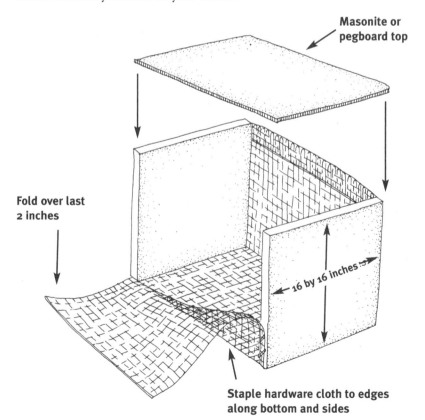

Masonite or pegboard top

Fold over last 2 inches

16 by 16 inches

Staple hardware cloth to edges along bottom and sides

2. Cut two 16-by-16-inch squares out of ¾-inch plywood. These will form the sides of the hutch.

3. Fold over the first 2 inches of the mesh hardware cloth. Staple the cloth to the two plywood squares, as shown at left. The mesh hardware cloth will form the back, bottom, and front of the hutch.

4. When you get to the last side, bend over the cloth where it meets the top, leave 2 inches for the fold, and trim off the excess.

5. Cut a piece of Masonite or pegboard for the top. It should be 16 by 30 inches, but measure first to be sure.

6. When the hutch is finished, cut the 2-by-4s in half and set the cage up off the floor on the two pieces as shown.

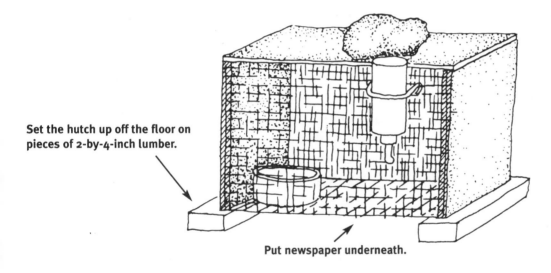

Set the hutch up off the floor on pieces of 2-by-4-inch lumber.

Put newspaper underneath.

7. Cover the area under the cage with six layers of newspaper. Install a water bottle on one wall, set a food dish inside, and place a rock weight on top.

- ¾-inch exterior-grade plywood, 16 by 40 inches
- ½-inch-mesh hardware cloth, 36 by 54 inches
- 6-inch shelving board, 30 inches long
- Common nails, 1½ inches long
- ½-inch exterior-grade plywood, 18 by 32 inches
- Two 6-inch T-hinges
- 3-inch screw-in hook
- 1 pint of shellac
- 1 quart of exterior enamel paint
- 2-by-4-inch lumber, 36 inches long; or four bricks

Tools

- Yardstick or long ruler
- Circular saw
- Wire shears
- Staple gun and wire staples
- Screwdriver
- Paintbrush

Accessories

- Water bottle and wire bracket
- 6-inch crockery food dish

Outdoor Hutch

The roof of this outdoor hutch is sloped down so it will shed rain. In bad rainstorms and temperatures below 20 degrees, throw a tarpaulin or a heavy plastic drop cloth over the hutch to give your pets better protection.

1. From ¾-inch exterior-grade plywood, cut the two sides so that they are 16 inches wide, 16 inches high on one side, and 20 inches high on the opposite side, as shown in the illustration at right.

2. Fold 2 inches of one end of the mesh hardware cloth over onto itself and staple it to the edge of the lower sloped end of the two side pieces. Stapling as you go, wrap the mesh around the edges, across the bottom, and up the front, ending at the upper sloped end of the two side pieces. You don't have to fold the wire mesh over here at the high end, because it will be covered with a board.

3. On the higher side of the hutch, from the top of one side to the top of the other, nail the 6-inch shelving board in place across the hardware cloth, as shown.

4. Set the piece of ½-inch plywood over the frame; you have to make sure it fits as a top. It should overhang at least an inch on each side.

5. Install the hinges so that they connect the top to the shelving board, as shown. Because the boards are coming together at an angle, the hinges won't fit just right, but it doesn't matter — they'll get the job done.

6. Predrill a hole in the lower end of the top for the screw-in hook, then screw the hook into place. You should be able to secure the hook around the wire mesh to hold the roof closed. If you have trouble getting the hook to stay put, loop a small ring of wire through the mesh at the right distance for the hook to grab on to.

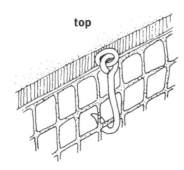

Hook grabbing directly into mesh

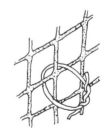

Small wire ring as alternative hooking site

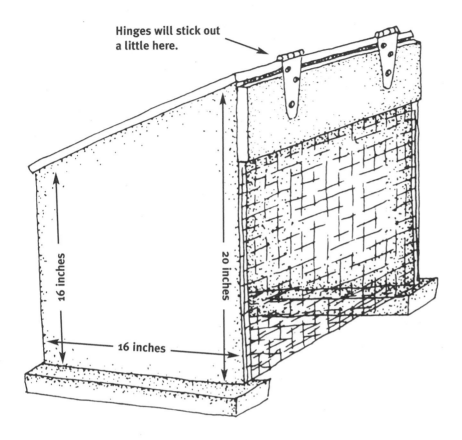

Hinges will stick out a little here.

16 inches

20 inches

16 inches

7. Apply several coats of shellac to both the inside and the outside of the hutch.

8. Paint the outside of the hutch with one or two coats of exterior enamel paint.

9. Saw the 2-by-4-inch lumber in half and place one under each side of the hutch, or set one brick at each corner. If the hutch is wobbly on its supports, remove dirt from or add dirt under the 2-by-4s or bricks until the hutch is steadily balanced.

- ½-inch interior-grade plywood, one 4-by-8-foot sheet
- White glue
- Common nails, 1¼ inches long for nailing plywood and 3½ inches long for nailing door frame
- 1-by-2-inch lumber, 14 feet long
- Corner braces
- Screws
- ½-inch-mesh hardware cloth, 36 by 18 inches
- Two 6-inch T-hinges
- Hook and eye
- 1 pint of shellac, and paint if you wish

Tools

- Yardstick or long ruler
- Circular saw

Accessories

- Water dish or water bottle and bracket
- Newspaper to cover floor or litter box
- Silicone gel

Ferret or Skunk Home

This cage is made complete with a private den separated from the rest of the cage by a sliding panel. For a ferret, the triangle you saw off the den panel to make an entrance hole should be quite small, as ferrets like sneaking through small spaces. You will have to cut off a larger triangle to accommodate the bulkier skunk. The steps for building this home are somewhat complicated; recruit your favorite adult to help you build it.

You can mount a water bottle through the wire door on this cage just as you would for a cake-pan cage (page 330) or a hutch (page 332). Spread newspaper on the floor outside the den area, or use a small litter box, as discussed for ferrets. You might add some rags, in case your pet wants to pull them into its den to make a bed.

Change the newspapers or box when soiled, and wash the inside of the cage with soap and water when necessary. To clean the den area, pull the panel out. If the panel is hard to slide, a silicone gel (available in hardware stores) can be squeezed into the grooves as a lubricant.

1. Cut two sides, a top, a bottom, and a middle panel from a sheet of ½-inch plywood, using the cutting plan below.
2. Glue and nail together the two sides, the top, and the bottom.

CUTTING PLAN FROM A 4'-BY-8' PLYWOOD SHEET

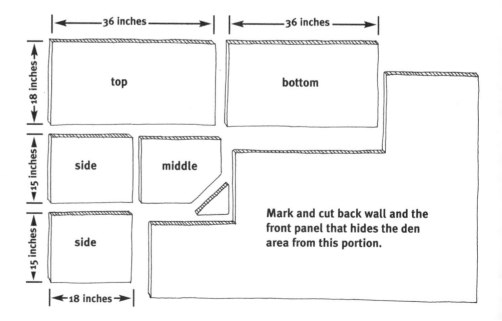

36 inches | 36 inches

18 inches

top

bottom

15 inches

side | middle

15 inches

side

18 inches

Mark and cut back wall and the front panel that hides the den area from this portion.

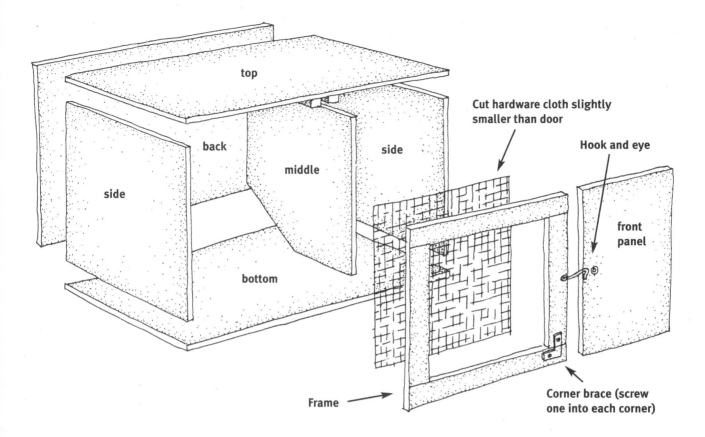

top

back

middle

side

side

bottom

Cut hardware cloth slightly smaller than door

Hook and eye

side

front panel

Frame

Corner brace (screw one into each corner)

3. Use the assembled box as a guide to measure and cut the back wall. Glue and nail it into place.

4. Position the middle panel about one third of the way from one side to make a small den area. Mark the position of the panel on the top and glue two 1-by-2-inch strips of lumber to either side of this mark, as shown in the illustration. The middle panel will fit in the groove between these two strips of wood. If the panel is wobbly, glue similar strips to the bottom, too.

5. Measure carefully to mark, then cut pieces for the door frame from 1-by-2-inch lumber. The door should line up with the side wall and extend just past the den panel so that the panel can slide out when the door is open.

6. Use corner braces to secure the door pieces together in a square frame, as shown. Cut ½-inch-mesh hardware cloth to fit the door and staple it to the inside of the door frame.

7. Measure and cut the plywood panel that will cover the front of the den area. Glue and nail it in place.

8. Attach the door to the front of the box with T-hinges at the top (so the door swings up) or the side (so the door swings open to the side).

9. Install a hook on the door and the eye on the front panel, as shown, so that the hook can be set in the eye to keep the door closed.

10. Shellac all inside surfaces with three coats. If you wish, paint or varnish the outside.

Poultry Sheds

A shed the size of a small doghouse can house six chickens, a pair of geese, or, with some adjustments, a dozen pigeons. The shed should be located on dry, raised ground and should face south. The inside and outside should receive several coats of shellac, and the outside should be painted with an exterior-grade paint. A poultry shed can be as simple as a lean-to-type construction — three walls and a one-piece roof. Unless you want to confine your birds, you don't really need anything more than this basic shelter.

Building a poultry shed from scratch is a major project. The shed's exact dimensions will depend on, among other things, where you want to put it, how many birds you are going to keep in it, whether or not you want to keep the birds confined, and how much time you can devote to keeping it clean. For this reason, we're not going to give specific step-by-step instructions for building a shed. Instead, we'll encourage you to use your imagination in converting an existing shed or working with your family to build a new one, always keeping in mind the health, safety, and happiness of your birds.

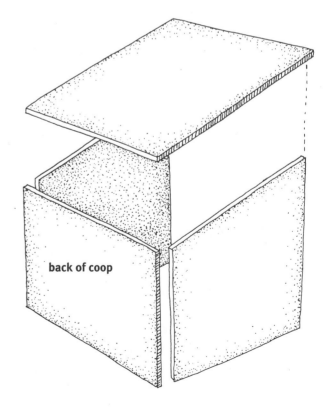

An open lean-to shed is easy to construct and offers adequate shelter for birds that are allowed to wander about the yard. A sloping roof that overhangs the shelter on all sides is best because it diverts rain away from the inside of the shelter.

back of coop

POULTRY SHED FLOOR

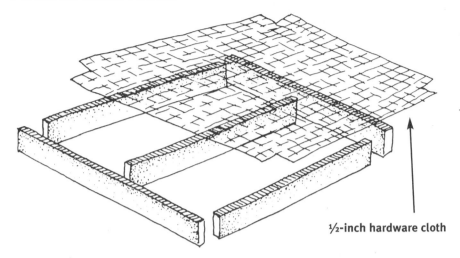

½-inch hardware cloth

Any poultry shed should have a thick layer of hay on its floor. With confined birds, cleaning the bedding hay is a daily chore. If the shed has a raised mesh floor, droppings will fall through the holes, as in a hutch, and the ground beneath need be raked out only once a week.

POULTRY YARD

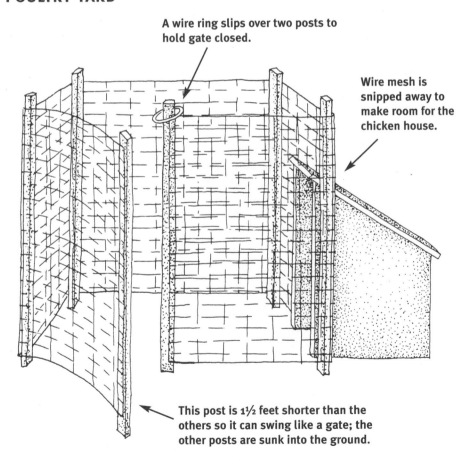

A wire ring slips over two posts to hold gate closed.

Wire mesh is snipped away to make room for the chicken house.

This post is 1½ feet shorter than the others so it can swing like a gate; the other posts are sunk into the ground.

If you want to confine your birds, use 1-by-2-inch garden netting (wire mesh) to enclose a yard for them attached to the shed. Chickens don't need a lot of exercise, so you can make this yard as small as 6 feet by 6 feet, and only 3 to 4 feet high.

Pigeon Coops

Pigeons need to have a roosting place set high up off the ground. Unlike geese and chickens, they are not ground birds — notwithstanding the number of city pigeons that spend most of their time browsing sidewalks for treats! A simple pigeon coop can be made from a lean-to-type shelter outfitted with roosting shelves and installed on a wall 5 to 6 feet off the ground.

A pigeon coop should have a door so that you can confine the birds. A mesh door with a wooden frame that's held in place by T-hinges, like the door to the ferret or skunk home (see page 337), is ideal.

The base of the pigeon coop should extend out in front of the door. When the pigeons come home to roost, the base will serve as a landing ledge for them.

Inside the coop, you'll want to install roosting shelves for your birds. The shelves can be attached to the back wall of the coop. They should have a small lip on the front edge to help the birds feel securely settled on the shelf.

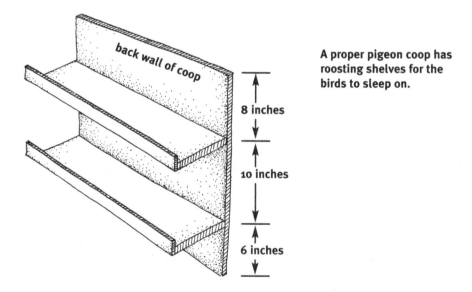

back wall of coop

8 inches

10 inches

6 inches

A proper pigeon coop has roosting shelves for the birds to sleep on.

Like the chicken coop, the pigeon coop should have a sloping roof to keep rain out of the shelter. The roof should overlap the coop on all sides except the back. (Because you're going to attach the back of the coop to a wall, the back needs to be flat.)

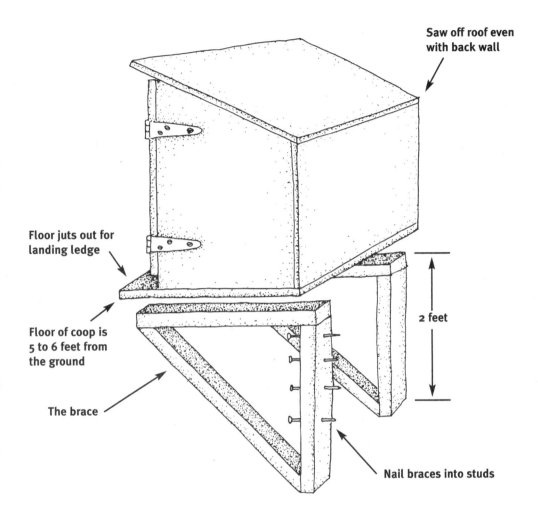

Saw off roof even with back wall

Floor juts out for landing ledge

Floor of coop is 5 to 6 feet from the ground

The brace

2 feet

Nail braces into studs

The best way to attach a pigeon coop to a wall is to set it on braces. To make a brace, you simply nail together two pieces of 2-by-4-inch lumber at a right angle. Use a square to make sure that the angle they form is exactly 90 degrees, and then nail on a diagonal brace to form a triangle, as shown. The braces themselves should be secured to studs in the wall. (An adult should be able to help you find the studs.)

Once the braces are nailed firmly into the wall studs, lift the coop up onto them. If you want, you could drive a few nails through the coop floor into the braces, and a few more through the back wall of the coop into a wall stud. Probably neither is really necessary, and it's not a bad idea to be able to lift the coop down when you want to give it a good scrubbing.

Coat both the inside and outside of the coop with several coats of shellac, and paint the outside with an exterior-grade paint.

Goat Homes

Goats have to be confined at all times, unless you want to live in a desert devoid of leaves, grass, and flowers. They are formidable eaters and are stubborn besides. For many people, a simple stall in a corner of the garage is the best place to keep a goat. Other people keep their goat in a freestanding shed. We won't give exact instructions for building a goat stall or shed here, because these are complicated projects that are best left in the hands of an experienced builder. However, you, as the goat owner, should certainly weigh in on the stall or shed design considerations and could volunteer to assist with the project. (Imagine the carpentry skills you'll learn!)

Whether you keep your goat in a stall or a shed, cover the floor of the enclosure with hay. Add a little hay over the surface every day. Goat droppings and urine don't smell much, and goat keepers have to clean the bedding and floor only twice a year — spring and fall. The daily layer of hay keeps the goat clean and dry. Of course, the floor gets higher and higher, but it will all make excellent compost in the long run.

If you are planning to keep your goat in a shed, make sure the shed is in a good site. The door of the shed should face south to offer your goat the best protection from bad weather. The area should be level and on high dry ground, as goats object to any dampness underfoot.

When you are finished preparing the stall or shed, either attach to it a fenced-in goat yard or plan to chain your goat to a stake in the ground. If you have more than one goat, a fenced yard is a more practical way to confine them than is staking. A goat yard is usually attached to the shed so goats are free to come and go as they wish when the shed door is open. Sand is the best flooring for the yard. Water drains from it easily and it can be raked clean of droppings from time to time. The fencing should be at least 4 feet high. If your goat is a jumper — and many are — the fencing should be higher.

GARAGE GOAT STALL

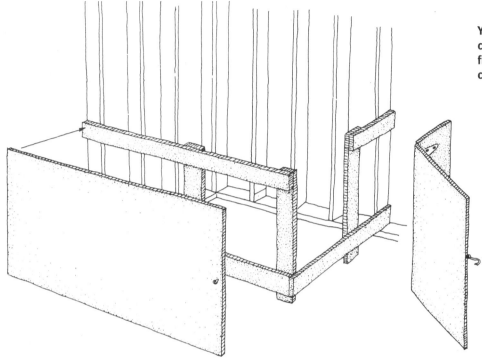

You can install a stall for your goat in a corner of the garage. The frame is made from 2-by-4-inch lumber, which is then covered with interior-grade plywood.

FREESTANDING GOAT SHED

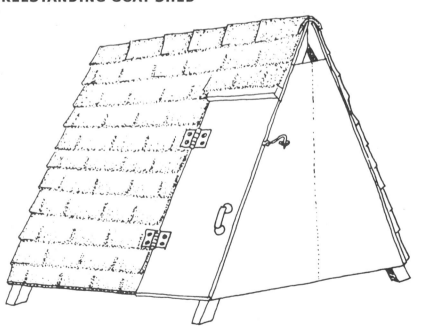

An A-frame is one of the easiest-to-build and strongest shapes in construction. A small A-frame shed, shingled on both sides and with a sturdy door, makes a good, inexpensive goat shed.

last words

These last words are important. They are about some of the troubles the owner of any sort of pet has to go through. One trouble is vacations: How do you go away without taking your pets with you? Another trouble is escapes: How do you find a lost pet? And the last trouble is death. Sooner or later, every pet dies.

As for vacations, many of the animals in this book can get along for a few days without you, provided you leave a larger amount of food and water than usual. Any reptile, bird, amphibian, insect, mollusk, spider, fish, or crustacean can be left over a long weekend.

For longer vacations, you have three choices. If most of your animals are temporary ones like salamanders, tadpoles, garter snakes, and grasshoppers, you could let them go and start all over again when you return. If most of your animals are small, caged, permanent, and portable, like pet turtles and fish, a pet store may board them, usually at a reasonable price. Many veterinarians board cats and dogs, though the cost is not cheap.

If permanent pets include nonportable members like geese and goats, or if you have many pets, you will have to hire a pet sitter. It is cheaper to find a child who has always wanted to keep pets to do the sitting, rather than hiring an adult. The price is up to you and the pet sitter. Estimate the time it takes to do daily cleaning and feeding, add up the total number of hours, and settle on something like five dollars an hour. Chances are this rate, even for quite a few pets, won't run more than fifteen dollars a week. Be sure to start showing your sitter how to take care of things well ahead of time, though, and let him or her go through the whole routine once or twice before you leave so any questions that come up can be handled. Written instructions are helpful too. Be sure to leave enough food for the whole time you will be away. And leave a way to reach you, just in case.

Escapees and runaways are a bigger problem. There is no such thing as a cage that prevents an animal from ever escaping, not because there is anything wrong with the cage, but because you will forget to close it correctly, or will think the animal can't climb or jump or squeeze as well as it really can. And some animals will run — or perhaps only wander — away from home.

The first thing to do is control your own behavior. Don't panic and carry on. Adults will be sorry they ever let you have a pet if it's going to cause all this fuss. Don't make a joke of it,

either. People don't think a garter snake in the closet is funny, and the garter snake doesn't think it's funny either.

For the smallest animals, make the search easier by shutting everything that can be shut — doors, windows, boxes, closets, drawers, cupboards. Start looking. The most likely place for an escaped animal to be is close to its cage, in the nearest natural hiding place. For instance, a snake that was "lost" for two weeks was found exactly 12 inches from his cage, curled up inside an amplifier. A mouse that was gone for days was hidden in a school bag that was kept right next to his cage. He took three trips to school and back before anyone noticed him.

In other words, animals seldom really try to escape. They simply get out of their cages. But once they have made the mistake of leaving their cages, they simply try to live as conveniently as

they can. Do your searching methodically, starting right next to the cage. Strip beds and lift mattresses. Remove books from shelves. Go through drawers, and then shut them. Take everything off the closet floor and search each shoe and boot. If you can't find your pet this way, try leaving the cage open with some food in it for a few nights. Stay up for a while in the evening and watch. The animal might come during the night to eat. If it does, slam the cage shut once it's inside.

If your pet is not in hiding near its cage and refuses to come back of its own accord, it may still turn up within the next few weeks. For rodents there is one other technique — trapping. A Havahart animal trap is specially designed to catch small animals like rodents without harming them. Bait the trap with your pet's favorite food and put it in an out-of-the-way spot. If your pet really is nowhere near his cage, the next most likely spot is the kitchen, so you might try placing the trap under the sink, behind the garbage can, or anywhere you have seen wild mice come to eat. Keep trying for at least a few weeks.

So much for animals that escape indoors. Animals that escape outdoors are in greater danger, both from cars on the street and from neighboring dogs. Before you dash around, think through the animals' habits. Most animals head for logical places — a goose to water, a goat to the nearest flower bed. Chickens are most likely to be close by, happily pecking for worms. Rabbits are most likely to be just as close by, nibbling grass. Guinea pigs, however, go into hiding under shrubbery, in woodpiles, or under porches. They can be difficult to find.

If you don't see your pet in a logical place on your own property, start calling neighbors. Word of stray goats and tame bunnies gets around fast.

Your mail carrier, newspaper delivery person, or garbage collector may also be helpful in looking for and spreading word about your lost pet.

Once you've located your pet, the next problem is getting it back into its proper home. Herding seems to work better than catching for geese and chickens, and often for rabbits. Get someone to help you. Start the animal in the right direction, then crowd it toward home calmly and quietly. Goats will no doubt come to you for food. Put a rope or a leash around the goat's neck and drag it home. Guinea pigs probably should be caught with your hands, or under a carton or wastebasket.

For runaway or lost cats and dogs, each community has its own finding methods. Some local radio stations broadcast descriptions of lost and found animals at specific times each day. Call the stations near you and find out if they have such a service. Any newspaper will run classified ads for lost or found pets, the cost of the ad depending on the number of words you use. And there is always the ASPCA and other animal shelters that accept lost pets. You have to call them as soon as you notice your cat or dog is missing, since many of them will keep a cat or dog only three days before they'll "put it to sleep" (kill it by painless injection). If all else fails, put up notices on bulletin boards or in windows of local stores, veterinary offices, or wherever else your neighborhood allows such free ads.

If a lost pet isn't found within a week or two, you'll wonder if it's dead. That depends on the pet. Lost reptiles, unless they are native to your area, will probably not survive without your care. Rodents, on the other hand, can usually get along on their own unless there is a native population of rats nearby, which may kill any other rodent intruding into their territory. Birds that escape outdoors in warm climates will be fine, but none of the pet birds in this book can survive cold weather. Escaped rabbits, guinea pigs, skunks, and ferrets may get along for a while, but are often too domesticated to keep out of the way of dogs. Runaway cats have probably run away on purpose, in a snit about something. They tend to find a home sooner or later, or even get along without humans in the wild. Dogs — especially the wandering types like hounds — may also adopt a new family (no one knows why). The greatest worry about a dog or cat is whether it has been run over. You can check out this possibility with the highway department, since it is responsible for picking up animal carcasses from the road. It's a sad thing to have to do, but it's better to get an answer one way or the other.

Dealing with Death

Death is the most difficult thing of all. When you find the limp corpse of your pet gerbil that only yesterday munched its lively way through life, your heart sinks and your fingers are reluctant to touch. Worse yet, you feel guilty, as though there was no way your pet could die without you having done something wrong. But plenty of pets die from old age, not mistreatment. Old age for a mouse, after all, is only a couple of years; for a cricket, a winter's span. Plenty of pets die from sicknesses you could not have cured even if there had been a way to notice them.

But of course pets may die from mistreatment, too. Anybody who has had a lot of pets has killed some by not caring for them well enough, by not understanding all their needs, or by not protecting them from enemies. We were responsible for the death of a rat by not cleaning its cage often enough, of a tortoise by not understanding its need for warmth, and of a hamster by not securing its cage from the cat. Those deaths were our fault. We tried to learn from them.

There are other deaths for which you might have to accept responsibility. If you want to keep a tarantula or a boa constrictor alive, you must be ready to take on responsibility for the killing of crickets and mice, both of which might have become pets themselves. A woman once asked one of my children whether he didn't feel sorry for "those poor defenseless mice" when he fed his snake dinner. He asked her if she felt sorry for "those poor defenseless cows" when she fed herself dinner. Responsibility for certain deaths is a fact of life that everyone must face.

When any pet dies, whether or not you had anything to do with it, you will feel awful. You will feel even worse if you get rid of the body — down the toilet, in the garbage, or by burial — without formalities, and without farewells. Whether your pet is a tiny salamander or a dear big old dog, you will need a way to acknowledge death and say good-bye the way humans have always done it — with a funeral.

If your pet is small, find a box that its body will fit into nicely, or find something soft to wrap your pet in. It might feel right to you to wrap a hamster in the sock it loved to burrow into, or nestle a turtle into moss or leaves, or wrap a cat in a soft old towel. People often feel better if they put a little food or a favorite toy in with their pet too, even though they know it will not eat or play anymore.

A funeral is not a difficult thing to arrange. Everybody we think will care about the pet's death comes together. We talk about the pet. We say nice things we remember; we apologize for things we feel sad about; we say we will miss our pet. If we have a place to bury it, we put a stone or flowers on the grave. If we don't — if the veterinarian must take care of it, or the garbage man — we have still said good-bye in sad, proper, ancient human fashion.

index

Italicized page numbers indicate illustrations or photographs.